A MANUAL

OF

INTERNATIONAL LAW

BY

GEORG SCHWARZENBERGER

FOURTH EDITION
IN TWO VOLUMES

VOLUME 1

Published under the auspices of
THE LONDON INSTITUTE OF WORLD AFFAIRS

LONDON · STEVENS & SONS LIMITED
NEW YORK · FREDERICK A. PRAEGER

First Edition - - 1947
Second Edition - - 1950
Third Edition - - 1952
Fourth Edition - - 1960
(Translated into German, 1951)

Published by
Stevens & Sons Limited
of 11 New Fetter Lane
in the City of London and
printed in Great Britain
by The Eastern Press Ltd.
of London and Reading

Published in the U.S.A. by
Frederick A. Praeger, Inc.
of 64 University Place
New York 3, N.Y., U.S.A.

THE LIBRARY OF WORLD AFFAIRS

Editors:
GEORGE W. KEETON
AND
GEORG SCHWARZENBERGER

Number 3

A MANUAL OF INTERNATIONAL LAW

VOLUME 1

TO

H. A. SMITH

PREFACE

THIS fourth edition of the Manual is, and is not, a new book. It is not a new book in that it maintains its continuity with the earlier editions in a number of ways. The presentation of the rules of international customary law is based primarily on international law as applied in international judicial and Anglo-American practice. Although further developed, the systematic arrangement of the material adopted in the earlier editions has been retained. As before, international law is viewed as a system of fairly stable and interlocking rules of international customary law on which, from time to time, more ambitious superstructures, varying in permanence and significance, have been grafted by way of treaty.

As in previous editions, the Study Outlines form an integral part of the Manual. To facilitate the use of the Manual, it has been decided to bind the text and the Study Outlines (together with the other supplementary material) separately. The Study Outlines give expression to a three-fold belief, increasingly strengthened by further teaching experience. First, as in any other field of knowledge, insight into international law is best acquired layer by layer. Secondly, once the foundations are laid, the reader should be enabled to deepen and widen his knowledge in accordance with his own predilections. Thirdly, a liberal selection of material on the main issues has considerable protective value for anybody exposed to attacks of " ipse-dixitism " (Bentham) and, generally, appears to assist in raising the standards of discussion.

At the same time, the Manual is a new book; for, with the exception of the concluding chapter, it has been largely rewritten and, in the process, enlarged into a medium-sized presentation of international law. The drastic overhaul required by the decision to attempt to meet the need for a book of this type has also provided an opportunity to incorporate in the Manual experiments made since the previous edition.

It may be helpful to list at least the more significant of these. They include greater emphasis on the inter-disciplinary approach to the study of international law and the three perspectives in which the subject as a whole can then be viewed as it were from the outside; the development of views expressed more tentatively in earlier editions on the inductive approach to international law and its " sources," in particular the critical assessment of inter-national judicial material; elaboration of the thesis of the exclusiveness, rather than supremacy, of international law in relation to municipal law; clarification of the relations between legal rules, principles and maxims and application of these distinctions to international law; differentiation between the fundamental rules and principles of international law on the one hand, and, on the other, rules and principles of a subsidiary character; presentation of international customary law as a system of rules governing seven funda-mental principles; exemplification of this technique by reference to, for instance, the so-called principle of State succession, title to territory or the nascent field of space law; even greater emphasis than in previous editions on the relativity of truth in any statement according to its intended application to the levels of unorganised or organised inter-national society; illustration of the growing significance of the consensual superstructures in international law by refer-ence to new branches such as, for instance, international economic law, international social law, international air law, international criminal law and the law of international institutions and, finally, a distinction between four different types of rules of warfare to assist in the critical evaluation of the laws and customs of war.

As in previous editions, I am greatly indebted to a growing number of academic colleagues as well as reviewers in this country and abroad for their helpful and constructive criticism. My own students have also splendidly risen to what they have considered a novel challenge, and I have taken full advantage of the comments made at first shyly, and then with commendably decreasing inhibitions, from the " consumer's " point of view.

Even more than in the past, I am under a debt of gratitude to my three trusted friends and colleagues in the field of international law at University College, London, Dr. Cheng, Mr. Green and Mr. Parkinson. With characteristic zeal and generosity, they have thrown themselves into the task of helping me to refashion the Manual. Beyond giving me the benefit of eager and thoughtful co-operation, they have also relieved me of the major part of the burden of proof-reading, revising and checking the Study Outlines, and preparing the table of cases, the table of treaties and the index.

Since its first edition, the Manual has been dedicated, both as a token of friendship and as a tribute to a British pioneer in the application of the inductive method to international law, to Professor H. A. Smith, who, until his retirement in 1946, held the Chair of International Law in the University of London.

Finally, it is a pleasure to thank the publishers and printers for their exemplary co-operation and, in particular, my friend, Hilary Stevens, for the helpful counsel which I have received from him at every stage of the production of this Manual.

G. S.

UNIVERSITY COLLEGE, LONDON.
     January 14, 1960.

CONTENTS

VOLUME ONE

PART ONE: ELEMENTS OF INTERNATIONAL LAW

xi

Contents

VOLUME TWO

PART TWO: STUDY OUTLINES

PART ONE

ELEMENTS OF INTERNATIONAL LAW

CHAPTER 1

INTERNATIONAL LAW IN PERSPECTIVE

"It is a process of inductive reasoning" (*Re Piracy Jure Gentium*—Judicial Committee of the Privy Council *per* Viscount Sankey L.C., 1934).

INTERNATIONAL law is the body of legal rules which apply between sovereign States [1] and such other entities as have been granted international personality.[2] The term *international law* was coined by Bentham and is synonymous with the term *law of nations* and its French and German equivalents (*droit des gens—Völkerrecht*).

I—DISTINCTIONS

International law may be contrasted with *municipal law*. While international law applies only between entities which can claim international personality, municipal law is the internal law of States which regulates the conduct of individuals and other legal entities within their jurisdiction.[3]

It is also helpful to distinguish international law from *quasi-international law*, that is to say, the law governing relations on a footing of relative equality and, therefore, akin in substance to those under international law, but outside the realm of international law because one at least of the parties is not a subject of international law. This type of legal relations is illustrated by a loan contract between an international banking consortium and a sovereign State. In fact, such relations are governed by municipal law.[4]

International law must also be kept apart from *private international law* or the *conflict of laws*. These are synonymous terms to describe the body of rules of municipal law which regulate legal relations with a foreign element such as, for instance,

---

[1] See below, p. 57 *et seq.*
[2] See below, p. 62 *et seq.*
[3] See below, p. 39 *et seq.*
[4] See below, p. 142 *et seq.*

1

contracts of sale or service between persons in different countries. Rules of conflict of laws are only exceptionally rules of international law. Unless postulated by rules of international customary law, treaties or general principles of law recognised by civilised nations,[5] they are rules of municipal law. Thus, for instance, the statutory rules which give effect to the Copenhagen Convention on the Reciprocal Enforcement of Foreign Judgments, 1932, do embody international obligations of the United Kingdom. The same is true of the obligations created for the contracting parties by the Havana Convention on Private International Law, 1928, the so-called Bustamante Code.

International law differs from *comparative law* in that the latter is not a separate branch of law at all, but has as its object the comparative study and evaluation of the rules, principles and techniques applied in different legal systems.

It is less easy to differentiate accurately between international customary law and *international morality, international comity* and *international usage*. A possible test is whether, at a specific moment, the subjects of international law [6] who are supposed to be bound by a particular rule of international law, consider the rule in question legally binding or as one which they are prepared to accept only as a moral duty (*international morality*), as an act of courtesy (*international comity*) or as a mere habit (*international usage*). At one time, a particular rule may fall into one, and at another time, into another category. Thus, the spoliation of shipwrecks was for a long time a well established maritime practice. Since, the Middle Ages, however, the Church treated it as a moral sin. Subsequently, interference with wrecks was first prohibited by bilateral treaties and, in the end, this prohibition became incorporated into the body of international customary law.[7] Similarly, a good many rules may be common to different types of normative systems. The rule, for instance, on the duty to observe international treaties is both a moral and a legal obligation.[8]

Admittedly, to decide the legal or non-legal character of a rule by reference to the attitude taken towards it by the

---

[5] See below, p. 24 *et seq.*
[6] See below, p. 47 *et seq.*
[7] See below, p. 27 *et seq.*
[8] See below, p. 137 *et seq.*

addressees of the norm is to apply a somewhat subjective test. The difficulties arising from this element of uncertainty must not, however, be exaggerated. There is a fair number of rules of international customary law the legal character of which is not in dispute. In particular, this is true of the central rules governing the seven fundamental principles of international law.[9] In the case of consensual engagements, it is anyway accepted that their legal character depends entirely on the intention of the contracting parties.[10] Yet, the presumption is that if parties define their mutual obligations in the form of a written treaty, they intend to create legal obligations towards each other.[11]

Finally, in so far as rules abstracted from general principles of law recognised by civilised nations are concerned,[12] other elements of possible subjectivity require watching, but there is no need at all to apply the test discussed above. This is a criterion that matters only in relation to rules of international customary law.

II—THE PERSPECTIVES OF INTERNATIONAL LAW

To comprehend the genesis, peculiarities and the place of international law in international society, it is helpful to view the subject in its historical, sociological and ethical perspectives.

A. International Law in Historical Perspective

There is scope for international law whenever two conditions are fulfilled. First, the entities concerned must be prepared to grant each other at least equality of status if not substantially reciprocal treatment. Secondly, there must be sufficient contact between them to make legal regulation of some of their relations desirable.[13]

Thus, in the fourteenth century B.C., Pharaoh Rameses II of Egypt concluded a Treaty of Peace, Alliance and Extradition with the King of Cheta, and Suppiluliuma, King of the Hittites, entered into an alliance with Nigmad, King of Egarit. The

---

9 See below, p. 37 *et seq.*
10 See below, p. 138 *et seq.*
11 See below, p. 149 *et seq.*
12 See below, p. 29 *et seq.*
13 See also below, p. 7 *et seq.*

second of these treaties contains a passage which, by more than a millennium, anticipates the teachings of Kautilya (*Arthasastra, c.* 300 B.C.), and by nearly 3,000 years those of Machiavelli (*The Prince,* 1532): " Just as formerly thy ancestors were friends and not enemies of the Hittite country, now thou, Nigmad, shouldst be the enemy of my enemy and the friend of my friend." Many other treaties were concluded between States in ancient times, whereby, on a footing of at least formal equality, they settled temporarily political and economic issues between each other.

More frequently matters were settled by the sword. Policies of force were encouraged by the disinclination of States in antiquity to consider any community other than those closely related to themselves as civilised and, therefore, worthy of being treated on a footing of equality. The Hebrews waged many of their wars as wars of extermination. The Greek city States were willing to establish close relations only among themselves and, whenever there was a choice, the Romans treated none but their Latin cousins as equals. The rest of the world were barbarians to whom the Roman Empire brought *arma et leges.* They were merely fit to become incorporated into the Roman world empire or to be objects of policing operations on its fringes.

Although several systems of international law, in various stages of arrested development, existed in antiquity and, simultaneously or subsequently, in other parts of the world, present-day international law has its roots in medieval Europe. It might be thought that the hierarchical order of the Middle Ages was incompatible with the existence of international law, which requires the co-existence of equal and independent communities.[14] Actually, the pyramidal structure of feudalism, culminating in Pope and Emperor as spiritual and temporal heads of Western Christendom, was hardly ever fully realised. It left ample scope for relations on a footing of equality between what were often in fact independent States. This applied especially to kingdoms like England and Scotland which existed on the fringe of the Holy Roman Empire. Even within the Empire, relations between the more powerful feudal princes, independent knights and free cities were regulated by rules which

---

[14] See above, p. 3 *et seq.,* and below, p. 57 *et seq.*

in all but form were indistinguishable from those of international law and formed a system of quasi-international law.[15]

In the absence of specific rules, Roman law and canon law, in the guise of natural law, were adapted to the relations between such entities. In a number of treaties, principles and standards [16] were developed which, at a later stage, were taken for granted and gradually grew into rules of international customary law.[17] When the Holy Roman Empire began to crumble and an increasing number of States became independent of the Emperor in law as well as in fact, chancelleries had at their disposal a reasonable number of standard forms of treaties and even fragmentary rules of international customary law which had long been in use, even though they were not yet necessarily considered as a branch of law separate from municipal law. This continuity, as well as the gradual character of the transition from the medieval order to the modern State system, deserves being emphasised, as these significant aspects of the evolution of present-day international law have been unduly neglected.

At the same time, the *disintegration* of the Christian Commonwealth of Europe greatly stimulated the growth of international law and its development both as a separate branch of law and as an alternative to international anarchy. Two other major trends also contributed to the shaping of international law. Under the impact of political, spiritual, economic and technical revolutions, by which the medieval community was transformed into the capitalist world, strong incentives were created towards greater *expansion* and *centralisation* [18] of the then existing European inter-State system. Compared with the Europe of the sixteenth century, only a relatively small number of independent States have survived. But, as European States spread their nets all over the globe, other States formed themselves on their pattern in other continents. They now form part of *one* world society, governed, in at least some of their mutual relations, by a world-wide legal system.[19]

In the course of the expansion of international law from the " public law of Europe," as it was often called in State papers

---

[15] See above, p. 1, and below, p. 47 *et seq.*
[16] See below, p. 39 *et seq.*   [17] See below, p. 27 *et seq.*
[18] See below, p. 361 *et seq.*
[19] See below, p. 7 *et seq.*

of the eighteenth and early nineteenth centuries, intermediate stages were frequently preferred to either outright subjection and incorporation of the territories of outsiders or their acceptance as full subjects of international law.

In some cases it was impossible or inopportune to conquer such countries. Nevertheless, it appeared desirable to settle in a binding form questions of interest to European States as, for instance, in their relations with the Barbary States. It was then assumed that such States could be parties to treaties, but that they were not bound by the more intimate rules of international customary law as applied between European powers.

In other cases, European States considered it desirable to establish trade relations or to give protection to what were called appropriately enough merchant adventurers or to missionaries who were sent out to countries with different civilisations in the Near, Middle and Far East. Capitulation treaties provided means of harmonising discrepancies in standards of conduct, especially in the administration of civil and criminal law. In this way, foreigners resident in Asian and African countries were exempted from local territorial jurisdiction and made amenable to that of their home States, which exercised jurisdiction on the spot through their consular courts or in their own colonial possessions nearby.[20]

Finally, matters might be left in the hands of colonial companies such as the Dutch and English East India Companies. They were not considered as themselves endowed with international personality, but were regarded as organs of the States which had granted them their charters.[21] They had, however, wide discretionary powers and used them in concluding treaties with, or making war on, local rulers. Some of these treaties make sense only on the assumption that the colonial company acknowledged the sovereignty and international personality of the local princes concerned. Others are more akin to public contracts under the municipal law of the colonial power concerned. Today, these aspects of international law are primarily of historical significance. They are by-products of the transition of the European State system from periods of early

<hr>

20 See below, p. 86 *et seq.*
21 See below, p. 434 *et seq.*

colonialism and imperialism to the era of a slowly maturing world society.

B. International Law in Sociological Perspective

1. *The Structure of International Law*

Three features characterise the structure of contemporary international law: (a) its universality on the level of unorganised international society, (b) its exclusiveness and (c) its individualistic character.

(a) *The Universality of International Law.* On the level of unorganised international society, the geographical scope of international law is universal, in the sense that it extends to the whole world. International law on this level comprises the sum total of the rules from which the seven fundamental and interrelated principles of sovereignty, recognition, consent, good faith, responsibility, self-defence, and the freedom of the seas can be abstracted.[22]

The subjects of international law are, however, free to organise themselves on higher levels of integration. They may, for instance, become parties to a general agreement for the renunciation of resort to war, such as the Kellogg Pact of 1928[23] or join regional or universalist international institutions, such as the Organisation of American States or the United Nations.[24] They may even coalesce into territorial or functional federations on the model of Switzerland or the European Coal and Steel Community.[25] Within such institutional super-structures, international law may develop to an extent not feasible on the level of unorganised international society. Whether the integration of international society follows regional, functional or ideological patterns, treaties are the chief instrument of such closer international co-operation.

(b) *The Exclusiveness of International Law.* Whatever the level of integration, international law remains as yet essentially a law the typical subjects of which are territorially organised

---

[22] See below, p. 37 *et seq.*
[23] See below, p. 174.
[24] See below, pp. 265 *et seq.*, and 330 *et seq.*
[25] See below, pp. 50 and 343.

units.[26] Non-typical subjects are other entities which, for some or all purposes, these sovereign States choose to endow with international personality.[27] Thus, for purposes of international law, every entity that is not recognised as a subject, is merely an object of international law.[28] So long as this is so, the individual, although the basic unit on which all social relations rest, is as much an object of international law as any inanimate object under the jurisdiction of a subject of international law. Yet, this does not exclude that organised groups which are subjects of international law co-operate with each other, for instance, by way of treaty, for the benefit of the individual or particular categories of human beings.[29]

(c) *The Individualistic Character of International Law.* On the level of *unorganised* international society, subjects of international law are bound only by the rules underlying the fundamental principles of international law [30] and, perhaps, also by the general principles of law recognised by civilised nations.[31] Without their consent or acquiescence, however, it is not possible to obtain any binding statement regarding any of their international obligations or, in relation to any subject of international law, to develop the law as it stands.

On the international plane, no institutions comparable to the legislature, judicature or government of a mature State can be brought into existence without the consent of the subject of international law that is to submit to such jurisdiction. Consequently, unorganised international society lacks any central authority. This is true of the exercise not only of the legislative or executive functions but also of judicial authority. Thus, without the consent of States concerned, no international organ is competent to give an authoritative interpretation of international law.[32]

It is apparent that this state of auto-interpretation of international law by each subject of international law is easily open to abuse.[33] States, however, are free to establish

26 See below, p. 48 *et seq.*
27 See below, p. 71 *et seq.*
28 See below, p. 63 *et seq.*
29 See below, p. 100 *et seq.* and p. 128.
30 See above, p. 7, and below, p. 37 *et seq.*
31 See below, p. 24 *et seq.*
32 See below, p. 137 *et seq.*
33 See below, p. 10.

by agreement among themselves international institutions endowed with legislative, judicial or executive powers on either an *ad hoc* or a permanent basis. We then move to international law on the levels of partly or fully *organised* international society.[34]

2. *The Functions of International Law*

Law in any social environment may serve one or more of three different purposes. It may be an instrument of power, a regulator of reciprocal interests or a means of co-ordinating common efforts. While the first function of law is likely to be predominant in extreme society relations, the third function tends to prevail in correspondingly extreme community relations.

It is essential to realise that sociological terms such as society or community represent ideal or pure types of social relations. In actual life none of these groups exists in undiluted form; they are hybrids. Communities such as the family, nation or church may suffer from greater or smaller admixtures of society elements. Conversely, societies such as a joint-stock company, cartel or even a gang of thieves must accept a minimum of community standards, at least in the relations between members of such groups. Otherwise, they cannot even fulfil their own limited social or anti-social functions. Yet community aspirations remain necessarily dwarfed in such uncongenial surroundings. Relations between sovereign States, especially on the level of unorganised international society,[35] are more typical of those to be found in a society than in a community.

Unorganised international society is conditioned primarily by power politics with its typical objects, motivations, tactics and strategies. Thus, armaments, alliances, counter-alliances, balance of power systems and war are its typical concomitants. International law when operating on this level tends to present the characteristics of an extreme type of society law, that is to say, it is preponderantly, but not necessarily exclusively, a law of power.[36] Dependent upon the degree of integration among the States concerned, international law on the levels of partly or

---

[34] See below, p. 227 *et seq.*
[35] See above, p. 8, and below, p. 23.
[36] See below, p. 10.

fully organised international society may change into a hybrid
between society and community law—a law of reciprocity [37]—
or a fully fledged community law—a law for the co-ordination of
joint efforts on the basis of voluntary co-operation.[38]

(a) *The Law of Power.* International law may become a
direct instrument of power politics. This, for instance, happens
when peace treaties formalise power positions brought about by
resort to war. Each of the great peace settlements since the
Treaties of Westphalia (1648) has rested on, and given legal
expression to, an equilibrium that had been achieved in the
preceding major war. Another illustration of the law of power
is the institution of reprisals.[39] In particular, military reprisals
are open only to the strong against the weak.

In the absence of international organs entitled to impose upon
States an authoritative interpretation of their rights and duties
under international law, States may be tempted to employ international law as a quasi-legal garb to disguise designs that may
well run counter to their international obligations. Until world
society has developed commensurate international institutions,[40]
such abuses of international law cannot easily be avoided. Yet,
to be effective, institutions comparable to those of a well
functioning State machinery presuppose the existence of a highly
integrated community. On a world scale, this appears as yet a
far cry.

(b) *The Law of Reciprocity.* Even within an international
society engulfed in a system of world power politics, States find
it continuously to their benefit, on a basis of reciprocity, to
limit the crude play of power and force. The law of reciprocity
can be seen at work especially in spheres which are irrelevant or
peripheral from the point of view of power politics.

In matters such as diplomatic immunity,[41] extradition of
criminals,[42] commerce,[43] communications and transport,[44] rules

---

[37] See below, under (b).   [38] See below, p. 11.
[39] See below, p. 173 *et seq.*
[40] See below, p. 359 *et seq.*
[41] See below, p. 93 *et seq.*
[42] See below, p. 108.
[43] See below, p. 102 *et seq.*
[44] See below, pp. 102 and 109 *et seq.*

of international law freely and beneficially develop on a footing of reciprocity. On the levels of partly or fully organised international society, international law is primarily a law of reciprocity. Yet, even in the very thick of power politics, that is to say, in time of war, some scope exists for the law of reciprocity. The laws of war and neutrality owe their existence to typical considerations of this kind which tend to impose restraints on belligerent and neutral States alike.[45]

(c) *The Law of Co-ordination.* Although in a world society based on power sovereign States are primarily concerned with their own preservation and well-being, signs of a community law proper are not entirely lacking. The law of co-ordination does not seek either to exploit disparities in power positions or to adjust antagonistic interests on a basis of reciprocity. It serves as a means of co-ordinating individual efforts for the better achievement of common purposes. The treaties for the suppression of the African slave trade, concluded and observed mainly as a result of pressure exerted on other powers by successive British Governments during the nineteenth century,[46] the conventions in the interest of refugees,[47] and the work of the United Nations International Children's Emergency Fund [48] may be cited as illustrations.

Nevertheless, this type of international law is the exception which, until now, has confirmed the general rule. It is likely to remain so until nations are willing to consider the interests of the world as overriding their own parochial or sectional interests. So far, any development on lines of an international community has been limited to States which have very much more in common than the members of world society at large. On such levels of interdependence or inter-penetration, international and municipal relations tend to become increasingly mixed up, and the group of States concerned may then well be on the way to coalesce into some form of multinational State. This is where, at least for internal purposes, municipal law comes into its own again. A new, and larger, unit is born and, if experience is any

[45] See below, p. 170.
[46] See below, pp. 107 and 500 *et seq.*
[47] See below, pp. 132 and 503 *et seq.*
[48] See below, pp. 503 and 654.

guide, faces the outside world in hardly less individualistic, if
not aggressive, a manner than its own components had, in the
past, adopted towards one another.

C. International Law in Ethical Perspective

As long as international law applied only between European
States, their common Christian background and tradition
nourished continuously and imperceptibly the more formal and
technical aspects of their relations.   However precarious, during
this period, the observance of international law might have been,
it incorporated an appreciable minimum of the values cherished
by the members of this Christian Commonwealth (*una Christiana
res publica*).   When the European family of nations developed
into a world society, this common ethical foundation could no
longer be taken for granted.

During the initial period of the expansion of the West,
European States, with their superior military and naval forces,
compelled rulers in the Near, Middle and Far East to open their
countries to the Western nations and to accept relations with
them on their own terms.   Some were immediately reduced to a
state of colonial dependency.   Others, especially those African
and Asian States which had assimilated themselves to the
Western pattern of political organisation, were treated as subject
to a simplified system of international law that was free from its
peculiarly European features and considered by the Western
States to be congenial to all civilised nations.   In cases where a
country was regarded as approaching, rather than having
reached, a phase in its development in which it could be relied on
to comply with the standard of civilisation as embodied in international customary law, capitulation treaties assisted further in
bridging remaining discrepancies in social and legal values.[49]

The standard of civilisation as applied in these relations was
identified with a certain minimum of efficiency in running the
State machinery, a modicum of independence of the judiciary
from the executive, and adequate protection of the safety, life,
liberty, dignity and property of foreigners.   On this basis, the
Christian law of nations was transformed into international law

[49] See above, p. 6, and below, p. 86 *et seq.*

as applied between civilised States all over the world, at the price, however, of increasing separation from its metaphysical foundation and dilution of its traditional ethical contents.

The secularisation of international law was pushed further by the rise of coherent and increasingly powerful nation-States. They tended to resent any outside authority which might challenge their complete freedom of action and became increasingly unwilling to acknowledge the existence of any legal commitment other than treaties to which they had expressly agreed [50] or rules which, on the nourishing grounds of prolonged treaty practice or roughly parallel domestic usages, had become generally recognised as rules of international customary law.[51]

This development coincided with the eclipse of the naturalist approach to international law by a positivist treatment of the subject. This means the exclusion of rules resting on metaphysical, religious or ethical foundations unless corroborated by evidence that such rules are the products of one or more of the generally recognised law-creating processes.[52]

In its turn, the positivist movement in international law encouraged a further shift in emphasis, this time from international law as the law between *civilised* States to international law as the law between *sovereign* States and other entities recognised as subjects of international law by these sovereign States.[53] This became evident when, in rapidly growing succession, States like Russia, Italy, Germany and Japan adopted against sections of their own populations barbarous practices which in any but a largely amoral age would have put them automatically beyond the pale of civilisation. Yet, in fact, the rest of the world did not treat these acts during the interval between the First and Second World Wars as glaring abuses of sovereign power on the part of these totalitarian States, nor did it draw from this state of affairs the possible conclusion that these States had forfeited their international personality and had become international outlaws.[54] Thus, in pre-1939 international law, the standard of civilisation had almost reached vanishing

---

[50] See below, pp. 26 and 140 *et seq.*
[51] See above, p. 5, and below, p. 27 *et seq.*
[52] See below, p. 24 *et seq.*
[53] See above, p. 1, and below, p. 48 *et seq.*
[54] See below, p. 66.

point. It is a matter of some doubt how far the efforts made since 1945 to incorporate clauses for the protection of human rights on the levels of the United Nations and regional organisations have changed this picture.[55]

III—THE DOCTRINE OF INTERNATIONAL LAW

In the early stages of international law, the day-to-day work of European chancelleries was carried on by lawyers trained in the canon and civil law. The knowledge that was required for these purposes was specialised and treated as part of the secrets of statecraft. There was little demand for any scientific treatment of the subject. The more intensive inter-State relations became, and a growing body of public opinion regarded international law as a promising means of furthering the cause of international peace, the more such a need made itself felt.

A. The Place of the Doctrine of International Law

The value of any exposition of international law depends upon a test as simple as it is exacting: the degree of accuracy with which it reflects the true state of the law as it stands at a given moment. In this respect, writers in any age can at the most hope to approximate closely to this goal. Some may be thought to have succeeded better than others in this endeavour. Nothing could, therefore, be more dangerous than, without the most careful scrutiny, to treat the history of the doctrine of international law as a true mirror of the history of international law.[56]

B. History of the Doctrine of International Law

The beginnings of European international relations can be traced back to the microscopic inter-State system of the Italian city States. It is not, therefore, surprising to find here also the first signs of a doctrine of international law.

1. *The Italian School*

The Italian post-glossators, especially Bartolus (1314–1357) and Baldus (1327–1400), may claim to be among the first

---

[55] See below, p. 265 *et seq.*
[56] See above, p. 3 *et seq.*, and below, p. 35.

expositors of international law even though their treatment of the subject was fragmentary.

They conceived the law of nations as a universal and natural law applicable between independent princes and free commonwealths. Special mention may be made of Guido de Succaria, a professor of law at Naples. This upright civilian was among those lawyers and notables who, in 1268, were summoned to the court of Charles of Anjou to try and condemn Conraddin after he had fallen into Charles' hands. Succaria held that, as an independent prince, Conraddin was entitled to bear arms and was not subject to the jurisdiction of Charles. Although without success, he and most other lawyers present at the gathering advised the King of Sicily that he was not entitled to try his prisoner on the alleged ground of high treason under his own municipal law.

2. *The Spanish School* & ANGLO-DUTCH SCHOOLS

When, in the late fifteenth and early sixteenth centuries, WHEN Spain became the leading power in the Western State system, the centre of learning in international law shifted to that country. Vitoria (about 1480–1546) became the founder of the Spanish school of international law. In his *Relectiones de Indis noviter inventis* (1532) he maintained the tradition of the post-glossators in insisting on the universal validity of international law. In the face of royal disapprobation, he held that international law applied no less between Spain and the Indian principalities in America than between Christian States.

3. *The Anglo-Dutch School*

Elizabethan England adopted Gentili (1552–1608), a Protestant international lawyer of Italian origin. His works, *De Legationibus* (1588), *Commentationes de Jure Belli* (1589) and *De Jure Belli Libri Tres* (1598), show the shift in emphasis which is likely to occur when a jurist is not only an academic lawyer, but also is versed in the art of arguing cases in court, and especially in courts relying on precedents. Gentili acted as counsel in several major cases, and his work greatly benefited from this practical experience. Like other naturalists, he relied as authorities on classical writers, the Bible and the church fathers. In addition, he fortified himself by frequent references to Justinian's *Institutes* and *Digest* and to State practice. For him international law was not merely a moral standard to which the behaviour of States ought to conform, but a living body of law that was actually applied between States.

Greatly relying on Gentili, but sooner and more widely recognised in his significance, was Grotius (1583–1645). Only ignorance of the continuity in the development of the doctrine of international law can explain the statement that Grotius is the father of modern international law. Nevertheless, he can claim to be its expounder on a scale that was not previously reached. In the service of the United Provinces and as Swedish Ambassador in Paris, Grotius had acquired an intimate insight into the diplomatic affairs of his time. Nevertheless, or perhaps for this very reason, Grotius did not pay as much attention to State practice as Gentili had done.

In *Mare Liberum* (1609), a chapter from the long unpublished major work *De Jure Praedae* (1605), Grotius advocated the principle of the freedom of the seas.[57] This should be compared with Selden's (1584–1654) *Mare Clausum* (1618–first printed in 1635), in which the claim of Charles I to sovereignty over the seas adjacent to the British Isles was ably advanced, even though this proposition involved a striking departure from the policy of Elizabethan England in favour of the freedom of the seas. A comparison of *Mare Clausum* with *Mare Liberum* shows how closely they reflect the political and economic interests of their respective patrons and how easy it is, in particular with the assistance of enjoyably elastic notions of natural law, to arrive at predestined conclusions.

The remarkably swift and lasting success of Grotius' *De Jure Belli ac Pacis Libri Tres* (1625) is rightly attributed to factors such as the general realisation in the mid-sixteenth century that war without limits in the last resort defeats itself, and the willingness of Grotius to accept the sovereign State as the basic unit of international law. It is equally relevant to stress in this connection Grotius' skilful blend of natural law, Roman law and State practice, which left in vital matters a sufficient amount of discretion to governments to do, without legal hindrance, what

57 See below, p. 122 *et seq.*

they thought opportune. It should also not be overlooked that
the powers that upheld the Peace Treaties of 1648, and especially
France, hailed the Peace Treaties of Westphalia as the beginning
of a new epoch which had eliminated the supremacy of Pope and
Emperor. In an era of deep-seated ideological antagonism
between Protestant and Roman Catholic countries, the former
could hardly be expected either to underline the continuity of
doctrine or acknowledge the debt which they owed to " Popish "
civilians and canonists.

4. *The Naturalist School*

There was little future in the attempts of Continental
naturalists who, following in Pufendorf's (1632–1694) footsteps,
completely identified international law with natural law. Their
propositions were either so vague as to become practically
meaningless or they elevated assertions of somewhat transient
significance into eternally valid principles and, thus, reduced
natural law to the level of an ideology in the service of sectional
vested interests.

5. *The Positivist School*

It was left to Zouche (1590–1660), like Selden an Englishman,
to lay the foundations of positivism in international law. Without
denying the existence of natural law, Zouche drew a clear
distinction between natural law and positive international law,
the latter being illustrated by numerous instances from European
State practice.[58] More significant still, he paid due attention to
the legal problems arising out of relations between subjects of
international law in a state of peace as distinct from those of war
and neutrality. Bynkershoek (1673–1743), a Dutch international
lawyer, and Moser (1701–1785), a German jurist, further
developed this approach to international law. The great short-
coming of this type of positivism was its complete lack of any
measuring rod by which the moral or immoral character of State
practice could be judged.

6. *The Eclectic School*

A school, sometimes described as " Grotian," tried to hold a
golden mean between the extremes of naturalism and positivism

[58] See below, p. 34.

by paying attention both to natural and positive law. Wolff (1679–1754) and Vattel (1714–1767) are famous eighteenth-century exponents of this technique which is still in vogue today. The chief deficiency of this method lies in its arbitrariness. It justifies the description of " Grotians " as the eclectic school. The followers of this school select from natural law, legal maxims, incidents of State practice and the decisions of national and international courts what appears to fit into their *a priori* images of international law. Thus, the exponents of this treatment of international law are apt to consider themselves " sources " of international law [59] and tend to make the law fit their own preconceived conclusions.[60]

7. *Present-Day Opportunities*

This state of affairs calls for a different treatment of international law. The one chosen in this *Manual* is characterised by an inductive, inter-disciplinary and relativist approach to the subject.

(a) *The Inductive Method*. In the analytic field, the need for a change in emphasis from deductive and eclectic techniques to the inductive method is increasingly recognised. Its essence consists in ascertaining the rules of international law exclusively by means of rationally verifiable evidence.

To proceed in this way means to realise first of all that rules of international law are the only legal norms of international conduct. Principles of international law are further abstractions from these rules.[61] Legal maxims are even more remote from the reality of international law and, frequently, dangerously fragmentary epitomes of both rules and principles.[62] So-called principles of natural law and other ethical notions cannot create rules of international law. Unless clear evidence of their reception into the body of *lex lata* exists, they must be ignored in the formulation of legal rules and principles.

Moreover, rules of international law can be created only by means of generally recognised law-creating processes: treaties,

---

[59] See below, p. 23 *et seq.*
[60] See, *e.g.*, p. 16 above, and p. 99 below.
[61] See below, p. 38.
[62] See below, pp. 37 *et seq.*, 409 and 412.

international customary law and general principles of law recognised by civilised nations.[63] By way of contrast, international and municipal judicial decisions, the practice of individual subjects of international law and the doctrine of international law are not law-creating processes. They are merely evidence of international law or, to be more exact, law-determining agencies for ascertaining the contents of the actual rules of international law.[64]

It will assist in the evaluation of the views expressed by any of the elements of these law-determining agencies—judgments rendered by individual courts and opinions expressed by particular States or writers [65]—to test them in the first place in the light of the generally accepted rules which govern the seven fundamental principles of international law.[66] These offer, at least relatively, the most objective guide that is available for assessing accurately the evidential value of views on international law expressed by individual courts, States and writers.

As will be explained in due course,[67] among the elements of law-determining agencies, the decisions of international courts and tribunals, especially those of the World Court, provide a body of exceptionally persuasive authority. On a surprisingly varied number of topics, they offer further tests by which views expressed on international law by the other elements of law-determining agencies can be judged.[68]

In the systematic exposition of the practice of international courts and tribunals, American scholars, such as Moore, Ralston, Scott, Hudson and Professor Carlston have broken new ground. In other countries also, a growing number of writers are gradually concerning themselves with this rewarding material. In the United Kingdom, Lord McNair, the former President of the International Court of Justice, Sir Hersch Lauterpacht, a member of the Court, Sir Eric Beckett and Sir Gerald Fitzmaurice, former and present Legal Advisers to the Foreign Office, and Dr. Cheng may be singled out. Among Continental scholars, Anzilotti, A. de La Pradelle, Schücking, Max Huber, Professors

---

[63] See below, p. 24 *et seq.*
[65] See below, p. 31 *et seq.*
[66] See below, p. 38 *et seq.*
[67] See below, p. 31.
[68] See below, p. 33 *et seq.*

[64] See below, p. 30.

Charles de Visscher, Verdross, Carlo Schmid, Guggenheim and Hambro stand out among others.

In order to avoid the eclecticism which necessarily results from the indiscriminate use of diplomatic material, such material is used to the greatest advantage for the systematic analysis of the attitudes taken towards international law by various countries. It then becomes possible to achieve one of the primary objects of positivism, that is to say, to find out what the practice of States actually is, and whether a specific rule can be claimed truthfully as a universally or generally accepted rule of international law. It may, therefore, be advisable to repeat that the generalisations found in this *Manual* are based primarily on the practice of international courts and tribunals, supplemented where indicated by reference to Anglo-American State practice.[69]

The lead in the systematic study of State practice has again been given by American scholars such as Moore, Hyde and Judge Hackworth, who have concentrated on the systematic exposition of international law as applied by the United States of America. In the United Kingdom, valuable spade work has been increasingly done in recent years on corresponding material by, among others, Professor H. A. Smith and Lord McNair, as well as a growing number of younger scholars. In this context, attention should be drawn to the *International Law Reports,* the culmination of a joint enterprise launched in 1929 by Dr. McNair and Dr. Lauterpacht as they then were. The chief value of these Reports, first known as *Annual Digests of Public International Law Cases,* lies in making conveniently available the judgments of a growing number of foreign courts on points of international law, over and above those of international courts and tribunals.[70]

The main task of analysis never ends. It means constant revaluation of the rules and principles of international law in the light of new material which some of the elements of the law-determining agencies so generously provide. Necessarily, every such analysis and systematisation is always provisional. At the most, it represents a true picture of international law at a given

[69] See below, p. 34 *et seq.*
[70] See below, p. 33 *et seq.*

moment. It requires continuous adjustment as new developments take place or new material comes to light.

In particular, the functional and systematic exposition of the treaty practice of States is as yet largely virgin land. Studies on these lines open up entirely new fields of special branches of international law, such as international economic law, international labour law, international air law and the law of international institutions.[71]

(b) *Inter-Disciplinary Treatment*. The analytical work of the doctrine of international law requires to be supplemented by inter-disciplinary studies. They alone enable us to view international law in perspective. The *History of International Law* furnishes the international lawyer with insight into the evolution of this legal system over more than nine hundred years and assists him in assessing more accurately than he otherwise could the significance of more recent additions to, and modifications of, international law on the various levels of organised international society.[72]

The *Sociology of International Law* provides the international lawyer with the tools to determine the functional frontiers of his subject.[73] Last, but certainly not least, awareness of the existence of relevant religious and ethical perspectives makes it possible to evaluate international law in the light of metaphysical and moral values. Open use of these tests makes unnecessary any pretence that selective postulates of particular religious or ethical systems form automatically part and parcel of positive international law.[74] Such inter-disciplinary studies of international law in related wider contexts provide the synopsis which is the indispensable counterpart to unavoidable specialisation in the analytical field.

(c) *The Relativist Approach*. Finally, international lawyers may be expected to pay attention to the problem of the development of international law and to elaborate the conditions on which an overriding and effective rule of law between nations depends. Fulfilment of this task forms the province of a

---

71 See below, p. 101 *et seq.*, and p. 227 *et seq.*
72 See above, p. 3.
73 See above, p. 7.
74 See above, p. 12.

branch of international law which may be termed the science of *International Legislation*. As there is always more than one constructive solution of any social problem, this discipline calls for a relativist approach. It eschews any patent solution, but prides itself in making available, side by side, a number of patterns which are always available for any desired improvement in the organisation of international society, and each of which can be realised—at a price.

The international lawyer is entitled, and probably not least qualified, to point out the inherent advantages and shortcomings of any particular blue-print as well as the conditions on which its attainment depends.[75] The choice, however, is for governments and public opinion. It involves political decisions which are outside the lawyer's province.

---

[75] See below, p. 359 *et seq.*

CHAPTER 2

THE FOUNDATIONS OF INTERNATIONAL LAW

" Valuable as the opinions of learned and distinguished writers
must always be, as aids to a full and exact comprehension of a
systematic law of nations, Prize Courts must always attach chief
importance to the current of decisions, and the more the field is
covered by decided cases the less becomes the authority of com-
mentators and jurists " (*The Kronprinsessan Margareta*—Judicial
Committee of the Privy Council *per* Lord Sumner, 1921).

UNORGANISED international society lacks any central law-making
authority.[1] The subjects of international law comprise sectional
and conflicting loyalty areas of high potency. They cannot
easily be persuaded to transfer to the international society
functions which, however inadequately, they can discharge
themselves. In particular, this applies to their means of self-
defence. This type of environment is hardly conducive to the
growth of either an extensive or a strong legal system. Thus, it
is tempting to compare international law with municipal law in
the early stages of its development.

There are, however, important differences between primitive
or archaic systems of municipal law and international law. They
result from the basically different social environments of these
legal systems.[2] That this is the case becomes evident from the
fact that civilised States operate *simultaneously* systems of
highly developed community laws in their internal relations and
in their association with other closely related communities, but
rest content with a remarkably loose society law on the global
level.

In order to understand the legal foundations of the rules of
international law, a basic distinction, half-hidden but, none the
less, clearly discernible, in Article 38 of the Statute of the World
Court[3] must be mastered. It is between the law-creating
processes and law-determining agencies of international law.
While the former comprise the different processes whereby rules

[1] See above, p. 8.
[2] See above, p. 9.
[3] See below, p. 733.

of positive international law are *created*, the latter constitute the evidence by reference to which the existence and content of these rules are *determined*.

I—The Law-Creating Processes

In the early development of international society, international law consisted primarily of express agreements whereby the parties freely accepted rules of conduct as legally binding between themselves. Little was taken for granted, and everything that was considered if only remotely relevant was incorporated into the texts of these treaties. Gradually, however, some of these rules were found so convenient and generally acceptable that their inclusion in treaties was no longer considered essential. They were taken for granted or regarded as implied in every treaty.

When new States or outsiders were gradually co-opted as members of this legal system by way of recognition [4]—first, on the part of the Holy See, and, subsequently, by the existing subjects of international law—the newcomers were treated as having consented to be bound by these assumed rules, and these gradually hardened into rules of international customary law.[5] This, for instance, is the way in which the international law of tort has come into existence.[6] In other fields, such as the law of war [7] or the law of the sea,[8] rules of international customary law also grew out of roughly parallel municipal practices of the leading powers.

Treaties and rules of international customary law constitute the two chief law-creating processes of international law.[9] A third, and subsidiary, law-creating process, that is to say, the general principles of law recognised by civilised nations, will call for consideration at a later stage.[10]

The multitude of the rules of international customary law calls for classification into sets of related rules. These differ in

---

4 See below, p. 61 and p. 71 *et seq.*
5 See below, p. 27.
6 See below, p. 163.
7 See below, p. 185.
8 See below, p. 122.
9 See above, p. 18.
10 See below, p. 29.

relative significance, and from those of primary importance, seven fundamental principles can be abstracted.[11]   They represent the body of the rules of international law on the level of unorganised international society.   As they are merely abstractions from the rules of international law, they are not in themselves binding unless incorporated into international law through one of the three law-creating processes.   Even more is this true of legal maxims,[12] principles of natural law or any other moral precepts.[13]

In the individualistic environment in which international law has developed it has set out on its course primarily as *jus strictum*, that is to say, a system of legal rules which must be strictly and literally interpreted.   In the course of a treaty practice extending over centuries, however, clauses stipulating good faith or equitable treatment have gradually come to be regarded as implicit in international transactions of a consensual character.   Thus, today it is true to say that in international treaty law and that part of international customary law which has its origin in treaties,[14] *jus strictum* has been largely transformed into *jus aequum*.   In other words, these rules of international law have to be interpreted and applied in a reasonable and equitable manner.   It follows from the rules underlying the principle of Recognition that new entities acquiring international personality must be deemed to have accepted such *jus aequum* to any extent to which it has become embodied in international customary law.[15]

On the level of international courts and tribunals, even greater scope exists for the interpretation and application of international law as *jus aequum*.   The parties to international disputes submit by their own volition to the jurisdiction of international judicial institutions.[16]   It follows from the consensual character of the *compromis* that the parties themselves, and the judicial organs which enjoy but a delegated authority, must exercise their rights and duties in a reasonable and fair manner.   Thus, it is not surprising that international courts and tribunals tend to treat the whole body of international law as

[11] See above, p. 7, and below, p. 39.
[12] See above, p. 18, and below, pp. 409 and 412.
[13] See above, pp. 13 and 17.
[14] See above, p. 5.
[15] See below, p. 66 *et seq.*
[16] See below, p. 238 *et seq.*

jus aequum. The express incorporation in the Statute of the World Court of the general principles of law recognised by civilised nations as a third law-creating process [17] further encourages this shift in international law from *jus strictum* to *jus aequum.*

A. Treaties

Treaties are agreements between subjects of international law creating binding obligations in international law. They may be bilateral (*i.e.,* concluded between two contracting parties) or multilateral (*i.e.,* concluded between more than two contracting parties). In the absence of any overriding international authority or any accepted rules of international public policy, international customary law does not limit in any way the conceivable contents of any particular treaty.[18] The parties are free to adopt whatever rules they wish to govern their own conduct.

By the same token, the subjects of international law may limit their freedom and, by treaty, establish an international public order or quasi-order in a truly functional sense on the level of institutional integration.[19] Again, with effects limited, as a rule, to the contracting parties,[20] treaty obligations supplement, modify and override obligations arising from international customary law. For instance, in the *Wimbledon* case (1923), the World Court held that Germany's obligation under the Peace Treaty of Versailles of 1919 to open the Kiel Canal to traffic of all countries at peace with Germany prevailed—at least in relation to other parties to the Peace Treaty—over Germany's duties as a neutral power under international customary law.[21]

From this angle, treaties may be viewed as the primary law-creating process in international law. As, however, the binding character of any individual treaty rests on governing rules of international customary law, that is to say, the rules underlying the principle of consent,[22] the question of the priority of any one law-creating process over any other *in the abstract* is somewhat pointless. What matters is how, in any *concrete* case, a conflict

17 See below, p. 29.   18 See below, p. 150.
19 See below, p. 343 *et seq.*
20 See below, p. 149 *et seq.*
21 See below, pp. 208, 210 *et seq.*
22 See below, p. 138.

between a treaty and a relevant rule of international customary law is decided, and this is an issue which cannot be settled once and for all.

Treaties regulate only the rights and duties of the contracting parties.[23] They cannot, therefore, modify the legal position of non-parties without their consent.[24] However large the number of parties to an international treaty, it is more akin to a contract than to a statute in municipal law. Yet, in the absence of any world legislative authority on the level of unorganised international society,[25] treaties perform of necessity also legislative functions between parties so inclined.

Within the same limits, it is possible to speak even of delegated international legislation. This happens, for instance, when States, by means of treaties, establish international institutions which are authorised to make rules binding on the member States.[26] Thus, the International Civil Aviation Organisation (ICAO)[27] is empowered to adopt international standards governing technical aspects of international civil aviation, which are binding on all its members unless they notify their inability to comply with such standards. The powers of such an organisation are, however, strictly limited to those conferred on it by its constitution and, ultimately, the member-States.

B. International Customary Law

The second law-creating process is international customary law. It has two constitutive elements: (a) a general practice of States and (b) the acceptance by States of this general practice as law. It is not sufficient to show that States follow habitually a certain line of conduct, either in doing or not doing something. In order to prove the existence of a rule of international customary law, it is necessary to establish that States act in this way because they recognise a *legal* obligation to this effect. This was made clear by the World Court in the *Lotus* (1927)[28] and *Asylum* (1950)[29] cases.

---

[23] See below, p. 149.   [24] See below, p. 149.
[25] See above, p. 8.
[26] See below, p. 257 *et seq.*
[27] See below, pp. 109 and 252.
[28] See below, p. 398.
[29] See below, p. 402.

For purposes of ascertaining the two constitutive elements of international customary law, the various law-determining agencies come into play.[30] A growing body of decisions by international courts and tribunals and by national courts, as well as an abundance of material in diplomatic notes and other evidence of State practice, assists the student of international law in this arduous task.[31]

It must also be recalled in this context how many rules of international customary law have their origin in standards of conduct which were developed over centuries in a multitude of international treaties.[32] The rules governing the international minimum standard in favour of foreigners [33] and those underlying the principle of the freedom of the seas [34] are signal illustrations of this proposition. While, at one time, such rules had to be expressly stipulated in treaties in order to be regarded as binding, subsequently, they became so widely accepted that, even in the absence of an express treaty stipulation, they were regarded as automatically binding.

Thus, past treaty practice may constitute invaluable evidence of particular rules of international customary law. If, from any particular date onwards, particular clauses tend to be omitted from the text of treaties as it were by general consensus, this may well constitute telling evidence of their transformation into compulsory standards of international customary law.[35]

The interplay of the rules of international customary law brings about what may be described as the creation of secondary law-creating processes. Acquiescence [36] and recognition [37] may create estoppels in the sense that, in good faith,[38] a party can no longer rely on otherwise relevant rules of international law nor on their non-existence.

It is, for instance, an arguable view that, by adopting unanimously the Resolution on the Nuremberg Principles,[39]

---

30 See above, p. 19, and below, p. 30 *et seq.*
31 See above, p. 19, and below, p. 32 *et seq.*
32 See above, p. 5.
33 See below, p. 99.
34 See below, p. 122.
35 See below, p. 400 *et seq.*
36 See below, p. 160.
37 See below, p. 62.
38 See below, p. 137 *et seq.*
39 See below, pp. 183 and 200.

members of the United Nations have estopped themselves from contesting the existence of crimes against peace and humanity as war crimes in international law. If this were so, it would amount to very much the same thing as saying that, for subjects of international law so committed, new rules of international law have come into existence.

By attaching estoppels to the action or non-action of subjects of international law in appropriate situations, the rules governing good faith, in conjunction with those on consent or recognition, create situations distinguishable only in degree and scope from those of actual rules of international law.

C. The General Principles of Law

The general principles of law recognised by civilised nations form the last of the three law-creating processes. In order to qualify as a product of this subsidiary law-creating process, a principle of law must fulfil three requirements. It must be, first, a *general* principle of law as distinct from a legal rule of more limited significance.[40] Secondly, it must be recognised by *civilised* nations as distinct from barbarous or savage communities.[41] Thirdly, it must be shared, in substance, by a fair number of civilised nations, and it is arguable that these must include at least the principal legal systems of the world. The fact that a legal principle is recognised in one's own country does not necessarily mean that it has been accepted elsewhere. This is a matter for verification in each individual case.

According to the intention of the parties to the Statute of the World Court, the general principles of law recognised by civilised nations are a subsidiary law-creating process. In other words, they come into operation only in the absence of relevant treaty obligations and of applicable rules of international customary law. While bilateral arbitral tribunals have relied to some extent on this law-creating process, the World Court, as distinct from individual judges, has shown a distinct reluctance to fall back on the general principles of law recognised by civilised nations. Even so, they are not without value. Their existence in the background forestalls any argument that there are gaps in

---

40 See below, p. 38.
41 See above, p. 12.

international law which prevent an international judicial institution from rendering a judgment on the substance of any dispute submitted to its jurisdiction.[42]

Thus, if it were contested that rules such as those underlying the principle of good faith [43] or rules on the extinction of claims by lapse of time (*extinctive prescription*) [44] formed part of the body of international customary law, it would be possible to argue their existence on the level of the general principles of law recognised by civilised nations.   The hesitation of even advanced systems of municipal law to incorporate the doctrine of the abuse of rights shows, however, that it is advisable not to jump to hasty conclusions.   It is necessary first to sift carefully whether any particular legal principle is not only general, but also accepted by a representative group of systems of municipal law.   Conversely, if it is established that a legal principle forms part of international law as a rule of treaty law or international customary law, no further need exists to examine whether it also complies with the requisites of a general principle of law recognised by civilised nations.

II—THE LAW-DETERMINING AGENCIES

It is necessary to distinguish from the three international law-creating processes the law-determining agencies, or what are called in Article 38 of the Statute of the World Court the " means for the determination of rules of law."

A. Primary and Subsidiary Law-Determining Agencies

The law-determining agencies mentioned in Article 38 of the Statute of the World Court are judicial decisions and the teachings of the most highly qualified publicists of the various nations. These are rightly referred to as *subsidiary* law-determining agencies.   It follows that there must be corresponding *principal* law-determining agencies.

The principal law-determining agencies are always groups of subjects of international law.   The composition of these groups

---

42 See below, p. 234 *et seq.*
43 See below, p. 137 *et seq.*
44 See below, p. 162.

varies according to the character of the rule of international law in question. If the rule is one of treaty law, the States which are parties to the treaty form, collectively as regards that treaty, its principal law-determining agency, and each of the States concerned constitutes an element of this law-determining agency. In the case of rules of international customary law and of the general principles of law, the principal law-determining agency is composed of all the international persons who recognise the rule of international customary law or the general principle of law in question.

Compared with any of the various primary law-determining agencies—all composed of varying numbers of subjects of international law—the place of courts, international as well as national, and writers is more subordinate. If the *dicta* of courts or the propositions of writers on international law all happen to go in one direction, they represent valuable evidence which may greatly assist in clearing up uncertainties that may exist on the level of the primary law-determining agencies. Then, these subsidiary law-determining agencies come into their own.

As a matter of fact, it hardly ever happens that there is consensus in any of the law-determining agencies. The question therefore arises how to determine the relative value of the views expressed by individual *elements* of any of these agencies. The test must be as objective as any valuation can be. It must enable the student of international law to grade elements of such law-determining agencies in accordance with their intrinsic value as means of determining rules of international law.

A threefold scrutiny of these elements appears to achieve this end. It must take into account the degree of generic and individual independence, the international outlook and the technical standards of any of these elements.

B. Elements of Law-Determining Agencies

If the three above-mentioned tests are provisionally applied in a rough and ready manner, then a prima facie hierarchy of these elements emerges. It is from international courts and tribunals to national courts, individual subjects of international law and individual representatives of the doctrine of international law.

(a) *International Courts.* In the light of the tradition which international courts and tribunals have established, their subjective impartiality and the absence of any personal interest in the decision of any particular case may be taken for granted. Thus, they may claim to comply as far as is humanly possible with the first of the three tests laid down. International courts and tribunals, in particular the World Court, fulfil also to a remarkable degree the second and third requirements. The World Court has attained, although perhaps with over-representation of some, representation of the world's main legal systems. By and large, its members are also in the front ranks of international lawyers. Thus, there is little doubt that international courts such as the World Court should have pride of place in the hierarchy of elements of law-determining agencies. The relative status of other international judicial institutions depends on the degree to which they comply with the three tests discussed.

Decisions of international courts and tribunals are binding only on the parties to a dispute and only in respect of the subject-matter of that dispute.[45] The principle of *stare decisis* does not apply in the international sphere.[46] Nevertheless, it would be a mistake to overestimate the difference between the merely persuasive authority of international judgments and the binding character of national judgments. Especially in the case of a permanent judicial institution such as the World Court there is a strong tendency towards continuity in the interpretation and application of the law. Moreover, even *ad hoc* international tribunals frequently refer to, and adopt, the reasoning of earlier international decisions in similar circumstances.

It may be asked why the views expressed by international judges in their judicial capacity should carry greater weight than those voiced in their private capacity. In the first place, the average lawyer shows probably a greater degree of detachment and care in his formulation of the relevant rules of international law when dealing with concrete and real issues in a judicial capacity, as compared with situations in which he comments on purely hypothetical cases or actually represents overtly or

45 See below, p. 244.
46 See below, p. 244.

otherwise a party interest. Secondly, before a decision is rendered, the case has been exhaustively argued by counsel from both sides and, in the more representative international courts, examined by judges of widely varying background and experience. Finally, the technical assistance placed at the disposal of international courts and tribunals, especially when sitting at places such as The Hague or Geneva with their well equipped international law libraries, should not be minimised.

At the same time, even international courts and tribunals are but elements of law-determining agencies. Their work is entitled to respectful examination. It is not, however, sacrosanct. It calls for critical study primarily in the light of the established rules governing the fundamental principles of international law [47] and, secondly, the three perspectives of international law.[48] The more daring any particular judgment happens to be the less it is likely to constitute reliable evidence of international law as it stands.

(b) *National Courts.* Municipal courts are not in the same category as international courts and tribunals. Viewed in the light of the threefold test set out above, there is also a considerable difference between the standing of the courts of different countries. Those which can claim a long tradition of respect for rules of international law merit particular attention. Yet even in countries which unquestionably accept the independence of the judiciary from the executive and treat accepted principles of international law as part of the law of the land, municipal courts are faced with serious handicaps as compared with international courts and tribunals.

In the first place, they normally may not apply international law which runs counter to the constitution—if there is a written constitution—or even to ordinary statute law. Secondly, British courts, for instance, may not automatically apply treaties concluded between the Crown and foreign States if such treaties would modify the Common Law or otherwise affect the rights of individuals. Thirdly, in many countries, the doctrine of act of State imposes restrictions on the judicial freedom of municipal courts. Fourthly, national courts may be bound or tend to

[47] See below, p. 37.   [48] See above, p. 3.

accept of their own accord the word of the executive as conclusive on issues which they treat primarily as matters of policy. Whether the home State has recognised a foreign State or government or whether a state of war exists between certain countries is a question of this type.[49] Fifthly, in systems of municipal law in which the principle of *stare decisis* applies, municipal courts are inclined to follow previous decisions involving application of the same rules of international law.

Nevertheless, a difference in their value as evidence of the rules of international law may well exist between the decisions of the courts of a country and its diplomatic practice. Admittedly, this distinction may become entirely hypothetical in totalitarian and authoritarian States. It applies, however, wherever the independence of the judiciary from the executive is respected. Thus, only on the lowest level are judgments of municipal courts merely evidence of national attitudes to international law. Where decisions of municipal courts of different countries show a general consensus of opinion on topics of international law, their views become of especial interest. The same applies to fields which, in the present stage of the development of international law, are not likely to give rise to litigation before international courts, and to cases in which national courts examine critically the State practice of their own countries.

(c) *The Diplomatic Practice of Individual States.* Compared with the detachment which is taken for granted in judicial institutions, foreign offices are prima facie suspect of bias and subjectivity. But due regard must be paid to the context in which views are expressed. For what is said in answer to an inconvenient question in a national legislature or stated in pleadings before an international court may differ considerably from replies to a questionnaire on topics that are likely to be covered by a codification conference.

Moreover, the extent to which States indulge in special pleading and in the invention of *ad hoc* principles considerably varies. Senior legal advisers to foreign offices tend to view cases submitted to them in the light of the remarkably stable permanent interests of their countries and, against this

---

[49] See below, pp. 65 and 179 *et seq.*

background, formulate their views on controversial or unsettled legal points.

From a formal point of view, it may be thought to follow from the principle of State equality [50] that the view of any one State on any subject of international law is as good as that of any other. Such purism is certainly preferable to the opinion that great or world powers as such are entitled in this respect to a privileged position. Power in itself is no title deed to preferential treatment. There are, however, intrinsic reasons why more attention may legitimately be paid to the practice of some States as compared with that of others.

States which are connected with more than one continent and are both land and sea powers are likely to take a more balanced attitude towards issues of a controversial character than States which are either in one or the other category. Views of individual States which may claim to be of exceptional evidential value are those expressed against their own interest. They bear the most impressive testimony of true respect for law.

(d) *Individual Writers.* It is not easy to determine who, in the words of Article 38 of the Statute of the International Court of Justice, are the "most highly qualified publicists in the various nations." It is apparently easier to be fair to the dead than to the living or to those who are "extraterritorial" than to those who are in one's own country—to mention only two of the many considerations to which subjective colouring of judgment may be due. Perhaps the generals of the Greek city States were merely honest when, after their victory over the Persians at Salamis, each voted the first prize for distinguished merit to himself, but all of them graciously consented to give second place to Themistocles, the architect of their victory.

In any case, this most subsidiary of all the law-determining agencies has considerably decreased in significance. This is due both to the growing volume of international and national case law and the increasing flood in easily accessible form of relevant State papers. To the extent that the views of writers have been expressly adopted by States or courts, as is the case with Grotius and Vattel, their place is assured by such a process of reception.

[50] See below, p. 58 *et seq.*

For the rest, their significance has tended to be overrated. During the naturalist period,[51] they often laid down unconsciously the law which they thought they were merely expounding. Until it became possible to cross-check their views with judicial dicta and those expressed in State practice, they enjoyed a monopoly which, in our time, has rapidly vanished.

(e) *The Risk of Evaluation.* To weigh and not merely to count the elements of the various law-determining agencies, assessing the significance of one as compared with another, may be suspect as a new type of voluntarism. If, however, this approach is consciously adopted, and the criteria of assessment are articulately stated, such evaluation can do little harm. It is implied or unconscious eclecticism which constitutes the danger.

III—The System of International Law

The systematic presentation of the rules of international law has undergone considerable changes through the centuries.

In the earliest stage, international law was but a commentary on the customs of warfare between Christian States, with emphasis on their humanisation and limitation. If considered at all, the law of neutrality marked the beginning of a systematic treatment of the law of peace. In this way, the rights and duties of States at peace, at least in their relations to belligerents, received some attention. Gradually, the emphasis changed until, in the eighteenth century, the international laws of war and of peace stood side by side.

From the nineteenth century onwards, it has become fashionable to give priority to the Law of Peace as compared with the Laws of War and Neutrality and to assume that, in the international sphere, war is analogous to litigation within the State. Once it is realised that, in a system of power politics, war is but the last resort in an ascending scale of pressure politics, the unreality of this view becomes painfully obvious. While war has been waged for the realisation of moral or legal claims which cannot otherwise be secured,[52] it has frequently also served ends which cannot be so justified. The test of the seriousness of the

---

[51] See above, p. 17.
[52] See below, p. 170 *et seq.*

claim that peace is the normal state in international society, is whether writers define the exception by reference to the rule, that is to say, war by reference to peace. Yet writers hardly concern themselves with this hopeless task, and for good reason. In a system of power politics, peace is merely a negative state, *i.e.*, the state in which subjects of international law are not at war with each other. It is, therefore, more usual for writers to concentrate on the apparently more rewarding task of defining the basic notion of war.[53]

In the light of the legal restrictions placed upon the resort to armed force since 1919 in a growing number of multilateral treaties,[54] the relative importance of the laws of war and neutrality in a systematic exposition of international law must remain controversial.[55] It appears justifiable to put less emphasis on these topics than was customary in pre-1914 days. At the same time, it would probably mean anticipating events to eliminate these topics altogether, even from an introductory exposition of international law.

The international lawyer's answer to the challenge of nuclear war can be neither the policy of the ostrich nor the tenets of *Couéism*: a chorus of mutual reassurance on the slow but sure progress on the road towards the rule of law in world affairs. It demands continuous checks of the adequacy of the transition made on a *world scale* from unorganised to organised international society. This is the reason why international law on the institutional level—its achievements, shortcomings and potentialities—receives such liberal attention in this Manual.

IV—THE FUNDAMENTAL PRINCIPLES OF INTERNATIONAL LAW

Arguments " from principle " are notoriously unreliable. It is, therefore, advisable to establish clearly the character of both the rules and the principles of international law and to elaborate the differences between the two.

A. The Rules of International Law

These are legal norms which can be inductively verified as the products of one, or more, of the three generally recognised

---

[53] See below, pp. 171 and 179 *et seq.*
[55] See below, pp. 185 and 208 *et seq.*

[54] See below, p. 171.

law-creating processes.[56] For instance, subject to the operation
of other relevant rules,[57] a subject of international law exercises
exclusive jurisdiction inside its own territory.[58] Another undisputed rule is that the jurisdiction of international judicial
institutions depends on consent.[59] The fact that both rules are
universally recognised makes it possible to formulate these rules
confidently as operative rules of international law.

Some rules are of wider scope and greater significance than
others. The former may be termed *primary* rules and the latter
subordinate rules. Subordinate rules are of two kinds. They
are either sub-rules of a primary rule or secondary rules.

Sub-rules spell out in detail specific applications of primary
rules as, for instance, the application of the rule on territorial
jurisdiction to individuals, property and ships in areas under the
exclusive jurisdiction of the territorial sovereign.[60]

As distinct from sub-rules, *secondary* rules are not contained
in any one primary rule. They are products of the interaction
between two or more of the primary rules. Rules such as those
on diplomatic immunity [61] or the breadth of the territorial sea [62]
belong to this category.

B. The Principles of International Law

For purposes of systematic exposition and legal education it is
valuable to abstract principles from legal rules. Thus, it is
possible to extract a principle from the rules on diplomatic
immunity.[63] Principles provide the common denominator for a
number of related rules. The more fundamental the underlying
rules, the more fundamental is the legal principle that is extracted
from these rules. Whether fundamental or not, principles are
mere rubrics and give merely a general indication of the contents
of the rules under their respective headings.

C. The Fundamental Principles of International Law

It may be a matter of argument which rules and principles should
be singled out from others and described as fundamental. There

---

[56] See above, p. 24.
[58] See below, p. 89.
[60] See below, p. 86
[62] See below, p. 120.

[57] See below, p. 84.
[59] See below, p. 238.
[61] See below, p. 93.
[63] See below, p. 93.

is an unavoidably subjective element in any such evaluation. All that can be attempted here is to enumerate the tests applied in the selection of the fundamental rules and principles of international law.

To rank in this class, rules and principles must fulfil three conditions:

(1) They must be exceptionally significant for international law.

(2) They must stand out from others by covering a relatively wide range of issues and fall without artificiality under one and the same heading.

(3) They must either form an essential part of any known system of international law or be so characteristic of existing international law that if they were ignored we would be in danger of losing sight of a characteristic feature of contemporary international law.

If these tests are applied, seven fundamental principles emerge on the level of international customary law. They are those of sovereignty,[64] recognition,[65] consent,[66] good faith,[67] self-defence,[68] international responsibility[69] and the freedom of the seas.[70]

D. Optional Principles and Standards

By means of bilateral and multilateral treaties,[71] subjects of international law are free to create additional principles as, for instance, those of freedom of commerce and navigation.[72] Unless parties desire to give effect without any qualification to any such optional principle, they have at their disposal counterparts to compulsory rules in the form of optional standards. It is the function of these standards to express in more concrete ways than would otherwise be possible how the principle in question is to be attained. The standards of most-favoured-nation and national treatment are classic illustrations of such optional standards in the field of international economic law.[73]

[64] See below, p. 57.
[66] See below, p. 138.
[68] See below, p. 172.
[70] See below, p. 122.
[72] See below, p. 106.

[65] See below, p. 61.
[67] See below, p. 137.
[69] See below, p. 162.
[71] See below, p. 141.
[73] See below, p. 102.

V—INTERNATIONAL LAW AND MUNICIPAL LAW

International law applies in the relations between the subjects of international law.[74] The relations between subjects and objects and between objects of international law are governed by municipal law [75] or, at the most, approximations of municipal law to international law which amount to rules of quasi-international law.[76]

Individuals and corporate entities are the bearers of rights and duties under municipal law. If a number of systems of municipal law insist on regulating legal relations in this category, conflicts between them are likely to arise. In the absence of treaties by which such contradictions are ironed out, each system of municipal law deals as it sees fit with questions of the conflict between its own and foreign systems of municipal law.[77]

If the bearers of rights and duties under international law and municipal law were necessarily different,[78] a plausible case could be made out for the proposition that any conflict between international law and municipal law was impossible. Yet, the existing subjects of international law are free to transform any objects into subjects of international law and create new subjects as they wish.[79] For this reason alone, conflicts between international law and municipal law are always possible.

Even if this were otherwise, the chief substantive problem would remain. This is not a question of a true conflict between different legal systems, but one of the issues of the effectivity of international law: the willingness of the subjects of international law so to adjust their own internal laws as to be able to carry out their obligations under international law.

A. Conflicting Doctrines

The problems arising from potentially conflicting rules of international and municipal law have been unduly magnified by doctrinal disputes. Two schools—the monist and dualist—hold diametrically opposed views on this issue.

In the monist view, led by Professor Kelsen, a theoretical alternative exists. International law is either superior or inferior

---

[74] See below, p. 47.
[76] See above, p. 5.
[78] See above, p. 1.

[75] See above, p. 1.
[77] See below, p. 391.
[79] See below, p. 62.

to municipal law. As the dualists see it, international and municipal law are separate and self-contained legal systems. Contacts between them are possible but require express or tacit recognition of the rules of the one legal system by the other. To do justice to the problem, it is advisable to take a somewhat detached attitude towards both schools and let the material speak for itself.

B. The Struggle for Supremacy

The doctrine of the supremacy of international law over municipal law appeals to the *amour propre* of international lawyers and has its attractions *de lege ferenda*. In *lex lata*, it corresponds to reality on the—always consensual[80]—level of international institutions, in particular international courts and tribunals.[81]

To some extent, this proposition is also borne out by the practice of a considerable number of States. Thus, according to English law, international law is part of the law of the land. Similarly, in a good many written constitutions, the generally recognised rules of international law are given priority over conflicting rules of municipal law. This argument does not, however, bear being pressed too hard.

The automatic reception of international law into any of these systems of municipal law means international law as recognised and practised by each of the countries concerned. Moreover, little doubt exists that if any United Kingdom statute were to run counter to international law, British courts would, in the first place, do their best to harmonise it with their own views of the United Kingdom's international obligations. If, however, such a construction proved impossible, they would be bound to give full effect to the statute.

Similarly, in the United States Constitution, treaties approved by the Senate are put on a par with the laws of the United States. This means no more than that they override conflicting state law and prior federal legislation. Yet such treaties them-selves—like rules of international customary law—may be made ineffective by subsequent federal legislation.

80 See below, p. 227.
81 See below, p. 229.

Finally, State organs operating under municipal law may apply what they imagine to be rules of international law. In fact, as on matters such as diplomatic immunity,[82] prize law [83] or war crimes,[84] they may well apply rules of municipal law which may or may not coincide with the governing rules of international law. In situations of this type the variant of the monist doctrine which reduces international law to the external branch of municipal public law attains a semblance of confirmation. It is, however, merely a semblance, for, from the point of view of international law, it does not matter whether there is a conflict or not. All that is relevant is whether a subject of international law complies with its obligations under international law.

C. The Exclusiveness of International Law

It becomes evident that the relation between international law and municipal law looks different according to whether the issue is viewed from the angle of municipal or international law. While municipal organs are ultimately governed by their own municipal law, international organs are entitled or, as the World Court,[85] bound to apply international law. Thus, international organs are free to follow in the footsteps of the World Court and refuse altogether to treat municipal law as law. In the eyes of international organs, it can be reduced to a set of facts which either are in conformity with international law and then are unobjectionable or conflict with international law and then are merely relevant as potentially tortious activities on the part of a subject of international law.[86]

It follows that, before any international organ, municipal law cannot prevail over a State's international obligations, whether these are founded on international treaties, rules of international customary law or general principles of law recognised by civilised nations.[87] On the international level, a State is estopped from arguing that its own constitution or any of its own constitutional

---

[82] See below, p. 93.
[83] See below, pp. 217 and 219 *et seq.*
[84] See below, pp. 198 and 199 *et seq.*
[85] See below, p. 233.
[86] See below, p. 163.
[87] See above, p. 29.

organs prevent it from complying with international law.[88] Any international entity which has contracted international obligations must, if necessary, change its domestic law so as to be able to fulfil its international commitments.[89] The fact that a State applies a measure which is contrary to international law to its own citizens is neither a justification nor an excuse for a breach of international law.[90] The same is true of any measure under municipal law which amounts to an evasion of international obligations[91] or the infliction of indirect damage on other subjects of international law.[92]

This relativist view of the relations between international law and municipal law is confirmed by wider considerations. The unity of law and the hierarchical order of legal norms, which the monist doctrine postulates, is a relation between abstractions on incommensurate levels. There is international law, but there is not *one* corresponding system of municipal law. This concept is an abstraction from a plurality of legal systems which have the negative feature in common that they are not international law.

It is perfectly possible for any of the subjects of international law to fulfil its own obligations under international law without subjecting its own legal system to a hierarchical relationship with international law. Actually, considering the different social background of international customary law as a loose society law as compared with the highly integrated systems of community law which the most advanced systems of municipal law represent,[93] it would be surprising if such a society law formed the apex of this imaginary pyramid.

D. The Formative Influence of Municipal Law on International Law

In the historical evolution of international law, municipal law, in particular Roman and canon law, exercised a considerable influence on the moulds and patterns of international law. Thus, whenever, in these formative stages, a need for new rules of international law arose, it was to be expected that international

---

[88] See below, p. 413 *et seq.*
[90] See below, p. 99.
[92] See below, p. 164 *et seq.*

[89] See above, p. 23 *et seq.*
[91] See below, p. 163 *et seq.*
[93] See above, p. 11.

lawyers would adapt suitable concepts and institutions of municipal law to their own needs and rely heavily on analogies from municipal law.

The doctrinal treatment of topics such as titles to territory,[94] State servitudes[95] or mandates[96] abounds with terms borrowed from Roman law. Occasionally, an Anglo-Saxon law term like trust territory[97] makes its appearance. The rules on the interpretation of treaties which, in close analogy to the construction of contracts, were gradually evolved by international courts and tribunals[98] provide further evidence of the debt owed by international law to municipal law.

In a regulated manner, this process still continues legitimately through the medium of the last of the three law-creating processes: the general principles of law recognised by civilised nations.[99] Otherwise, the task in this field is rather to reverse the process and to guard against the uncontrolled use of analogies from municipal law. It will assist in the task of emancipating international law from this state of dependence to eliminate from international law such municipal law terms as obscure rather than clarify the rules of international law which have meanwhile matured behind this nomenclature. Notions such as State servitude[1] and Roman law terms in the field of titles to territory[2] rank high in this list.

E. The Application of Municipal Law by International Organs

It may fall to international organs, in particular courts and tribunals, to have to apply municipal law. As all international institutions exist only by the consent of the subjects of international law who are its members,[3] such organs discharge this function necessarily by way of delegated authority. It follows that if such bodies apply municipal law, it is only because they are charged to do so by subjects of international law and, in this respect, international law grants them complete freedom.[4]

In particular, international judicial institutions may be faced with this task when they have to decide incidental questions such

---

94 See below, p. 114.
96 See below, p. 55.
98 See below, p. 152.
 1 See below, p. 515 *et seq.*
 3 See below, p. 229.

95 See below, p. 515 *et seq.*
97 See below, p. 56.
99 See above, p. 29.
 2 See below, p. 115.
 4 See below, p. 229.

as the nationality of an individual [5] or a corporation [6] involved in an international claim.[7] Similarly, they may have to pronounce on the rights and duties acquired by foreign nationals under concession contracts [8] or State loans.[9]

It may even happen that organs, such as the Mixed Arbitral Tribunals under the Peace Treaties of 1919–23 [10] or the Conciliation Commissions under the Peace Treaty with Italy of 1947,[11] are primarily concerned with questions of municipal law. For such purposes, international institutions may not only have to apply rules of any one system of municipal law, but also may have to evolve rules of their own on deciding conflicts between competing systems of municipal law.[12]

F. The Blending of International Law and Municipal Law

In a growing number of fields, international law and municipal law tend to become interwoven. In matters ranging from labour relations,[13] copyright,[14] peaceful and other uses of nuclear energy,[15] and the industrialisation of underdeveloped countries [16] to public health,[17] international law increasingly affects the life of the individual and leads to the enactment of internationally prescribed municipal law. Some of the achievements in this type of functional co-operation are more substantial than others. However encouraging, they must not be allowed to lead to a loss of perspective.

Close co-operation exists between some States, but it is closer between some than between others. It is even arguable that some of the integration attained in each of the two world camps is but the complement of the gulf that separates the world camps from each other. Moreover, interpenetration, as this process has also been termed, may be somewhat one-sided and stand primarily for a position of hegemonical pre-eminence of a leading power over some of its equals in law.[18]

Similarly, the approximation of international law to municipal

---

5 See below, p. 129.
7 See below, p. 164.
9 See below, p. 140.
11 See below, p. 231.
13 See below, p. 107.
15 See below, p. 346.
17 See below, p. 654.

6 See below, p. 133.
8 See below, p. 140.
10 See below, p. 231.
12 See above, p. 414 *et seq.*
14 See below, p. 258.
16 See below, p. 293 *et seq.*
18 See below, p. 358.

law in relations governed by supra-national institutions [19] is not necessarily striking evidence of a glorious movement in this direction on a global scale. In Western Europe, it is hardly more than a belated attempt to achieve by way of functional federation a degree of unity which it has proved impossible to attain by means of more traditional devices.

International law is a universal law.[20] Thus, the relations between powers in different blocs or between such powers and non-committed States are probably a more commensurate testing ground for the accuracy of the thesis of the growing inter-penetration between international law and municipal law.

[19] See below, p. 343.
[20] See above, p. 7.

CHAPTER 3

INTERNATIONAL PERSONALITY

" The principle of the independence of States is a fundamental principle of international law " (*The Status of Eastern Carelia*— The Permanent Court of International Justice—1923).

INTERNATIONAL personality means capacity to be a bearer of rights and duties under international law. Any entity which possesses international personality is an international person or a subject of international law, as distinct from a mere object of international law.[1] International personality may be unlimited (*full capacity*), as is the case with independent States, or restricted (*limited capacity*), as in the case of dependent States [2] or international institutions.[3]

I—INTERNATIONAL PERSONALITY IN HISTORICAL PERSPECTIVE

To understand why certain entities are, and others are not, endowed with international personality, it is helpful to view the issue in historical perspective.[4]

The feudal nexus between Emperor, kings and princes within the Holy Roman Empire continued to exist in form for a long time after, in fact, some of these rulers had already firmly secured a high degree of actual independence and were treated by the Emperor on a footing of equality in all matters except those of a merely ceremonial character. Furthermore, on the fringes of the Holy Roman Empire, a number of kingdoms existed which either had broken loose from it or never acknowledged the Emperor's overlordship. These European States which recognised each other as substantially equal, form the historical nucleus of the over eighty subjects of full capacity in present-day international law.

In the course of the political and military upheavals which accompanied the formation and growth of European polity, some

---

[1] See below, p. 113 *et seq.*   [2] See below, p. 54 *et seq.*
[3] See below, p. 72 *et seq.*
[4] See above, p. 3 *et seq.*

of these international persons, like the King of Aragon or the Duke of Ferrara, disappeared from the international scene. Others, such as the Kings of Spain, France or England, grew in stature in proportion to their increase in power and influence.

For a long time, these crowned heads rather than their States were considered to be subjects of international law. During the period of absolutism, monarch and State were for all practical purposes treated as identical in most European countries. Thus, in some instances until the nineteenth century and later, the personification of the State in the ruler corresponded to the actual position.

The existence of aristocratic free cities within the Holy Roman Empire and in Italy made political scientists and lawyers familiar with the existence of political entities other than absolutist monarchies or principalities. When, in the seventeenth century, States such as the United Provinces of the Low Countries or Cromwell's Commonwealth claimed, and received, international personality, additional precedents were created. In a more liberal age, their existence assisted in gradually shifting the emphasis from the head of State to the State itself as an international person.

II—Typical Subjects of International Law

The typical subjects of international law are organised on a territorial basis. Three groups call for consideration: independent States, dependent States and, finally, mandates and trust territories.

A. Independent States

In accordance with their central position in international society,[5] independent or sovereign States are the foremost category among the territorially organised subjects of international law.

1. *Criteria of Independent Statehood*

Before recognising an entity as an independent State,[6] the existing subjects of international law usually require a minimum

---

[5] See above, p. 7.
[6] See below, p. 65 *et seq.*

of three conditions to be fulfilled.[7] The State in quest of recognition must have a stable government, which does not recognise any outside superior authority; it must rule supreme within a territory—with more or less settled frontiers—and it must exercise control over a certain number of people. These features have come to be taken as the essential characteristics of independent States. This degree of governmental stability, extent of territory and size of population may vary as considerably as they do between China, at one end of the scale, and, at the other, small Central American or European States.

On a basis of reciprocity, sovereign States as a rule treat each other's internal structure as a matter which is no concern of theirs, that is to say, as a matter of exclusively domestic jurisdiction.[8] Thus, each sovereign State decides for itself whether it wishes to organise itself on democratic, authoritarian or totalitarian patterns or to run its economy on lines of *laissez-faire*, State planning, State socialism or communism.

Similarly, subjects of international law do not necessarily concern themselves with the question whether the government of another sovereign State has come to power in accordance with its own constitution. At the same time, international law enables its subjects to take notice of such happenings. If a new entity wishes to be recognised as a subject of international law, existing subjects are free to make their recognition dependent on any conditions they see fit to lay down.[9] The same applies to the recognition of a new government of an already existing sovereign State.[10] If a government is sustained in power chiefly by the armed forces of another sovereign State, this may indicate that the government concerned has been reduced to a puppet government, and the State which it purports to represent has ceased to be a sovereign State.[11] Revolutions may lead to breaches of the minimum standard of international law for the protection of foreigners [12] or of treaty stipulations in favour of the inhabitants of a State irrespective of their nationality.[13] In such cases, sovereign States may, by the exercise of their discretionary power

[7] See below, p. 424 *et seq.*
[9] See below, p. 66 *et seq.*
[11] See below, p. 645 *et seq.*
[13] See below, p. 617 *et seq.*

[8] See below, p. 84 *et seq.*
[10] See below, p. 67 *et seq.*
[12] See below, p. 99 *et seq.*

of recognition, seek to attain compliance with political or ethical standards which they consider essential.[14]

Again, the degree of constitutional and political cohesion of an independent State is primarily its own affair. What matters to other subjects of international law is the existence of a body politic which can be held directly responsible under international law [15] in respect of a given territory, whether under a treaty [16] or in tort.[17]

2. *Composite States*

An entity may be so loosely organised that it is doubtful whether it alone possesses international personality or some of its constituent members do so as well. This is especially true of composite States. In accordance with a terminology borrowed from political science, which tends to be belied in individual cases, it is possible to distinguish between different types of such States.

A *personal* union consists of two separate States which happen to share the same Head of State. The personal union which existed between Great Britain and Hanover from 1714 until 1837 belongs to this category. In a *federation*, normally, the federal State possesses international personality, but not its constituent members. The United States of America and Canada illustrate this type of State. The existence of limited rights of legation and treaty-making power reserved to some of the member States of the German *Reich* between 1871 and 1918 proves that this typology serves merely purposes of classification, but is not a matrix of legal rules.

In a *real* union, such as the Austro-Hungarian Empire, or a *confederation*, such as Switzerland from 1815 to 1848, international personality is primarily or exclusively vested in each of the constituent members. As, however, is shown by other confederations, that is to say, the League of Nations and the United Nations,[18] nothing prevents the members of a confederation from endowing the confederation as such with an international

---

14 See below, p. 63 *et seq.*
15 See below, p. 58 *et seq.*
16 See below, p. 149 *et seq.*
17 See below, p. 162 *et seq.*
18 See below, p. 265.

personality of its own, or non-members from recognising it in this capacity.[19]

Similarly, in a *personal* union—such as that between Great Britain and Hanover from 1714 to 1837—the constituent members have in common the same head of State, but remain separate States with distinct international personalities. If the reality of international law could be pressed neatly into the straitjackets of these classificatory notions, a *real* union would be an association of States the constituent members of which lack international personality. Actually, it depends entirely on internal arrangements in any real union, and the attitude of third States taken towards it and its member States, whether the union alone or both the union and the member States possess international personality. Thus, from 1723 to 1849 and 1867 to 1918, the Austro-Hungarian Dual Monarchy was regarded as a real union. Nevertheless, in contrast to the more conceptualist doctrine of international law, the Permanent Court of International Justice found that each of the two constituent members of this real union was not only a separate State for internal purposes, but also had distinct international personality.

The position of the *British Commonwealth* calls for separate comment. While, originally, the British Empire was a unitary State—and this description still applies to the United Kingdom and its colonial dependencies—the Dominions have gradually developed into sovereign States and subjects of international law in their own right. For some purposes, they make use of their international personality; for others, they may prefer to be treated as part of the more comprehensive unit formed by the British Commonwealth.

A body which is involved in such a process of devolution presents anomalies. Yet, in so far as treaties are concerned, a procedure has been elaborated which leaves no doubt as to the individual members of the British Commonwealth which are parties to a treaty. Similarly, no difficulties appear to arise regarding tortious liability.[20] The members of the Commonwealth are anxious to affirm their international personality. They, therefore, are not likely to shirk the consequences which

---

[19] See below, p. 277 *et seq.*
[20] See below, p. 432 *et seq.*

follow from this status even if, in individual cases, they may deny the existence of any liability. Thus, third States have little reason to challenge a position which amounts to saying that the British Commonwealth and Empire is *one* subject of international law for all purposes for which its constituent members wish to act as a single unit.

3. *Condominium and Co-imperium*

Territories under *condominium* of two or more sovereign States possess no international personality of their own, but are under the joint sovereignty of the States in charge of their administration. Examples are the *condominium* exercised jointly by the United Kingdom and the United States over the Pacific islands of Canton and Enderbury and that of France and the United Kingdom over the New Hebrides.

An analogous situation arises if, after their enemy's *debellatio*,[21] the victors decide not to annex the territory of their defeated enemy nor to leave it in a state of international no man's land, but to govern the territory jointly as a distinct international entity. This happened after Germany's defeat in 1945 when it was decided to establish there an inter-Allied government. This type of situation may be distinguished from one of *condominium*, because the administering powers do not treat the area as their own, and termed *co-imperium*.[22] The same description is probably also appropriate to describe the status of the Republic of Andorra which has two co-princes, the President of the French Republic and the Spanish Bishop of Urgel.[23]

4. *Neutralised and Guaranteed States*

A sovereign State may commit itself in an internationally binding form [24] to remain permanently neutral or not to alienate its independence. This undertaking can be strengthened by other subjects of international law agreeing among themselves, and with the State directly concerned, to respect or guarantee collectively (*joint* guarantee) or both collectively and individually

---

21 See below, pp. 116 and 203 *et seq.*
22 See below, p. 249 *et seq.*
23 See below, p. 424.
24 See below, p. 160 *et seq.*

(*joint* and *several* guarantee) the neutrality or independence of such a State. Without committing themselves to this extent, third parties may, however, limit themselves to recognising such a state of neutrality, that is to say, to treating it as *opposable* to themselves.[25] This result can also be attained by bringing a new sovereign State into existence, subject to corresponding conditions.

The former type of limitation of the exercise of State sovereignty is illustrated by permanently neutral States, such as the Vatican City (1929)[26] or Austria (1955),[27] or neutralised States, such as Switzerland (1815),[28] Belgium (1831–1919)[29] and Luxembourg (1867–1919).[30] The latter is exemplified by the Geneva Declaration of Austria (1922) not to alienate her political or economic independence[31] and the undertakings to be given by the Republic of Cyprus under the Cyprus Settlement of 1959 to refrain from total or partial union with any other State or from separatist independence, that is to say, partition of Cyprus into two independent States.[32]

The distinction between permanently neutral and neutralised States is metalegal. The passive tense in the latter case puts the emphasis on the initiative having come from a Great Power oligarchy like the Concert of Europe. What matters in law is whether, as in the typical case, policies of neutrality[33] or the maintenance of independence[34] remain matters of sovereign decision—as they are under international customary law—or whether this freedom is limited by internationally binding undertakings as in the case of permanently neutral as well as neutralised States. Yet, limitations of this type do not differ in substance from other restrictions of the exercise of State sovereignty as, for instance, those undertaken by members of the United Nations.[35] Thus, the distinction between neutralised or guaranteed States and others has lost much of the significance it had at a time when Great Powers refused to undertake comparable commitments.

[25] See below, p. 62.
[27] See below, p. 207.
[29] See below, p. 168.
[31] See below, p. 418.
[33] See below, p. 209 *et seq.*
[35] See below, p. 271 *et seq.*

[26] See below, pp. 71 and 434.
[28] See below, p. 209.
[30] See below, p. 209.
[32] See below, p. 428.
[34] See below, p. 57 *et seq.*

Whether permanent neutrality or neutralisation is compatible with membership of institutions based on the principle of collective defence [36] is a question of interpretation of potentially conflicting international obligations.[37] Switzerland does not consider her status compatible with that of a member of the United Nations. Austria, however, has joined the United Nations, on the assumption that her duties as a permanently neutral State take precedence over those of a member State under the Charter.[38]

B. Dependent States

Dependent States are subjects of international law with a limited capacity. They are the products of particular circumstances on which it is difficult to generalise. In each case, the matter is governed by the rules underlying the principles of consent, recognition and good faith; or, in other words, by treaties and, in relation to third parties, by recognition or non-recognition of the situation.[39]

1. *International Protectorates*

An independent State may have surrendered so much of its sovereignty or the exercise thereof that, for all practical purposes, it becomes a dependent State under the suzerainty or control of another international person, without losing the empty shell of its sovereignty. States in this position are termed *international* protectorates. If not even a semblance of sovereignty survives, the protectorate becomes a *colonial* protectorate. In other words, the protected State loses its international personality.

Protectorates such as that exercised by the United Kingdom over Zanzibar [40] and the Kingdom of Tonga [41] or those formerly held by France and Spain in Morocco [42] belong to the first category. Their exact position can be determined only by reference to the treaties establishing such protectorates, and by the extent to which third States recognise this hierarchical nexus. The protecting power usually makes itself responsible for the

[36] See below, p. 356 *et seq.*
[38] See below, p. 209 *et seq.*
[40] See below, p. 422.
[42] See below, p. 422.

[37] See below, p. 150.
[39] See below, p. 62 *et seq.*
[41] See below, p. 431.

conduct of the foreign affairs of the protected State and becomes internationally responsible for it to the extent to which third States are debarred from making their claims against the protectorate itself.

2. *Colonial Evolution*

An intermediate State on the road from dependence to independence may also lead to a stage of limited international personality. This was the position in the post-1919 period when India became an original member of the League of Nations. In some respects, the separate membership of Byelo-Russia and the Ukraine in the United Nations is a comparable phenomenon. It can, however, also be explained as the grant of a limited international personality to member States of a federation.

3. *Free Cities*

Areas which, for special reasons, peacemakers do not desire to leave under the sovereignty of their former territorial rulers nor to transfer to another sovereign State, may be endowed with a limited international personality.

The Free City of Danzig was established in this way under an international régime laid down in the Peace Treaty of Versailles and a bilateral Convention of 1921 between Danzig and Poland.[43] In the Peace Treaty of 1947 with Italy, a similar régime was envisaged for Trieste, but remained abortive.[44]

4. *Diminutive States*

In the nature of things, extremely small States such as Andorra,[45] Liechtenstein,[46] Monaco [47] and San Marino [48] tend to fluctuate in a twilight region between independent and dependent international persons.

C. League Mandates and United Nations Trust Territories

After the First World War the mandates system was created. The territories detached from the Central Powers were not

[43] See below, p. 249.
[45] See above, p. 52.
[47] See below, p. 418.

[44] See below, p. 431.
[46] See below, p. 449.
[48] See below, p. 449.

annexed by the Principal Allied and Associated Powers but placed under the administration of various mandatory Powers in accordance with Article 22 of the Covenant of the League of Nations and treaties concluded between the League and the individual mandatory Powers. Three categories of mandates were established: A-, B- and C-mandates. This classification took into account both the political development of the areas concerned and the willingness—or lack of it—of the prospective mandatories to accept more than a nominal control of their activities.

The international régime of each mandated territory depended upon the treaty establishing it, but the treaties in each of the three categories were largely similar. The administration of all three categories of mandated territory was subject to supervision and control by the League of Nations.[49] At least in so far as the A-mandates were concerned, a limited international personality was granted by the mandate treaties to these territories and recognised also by other League members and a number of non-member States.

The A-mandates have since acquired independence. All the other mandates but one have become trust territories under agreements between the former mandatory Powers and the United Nations. The exception is South-West Africa. In the absence of a trust agreement, this territory ought to be administered by the Union of South Africa as a League mandate, but she acts with scant regard for the mandate treaty. In the view of the Union, however, the mandate treaty has lapsed with the dissolution of the League of Nations.

In its Advisory Opinion on the *International Status of South-West Africa* (1950),[50] the International Court of Justice found that the powers formerly exercised by the League of Nations in relation to the C-mandate of South-West Africa had automatically devolved upon the United Nations because of the intrinsic similarity between the mandate and the trusteeship systems. The Court attached little importance to the break in continuity between the League of Nations and the United Nations. Actually, the undertakings given by the Union of

---

[49] See below, p. 298 *et seq.*
[50] See below, p. 303.

South Africa at the last session of the League Assembly in 1946 and to the United Nations appear to provide a more secure legal basis for the assumption, however ineffective, by the United Nations of a controlling function corresponding to that exercised by the League of Nations.

The trusteeship system of the United Nations does not apply to specified territories or specific categories of territory as did the mandates system. By Article 77 of the Charter of the United Nations, the trusteeship system is entirely optional. It is left with member States whether they wish to place any of the three categories of territory enumerated in the Article under the trusteeship system.

Two types of trust territory are provided for in the Charter: strategic and non-strategic. Both are placed under the administration of the administering Power by agreement with the United Nations, the initiative being left in practice—but, with the exception of former mandated territories, not yet forthcoming —with the States responsible for the administration of dependent territories. Supervision of territories designated as *strategic areas* is carried out by the Security Council and that of other trust territories by the General Assembly, in both cases with the assistance of the Trusteeship Council.[51] In contrast to A-mandates, none of the trust territories has even a limited international personality of its own. Like any other territories,[52] they are objects of international law. They must, however, be administered in accordance with the beneficial purposes laid down in the Charter of the United Nations and the individual trusteeship agreements.[53] The first trust territory to relinquish this position was the part of Togoland under British administration. In 1957 it was united with the Gold Coast in the independent State of Ghana.[54]

III—The Principle of Sovereignty

The concept of sovereignty has been employed by theologians, lawyers and political scientists ever since the days of St. Thomas Aquinas.

---

[51] See below, p. 298 *et seq.*   [52] See below, p. 114.
[53] See below, p. 301.   [54] See below, p. 442.

A. Meanings of Sovereignty

In the context of theology and the constitutional theory of the unitary State, sovereignty means *omnipotence*. But if several entities none of which is able to attain supremacy over any of the others resign themselves to co-existence with each other, the meaning of sovereignty in their mutual relations changes. Each will still refuse to recognise the superior authority of any other outside authority. It will, however, be prepared to accept on a basis of reciprocity the claim by others in a similar position to be also *free from external control*.

The stratification of world society in hierarchies of world Powers, medium Powers and small States—as well as groupings under leading Powers inside antagonistic camps—indicates that *political* sovereignty still means, if not necessarily omnipotence, at least *pre-eminence* and *leadership*. This state of affairs is fully compatible with any of such entities enjoying *legal* sovereignty, that is to say, equality in, and before, international law or, as it is put in the Charter of the United Nations, with the principle of *sovereign equality*.[55]

In the dynamics of international law and relations, co-ordination between political and legal sovereignty—sometimes termed interdependence[56]—is attained by way of consent or acquiescence,[57] that is to say, acceptance by those who must of " advice " which it is inopportune to reject.

B. The Governing Rules

The principle of legal sovereignty is an abstraction from a number of relevant rules :

(1) Without its consent, a subject of international law is bound by applicable rules of international customary law[58] and general principles of law recognised by civilised nations.[59]

(2) Additional international obligations can be imposed on any subject of international law only with its consent.[60]

[55] See below, pp. 270 and 319.
[56] See below, pp. 270 *et seq*, and 418.
[57] See below, p. 138 *et seq*.
[58] See above, p. 27 *et seq*.
[59] See above, p. 29 *et seq*.
[60] See below, p. 138 *et seq*.

(3) Unless the territorial jurisdiction of a State is excluded [61] or limited [62] by rules of international law, its exercise is exclusively the concern of the State in question.

(4) Subjects of international law may *claim* jurisdiction over persons or things outside their territorial jurisdiction.[63] In the absence of permissive rules to the contrary,[64] however, they may actually *exercise* such jurisdiction in concrete instances only within their territories.[65]

(5) Unless authorised by permissive rules to the contrary,[66] intervention by subjects of international law in one another's sphere of exclusive domestic jurisdiction constitutes a breach of international law.[67]

C. The Co-Existence of Sovereign States

It is the purpose of the fourth rule outlined above [68] to make possible the co-existence in law of a number of entities with so far-reaching a jurisdiction as, in unorganised international society, is left in the hands of each sovereign State. The territoriality principle assists in adjusting competing claims by limiting the exercise of State jurisdiction to areas which are generally recognised to be under the exclusive jurisdiction of individual subjects of international law.[69]

This leaves unsolved the problem of competing jurisdictional claims on, and above, the high seas. These spaces are governed by complementary rules which, at least in time of peace, restrict sovereign States on the high seas to an exclusive control over ships entitled to sail under their own flag.[70] On a treaty basis, these rules have been extended to aircraft.[71]

D. The Complementary Character of the Rules of International Law

The equilibrium between the rules governing the principle of sovereignty and those underlying the other principles of international law is never static. For instance, under a peace treaty,

[61] See below, p. 86 *et seq.*
[63] See below, p. 86.
[65] See below, p. 86 *et seq.*
[67] See below, p. 84 *et seq.*
[69] See below, p. 86 *et seq.*
[71] See below, p. 135 *et seq.*

[62] See below, p. 92 *et seq.*
[64] See below, pp. 87 and 88.
[66] See below, p. 271 *et seq.*
[68] See above, under B.
[70] See below, pp. 90 and 134 *et seq.*

a State may acquire far-reaching concessions of a unilateral character. It is then easy to see that the limitation or exclusion in favour of the victor of any jurisdiction which the defeated had previously enjoyed involves a corresponding extension of the victor's jurisdiction.

When, as in the case of new rules of international customary law or mutual treaty obligations, each party concerned accepts limitations of its own jurisdiction so as to obtain corresponding concessions from others, the reciprocal character of the situation tends to obscure the real nature of the change which has occurred. In the first place, any new rule which is added to the body of international law changes the previously existing equilibrium between the rules governing the principle of sovereignty and the other principles of international law in favour of the latter. Secondly, *negative* sovereignty so limited does not vanish. Potential or actual jurisdiction is transferred to the potential or actual beneficiaries of these rules and transformed into *positive* sovereignty. In other words, each subject of international law concerned acquires additional rights under compulsory or optional rules of international law to command any of the other subjects in the same nexus to behave in accordance with the rule invoked.

On the level of *unorganised* international society, international law lacks any rules corresponding to those of *jus cogens* in Roman law or public policy in Anglo-Saxon law.[72] Thus, each subject of international law is free to limit as it sees fit the exercise of its own sovereignty in favour of another sovereign State or an international institution or to extinguish its own sovereignty in favour of another.[73]

It follows that, on a basis of consent, it is even possible to imagine a world State coming into existence in one of two ways and fully in accordance with international law. Sovereign States may renounce their spheres of exclusive jurisdiction in favour either of one of them or of one or more supra-national institutions.[74] In both cases, all the negative sovereignty enjoyed by its former bearers will have been transformed into positive

---

[72] See below, p. 411.
[73] See below, p. 138 *et seq.*
[74] See below, p. 343 *et seq.*

sovereignty, wielded by a world State or supreme world authority.

E. The Significance of Negative Sovereignty

The implication of so wide a sphere of exclusive jurisdiction as, in unorganised or partly organised international society, is left with the sovereign State can hardly be overrated.

Matters as important as territorial issues, customs duties, import quotas, exchange regulations or access to raw materials and markets are all primarily the exclusive concern of the territorial sovereign concerned. Beyond this, each sovereign State decides for itself the scope of its armaments. In the absence of consent or acquiescence, it is under no legal obligation to submit disputes with other sovereign States to procedures for the pacific settlement of international disputes [75] or to agree to changes in the existing international status quo.[76]

This situation puts other sovereign States into a quandary. If a State is not willing to be co-operative in matters vital to others, but within its own exclusively domestic jurisdiction, these States are faced with a difficult choice. They may have to be content with the state of affairs as it is. They may, however, consider this intolerable and then have to contemplate resort to various forms of pressure, including war.[77]

Thus, unless resort to armed force is outlawed by treaty and adequate means for peaceful change have been created,[78] the principle of sovereignty fulfils a dual function. State sovereignty is one of the seven fundamental principles of international law. Yet, it also constitutes a potent guarantee of the supremacy of the rule of force over the rule of law in international relations.[79]

IV—THE PRINCIPLE OF RECOGNITION

The growth of international law is best understood as an expanding process from a nucleus of entities which have accepted each other's negative sovereignty [80] and, on a basis of consent, are prepared to maintain and possibly extend the scope of their legal relations. Like most clubs, the society of sovereign States

---

[75] See below, p. 229 *et seq.*
[77] See below, p. 179 *et seq.*
[79] See above, p. 10 *et seq.*

[76] See below, p. 311 *et seq.*
[78] See below, pp. 171 and 311 *et seq.*
[80] See above, p. 58.

is based on the principle of co-option. In exercising this prerogative, the existing subjects of international law employ the device of recognition.

A. The Functions of Recognition

The generality and importance of this device is such as to justify treating recognition as one of the fundamental principles of international law.

Recognition may be employed not only for the purpose of acknowledging the existence of a new subject of international law [81] or its organs,[82] but also for a variety of other purposes. These range from the recognition of territorial claims,[83] changes in the title of sovereigns,[84] and the grant and withdrawal of nationality [85] to the recognition of the maritime flag of a land-locked State,[86] of a sphere of exclusive influence [87] or of the validity of a pacific blockade.[88]

In each case, recognition is a means by which States express their willingness to acknowledge *vis-à-vis* themselves the existence, and legal effect, of a situation or transaction which, in the absence of such recognition, would not be *opposable* to them.

B. Underlying Rules

Whenever recognition is at issue, five rules are taken for granted:

(1) In the absence of established rules or treaty obligations to the contrary, recognition of any situation or transaction which would not otherwise be *opposable* to a subject of international law, is a matter of discretion.

(2) The scope and effect of recognition is a matter of intent which, in each case, has to be ascertained according to the tenor of the act of recognition and its context.

(3) Recognition may be unconditional or conditional and may be express or implied.

(4) The devices of protest and reservation of rights may be used, *inter alia*, for the purpose of express refutation of the

---

[81] See below, p. 65 *et seq.*
[82] See below, p. 67 *et seq.*
[83] See below, p. 116.
[84] See below, p. 443.
[85] See below, p. 130.
[86] See below, p. 127.
[87] See below, p. 445.
[88] See below, p. 446.

intention of granting implied recognition to a situation or transaction which might otherwise be *opposable* to the State in question.

(5) Notification is a device by which a situation or transaction is communicated to a third Power with the intention of making it *opposable* to such a third Power.

Unless limited by prohibitive rules of international customary law,[89] the subjects of international law are entitled to use their discretion in granting and refusing recognition of any kind. They are, therefore, also free to limit this discretion either by standards of conduct which each of them lays down for itself or by way of treaty. Thus, in reliance on the Kellogg Pact,[90] the United States announced the Stimson doctrine, following the Japanese invasion of Manchuria in 1931. This meant that the United States would not recognise territorial changes brought about as the result of a breach of international obligations. The same principle is implied in Article 10 of the Covenant of the League of Nations [91] and Article 2 (4) of the Charter of the United Nations.[92] It is further reaffirmed in a Declaration adopted at the Inter-American Peace Conference of Buenos Aires (1936) and in the Bogotá Charter of the Organisation of American States (1948).[93]

V—The Acquisition of International Personality

The rules governing the principle of recognition regulate most of the questions arising in connection with the acquisition of international personality.

Occasionally, other rules may have to be taken into account. Thus, the rule prohibiting intervention in exclusively domestic affairs [94] makes illegal in relation to a recognised government any premature recognition of rebels as belligerents,[95] as an alternative government [96] or as a separate State.[97] Similarly, in relation to other parties to a treaty, a subject of international law may have committed itself not to exercise its discretion to recognise a new entity as a subject of international law or to do so only if

[89] See above, p. 60, and below, p. 411.
[91] See below, p. 584 *et seq.*
[93] See below, p. 330.
[95] See below, p. 70 *et seq.*
[97] See below, p. 65 *et seq.*

[90] See below, pp. 117 and 174.
[92] See below, p. 700.
[94] See above, p. 59.
[96] See below, p. 68 *et seq.*

stipulated conditions are fulfilled.[98] Finally, the rules on good faith [99] may create an estoppel and preclude a subject of international law from asserting that it has not recognised another entity as a subject of international law.[1]

A. Modes of Acquisition of International Personality

International personality may be accorded provisionally or definitely, conditionally or unconditionally, completely or incompletely and expressly or by implication. The scope of the international personality granted is a matter of intent.

There is no fixed form for the grant of international personality. The usual method is by a unilateral act of recognition. This may be formal or informal. Of necessity, the acquisition of international personality both by way of implied recognition and by estoppel through conduct is a matter of inference. The practice of States is understandably hesitant to infer recognition.

Thus, for example, contact with a foreign *de facto* authority for the purpose of protecting the lives or property of nationals abroad does not necessarily imply recognition of this authority as the *de facto* or *de jure* government of a new State or of an existing State.[2] The *de facto* authority is, however, equally free to refuse to entertain relations on such an informal basis.

Equivocal borderline cases remain. A member of an international institution may abstain from voting on, or vote in favour of, the admission of a State which it has not recognised. Two States which do not recognise each other may take part in an international conference or become co-signatories to a multilateral agreement. They may be parties to multilateral agreements to which non-parties may accede or be admitted by a majority of the existing contracting parties, as is provided for in the Statute of the World Court and the Charter of the United Nations.

If two States which do not recognise each other are co-parties to a multilateral treaty or co-members of an international institution, they have undertaken, by the consent given to

98 See above, p. 63.
99 See below, p. 137 *et seq.*
1 See below, p. 65.
2 See below, p. 65 *et seq.*

the treaty or to the establishment of the international institution, to fulfil towards any original or subsequent party all the obligations under the multilateral agreement concerned, however they may choose to treat each other outside the treaty nexus. Thus, they must be taken to have recognised each other at least for all purposes which fulfilment of their treaty obligations or co-operation as co-members of an international institution necessitates. Whether, by being co-parties or co-members, they have also implicitly recognised each other for other purposes is a matter of intent. This can be determined only in each individual case. The device of express reservation makes it possible to avoid any possible misunderstandings.[3]

Until the existing subjects of international law choose to transfer the function of recognition of new subjects of international law to a world authority, the effect of recognition is necessarily *relative*. It is limited to the relations between the recognising and recognised entities. As with titles to territory [4] or with multilateral treaties,[5] their initially relative effects tend to become absolute in the course of a gradual process of consolidation.

B. Recognition of States

The normal method for a new State to acquire international personality is to obtain recognition from already existing States. Such recognition may be recognition as a *de facto* or *de jure* State or, more briefly, *de facto* or *de jure* recognition. A State grants another *de facto* recognition if, for any reason, it wishes to delay full recognition. Typical reasons are doubts on the stability of the new State, reluctance of the new State to accept its obligations under international law or its refusal to settle outstanding issues.

De facto recognition means that, in relation to State activities in areas under the effective territorial control of the new entity, it is entitled to be treated as a subject of international law. The effects of *de jure* recognition are more far-reaching. The new entity is recognised as a subject for all purposes of international law.[6]

---

[3] See above, p. 62.
[5] See below, p. 141 *et seq.*

[4] See below, p. 114 *et seq.*
[6] See above, p. 48.

If a State is merely recognised *de facto*, its claims to public property situated abroad may well be ignored by the recognising State, especially if it is faced with competing claims on the part of another entity still recognised *de jure*. By way of contrast, the property situated abroad of a State which is recognised *de jure*, and in a state of peace with the recognising State,[7] is fully protected and entitled to immunity from local jurisdiction.[8] Moreover, as distinct from *de facto* recognition, the typical intention in the case of *de jure* recognition is to avoid any legal vacuum. The recognising State is, therefore, taken to let *de jure* recognition date back to the time when the newly recognised entity first proclaimed its existence as a new State.

Although exceptions which confirm the rule exist, it is also still true that, until *de jure* recognition is granted, diplomatic relations between the States concerned fall short of the appointment of fully accredited diplomatic envoys.[9] Thus, in case of doubt, diplomatic representation implies *de jure* recognition. A growing tendency exists to assimilate the effects of *de facto* and *de jure* recognition in a number of fields. This applies in particular to the grant of diplomatic and State immunities and the extraterritorial effects of municipal acts, such as legislation and judicial decisions by organs of an entity which has obtained *de facto* recognition. This is particularly so if there is no competing entity which is still recognised *de jure*.

The recognition of a new State means more than the confirmation of the political independence of an entity in relation to a given territory. Recognition is granted for a purpose and on an assumption. The purpose of recognition is to endow the new entity with capacity, *vis-à-vis* the recognising State, to be a bearer of rights and duties under international law and to participate in international relations on the footing of international law. The assumption is that the new entity on which such capacity has been conferred is capable and willing not only to claim the benefits of international law, but also to abide by its rules.

If a State, whether an original or a co-opted subject of international law, persistently violates international law, it is

---

[7] See below, p. 450 *et seq.*
[9] See below, p. 76 *et seq.*

[8] See below, p. 96 *et seq.*

arguable that, by way of reprisal,[10] other States are entitled to withdraw recognition of the offender as a subject of international law and treat it as an international outlaw. As in municipal law, outlawry in international law is a confession of weakness. Unless followed by war and annexation [11] or complete ostracism of the law-breaker, this form of retaliation is primarily of symbolic significance.

Compliance with legal duties towards existing subjects of international law may *prevent* an existing subject of international law from recognising an entity as a new subject of international law. International customary law does not, however, know of any duty to *grant* recognition to any entity. The principle of national self-determination is a formative principle of great potency, but not part and parcel of international customary law. In their *inter se* relations, States are free to incorporate the principle into international law and to commit themselves towards each other to apply the principle in relation to territories under their control. While, in the Charter of the United Nations, the principle of national self-determination remains one of a number of desirable objectives, the Trust Agreement on Somaliland (1950) [12] and the Anglo-Egyptian Agreement on the Sudan (1953) [13] illustrate the potentialities of the principle as an optional principle of international law.

C. Recognition of Governments and Heads of State

Whereas recognition of an entity as an independent State confers upon it international personality *vis-à-vis* the State granting such recognition, the recognition of a government or rival governments normally means something different. When a foreign government is recognised, the international personality of the State which it represents is, as a rule, taken for granted. The typical intention is to acknowledge that an existing subject of international law considers the head of State or government recognised as entitled to speak for, and enter into legal commitments on behalf of, the State concerned. In exceptional cases only—as with the British recognition of Israel—is recognition

[10] See below, p. 173 *et seq.*
[11] See below, p. 203 *et seq.*
[12] See below, p. 300 *et seq.*
[13] See below, p. 419 *et seq.*

of a government intended to convey an implied recognition of the international personality of a new State.

Similar to the *de facto* and *de jure* recognition of new States,[14] it is possible to recognise a government of a State, the international personality of which is not in doubt, as a *de facto* or *de jure* government. The distinction is not meant to refer to the constitutionality of the government so recognised under its own municipal law. It expresses different degrees of confidence in the stability of the régime concerned and of desire for diplomatic relations.

While *de facto* recognition is provisional and lapses automatically with the overthrow of the government thus recognised, *de jure* recognition is intended to be final and, if its conditions cease to be fulfilled, must be expressly withdrawn. While, normally, full diplomatic relations are not maintained with a government which has not been accorded *de jure* recognition, once this has been granted, diplomatic relations are either maintained on this footing or suspended. Suspension of diplomatic relations as such does not imply withdrawal of recognition.

If rival governments in one and the same country struggle for power, it may well happen that, at one stage, another State may have to grant *de facto* recognition to the government contending with that hitherto recognised *de jure*. This means in effect that the authority of each is recognised but only in relation to the territories under its effective control. So long as the claims of both governments are fairly evenly balanced, those of the *de jure* government tend to prevail. Moreover, only the diplomatic representatives of the *de jure* government are normally granted diplomatic privileges.

If a change of government occurs in accordance with normal constitutional processes, the issue of recognition does not usually arise. After a *coup d'état* or revolutionary upheaval, however, diplomatic representatives may require new credentials. Then, other States have to face the issue.

De jure recognition of a government is normally considered as retroactive, dating back in case of doubt to the time when the new government was first proclaimed. It does not, however,

---

[14] See above, p. 65.

have the effect of invalidating the acts of the previously recognised *de jure* government in spheres within its jurisdiction.

States may bind themselves either to recognise any government which may be in power in another State or not to recognise any government which has come into power by unconstitutional means or whose assumption of authority has not been confirmed by a free popular vote. In the absence of such consensual undertakings, other States are under no obligation to grant recognition to any particular government. Yet all this means is that they refuse to maintain diplomatic relations with it. In granting recognition to a rival government, other States must, however, not act prematurely. This would amount to an illegal interference in the exclusively domestic affairs of an independent State.[15]

As foreign ambassadors and ministers are accredited to the head of State,[16] the recognition of a government is often inseparable from the recognition of the head of a foreign State. Again, in principle, this is a matter for each sovereign State to decide for itself. Thus, a head of State may be a monarch, a president, the chairman of a supreme council, or even a collegiate body, such as the Swiss Federal Council. So long as there is no change in the head of State, changes in the internal administration, whether brought about by constitutional or unconstitutional means, do not require recognition. They may, however, constitute good reasons why diplomatic relations should be suspended and diplomatic representatives withdrawn.

D. Recognition of Insurgency and Belligerency

Civil war and revolution may raise issues akin to both the recognition of new States and governments. If revolutionaries have secession in mind, their limited recognition may well be but the first step on the road to recognition of new independent States. This was what happened in the revolutionary wars fought by the Latin-American colonies against Spain during the first half of the nineteenth century. Conversely, limited recognition of rebels whose object is the seizure of power in a State may be but the forerunner of their *de facto* or *de jure* recognition as the government of the State concerned.

---

[15] See above, p. 59, and below, p. 271 *et seq.*
[16] See below, p. 76 *et seq.*

Until a revolution or civil war has reached serious proportions, any form of intervention by another State in favour of insurgents constitutes an illegal interference in the domestic affairs of a sovereign State.[17] If, however, revolutionaries effectively control large areas of a country, other States may find it unavoidable to establish contacts with them, if only for the protection of their own nationals and their property.

On the insistence of Great Britain and, subsequently, the United States of America, this exception to the rule of non-intervention has been accepted in State practice since the last century. If revolutionaries have shown a certain staying power in more than a purely local area, other States may grant them recognition as insurgents or belligerents. The difference between these two forms of limited recognition is one of degree.

In recognising revolutionaries as insurgents, the intention is to refrain from recognising any right to wage war on, or above, the high seas.[18] It can also not be taken to be the intention of the recognising State to give any extraterritorial validity to acts of insurgent authorities.

If a State intends to concede to revolutionaries the right to wage war against their own government not only inside their own country, but also on and over the high seas, in short all the rights of a sovereign State at war,[19] it recognises the revolutionaries as belligerents. This status was granted by Great Britain and other States to the Southern States of the United States during the American Civil War. This form of recognition gives to revolutionaries all the rights of a subject of international law while the war lasts, but is limited to its duration. If the revolutionaries are defeated, this limited recognition automatically lapses. If they are victorious, the problem becomes one of recognition of either a new State or a new government.[20]

The government which is faced with revolution may itself consider it advisable to recognise the revolutionaries as belligerents. Typical reasons are to ensure that hostilities are

17 See above, p. 59.
18 See below, p. 192 *et seq.*
19 See below, p. 179 *et seq.*
20 See above, p. 65 *et seq.*

conducted in accordance with rules of international law,[21] and to give to the " legitimate " government all the rights of a maritime belligerent in relation to third States, in particular the right to establish a wartime blockade.[22] It is also noteworthy that, in the Geneva Red Cross Conventions of 1949, some minimum standards are laid down which, regardless of recognition of revolutionaries as insurgents or belligerents, every party to these Conventions must observe.[23]

A somewhat different problem arises when States at war with each other recognise fighting units composed of nationals or former nationals of their enemies as co-belligerents. Enemy States are fully entitled to ignore this limited type of recognition and, in strict law, may treat any nationals whom they capture in accordance with their own criminal law as traitors or deserters.

During the First World War, some of the Allied and Associated Powers recognised as co-belligerents both the Czechoslovak and Polish National Committees and, in the Second World War, the Axis Powers granted recognition of a comparable character to the " Emperor of China," the State of Croatia, and the Provisional Government of Free India.[24]

VI—Non-Typical Subjects of International Law

Three types of entity call for consideration: the Holy See, international institutions and the individual.

A. The Holy See

The Holy See marks the transition from subjects of international law with an essentially territorial organisation to those of an entirely different character.

At times the Holy See has had a territorial basis; at other times it has not. Yet all the time, a considerable number of States have recognised the Holy See as a subject of international law. It is even arguable that recognition as practised by sovereign States in their relations with each other is but a secularisation of the right once claimed by the Papacy as a

[21] See below, p. 185 *et seq.*
[22] See below, p. 224 *et seq.*
[23] See below, p. 202 *et seq.*
[24] See below, pp. 202 and 619.

monopoly to grant recognition to kings and emperors. In any case, until their annexation by Italy in 1870, the Papal States were territories under the sovereignty of the Holy See.

By the Lateran Treaty of 1929 between Italy and the Holy See, the Vatican City was created, and the Holy See re-entered the list of sovereign States.[25] Nevertheless, the Holy See is a territorially organised subject of international law with special features of its own. Its territorial character is accidental rather than essential to its status as a subject of international law. This rests on the position of the Pope as the head of a world-wide organisation, the Roman Catholic Church. For this reason, and not because the Pope is the head of a merely symbolic State, the States which recognise the Holy See treat it as a subject of international law. In substance, the international status of the Holy See is the prototype of the recognition of an entity which is not a State as a subject of international law.

The treaties concluded between the Holy See and secular powers concerning relations between Church and State are termed *concordats.* They do not, however, differ in character from other treaties governed by international law.[26] Similarly, the Papal Nuncios, Internuncios and Apostolic Delegates accredited abroad are diplomatic representatives like those of other powers. By the Vienna *Règlement* of 1815, the Nuncio is accorded the position of doyen of the resident Diplomatic Corps. It is uncertain whether this Article is intended to refer only to courts to which, in 1815, a Nuncio was accredited or is meant to be of general application.[27]

B. International Institutions

It is within the discretion of the members of an international institution [28] whether, and to what extent, they wish to grant it international personality.

Even before the advent of comprehensive international institutions, such as the League of Nations and the United Nations,[29] administrative international institutions, such as

[25] See below, p. 434.
[26] See below, p. 140 *et seq.*
[27] See below, p. 76.
[28] See below, p. 227 *et seq.*
[29] See below, p. 265 *et seq.*

international river commissions,[30] were occasionally endowed with limited international personality.

The United Nations—as did the League—enjoys a large measure of international personality. It is competent to be a party to international treaties as, for instance, trusteeship agreements [31] or the agreements with Egypt as the host country of the United Nations Emergency Force.[32] It may also give functional protection to its officers [33] and is even entitled to establish a military command to take military action directly or through its members, as in Korea.[34]

It must still be regarded as controversial whether, in relation to non-member States which have *not* recognised an international institution such as the United Nations, the institution may claim international personality. It appears more consonant with the rules underlying the fundamental principles of international law to limit this personality to member States and to non-member States which by consent, recognition or acquiescence have estopped themselves from disputing such a claim.[35]

In other cases, members may decide that there is no need to endow international institutions with international personality. Thus, the Bank for International Settlements at Basle has been granted merely legal personality of an identical character under the various *municipal* laws of its member States.[36]

C. Individuals

The history of international law proves that the aristocracy of sovereign States is a co-option society. The rules governing recognition are so elastic that there is no limit to the objects which, by recognition, may be transformed into subjects of international law.[37] Thus, the international personality of the individual is not a question of principle, but simply of fact: Is there enough evidence to substantiate the claim that the individual, the basis of national and international life, is more than an object in international law as it stands?

Under classical international law, the individual benefits from important rules of international customary law as, for

30 See below, p. 491 *et seq.*   31 See above, p. 56, and below, p. 301.
32 See below, p. 480.   33 See below, p. 132.
34 See below, p. 288.   35 See above, p. 39.
36 See below, p. 253.   37 See above, p. 62.

instance, that on the minimum standard of international law regarding the treatment of foreigners.[38] By way of treaties of friendship, commerce and navigation his lot can be even further improved.[39] Yet, in every such case, he remains an object of international law. Whether he is entitled to benefit from these compulsory or optional rules of international law depends on his own link—primarily through nationality[40]—with a subject of international law who, on the international level, is alone competent to assert such rights against another subject of international law.[41] Attempts to prove that a somewhat seamy collection of individuals, ranging from pirates[42] and blockade-runners[43] to war criminals[44] qualify at least as duty-subjects of international law are perhaps the surest admission of a case as yet unproven on the level of international *customary* law.

On the level of organised *world* society, that is to say, the United Nations, the protection of fundamental human rights and freedoms is still so embryonic as not to alter the picture. If anything, official emphasis on the " merely " moral character of the Universal Declaration of Human Rights[45] and the grotesque formulation of the Genocide Convention,[46] both of 1948 vintage, are telling evidence of the unwillingness of the members of the United Nations to divest themselves of their monopoly of responsibility for their nationals or, more realistically, to become internationally accountable to them.

Matters tend to become different on levels of closer international integration as between members of the Council of Europe[47] or inside any of the Continental supra-national institutions.[48] The more international law approximates to national law, the more the individual has a chance to become a direct bearer of legal rights and duties. The test in each case is whether, without the concurrence of the individual or corporation concerned, contracting parties have reserved to themselves the power to withdraw such privileges.

---

[38] See below, p. 99 *et seq.*
[40] See below, p. 129 *et seq.*
[42] See below, p. 88.
[44] See below, p. 198 *et seq.*
[46] See below, p. 438.
[48] See below, p. 354.

[39] See below, p. 102 *et seq.*
[41] See below, p. 164 *et seq.*
[43] See below, p. 224 *et seq.*
[45] See below, p. 642.
[47] See below, p. 337.

VII—INTERNATIONAL REPRESENTATION

States and international institutions—so far, the only subjects
of international law—can act only through individuals. This is
why relations between them are based on the principle of
necessary representation.

A. Heads of State

The principal representative of a State is its head of State.[49]
Notwithstanding limitations of his powers under municipal law,
the head of a sovereign State is deemed by international law to
have plenary powers to commit his State.

For the representative of another subject of international law
to throw doubts on the plenary powers of a head of State on the
basis of his own interpretation of a foreign constitutional law
would be more than highly offensive. It would amount to an
illegal interference with the sphere of exclusive domestic jurisdiction of another sovereign State.[50] Thus, with the exception of
rare cases of estoppel, the rule on the unlimited international
power of the head of State, which crystallised in the era of
absolutism, is still good international law.

B. Ministers

The Foreign Minister or Secretary is historically the principal
assistant of the head of State. For this reason, a rule of international law has developed in accordance with which he also is
considered to have plenary powers in all matters within the
scope of his office. In the United Kingdom, each successive
Secretary of State for Foreign Affairs and each Permanent Under-
Secretary of State for Foreign Affairs receives, on taking up his
duties, a General Full Power which authorises him to treat with
any other State.

The office of the Prime Minister is a relatively recent institution and in some constitutions, as, for instance, that of the United
States, does not exist at all. It is, therefore, impossible to state
categorically that a Prime Minister has the same international
powers as a Foreign Minister, in particular if his government

[49] See above, p. 67.
[50] See above, p. 59.

includes a separate holder of this office. It is, however, at least arguable that a government in which, in fact and common knowledge, the Foreign Minister is but the Prime Minister's nominee, is estopped from pleading the Prime Minister's lack of international powers.

C. Diplomatic Representatives

Continuous disputes over the precedence of diplomatic envoys were settled in a manner which received general assent in a *Règlement* adopted at the Peace Congress of Vienna in 1815 and amplified in 1818 at the Congress of Aix-la-Chapelle.[51] In all other matters, diplomatic envoys as the agents of sovereign and equal States [52] are on a footing of complete equality with one another.

In accordance with these Regulations, the following three classes of heads of diplomatic missions are *accredited* to the head of the State to which they are sent: ambassadors extraordinary and plenipotentiary (first class); envoys extraordinary and ministers plenipotentiary (second class); and ministers resident (third class). While ambassadors *represent* their own heads of State, diplomatic envoys in the other two classes represent their governments.

Chargés d'affaires, the fourth class of diplomatic envoys, act in the absence of their head of mission. They are accredited to the Foreign Minister of their countries of residence and represent their own Foreign Office.

The personnel of diplomatic missions serve to assist the head of mission in the discharge of his duties. It is, therefore, not for them, but their head of mission, to waive, as he sees fit, their immunity.[53]

The powers of heads of mission depend upon their letters of credence which they present on arrival and any additional *lettres de pouvoir* which they may have received from their own government and duly presented to the State to which they are sent. In accordance with accepted practice, the acts of accredited representatives in foreign States can be repudiated

---

[51] See below, p. 469 *et seq.*
[52] See above, p. 58.
[53] See below, p. 94 *et seq.*

only if it can be shown that they have exceeded their powers or they have acted contrary to their instructions.

On the lapse of recognition of a State or government,[54] the credentials of its diplomatic representatives are automatically terminated. As each subject of international law decides for itself on the withdrawal of recognition, this act is of a strictly relative character and does not affect the position of other subjects of international law.

Thus, while, on the recognition in 1950 by the United Kingdom of the Communist government in Peking, the credentials of the then Chinese Ambassador at the Court of St. James's came to an end, this left entirely unaffected the position of diplomatic envoys with credentials from Generalissimo Chiang Kai-shek in countries which still recognised him as the President of the Chinese Republic.

D. Representation of, in and at International Institutions

International customary law does not know of international institutions. They are entirely the product of informal or formal understandings of a consensual character, and the same applies to all problems of international representation arising in this context.

1. *Representation of International Institutions*

Their constitution may provide for individuals or organs to represent them in their relations with member and non-member States. Such representation may also be entirely the result of a constitutional practice acquiesced in by member States and accepted by non-member States. Thus, under the Treaty on the European Economic Community of 1957, the Council is the Community's representative organ in its relations with non-member States and other international institutions.[55] By way of contrast, the representative functions of the Secretary-General of the United Nations and his exercise of a delegated treaty-making power on behalf of the United Nations are entirely the result of constitutional practice.[56]

---

[54] See above, p. 68 *et seq.*
[55] See below, p. 353 *et seq.*
[56] See below, p. 307.

2. *Representation in International Institutions*

It is a matter of interpretation of the constituent document of an international institution what functions the members of its organs are intended to fulfil. In the case of members of judicial international institutions, it is generally accepted, even if not expressly stipulated,[57] that their judicial office precludes them from acting as representatives of any particular State.[58] In the case of members of organs of other international institutions, however, the presumption is to the opposite effect. Delegates of member States—as distinct from international civil servants [59]—represent only their own States and are subject to any instructions received from their home governments.

This situation does not preclude any of the organs of an international institution, as, for instance, the Security Council of the United Nations, from being authorised by its constitution to act for all or certain purposes on behalf of all the members of the Organisation.[60]

3. *Representation at International Institutions*

It is necessary to distinguish from the representation of member States *in* international institutions their representation *at* such institutions. Thus, an increasing number of member States have found it advisable to be represented at the headquarters of the United Nations by permanent delegations with diplomatic status. In the Headquarters Agreement of 1947 between the United Nations and the United States of America, in which the immunities granted by the United States to these delegations are settled, reference is made to representatives with the rank of ambassador or minister plenipotentiary.[61] In a resolution passed by the General Assembly in 1948, it is recommended that the credentials of such permanent representatives should be issued by the head of State, the head of the government or the minister of foreign affairs.[62]

Similarly, non-member States may wish to maintain relations on a diplomatic footing with international institutions. Thus, in

---

[57] See below, p. 235 *et seq.*
[58] See below, p. 236.
[59] See below, p. 304.
[60] See below, p. 284 *et seq.*
[61] See above, p. 76.
[62] See below, p. 640.

1952, the Foreign Office of the United Kingdom, soon followed by the United States and other non-member States, accredited to the European Coal and Steel Community a permanent delegation headed by an envoy with the rank of ambassador.

E. Consuls

Consuls do not normally fulfil representative functions. They are resident officials stationed abroad with the consent of the receiving State—expressed in the form of an exequatur—for purposes of promoting trade and rendering assistance to nationals of the sending country, in particular seamen.

Consuls as such are not members of the Diplomatic Corps. Thus, they themselves—as distinct from their official acts and archives—are not entitled to diplomatic immunity. In view, however, of the growing integration between diplomatic and consular services in an increasing number of States, they may enjoy such privileges by virtue of a simultaneously held diplomatic appointment.[63] Moreover, in backward countries and under capitulation treaties,[64] their status has frequently been assimilated to that of diplomatic envoys.

In the post-1945 period, the United Kingdom has found it convenient to adopt the practice of bilateral consular conventions in which, on a basis of reciprocity, typical issues of jurisdiction, immunities, fiscal privileges as well as acceptable numbers and classes of consular officers are settled.[65]

VIII—CONTINUITY AND DISCONTINUITY OF INTERNATIONAL PERSONALITY

International Personality is a convenient term for classifying under the same heading rules concerned with the creation, attributes and extinction of entities which are directly subject to international law. The danger which is inherent in the personification of a collective entity is the temptation to apply by way of analogy rules developed in municipal law primarily for " natural " persons.

[63] See below, p. 93.
[64] See above, p. 6.
[65] See below, p. 472.

A. The Relativity of Continuity and Discontinuity of International Personality

The problem arises in international law in three typical situations: revolution, territorial changes and war.

By and large, State practice works on the assumption that *revolution* is a matter within the exclusively domestic jurisdiction of a sovereign State and, therefore, does not affect its international personality.[66]

In the case of *territorial changes*, different situations must be distinguished. If two States decide on the cession of a relatively insignificant portion of territory, the matter is governed between the parties by the rules on consent [67] and, in relation to third States, by those on recognition.[68]

If a State agrees to its own truncation or a composite State is dismembered, the relativity of continuity and discontinuity of international personality becomes patent. In practice, the legal consequences of such changes are settled by way of treaty, recognition or acquiescence.

In the case of *belligerent occupation*, the rules of warfare provide that, short of *debellatio*,[69] such changes are treated as merely temporary while the war lasts [70] and do not affect the territorial *status quo*.

B. The Legal Consequences of the Cession of Territory

As a rule, the parties to a cession treaty settle expressly the typical issues arising from the transfer of a territory. This situation is necessarily ambiguous. It is equally arguable that these treaties prove or disprove the existence of a rule of general succession to all rights and duties between subjects of international law. If a treaty incorporates rules affirming such continuity, the parties may have meant the treaty to be in the main declaratory of international customary law and they may have merely intended to settle details not covered by these rules. Yet, they may also have found it necessary to lay down optional rules because of the absence of governing rules of international

---

[66] See above, pp. 59 and 70, and below, p. 201.
[67] See below, p. 138 *et seq.*
[68] See above, p. 62 *et seq.*
[69] See below, p. 203.
[70] See below, p. 192.

customary law. If parties to individual treaties have departed from the principle of general succession, corresponding two-way arguments offer themselves.

International judicial practice proves that, while the principle of general succession can hardly be substantiated as part of the body of international customary law, some rules governing a number of relevant situations exist. They are not founded on analogies from municipal law, but the result of the interplay of the rules governing the fundamental principles of international law.

Thus, on cession the *public property* of the ceding State in the ceded territory becomes automatically the property of the cessionary State. This rule rests on the interpretation of the typical intentions of parties to cession treaties.

On the same basis, it is taken for granted that parties to cession treaties desire to avoid a legal vacuum. Therefore, on the cession becoming effective, the whole of the *public* law of the ceding State is presumed to be replaced by that of the cessionary State. Thus, unless anything to the contrary is agreed, the nationals of the ceding State living in the ceded territory acquire automatically the nationality of the cessionary State.[71]

In the case of the *private* law of the ceding State, the presumption works in the opposite direction. Until it is changed by the cessionary State, it remains in force. Private rights acquired under the law of the ceding State are not automatically affected by the cession. They must be respected by the cessionary State.

In the absence of express treaty obligations, a general rule imposing succession to the State *debts* of the ceding State by the cessionary State appears to be lacking. On equitable grounds, a different rule is often asserted regarding strictly *localised* debts. It is doubtful, however, whether sufficient evidence exists to bear out the conclusion that a hard and fast rule of international *customary* law on this topic exists. Cessionary States are under no obligation to assume any responsibility for *tortious* acts or omissions of the ceding State.

---

[71] See below, p. 132.

C. Subrogation and Treaties

Treaties are binding only between the contracting parties.[72]   If one of these cedes part of its territory, existing treaties between third parties and the ceding—as well as the cessionary—State are interpreted in accordance with the rule of movable treaty frontiers.   It is presumed that it is the intention of parties to treaties to adjust automatically the territorial scope of their treaties to such territorial changes as may subsequently occur.

If a subject of international law ceases to exist, any treaties concluded with it automatically lapse.   In cases such as the voluntary dissolution of a composite State or the fusion of a number of States in a union, the results of the application of this rule may be harsh.   They are, however, mitigated by the need of the new international entity to obtain recognition and by the discretionary power of existing subjects of international law to make such recognition dependent on compliance with justified expectations.[73]

The assumption by the United Nations of a supervisory jurisdiction over the Union of South Africa in relation to South-West Africa appears to rest on estoppel by consent and conduct rather than on any rule of international customary law providing for subrogation of one international institution for another.[74]

D. The Alleged Rule of General State Succession

The only rule of subrogation in the case of the transfer of territory for which some evidence exists is that postulating respect for acquired private rights.   Yet, this rule can also be explained as fulfilment by a cessionary State of its *own* obligations in accordance with the minimum standard of international law in favour of foreigners.[75]

Thus, it would be unsafe to attempt to abstract from somewhat scanty evidence a general rule of subrogation or State succession.   Yet, the rules underlying four of the fundamental principles of international law—sovereignty, recognition, good faith and international responsibility of a subject of international law for its own illegal acts—go a long way to cope effectively

---

[72] See below, p. 149 *et seq.*   [73] See above, p. 62.
[74] See above, p. 56, and below, p. 458.
[75] See below, p. 99.

with issues arising from any break in international personality. For the rest, what cannot be attained on the level of international customary law, can always be achieved by way of consent. This is the safe road which, more often than not, the practice of States has chosen.

CHAPTER 4

STATE JURISDICTION

" All that can be required of a State is that it should not overstep the limits which international law places upon its jurisdiction; within these limits, its title to exercise jurisdiction rests upon its sovereignty " (*The S.S. Lotus*—The Permanent Court of International Justice—1927).

STATE sovereignty in international customary law is an essentially negative concept.[1] State jurisdiction is its positive complement.

I—THE STATICS AND DYNAMICS OF THE PROBLEM

If international law were limited to the sum total of the rules of international customary law governing the seven fundamental principles,[2] State jurisdiction in parts of the earth subject to territorial sovereignty[3] would comprise any topics not covered by rules other than those on State sovereignty.[4] In the terminology of Paragraph 8 of Article 15 of the Covenant of the League of Nations, any of these matters would be " solely within the domestic jurisdiction " of each sovereign State.

Actually, this exclusive domain is further restricted by the general principles of law recognised by civilised nations and treaties. By means of bilateral and, even more so, multilateral treaties, the subjects of international law impinge continuously on one another's spheres of exclusively domestic jurisdiction. These optional rules—normally operative only among the parties to the consensual superstructures which have been created increasingly on the foundation of international customary law[5] —contribute further to the shrinkage of the sectors of State jurisdiction which remain unaffected by international law. Thus, the totality of the rules of international law can be explained as a constantly changing and dynamic interplay between the rules

---

1 See above, pp. 58 and 60, and below, p. 270.
2 See above, pp. 7 and 38.
3 See below, p. 86 *et seq.*
4 See above, p. 39 *et seq.*
5 See below, p. 27 *et seq.*

underlying the principle of sovereignty and those governing the other fundamental principles of international law.[6]

The conceptual counterpart of this interplay of the rules of international law is the distinction between those spheres in which State jurisdiction is not exposed to the impact of international law and others in which it is limited or excluded by impinging rules of international law. Whenever this happens, the jurisdiction so limited or excluded does not vanish into thin air. It accrues to other entities which become the actual or potential beneficiaries of such rules. Of necessity, these are other subjects of international law or entities endowed by them with international personality, in particular international institutions.[7]

II—The Forms of State Jurisdiction

The place and scope of State jurisdiction in international law is best understood if an attempt is made to classify the most significant forms of State jurisdiction.

The first classification of forms of State jurisdiction is based on the criterion of the *object* of jurisdiction. It furnishes the forms of *personal* and *territorial* jurisdiction.

The test applied in the second classification is the typical or non-typical *character* of the exercise of State jurisdiction. It provides the forms of *ordinary* and *extraordinary* jurisdiction.

The third classification draws its test from the *bearer* of jurisdiction. It leads to the threefold distinction between *exclusive, concurrent* and *limited* jurisdiction.

As each of these classifications is made from a different point of view, but comprises all possible forms of State jurisdiction, the seven forms of jurisdiction necessarily overlap. Those set out under any one heading can be used as sub-divisions under any one of the others.

A. Personal and Territorial Jurisdiction

Classification by reference to the potential object of State jurisdiction is the most important of these three typologies.

---

[6] See above, p. 39.
[7] See below, p. 227 *et seq.*

Personal jurisdiction is the authority asserted by a sovereign over individuals on grounds of allegiance or protection.[8] *Territorial* jurisdiction is the authority over a geographically defined portion of the surface of the earth and the space above and below the ground which a sovereign claims as his territory,[9] together with all persons and things therein.

In the evolution of contemporary international law, personal jurisdiction preceded territorial jurisdiction. Although this was always true only up to a point, the subjects of a sovereign were considered to remain under his authority wherever they went. On this assumption, the ruler of a territory through which a foreigner happened to pass was faced with a choice. He might refuse to recognise the foreigner's personal law and treat the stranger as rightless. Until the lot of foreigners was improved by means of individual safe-conducts and, subsequently, treaties,[10] this was what frequently happened. Another possibility was to apply to foreigners their own law or, at least, to take it into consideration to some extent. Again, in a number of medieval legal systems, traces of a movement in this direction can be discerned. The main trend was, however, towards an entirely different form of State jurisdiction.

In the practice, if not the theory, of feudalism, there was always an element of jurisdiction which was not based on the personal nexus created by allegiance and protection, but was of a distinctly territorial character. Corresponding to the consolidation of their position as undisputed masters in areas under their control, kings and princes insisted increasingly on exclusive jurisdiction over everybody and everything under their sway. Thus, territorial jurisdiction started on its career of ascendancy and pushed its rival into the background. It would, however, be a mistake to assume that personal jurisdiction has lost all significance in present-day international law. Though the emphasis is on territorial jurisdiction, it has not entirely superseded personal jurisdiction.

So long as the home State of an individual does not purport to exercise its personal jurisdiction *in* the territory of another

---

[8] See below, p. 129 *et seq.*
[9] See below, p. 114 *et seq.*
[10] See below, p. 99.

sovereign State,[11] it is entitled to claim a concurrent personal jurisdiction over its nationals abroad and to protect them against breaches of international law by the State of sojourn or residence.[12] Consular jurisdiction, as exercised by Western powers over a prolonged period from the Near East to the Far East and verging on the exercise of territorial jurisdiction inside other sovereign States, is perhaps the most extreme example of reliance by consent on the principle of personal jurisdiction.[13]

If State jurisdiction is exercised in areas which are not under the exclusive territorial jurisdiction of any single subject of international law, such as the high seas or the air space above the high seas, the principle of territorial jurisdiction is useless unless it is drastically adapted to so different an environment. Some semblance of order can be established only if each subject of international law is content to limit its jurisdiction to ships with which it can claim an especially close connection. This exists between a particular State and ships which, by international law, are recognised to have its nationality.[14] By way of treaty, this principle has been extended to aircraft.[15]

As this jurisdiction is exercised over entities endowed with nationality, it is possible to describe it as a mere extension of the principle of personal jurisdiction and to term it *quasi-personal*. The flag-State does not, however, exercise jurisdiction merely over the ship or aeroplane, its own nationals and their property on board, but also over any foreigners and their property aboard a ship or aircraft. Thus, a probably even stronger analogy to territorial jurisdiction can be invoked and this type of jurisdiction may be described as *quasi-territorial*.

B. Ordinary and Extraordinary Jurisdiction

The test applied in this classification is concerned with the normal or exceptional character of the exercise of State jurisdiction.

The illustrations selected so far represent instances of the exercise of *ordinary* personal and territorial jurisdiction. It

[11] See below, p. 89 *et seq.*
[12] See below, p. 164 *et seq.*
[13] See above, p. 6, and below, p. 462.
[14] See below, p. 134 *et seq.*
[15] See below, p. 135.

remains to provide examples of *extraordinary* State jurisdiction. Pirates [16] and war criminals [17] figure prominently in this category.

Piracy consists of acts of unlawful violence, detention or depredation for private ends against shipping or aircraft on, or over, the high seas or any other place outside territorial jurisdiction. If acts of violence of this type were covered by authority under the municipal law of a sovereign State, they would amount to international torts for which the State concerned would be responsible to the home State of the ship, aircraft or nationals thus injured.[18] If such acts are unauthorised, the home State of the pirates, or the pirate ship, if still entitled to sail under its flag, or of the pirate aircraft is estopped by international customary law from exercising the right of protecting its nationals, ship or aircraft against interference by the State which assumes such extraordinary jurisdiction. This estoppel enables other powers to extend their jurisdiction to ships other than those sailing under their own flag, as well as to foreign aircraft, to initiate criminal proceedings against the pirates and to impose on them any punishment considered condign, including that of death.[19]

Similarly, members of armed forces and civilians who fall into enemy hands are in principle entitled to the protection of the applicable customary rules of warfare and conventions.[20] Yet, if they themselves have violated these rules, then, under the laws and customs of war, the enemy is entitled to retaliate and, by way of reprisal, deny them the protection of the law which they themselves have violated. As in the case of piracy, it is entirely within the discretion of a belligerent whether he wishes to hold the prisoners responsible for their war crimes. If he decides to proceed against them, he must accord them some form of trial and may then impose any penalty that fits the crime. As in the case of pirates, the home State of war criminals is estopped from intervening on their behalf.[21]

---

16 See above, p. 74, and below, p. 90 *et seq.*
17 See above, p. 74, and below, p. 198 *et seq.*
18 See below, p. 162 *et seq.*
19 See below, p. 127.
20 See below, p. 190 *et seq.*
21 See below, p. 199 *et seq.*

Such limitations as exist regarding the exercise of this extra-ordinary jurisdiction over pirates and war criminals alike—the need for a trial and the prohibition of barbarous penalties—are the result of the impact of the standard of civilisation [22] on what were originally very much harsher customs of the sea and war.

C. Exclusive, Limited and Concurrent Jurisdiction

The distinction between exclusive, limited and concurrent jurisdiction is concerned neither with the object of jurisdiction nor with its typical character, but with its exercise in the nexus of a plurality of sovereign States. This classification assists in explaining how the relevant rules of international law serve to minimise conflicts of jurisdiction between the subjects of inter-national law and, if they cannot be avoided, how to determine the legality of any contested exercise of State jurisdiction.

The starting point in this discussion is the division among sovereign States of most of the world's land areas,[23] together with a belt of territorial sea adjacent thereto,[24] as well as the subsoil below, and the air space above.[25] Each sovereign State exercises *exclusive* territorial jurisdiction in respect of its own territory, subject only to such limitations as may be established by international customary law, treaties and the general prin-ciples of law recognised by civilised nations (*limited* jurisdiction).[26] Unless so restricted, a sovereign State may exer-cise in its territory, to the exclusion of other subjects of inter-national law, all the powers of a State, be they legislative, judicial or executive.

Limitation of this territorial jurisdiction cannot be presumed but must be clearly established and are likely to be narrowly construed.[27] The mutual recognition of one another's sovereignty means that in the absence of permissive rules of international law to the contrary, States accept a legal duty not to trespass on the territorial jurisdiction of other sovereign States.[28]

[22] See above, p. 12, and below, p. 186.
[23] See below, p. 114 *et seq*.
[24] See below, p. 119 *et seq*.
[25] See below, p. 118 *et seq*.
[26] See below, pp. 92 and 100 *et seq*.
[27] See above, p. 59, and below, p. 271 *et seq*.
[28] See above, p. 59.

Within each State's territory, its territorial jurisdiction over its possessions, its nationals and their property is, under international customary law, complete and exclusive. Over foreigners, whether temporarily or permanently resident in the territory, as well as their property, a State also exercises territorial jurisdiction. It is, however, limited by the international minimum standard in favour of foreigners [29] and may be further restricted by means of treaties. [30] This limited territorial jurisdiction is concurrent with the personal jurisdiction which foreign States may still claim over their nationals and their property while they are abroad (*concurrent* jurisdiction). [31]

International law prohibits appropriation of the high seas by individual States. [32] Consequently, no State may claim exclusive territorial jurisdiction over the high seas. Thus, States are limited to exercise their jurisdiction over ships and aircraft of their own nationality while sailing on, or flying over, the high seas, as well as over all persons and cargo on board. [33] This jurisdiction may be exercised either on the high seas or when the ship, aircraft or persons on board enter the flag State's territory. [34]

Illustrations of limited and concurrent jurisdiction on, and above, the high seas are not lacking. Thus, the exclusive jurisdiction of a State over its ships and aircraft on and above the high seas may be limited by other rules of international law as, for instance, those governing the principle of self-defence. [35] Finally, the assumption of jurisdiction on the high seas over pirates illustrates the exercise of concurrent jurisdiction. [36]

III—STATE JURISDICTION AND THE CO-EXISTENCE OF SOVEREIGN STATES

If sovereign States restricted their activities to areas and persons over which they exercise exclusive, limited or concurrent jurisdiction, the rules discussed above would suffice to resolve any conflict of jurisdiction. In the *Lotus* case (1927), however, the Permanent Court of International Justice has held by a narrow majority that, at least in the field of criminal law, international

---

[29] See below, p. 99.
[31] See above, p. 86.
[33] See above, p. 87.
[35] See below, p. 172 *et seq.*

[30] See below, p. 102 *et seq.*
[32] See below, p. 122 *et seq.*
[34] See below, p. 134.
[36] See above, p. 88.

customary law does not postulate the territoriality principle.[37] In other words, the criminal legislation of a sovereign State is not bound to keep within the limits of territorial and personal jurisdiction. It may attempt to cover acts of foreign nationals which have been committed abroad. The criminal law of most countries, including those which accept the territoriality principle, contains crimes which are based on the protective principle, that is to say, a claim to the exercise of universal jurisdiction for the protection of national interests. In particular, this applies to spheres close to the nerve centres of the State apparatus such as defence, security, currency and serious crimes committed abroad against nationals.

The World Court limited its ruling by distinguishing firmly between *general* assumption of such a universal jurisdiction in the *abstract*, which is compatible with international law, and its *actual* exercise in any *concrete* case. This is legal only if it takes place inside the territory of the State enacting such legislation or on its ships and aircraft on and above the high seas.

Thus, any State is entitled to legislate, for instance, on the collision of ships on the high seas. It may, however, assume jurisdiction over a foreign ship and her crew involved in an actual collision only if the ship or members of her crew happen to come under its territorial jurisdiction. Nothing prevents States which disapprove of this solution of the problem under international customary law from changing the law in their *inter se* relations by way of treaty. In relation to collision at sea, efforts to this effect have been made.[38] However, this leaves the general rule unaffected.

In extreme cases, the protective principle is liable to abuse. Yet, so long as the criminal law of a State and its administration of criminal justice do not fall below the minimum standard of international law,[39] the home State of a national who is caught in the meshes of the exercise of universal criminal jurisdiction by another State can do little about it. It may advise its nationals not to enter such a country, or apply measures of retorsion against the State concerned.[40] Beyond this, it must console itself with

[37] See below, p. 462.
[38] See below, p. 466.
[39] See below, p. 99.
[40] See below, p. 173 *et seq.*

the reflection that this is part of the price to be paid for the co-existence of sovereign States and that, one day, it may wish itself to exercise jurisdiction based on the protective principle.

IV—LIMITATIONS OF STATE JURISDICTION UNDER INTERNATIONAL CUSTOMARY LAW

The growing technological and economic integration of international society has made inevitable increasing contacts both between sovereign States and between their subjects.

A. The Evolution of the Governing Rules

In the early stages of this development, foreigners had to take the risks involved in entering foreign lands as emissaries of their sovereigns or as merchant adventurers.[41] Safe-conducts on the honour of a prince provided the matrix from which sprang the compulsory rules governing diplomatic immunity,[42] as well as the optional rules underlying principles such as those of freedom of commerce and transit.[43]

When safe-conducts were incorporated into consensual arrangements between princes, the next stage in this historical process was reached. At this point, legal protection was lifted from the levels of morality and municipal law to that of international law. Finally, some of these rules, like those on diplomatic immunity, were taken for granted and treated as rules of international customary law.[44]

Even so, most of these rules have preserved a consensual element. For instance, once foreign envoys are accredited, they are entitled to diplomatic immunity. Yet, each sovereign State remains free to decide for itself whether it wishes to maintain diplomatic relations with any other subject of international law.[45] Moreover, before the appointment of any individual is announced, the receiving State must signify to the sending State that the proposed envoy is *persona grata*. Finally, whenever he ceases to be acceptable (*persona non grata*), the sending State must recall its emissary.[46]

[41] See above, p. 6.   [42] See below, p. 93.
[43] See below, p. 103.
[44] See above, p. 10 *et seq.*, and below, p. 93 *et seq.*
[45] See above, p. 69.   [46] See below, p. 94.

Other rules, such as those governing the principles of international economic law [47] save that of the freedom of the seas,[48] have remained optional and still rest on a treaty basis.

B. Diplomatic and Consular Immunities

Since the late Middle Ages, it was found that occasional meetings between sovereigns and *ad hoc* missions no longer sufficed to maintain adequate relations between the leading States of Europe. Although, for fear of espionage, most rulers showed considerable hesitation in permitting the establishment of resident and permanent missions, they sooner or later found it advisable to follow in the footsteps of the Holy See, the first power to which resident missions were accredited, and the first to establish such missions abroad. Thus, the status of diplomatic envoys had to be settled beyond any possible doubt.

In the early stages of this development the local sovereign was free to treat such envoys as he wished. This, however, implied that he could not complain if his own envoys to another sovereign were treated in the same way. Sovereigns, therefore, could apply the principle of reciprocity either restrictively or liberally. To apply the principle of diplomatic immunity in a narrow sense would have stultified the objects which the maintenance of regular relations between sovereign States was intended to serve. In addition, ambassadors and ministers are representatives of their sovereigns.[49] Any wanton insult to which they are exposed is inflicted on their sovereign and may lead to serious complications. Thus, it was considered preferable to apply the principle of diplomatic immunity in a manner which would guarantee the maximum of personal inviolability and immunity to foreign diplomatic envoys.

Provided that they are accepted by the receiving State and, in the United Kingdom, their names have been entered in the diplomatic list, foreign diplomatic representatives, their families, staff and foreign servants, are inviolable and immune from the jurisdiction of local civil and criminal courts. They are also exempted from direct taxation. Their immunity from customs

---

[47] See below, p. 102 *et seq.*
[48] See below, p. 122 *et seq.*
[49] See above, p. 76.

duties, however, still rests on international courtesy, as distinct from international law.[50] This privileged treatment is granted to foreign envoys both as a token of respect for the sending State and to ensure that foreign envoys are able to function in the receiving State without fear of any pressure being brought to bear on them or members of their missions.

Diplomatic immunities are regarded as absolute in character and, therefore, are not used as an object of reprisals, unless in respect of a breach of such immunities.[51] Thus, for instance, by way of reprisal against Communist States which have limited the traditional immunities of foreign diplomats, Western States, including the United States and the United Kingdom, have reduced from time to time some of the privileges enjoyed by diplomats from these countries to a corresponding extent. The purpose of such identical reprisals has been to keep intact the operation of the underlying principle of reciprocity and to induce these States to return to the traditional law.[52]

The receiving State may at any time declare any member of a diplomatic mission *persona non grata*, ask for his recall, and " hand him his passport." [53] Although a receiving State may do so without disclosing any reason, this is done normally only in the case of serious misconduct. If this amounts to a criminal act, the sending State may also waive the immunity of the envoy concerned so that he becomes amenable to local criminal jurisdiction. As the right to immunity is enjoyed by the State and is not granted to any diplomat in a personal capacity, a head of mission cannot waive his immunity on his own authority. This can be done only by, or with the permission of, his own government. Correspondingly, the immunity of members of his staff can be waived only by the head of mission. The individual concerned may neither insist on, nor contest, the waiver.

Diplomatic immunity of a head of mission commences on presentation of his letter of credence and, in the case of a member of the staff, on notification of his arrival by the head of mission to the foreign office of the receiving State and acceptance by the latter. Diplomatic immunity continues after the termination of

---

[50] See above, p. 2.
[51] See below, p. 469 *et seq*.
[52] See above, p. 10, and below, p. 173.
[53] See above, p. 92.

the mission of a diplomatic envoy, whether this has been brought about by the voluntary action of the sending State or at the request of the receiving State, for a reasonable period so as to enable him to wind up his affairs and leave the country. This applies even in the case of a rupture of diplomatic relations between two countries.

The premises of diplomatic missions are accorded an immunity of their own. Without the consent of the head of mission concerned, the territorial State may not exercise jurisdiction therein, for instance, by entering and searching the premises.

Once the territoriality principle had taken root, lawyers found it difficult to imagine exceptions from the subjection of foreigners, however exalted, to the jurisdiction of the local territorial ruler. Thus, they invented the fiction of extraterritoriality. In other words, they pretended that the diplomats accredited to their own sovereign were not present in the State in which they actually resided, and that their diplomatic residences formed part of the territories of their home States. After the scope of diplomatic immunity had been defined on a basis of mutuality in roughly corresponding terms in civilised countries, these fictions could be discarded. It was then freely admitted that diplomatic immunity formed an exception to the principle of territorial jurisdiction, and that this exception rested on a rule of international customary law.

With the growth of international institutions, an increasing number of delegates and international civil servants have been granted immunities akin to those enjoyed by diplomatic envoys. Any of these privileges are entirely the product of treaties.[54]

Consuls as such are not as a rule diplomatic representatives.[55] They do not, therefore, enjoy diplomatic immunities and privileges. A limited immunity, however, attaches to them regarding acts performed in an official capacity, their archives and correspondence with their home governments. The immunities of trade delegations such as, since the Bolshevik Revolution of 1917, have been established by the Soviet Union in a number of other countries, rest exclusively on a treaty basis.

[54] See above, p. 78, and below, pp. 304 and 651.
[55] See above, p. 79.

C. State Immunity

With the change in emphasis from sovereign princes as subjects of international law in their own right to supreme organs of States,[56] their immunity, like that of other State organs, has come to be based on the social function they fulfil in this capacity.

1. *Heads of State*

A head of State travelling abroad is entitled to complete immunity from local jurisdiction in any country he visits and, during the period of his residence, any building occupied by him becomes extraterritorial. If he travels incognito, his immunity commences when his identity becomes known to the organs of the State visited. The consensual element in the rules relating to heads of State travelling abroad is preserved, but only on the level of international courtesy, by the convention that such visits take place only if, and when, they are not inconvenient to the host State.

2. *Armed Forces*

In time of peace, as distinct from *status mixtus* and war,[57] foreign armed forces may enter the territory of another sovereign State only with the latter's consent. The typical intention of parties to such arrangements—frequently, but hardly correctly, formulated as a rule of international customary law—is, in the absence of any express settlement,[58] to exempt such visiting forces from the jurisdiction of the host State.

3. *Men-of-War, Public Ships and other State Property*

The immunity of foreign men-of-war in national waters and ports is generally accepted. If members of the crew are ashore on official business, they also are probably entitled to immunity. It is more controversial whether mere shore leave suffices for this purpose. States reserve to themselves, however, the right to decide whether they are willing to admit any foreign warships and, if so, to determine their number. Thus, again, the consensual element in this rule must not be minimised.

---

[56] See above, p. 67.
[57] See below, p. 174 *et seq.*
[58] See below, p. 480 *et seq.*

In so far as State property, including *State-owned or operated merchant vessels* and *commercial aircraft*, is concerned, practice varies. British practice accepts the immunity of State-owned or operated ships and aircraft on the basis of both ownership and control as well as the immunity of any other kind of State property. Yet, some Continental countries, particularly Italy, and, more recently, also the United States of America, distinguish between foreign State activities *jure imperii* and *jure gestionis*. While in the former case they grant State immunity, in the latter they refuse it.

The distinction between these two types of State activity rests on the assumption that an adequate distinction between public and private State activities can be made. It has even been argued that the discrepancies in the practice of granting State immunity have become so far-reaching as to have had led to a complete breakdown of the rules on State immunity. Actually, even if immunities had to be scaled down to the level acceptable to Continental States and the United States, it would be possible, within these limits, to preserve the existing rules. In fact, no need exists for taking so rigid a view of reciprocity in this field. To any extent to which control of the State over economic and financial activities is extended, by nationalisation or in other ways, the field of State immunity widens and that of international State responsibility is correspondingly enlarged. Thus, in a more dynamic view, international law provides its own means for the automatic adjustment of international rights and duties in the law of State immunity.

States always remain free to renounce or curtail their immunities in relation to any of these pursuits. Thus, a number of Continental and South American States are parties to the Brussels Convention on the Immunities of State-owned Vessels (1926) whereby State-owned or State-operated merchant ships are placed in a position roughly equivalent to that of private merchant ships.[59]

D. Innocent Passage and Ships in Distress

On the basis of numerous treaties, a rule of international customary law gradually developed under which foreign

[59] See below, p. 134.

merchantmen have a limited right of innocent passage through
the territorial seas of coastal States.[60] It is controversial whether,
and on what grounds, the authorities of the coastal State are
entitled to arrest a foreign ship which merely traverses territorial
waters.   In the Geneva Convention of 1958 on the Territorial
Sea and the Contiguous Zone, this right is severely curtailed.[61]

It is also disputed whether foreign men-of-war may claim a
right of innocent passage. This appears, however, to be taken
for granted in the above Geneva Convention. In relation to inter-
oceanic straits,[62] the right of innocent passage of both merchant
ships and men-of-war has been established by the International
Court of Justice in the *Corfu Channel* (*Merits*) case (1949).[63]
Beyond this, the Court held that the coastal State has a positive
duty to warn users of an international strait as soon as possible
of any danger to shipping that comes to its knowledge.

Conversely, if a passage is not innocent, the coastal State is
entitled to assume jurisdiction over any ship inside its territorial
sea.   The practice is, however, to leave matters of internal
discipline on board the ship to the flag State,[64] unless the
authorities of the coastal State have been requested to render
assistance.

The right of innocent passage through the territorial sea does
not include access to national waters and ports.   In the absence
of treaty obligations to this effect,[65] it is still doubtful whether
any custom or courtesy of the sea has hardened into a rule of
international customary law. If a ship other than a public ship
has been admitted to national waters and ports, it is subject in
every respect to the jurisdiction of the coastal State.

Ships in distress are the only clear exception to this rule. If,
for instance, owing to bad weather or difficulties of navigation, a
ship is forced to enter national waters or a port, it does not
require any permission. If her cargo is not to be landed, it
remains exempt from local customs duties. Again, this rule of
equity has developed out of a prolonged and widespread treaty
practice which was gradually taken for granted and, at this
point, became embodied in international customary law.

[60] See below, p. 119.   [61] See below, p. 463.
[62] See below, p. 491.   [63] See below, p. 492.
[64] See above, p. 87, and below, p. 463 *et seq.*   [65] See below, p. 119.

E. Minimum Standards in Favour of Foreigners

Over centuries, innumerable treaties were concluded in which contracting parties granted a minimum of rights, first, to each other's merchants and, subsequently, to their nationals at large while they sojourned in territories of the other party. By way of most-favoured-nation clauses,[66] the range of the application of these optional minimum standards was even further enlarged. Since the middle of the nineteenth century, an admittedly elastic but, nevertheless, relatively objective standard for the treatment of foreign nationals has crystallised into a rule of international customary law.

In general, it demands compliance by any subject of international law in its treatment of foreigners with the rule of law as understood in Western countries. In more specific terms, this means a modicum of respect for the life, liberty, dignity and property of foreign nationals, such as may be expected in a civilised community, freedom of the judiciary from direction by the executive, unhindered access to the courts and reasonable means of redress in the case of manifest denial, delay or abuse of justice.[67]

In so far as the protection of the property of foreign nationals is concerned, the minimum standard of international law permits expropriation as distinct from confiscation. Expropriation means the transfer of ownership in a property to the State or one of its subordinate organs for reasons of public interest with prompt, effective and fair compensation. Failure to comply with any of these conditions makes an otherwise legal expropriation an illegal confiscation and amounts to an international tort.[68]

F. The Abuse of Rights

It is frequently suggested that, under international customary law or the general principles of law recognised by civilised nations, a general rule prohibiting the abuse of rights exists.

In the first place, it is somewhat difficult to establish what is supposed to amount to an abuse, as distinct from a harsh but justified use, of a right under international law. Secondly, the

---

[66] See below, p. 103.
[67] See below, pp. 165 and 167.
[68] See below, p. 162 *et seq.*

existence of the institution of retorsion [69] itself rather suggests that international customary law does not know of any general rule prohibiting the abuse of rights. Thirdly, such evidence as exists for the prohibition of bad faith and unreasonableness is chiefly drawn from material which appears to justify only the formulation of more limited rules of international customary law.[70]

Thus, it does not appear that a general prohibition of the abuse of rights is postulated by international customary law. In view of the diversity on this subject in the municipal laws of civilised countries, it would also be difficult to accept the proposition that the prohibition of the abuse of rights is a general principle of law recognised by civilised nations.

Matters are different on levels controlled by *jus aequum*, in particular on those of relations governed by treaties, and within international institutions. Thus, in a fair number of bilateral treaties between adjoining countries, rules have been incorporated which justify the abstraction from these treaties of a principle of good neighbourliness.[71] This principle has also found its way into the Charter of the United Nations and the constitution of the General Agreement on Tariffs and Trade (G.A.T.T.).[72] On the institutional level, scope for the application of the prohibition of the abuse of rights exists also in a more specialised form: prohibition of the abuse of institutional competences and discretions on the part of any organ as, for instance, in relation to members of the staff of international institutions.[73]

V—LIMITATION OF JURISDICTION BY WAY OF TREATY

The growth of international law by the addition of new rules of international customary law is imperceptible rather than spectacular.[74] Similarly, the more closely they are examined, the less remains of truly established general principles of law recognised by civilised nations.[75] Thus, such major advances as have been made have been secured directly or indirectly on the basis of bilateral and multilateral treaties.[76] On a basis of

---

[69] See below, p. 173.
[71] See below, p. 104.
[73] See below, pp. 305 and 651.
[75] See above, p. 29 *et seq.*

[70] See below, pp. 106 and 412.
[72] See below, pp. 104 and 699.
[74] See above, p. 27 *et seq.*
[76] See below, p. 140 *et seq.*

consent, superstructures of greater and lesser permanency have been erected on the foundations of international customary law. In particular, consent has made possible the accumulation of a considerable body of judicial case law on the international level. In this way, a remarkable enrichment of international law by way of judicial interpretation and formulation of the rights and duties of parties to disputes has been attained.[77]

All that is possible is to attempt within the confines of this Section to point to some of these limitations of State jurisdiction by means of treaties which have proved exceptionally fruitful and deserve to be treated as specialised branches of international law. The material in question can be conveniently assembled under the headings of the Law of International Institutions, International Economic Law, International Criminal Law and International Air Law. Finally, the picture may be rounded off with a glance at the legal régime of Outer Space. Although the subject is not yet covered by treaties, the contrast between what is and what might be forcibly drives home the potentialities of the expansion of international law on a treaty basis.

A. The Law of International Institutions

As this branch of international law will be discussed in subsequent chapters,[78] one point only calls for discussion at this stage. International *customary* law does not know of any rules comparable to considerations of public policy, public order or *jus cogens* in municipal law.

Admittedly, some of the rules underlying the fundamental principles of international law can be ignored only on penalty of reducing international law to a state of anarchy in the relations between those tampering with such rules. The decisive point, however, is that international customary law lacks any device which serves to prevent subjects of international law from undermining its very foundations.[79]

Any international constitutional law worthy of the name, therefore, rests of necessity on self-denying ordinances of a consensual character. The whole of the international public order

[77] See below, p. 233 *et seq.*
[78] See below, p. 227 *et seq.*
[79] See above, pp. 8 and 9, and below, p. 259 *et seq.*

or, more accurately, the precarious quasi-order that, so far, contemporary world society has been able to create is embodied in treaties and institutions founded on treaties. In particular, this is true of any restraints it has been possible to impose on resort to armed force.[80]

The world quasi-orders of the United Nations [81] and its specialised agencies [82] are considerably weaker than those of more restrictive associations: the antagonistic groupings which have arraigned themselves against each other behind the shields of the North Atlantic and Warsaw Treaties.[83] Thus, it behoves to be discriminating in any assessment of the value of existing international institutions. While some serve to strengthen universal international law without fear or favour, others merely deepen existing divisions or constitute but a means of creating by means of functional federation a supra-national integration that is otherwise unattainable between small States or middle powers.

B. International Economic Law

International Economic Law is that branch of public international law which is concerned with the production, circulation and consumption of goods and the status of the entities involved in these transactions.

With the exception of the principle of the freedom of the seas [84] and the minimum standard of international law,[85] the principles and standards of international economic law are of a purely optional character.[86] The principle of the freedom of the seas and the minimum standard of international law have outgrown the limits of their original habitat and become incorporated into international customary law. Although they are still predominantly of an economic character, this is no longer exclusively the case.

Yet, even the rules governing the principle of freedom of the seas are far too rudimentary to suffice for the solution of the manifold problems which have arisen from conflicting users of the high seas in an era of rapid technological change. Thus, in

---

[80] See below, p. 176 *et seq.*
[82] See below, p. 316 *et seq.*
[84] See below, p. 122 *et seq.*
[86] See above, p. 39.

[81] See below, p. 265 *et seq.*
[83] See below, p. 355.
[85] See above, p. 99.

this field also it has become necessary to supplement, modify or supersede some of the traditional rules by an extending network of multilateral treaties and the creation of an increasing number of international maritime institutions.[87]

If subjects of international law wish to secure any of the classical freedoms and equalities in the economic sphere for themselves or their citizens, they can achieve this only by way of treaty. Freedom of commerce, navigation, transit, road, rail and air transport as well as free access to the sea can be attained in this way.[88]

Any of these freedoms may be stipulated either in absolute or relative form. While, in the former case, the rights comprised in such a freedom are granted without any restriction, in the latter, they are limited to those covered by the standards incorporated in any particular treaty.[89] In a practice extending over nearly a millennium, seven classic standards have been evolved by way of treaties of commerce and navigation.

(1) *The Most-Favoured-Nation Standard* gives to a contracting party automatically any rights in the same field already granted, or to be granted at a future date, to any third State. Thus, most-favoured-nation treatment receives its contents from the rights granted to others. It creates equality with third parties, but only so long as third parties are entitled to demand such rights from the other contracting party.

(2) *The National Standard* provides equality of treatment between foreigners so privileged and the nationals of the State granting this type of equality. While most-favoured-nation treatment means *foreign* parity, national treatment involves *inland* parity.

(3) *The Standard of Mutuality* requires identical treatment of contracting parties and a literal application of the principle of reciprocity.[90]

(4) *The Open Door Standard* is an adaptation of the most-favoured-nation standard to situations in which contracting parties wish to establish equality among themselves in a territory

[87] See below, pp. 535 *et seq.*
[88] See below, p. 105 *et seq.*
[89] See above, p. 39.
[90] See above, p. 10.

which is not subject to their sovereignty. This may be a nominally independent State as, for instance, China in the pre-1914 period when the United States evolved this standard to thwart more exclusive designs of European powers.[91] In the post-1919 and post-1945 eras, the open door standard has fulfilled a corresponding function in relation to mandated and trust territories.[92]

(5) *The Standard of Equitable Treatment* serves to prevent arbitrary discrimination between foreign nationals in relations in which it is impossible to apply hard and fast objective tests. The allocation of foreign exchange or import quotas, for instance, may be regulated in this manner.

(6) *The Minimum Standard of International Law* takes its test from the behaviour expected in civilised communities. While it has first been developed in the context of treaties of commerce, it is the only one among the standards of international law which has widened its scope so as to have become a rule of international customary law.[93]

(7) *The Standard of Preferential Treatment* is the only standard of international economic law which does not aim at equality of some kind but at discrimination in favour of those entitled to invoke it. The object of treaties which are based on this standard, such as the Ottowa Agreements of 1932, is to make possible relations which may fall short of national treatment but are closer than those in a most-favoured-nation nexus.[94]

In the post-1945 period, another standard has come to supplement the classic standards of international economic law. This is *the Standard of Economic Good Neighbourliness*. It assists in making more concrete and real in this field a principle which, otherwise, tends to remain somewhat vague and abstract.[95] As good neighbourliness is symptomatic of a community attitude rather than expressible in clear-cut rules, the application of this standard is greatly assisted by the existence of institutional organs such as are provided in the General

[91] See below, p. 488 *et seq.*
[92] See above, p. 55, and below, p. 269.
[93] See above, pp. 28 and 99.
[94] See above, p. 103.
[95] See above, p. 100.

Agreement on Tariffs and Trade (G.A.T.T.) and the constitution of the Organisation of European Economic Co-operation (O.E.E.C.).[96]

The operation of these optional principles and standards may be illustrated by reference to the principle of the freedom of inland navigation. If States wish to establish freedom of navigation on inland waterways, they cannot rely on any compulsory rules authorising them to share in the use of rivers or artificial waterways in the territory of another State. If a river is a border river, that is to say, separates States, jurisdiction over it is usually divided between the two riparian States in the middle of the main navigable channel (*thalweg*), and each half of the river is under the exclusive control of one or the other of the neighbouring States. If a river is a multinational river, that is to say, passes through more than one State, each of its national segments is under the exclusive jurisdiction of the State through the territory of which it happens to flow. In the absence of treaty arrangements to the contrary, rivers are as much as any other land territory subject to territorial jurisdiction.

Attempts to impose compulsory limitations on State jurisdiction regarding multinational rivers on the basis of international customary law or general principles of law recognised by civilised nations—but short of consent—and, in this way, to transform them into international rivers rely on one or more of three reasonings. The *first* set of arguments is based on question-begging analogies from the rights of riparian owners in the municipal law of private property or limitations of such rights under public municipal law.[97] The *second* group is founded on analogies from quasi-international law on the federal level. To draw analogies from international law and apply these in the relations between federal States is entirely legitimate. Rules which exist and are helpful even on lower levels of social integration may well be taken for granted on levels of closer social cohesion. To reverse the process, however, means to infer that unorganised or partly organised international society has reached a degree of integration that may be expected only on a federal level.[98] The *third* line of attack stands and falls with the validity

---

[96] See below, pp. 322 and 339.   [97] See above, p. 44.
[98] See above, p. 7 *et seq.*

of the proposition that, on the level of international customary law, the doctrine of the prohibition of the abuse of rights is more than mere wishful thinking.[99]

Since the early Middle Ages, States have mitigated the inconveniences resulting from the absence of governing rules of international customary law by means of bilateral treaties between riparian States. More commensurate developments on a multilateral basis, however, had to await the nineteenth century. Beginning with the Peace Treaty of Vienna of 1815, a number of atomised river segments have been transformed into international river communities, greatly assisted in this continuous task of international co-operation by permanent river institutions.[1]

In some of these treaties, the principles of freedom and equality of navigation are formulated in absolute terms. In others, some of the traditional standards of international economic law, in particular those prescribing most-favoured-nation and national treatment have been employed.[2] Moreover, in the relations between any members of the United Nations, the principle of good neighbourliness is as applicable to uses and abuses of jurisdiction over inland rivers as to other matters which, otherwise, are still within their domestic jurisdiction.[3]

By the use of similar techniques, artificial waterways forming part of a sovereign State and linking portions of the high seas, such as the Suez, Panama and Kiel Canals, have been assimilated to the high seas[4]; fishery rights of foreign fishermen have been established in national and territorial waters[5], and rights of access to the high sea[6] and to national ports from the high sea,[7] as well as rights of transit on land and in the air,[8] have been created.

If international economic and financial co-operation requires co-ordination of efforts beyond the stage of primarily negative limitations of State jurisdiction in favour of economic freedoms, more elastic principles and standards, setting out common

[99] See above, pp. 30 and 99.
[2] See above, p. 103, and below, p. 150.
[4] See below, p. 122 *et seq.*
[6] See below, p. 445.
[8] See below, p. 512 *et seq.*

[1] See below, p. 497 *et seq.*
[3] See above, p. 100.
[5] See below, p. 528 *et seq.*
[7] See below, p. 528 *et seq.*

objectives and ways of attaining them, replace their classical predecessors. At this point, treaties alone no longer suffice. Yet, they still provide the constitutional framework for functional institutions such as the General Agreement on Tariffs and Trade in the sphere of customs tariffs, the International Bank for Reconstruction and Development in the field of international investment, the International Monetary Fund in matters of currency stability, or the three supra-national institutions of Little Europe, the European Coal and Steel Community, the Economic Community and Euratom.[9]

C. International Social Law

Under the impact of a variety of movements—religious, radical, liberal, humanitarian, rationalist and trade unionist—a growing number of bilateral and multilateral conventions have been concluded with the object of improving the position of at least some down-trodden groups of humanity.

The treaties for the suppression of the slave trade and the abolition of slavery, the protection of minorities and refugees as well as international labour conventions and social security agreements belong to this nascent discipline.[10]

While the self-isolated individual is a myth, in increasingly powerful and unscrupulous mass societies he is more than ever in need of protection against the impersonal might of the super-Leviathans. Thus the efforts, however feeble, made since the Second World War to anchor some of his fundamental rights and freedoms in international law also deserve a place in this branch of international law.[11] This treatment of the subject may claim two points in its favour. It puts the Human Rights movement of the post-1945 era in the necessary perspective of a long chain of related—and, frequently, more effective—efforts made since the post-Napoleonic period. Moreover, it emphasises that if these efforts are to be more than mere ideology-mongering, they must be embodied in binding treaties and be given commensurate institutional guarantees.[12]

[9] See below, p. 343 *et seq.*
[10] See below, p. 500 *et seq.*
[11] See below, p. 436 *et seq.*
[12] See below, p. 337 *et seq.*

D. International Criminal Law

In a few instances, international customary law authorises or postulates municipal criminal law. It authorises it in the cases in which, as with pirates and war criminals, subjects of international law may exercise an extraordinary jurisdiction.[13] It postulates it if, for instance, municipal criminal law and procedure are required to measure up to the minimum standard of international law.[14] In still rarer instances, international law may lead to a limitation of territorial jurisdiction. Thus, the right of diplomatic asylum, as practised on the basis of treaties and regional customs in Latin America, precludes the exercise of territorial jurisdiction, but only in relation to persons accused of, or condemned for, political offences who have found refuge in places endowed with diplomatic or State immunity.

On the present level of world organisation, occasional attempts to create substantive international crimes by way of treaty have necessarily remained of a somewhat freakish character.[15] The apparent exception of the London Agreement of 1945 for the Prosecution and Punishment of the Major War Criminals of the European Axis merely confirms the rule, for an international agreement is the simplest way for Powers which exercise *co-imperium* over a territory to co-ordinate their own policies in binding form.[16]

Yet, even on levels falling short of supra-national integration, a more modest type of international criminal law which is of practical significance does exist. Throughout the ages, rulers have been anxious to lengthen their own arm of criminal justice and secure the return of fugitive rebels and other offenders.

Extradition treaties provide the answer and allow contracting parties to demand the surrender of a suspected or convicted criminal from another State in which he has taken refuge. In States in which the rule of law in the Western sense applies, great care is taken to define precisely the offences for which extradition is to be granted. States which are otherwise willing to co-operate freely with others frequently make reservations regarding the non-extradition of their own nationals and

---

[13] See above, p. 88.
[14] See above, p. 99.
[15] See below, p. 506.
[16] See above, p. 52, and below, p. 200.

political offenders, unless these are charged with an attack on
life.[17]

E. International Air Law

Finally, the rapidly developing branch of international air law
deserves attention. Again, the starting-point is the unlimited
sovereignty of each sovereign State over the air space above its
own territory, including the territorial sea.[18] Any freedom of
the air is, therefore, dependent on the conclusion of treaties,
determining the scope of the right to fly of foreign aircraft, public
and private.

At this point, as long ago in relation to individuals,[19] the
need for a nationality of aircraft arises. It is the simplest way
to establish whether a particular aircraft is entitled to privileges
granted under particular treaties. Thus, in a series of multilateral
conventions concluded in the inter-war period, commencing with
the Paris Convention on the Regulation of Aerial Navigation of
1919, nationality was extended to aircraft, and the test of
registration adopted.[20]

In the Chicago Convention on International Civil Aviation of
1944, an attempt was made to codify some of the governing
principles in this field. Private aircraft which are not used for
commercial purposes enjoy a fairly liberally defined right to
fly into, or over, the territories of other contracting States.
The maximum of feasible concessions to aircraft engaged in
commercial, in particular scheduled, international air services are
not granted automatically even to members of the International
Civil Aviation Organisation. They are set out as optional
freedoms to be earned for due consideration and are known as
the five freedoms of the air:

(1) The right of transit.

(2) The right to land for non-traffic purposes.

(3) The right to put down passengers, mail and cargo taken
    on in the territory of the State whose nationality the
    aircraft possesses.

[17] See below, p. 510.
[18] See above, p. 86, and below, p. 118.
[19] See above, p. 73, and below, p. 129.
[20] See below, pp. 114 and 135.

(4) The right to take on passengers, mail and cargo destined for the territory of the State whose nationality the aircraft possesses.

(5) The right to take on passengers, mail and cargo destined for the territory of any other contracting State and the right to put down passengers, mail and cargo coming from any such territory.

Unless specifically granted to foreign aircraft, air cabotage, that is to say, the right to take on in the territory of a contracting party passengers, mail or cargo for remuneration or hire and destined for another point within the same territory, is reserved to national aircraft.

While the International Air Services Transit Agreement of 1944, embodying the first and second freedoms of the air, has been accepted by fifty-one members of the International Civil Aviation Organisation (January 1, 1960), the International Air Transport Agreement of 1944, embodying all five freedoms of the air, is binding only on eleven of the member States. Most of the member States have preferred to settle matters affecting international air transport by way of bilateral treaties.[21]

The International Civil Aviation Organisation, established under the International Civil Aviation Convention of 1944, provides the institutional framework for the further development of international air transport on a multilateral basis.[22]

F. Space Law

It is as yet uncertain where air space, that is to say, the atmosphere of our planet, ends and outer space begins. This does not mean, however, that international law is unable to cope with issues arising from the penetration of man or man-made missiles into this sphere. If anything, reflections on space law are a salutary exercise in demonstrating both the elasticity and the limits of the rules governing the fundamental principles of international law.[23]

---

[21] See below, p. 135.
[22] See below, pp. 253 and 512.
[23] See above, pp. 7 and 38.

Because of the rotation of the earth, the territory beneath a point in outer space, as distinct from a point in the atmosphere, is continuously changing. This may rule out the projection of territorial sovereignty into outer space. Yet, in law, outer space differs as much from the high seas as it does from the earth's atmosphere.

By consent expressed in innumerable treaties and gradually consolidated into rules of international customary law, the high sea has become *res extra commercium*, that is to say, excluded from areas that may be lawfully occupied and be subjected to exclusive jurisdiction by any international person.[24] In relation to outer space, no comparable limitation exists. It is *res nullius*, that is to say, it is so far unappropriated because, as yet, no subject of international law has been able to do so. So long as this situation exists, each subject of international law may exercise its own jurisdiction over, and in due course in, its own earth satellites, space ships or any other missiles it has launched. Extraterrestrial bodies are in the same position. Thus, if, for instance, occupation of the moon became a practical possibility, it would—in relation to other subjects of international law—become as much subject to the exclusive jurisdiction of the occupying power as any other territory on the earth.[25]

If the launching of earth satellites and other missiles—or their return journey if any—involves passage through the air space of other sovereign States, their consent is required. This may, however, take the form of acquiescence. If prolonged, silence may even amount to an estoppel of any subsequent protest that such activities if carried out without consent amount to a breach of territorial sovereignty.[26]

Should earth satellites or other missiles on their way to, or from, outer space inflict damage on life or property in the territory of any other subject of international law, the matter is governed by the rules underlying the principle of international responsibility.[27] Even if permission for passage through the air space of the State concerned has been granted, this cannot be

[24] See below, p. 122.
[25] See below, p. 114 *et seq.*
[26] See below, pp. 113 and 512.
[27] See below, pp. 162 and 565.

construed as an implied renunciation of claims for damage suffered through any subsequent mishap.

In so far as measures of retorsion,[28] reprisals [29] or self-defence [30]—all applicable as much as in any other case—are concerned, it is essential not to lose sight of the decisive point. This is that the subject of international law which is responsible for the launching and operation of space missiles is not itself in outer space but right here and liable to retaliation on this planet. A neutral State through whose air space missiles travel on their way to enemy targets certainly complies with its duties under international law if it shows due diligence in preventing such passage. Until anti-missile devices have reached greater accuracy than, at present, they appear able to command, the problem does not even arise whether, in any case, a neutral State must attempt such interference or is under an international duty to do so only if it happens to possess the requisite equipment.[31]

Adaptable though international customary law is, there are limits to what can be attained without invoking the principle of consent. It should, however, be remembered that the rules governing this principle are also part of classic international law. Once matters are considered in this perspective, it does not appear to require undue imagination to envisage a space law that corresponds to the needs of a nascent space age.[32] If this is the test, then any solution which falls short of entrusting a specialised agency of the United Nations with exclusive jurisdiction over all matters relating to outer space probably suffers from a touch of incommensurate parochialism.

---

[28] See below, p. 173.
[29] See below, pp. 163 and 173.
[30] See below, pp. 163 and 172.
[31] See below, p. 208.
[32] See below, p. 512.

CHAPTER 5

OBJECTS OF INTERNATIONAL LAW

" International law is a law regulating the rights and duties of States *inter se* and creating no rights and imposing no duties on individuals—a view which the Permanent Court of International Justice appears to have definitely adopted " (British Memorandum in the *Finnish Ships* case, 1932).

LACK of international personality is the common characteristic of all objects of international law.[1] In other respects, they may be of a somewhat disparate character: individuals, tribes, nations, cars, trains, ships, aeroplanes, land, lakes, rivers, seas, beasts, fish and fowl.

In so far as international customary law is concerned, the issues-in-chief are whether subjects of international law may place such objects under their exclusive jurisdiction[2] and, if so, what are the rules governing such appropriation. From this point of view, objects of international law fall into the following five categories:

(1) Areas subject to the territorial jurisdiction of an international person.

(2) Areas susceptible of territorial jurisdiction (*res nullius*).

(3) Areas not admitting of such appropriation (*res extra commercium*). This is the position in relation to the high seas.[3]

(4) Individuals and corporations subject to the territorial or personal jurisdiction of an international person.[4]

(5) Ships and aircraft subject to the territorial or quasi-territorial jurisdiction of an international person.[5]

It will be the main burden of this Chapter to examine the rules of international customary law which determine the links between international persons and each of the different classes of object of international law.

---

[1] See above, p. 47 *et seq.*
[2] See above, p. 89 *et seq.*
[3] See below, p. 122 *et seq.*
[4] See above, p. 86 *et seq.*
[5] See above, p. 87, and below, p. 184.

On the levels of treaty law and international institutions, it is possible to iron out conflicts such as may arise from operative rules of international customary law. Thus, for instance, by way of treaty, complications typical of dual nationality may be resolved.[6] Harsh rules of international customary law, such as the character of a stateless person as *res nullius*, may be mitigated.[7] Nationality may also be created for objects otherwise lacking it under international customary law, *e.g.*, aircraft.[8]

More effective protection than international customary law is able to offer may be granted by means of treaty to business enterprises abroad menaced by the danger of nationalisation,[9] to whales threatened with extermination by over-efficient whalers or to elephants in search of refuge from jaded film stars on safari.[10]

On these optional levels, it even becomes possible to approximate the status of an object to that of a subject of international law. Beyond this, an object of international law may be transformed into a direct bearer of rights and duties under an international law which, in all but name, itself then becomes the municipal law of a functional federation.[11]

I—TERRITORY

International law is universal in the sense that its geographical scope is world-wide.[12] Sovereign States have apportioned among themselves practically all the land areas of the world, together with a narrow maritime belt bordering on their coastal territories.[13] With the exception of portions of Antarctica and bodies in outer space,[14] scarcely any land territory that is free from sovereignty of an international person (*territorium nullius*) now remains.[15]

A. Titles to Territory

Owing to the preponderance in contemporary international law of territorial—as compared with personal—jurisdiction,[16] the rules on which titles to territory depend are of the greatest practical importance.

---

6 See below, p. 131.
8 See below, p. 135.
10 See below, p. 536.
12 See above, p. 7.
14 See below, p. 520.
16 See above, p. 86 *et seq.*

7 See below, p. 131.
9 See above, p. 99, and below, p. 485 *et seq.*
11 See below, p. 381.
13 See below, p. 119 *et seq.*
15 See above, p. 113.

In the formative stage of the evolution of these rules, international lawyers have shown an understandable tendency to express such issues in terms of private and, in particular, Roman law. Even then, titles *jure belli* [17] might have served as a warning of the inherent differences between the laws of real property as applied within highly integrated communities and supposedly " analogous " rules in the law of a loose and turbulent international society.

While the formative influence of the concepts of the Continental laws of property on titles to territory should not be minimised, operative rules of international law have matured behind this once beneficent façade. The time has now come to discard these misdescriptions and to make articulate the reality of the situation. It will then be found that the actual rules on territorial titles are identical with those governing the relevant fundamental principles of international law.

1. *Sovereignty*

The historical starting point of titles to territory is pre-legal sovereignty, that is to say, effective control of a territory by a prince in his own name and with power to defend it.[18] Similarly, under international customary law, a State may extend its sovereignty by the effective *occupation* of territories which are not under the jurisdiction of any other subject of international law. This status of a territory as *res nullius* may be due to the fact that no other international person wishes to appropriate the territory in question or that it has abandoned jurisdiction over it.

Effective occupation manifests itself by the establishment of adequate State machinery and the actual display of State jurisdiction. The degree of effectiveness required varies with circumstances, such as the size of the territory, the extent to which it is inhabited and, as in deserts or polar regions, even climatic conditions.

Under this heading must also be included the cases of addition by natural causes of new land to river banks and sea shores (*accretion*, *accession* or *alluvion*), and assumption of sovereignty

---

[17] See below, p. 117.
[18] See above, pp. 58 and 67.

over territories the State apparatus of which has been destroyed by *debellatio* (conquest).[19]

2. *Recognition*

The elasticity of recognition makes this device an eminently suitable means for the purpose of establishing the validity of a territorial title in relation to other States.[20]

However weak a title may be initially, recognition estops the State which has granted it from subsequently contesting the validity of the recognised title. Moreover, persistent non-recognition by State practice of certain titles may lead to their falling into desuetude.[21] This happened in the case of titles based on *discovery* and *contiguity* of territory. At most, they are still inchoate titles.

3. *Consent*

A treaty of *cession* is the clearest form in which a State may express its willingness to transfer a territory to another international person. Under international customary law, every subject of international law is free to cede to another a part or the whole of its territory. All that matters is the consent of the parties concerned. It may be indicated formally or informally, and even by way of implication. The typical intention of parties to a cession treaty is that the cession should become effective only with the actual transfer of sovereignty.

By consent, States may also impose on one another duties which go beyond those of international customary law regarding the acquisition of a valid title to territory. Thus, under Article 34 of the General Act of Berlin of 1885, the contracting parties are bound to notify one another of any assumption of territorial jurisdiction on the coasts of Africa so as to enable others to make good any claims of their own. However, between the parties to the St. Germain Convention of 1919 on the Revision of the General Act of Berlin, this Article has been abrogated and the situation under international customary law restored.[22]

[19] See above, p. 52, and below, pp. 203 and 619.
[20] See above, p. 62.
[21] See below, p. 122
[22] See below, p. 489.

A State may perfect a title to a territory by exercising peaceful and effective jurisdiction over the territory for a prolonged period. In virtue of the principle of good faith, prolonged inaction on the part of third States which, at one time, might have been in a position to contest the claims of the State now in effective occupation gradually comes to be viewed as acquiescence. Then, such States are estopped from contesting the occupant's title.[23] This title to territory, known traditionally as *acquisitive prescription*, is actually a title with multiple roots and is based on the interplay of the rules underlying the principles of sovereignty, consent and good faith.

4. *Other Fundamental Principles of International Law*

Although in a less direct manner, the other fundamental principles of international law also play their part in determining titles to territory. The uniform function of the rules on *good faith* is to create estoppels. In this way, subjects of international law are effectively prevented from contesting any longer titles which they have recognised, to which they have consented or in which they have acquiesced. The rules governing the principle of *self-defence*, coupled with the consensual engagements of the Kellogg Pact and the Charter of the United Nations, provide a workable test for judging the validity of titles *jure belli*.[24]

The operation of the principle of *international responsibility* [25] must heavily rely on effective territorial authorities, which can be held responsible to other subjects of international law. Thus, the rules under this head work in favour of territorial titles which are based on occupation as compared with any claims, however well founded, of a more ethereal character.

Finally, the rules governing the principle of the *freedom of the seas* are indirectly relevant. The refusal to recognise quasi-territorial claims to the high seas has been the decisive formative factor in shaping the rule that the high seas are *res extra commercium*, that is to say, incapable of appropriation by individual States.[26]

---

[23] See below, p. 117.
[24] See below, p. 172.
[25] See below, p. 162 *et seq.*
[26] See below, p. 122.

5. *The Consolidation of Territorial Titles*

Titles to territory are governed primarily by the rules underlying the principles of sovereignty, recognition, consent and good faith. Initially, as, for instance, in the case of the transfer by way of cession of a territory from one State to another, the validity of a title to territory is likely to be relative. If, however, other States recognise such a bilateral treaty, incorporate it into a multilateral treaty or estop themselves in other ways from contesting the transfer, the operational scope of the treaty tends increasingly to become more absolute. The more absolute a title becomes, the more apparent becomes the multiplicity of its roots. In its movement from relativity to absolute validity, it undergoes a process of historical consolidation.[27]

6. *Land Frontiers*

Once it is settled that a territory belongs to a particular subject of international law, it is advisable to delimit its exact extent with the greatest speed and accuracy. To serve this end is the legal function of frontiers.

Students of international morality have attempted to find criteria of " natural " or " just " frontiers. Examination of any particular claims to " natural " frontiers is likely to bear out Lord Balfour's sceptical observation on this subject: The only common feature of " natural " frontiers is that they are more extensive than the existing frontiers of the State claiming " natural " or " just " frontiers for itself.

Actually, it is impossible to assess objectively the relative significance of historical, geographical, strategic, ethnical or economic considerations which are likely to be relevant in determining a given frontier. Any such settlement amounts to the exercise of a legislative function [28] and, in systems of power politics or power politics in disguise,[29] this task is not always performed primarily with reference to moral standards.

B. National Air Space

The air space above—like the subsoil under—national territories, including the territorial sea, is treated as an appurtenance of the land territory.

---

[27] See below, p. 516.
[29] See above, p. 9, and below, p. 368.

[28] See below, p. 257 *et seq.*

This rule of international customary law is recognised in a number of multilateral treaties, in particular, the Paris Convention on the Regulation of Aerial Navigation of 1919 and the Chicago Convention on International Civil Aviation of 1944. In these treaties, and probably also under international customary law, air space is treated as being synonymous with atmospheric space.[30]

C. Internal Waters and the Territorial Sea

Internal waters include all lakes and rivers within a State's land territory, as well as the waters on the landward side of the base-line of the territorial sea,[31] ports, harbours and historic bays. These are bays which, irrespective of their width,[32] are treated on grounds of acquiescence or recognition as subject to the exclusive jurisdiction of the coastal State. Thus, they form part of its internal waters, and not of the territorial sea.

The justification for the distinction between internal waters and the territorial sea lies in the limitation under international customary law of the coastal State's territorial jurisdiction in the territorial sea. The coastal State must permit the innocent passage of foreign merchant ships through its territorial sea.[33] In other respects, the territorial jurisdiction of the coastal State over its territorial sea is not impaired. The coastal State also exercises full sovereignty over the air space above, as well as over the bed and subsoil below, its territorial sea.

In delimiting the territorial sea, it is necessary to take into account (1) the base-line, (2) the width and (3) the outer limit of the territorial sea. It is also advisable to consider in this context the question of a contiguous zone beyond the territorial sea.

1. *Base-line*

The normal base-line of the territorial sea is the low-water line along a State's sea coast. As a rule, it follows the sinuosities of the coast. Exceptions are permitted in regard to islands, bays and other curvatures of the coast. Under the Geneva

---

[30] See above, p. 106, and below, p. 520.
[31] See below, p. 521.
[32] See below, p. 120.
[33] See above, p. 98.

Convention on the Territorial Sea of 1958, low-tide elevations inside a territorial sea may not be substituted for the corresponding point of the coast line unless lighthouses or similar installations which are permanently above sea level have been built on them. Islands have their own territorial seas.

In the above-mentioned Geneva Convention, a bay is defined as a well-marked indentation whose penetration is in such proportion to the width of its mouth as to contain land-locked waters and constitute more than a mere curvature of the coast. Under international customary law, a bay may be closed, that is to say, treated as internal waters, only at points which are not farther away from each other than six miles (twice the traditional distance of the breadth of the territorial sea).[34] By treaty, this distance has occasionally been increased to ten miles from headland to headland. No such limitation exists in the case of historic bays.[35] In the Geneva Convention on the Territorial Sea of 1958, the limit for permissible closing lines has been extended to as much as twenty-four miles.

In the *Anglo-Norwegian Fisheries Case* (1951), the International Court of Justice has upheld the legality of the Norwegian system which selects a number of points along the coast not necessarily on the low-water mark, and connects them by straight lines, the longest of which is forty-four miles. In the case of Norway, the straight base-line method has been justified by the highly indented character of her coast. The only limitation to the coastal State's discretion which has been indicated by the Court—and incorporated into the Geneva Convention on the Territorial Sea of 1958—is that the base-line must follow the general direction of the coast.[36]

2. Breadth

A considerable number of maritime powers still accept the limit of three miles or one marine league. At one time, this distance corresponded to the range of coastal batteries. Thus, the rule is known as the cannon-shot rule. This distance is also approximately the limit of visibility from land in reasonable

---

[34] See below, p. 522.
[35] See above, p. 119.
[36] See below, p. 521 *et seq.*

weather. It is therefore likely that both these considerations have been major factors in shaping the three-mile rule.[37]

A number of States have refused to limit their territorial seas to three miles. In particular, this is true of the Scandinavian countries, Portugal, Spain, Italy, Greece and Russia. Their claims vary from four to twelve miles. Since the end of the Second World War, there has been growing support for the adoption of a wider limit of the territorial sea, and some Latin American countries have claimed extensive belts of internal waters or territorial seas up to 200 miles. Any departure from the general rule can, however, be accepted only if evidence of consent, acquiescence, recognition or other behaviour amounting to an estoppel can be adduced.

3. *Outer Limit*

The outer limit of the territorial sea, which constitutes also the frontier between national territory and the high sea, is drawn by reference to the base-line.[38] In maritime practice, two methods are used, neither of which is legally compulsory. Their results do not appreciably differ. The one is the method of intersecting circles whereby the breadth of the territorial sea is used as the radius to draw circles seaward along the whole of the base-line. The outer limit of the territorial sea is formed by the circumferences of these circles. The other method is known as that of a common tangent whereby, at whatever is the breadth of the territorial sea, lines are drawn parallel to the base-line.

4. *The Contiguous Zone*

A number of maritime powers claim the right to exercise a limited jurisdiction over foreign ships in a geographically limited zone of the high seas contiguous to their territorial seas. The United States of America, for instance, is one of these. For over half a century, however, the United Kingdom has repeatedly declared on the international level that it does not purport to exercise any such jurisdiction in relation to ships of foreign nationality.

---

[37] See below, p. 522.
[38] See above, p. 119.

The object of this jurisdiction is to prevent infringements of customs, fiscal, immigration or sanitary regulations of coastal States. It is possible to justify the exercise of this jurisdiction on the basis of the rules governing the principle of self-defence.[39] In the Geneva Convention on Territorial Waters and the Contiguous Zone of 1958, this jurisdiction is recognised in a zone extending to the maximum of twelve miles from the base-line of the territorial sea. Any such area remains, however, part of the high seas.[40]

II—THE HIGH SEAS

The high seas are those parts of the interlinking chain of oceans which lie to seaward of the territorial sea.

A. The Principle of the Freedom of the Seas

The rules governing the principle of the freedom of the seas can be conveniently grouped under two headings: the prohibition of appropriation of any portion of the high seas and the lawful forms of user of the high seas.

1. *Prohibition of Appropriation*

Until the régime of the territorial sea assumed its more definitive form in the eighteenth century, maritime powers were prone to purport to appropriate to themselves portions of the high seas. Inability of coastal States to control such areas effectively and growing awareness in the principal maritime nations of their own overriding interest in the non-recognition of any such exclusive claims led to their gradual abandonment. Once maritime powers refused to consent to, or recognise, claims to exclusive jurisdiction by any individual State over the surface of the high seas, it meant taking only one further step to establish the first of the rules governing the principle of the freedom of the seas. In accordance with this rule, the assumption of exclusive jurisdiction by any subject of international law over any portion of the high seas, as distinct from the bed and subsoil of the bed of the sea, is prohibited.

[39] See below, p. 172.
[40] See below, p. 125.

This rule does not preclude subjects of international law from renouncing by way of treaty or otherwise any of their rights of user of the high seas,[41] for none of these—nor any other rules of international customary law [42]—are exempted from the interplay of the rules on consent or other rules creating an estoppel. In the abstract, this freedom could be used to attain, by way of renunciation of all users in favour of one or several subjects of international law, a situation which would not materially differ from an appropriation of the high seas by the beneficiaries of such disclaimers.

2. *The Exercise of Jurisdiction*

The scope of jurisdiction which a subject of international law may exercise on the high seas varies with the state of international law which, at any time, exists between the subjects of international law concerned: peace, the state of intermediacy between peace and war (*status mixtus*) and war.[43]

In time of peace, each subject of international law exercises exclusive jurisdiction on the high seas over all ships which are entitled to fly its own flag, but not over others.[44] This rule is subject to a number of true and apparent exceptions.[45]

In a state of intermediacy between peace and war, subjects of international law are free, under international customary law, to interfere with each other's shipping by way of reprisal. Such reprisals as, for instance, a pacific blockade, must be limited to ships flying the flag of the State against which the retaliatory measures are taken.[46]

In time of war, permissible interference with enemy and neutral shipping is regulated by the rules of sea warfare and prize law.[47]

3. *Users of the High Seas*

The use of the high seas, the air space above the high seas and the sea bed includes, but is not limited to, freedom of

---

[41] See below, p. 124.
[42] See above, pp. 13 and 27.
[43] See above, p. 36, and below, pp. 174 and 179.
[44] See below, p. 134 *et seq.*
[45] See below, p. 124 *et seq.*
[46] See below, p. 173 *et seq.*
[47] See below, p. 192 *et seq.*

navigation and fishing, to lay submarine cables and pipelines, and to fly over the high seas. Naval manoeuvres, gunnery and bombing practice are also treated as being in this category. The latest addition to these riskier forms of user is the disposal of radio-active waste in the high seas.

It is probably the better view, which has also received recognition in the Geneva Convention on the High Seas of 1958, that the rights of user are not absolute, but must be exercised with reasonable regard to the interests of others. The only forms of user which are unlawful are those prohibited by international customary law or, between the parties, by international treaties. Piracy and, more recently, slave trading belong to the first category.[48] The second is illustrated by contraventions of the Whaling Agreements or other forms of prohibited overfishing. In the Geneva Convention on Fishing and Conservation of the Living Resources of the High Seas of 1958 an attempt has been made to strike an equitable balance between the right to fish and avoidance of the over-exploitation of marine life.[49]

B. Exceptions

Exceptions to the principle of the freedom of the seas fall into two categories: true and apparent. While the latter vanish on adequate analysis, the former are the result of the interplay of the rules governing the principle of the freedom of the seas and the other fundamental principles of international law.[50]

1. *True Exceptions*

These are the right of hot pursuit, the exercise of the right of self-defence, the right of flag verification, the right of arrest in case of flag abuse and, finally, interference by right of treaty.

(a) The right of *hot pursuit* is the right to continue the pursuit of a foreign ship from internal waters or the territorial sea into the high seas. The explanation of this rule is that a coastal State cannot be expected to allow a foreign ship to evade its jurisdiction by escaping into the high seas. Conditions and

---

[48] See above, p. 88, and below, pp. 126 and 532.
[49] See below, p. 536.
[50] See above, p. 38 *et seq.*

limitations of the lawful exercise of the right of hot pursuit are, however, that:

(i) the pursuit has commenced in internal waters, the territorial sea or, under the Geneva Convention on the High Seas, in the contiguous zone, provided that the offence is one that has been there committed [51];

(ii) the pursuit is continuous and has not been interrupted;

(iii) the ship pursued has not succeeded in entering the territorial sea of any other State;

(iv) no excessive force is used to secure the return of the ship to one of the ports of the pursuing State.

(b) Whenever the conditions of the exercise of the right of *self-defence* are fulfilled, this right may be exercised on the high seas as elsewhere.[52] The exercise of jurisdiction by coastal States in contiguous zones which remain part of the high seas also rests on this basis.[53] It is more doubtful whether in time of peace it is possible to justify in this way the Air Defence Identification Zones established by the United States of America and Canada on the approaches to their Atlantic and Pacific coasts.[54]

(c) *The Right of Flag Verification.* Men-of-war may verify in time of peace [55] the flag of a merchant ship in a number of circumstances: *first*, if a ship sailing under the flag of a foreign State is actually a ship of the same nationality as the investigating man-of-war, *secondly*, if a foreign ship sails under the flag of the flag State of the man-of-war, and, *thirdly*, if a ship of the same or foreign nationality sails under several flags.

If, in the first case, the suspicion is justified, the issue is one of municipal law. In the second case, the illegal use of the flag of another State estops the home State of the foreign ship from making any international claim. In the third case, the ship's use of a number of flags is intrinsically so suspect of illegal practices that such a ship lays herself open to be treated as a ship without nationality. This rule has been incorporated in the Geneva Convention on the High Seas of 1958.

---

[51] See above, p. 122.
[52] See below, p. 172 *et seq.*
[53] See above, p. 121.
[54] See below, p. 540.
[55] See below, p. 174 *et seq.*

The procedure in verifying the flag of a suspected ship is to send a boat under the command of an officer to the ship. If suspicion remains after the documents have been checked, further examination and search may take place on board the ship. If the suspicion proves unfounded, and the foreign ship has done nothing to justify it, the interference with the foreign ship amounts to an international tort.[56]

(d) *Rights of Interference by Consent.* The anti-slave-trade treaties—bilateral and multilateral—are the most famous illustration of the extension, originally by way of treaty,[57] of the powers of men-of-war in time of peace over foreign commercial shipping. On a basis of reciprocity, British men-of-war were granted the right to visit and search ships sailing under the flags of other contracting parties suspect of being engaged in the slave trade.[58]

Under the Convention for the Protection of Submarine Cables of 1884, men-of-war and ships specially commissioned for the purpose by any of the contracting parties may secure evidence of the nationality of ships other than men-of-war which are suspected of breaches of the Convention as well as evidence of any such breach.[59] Similar provisions are contained in the Convention regarding the Liquor Traffic in the North Sea of 1887.[60] Yet, neither of these Conventions grants any right of boarding or searching suspect vessels.

2. *Apparent Exceptions*

These cover action against ships sailing under the flag of a non-existing or not recognised State and against pirate vessels.

(a) Ships sailing under the flag of a *non-existing* State are objects of international law which lack an international person entitled to their diplomatic protection. Thus, they cannot partake of the protection of rules which exist only between subjects of international law.[61]

Vis-à-vis a State which has not recognised another State, ships sailing under the flag of a non-recognised State—or of revolutionaries not recognised as belligerents [62]—are in the same position.

---

[56] See below, p. 162 *et seq.*
[58] See below, p. 533.
[60] See below, p. 531 *et seq.*
[62] See above, pp. 47 and 59.

[57] See above, p. 124.
[59] See below, p. 535.
[61] See below, pp. 134 and 162 *et seq.*

It is a matter of argument whether maritime powers are bound to recognise the maritime flag of a sovereign, but land-locked State. The fact that, in the Barcelona Declaration of 1921, special provision is made for the recognition of the right to a maritime flag of States having no sea coast appears to speak against any such presumption. This interpretation is strengthened by historical considerations. In the past, maritime powers recognised the maritime flags of only those States which were considered able to control effectively ships sailing under their flags. The formulation of Article 3 of the Geneva Convention on the High Seas of 1958 adds further support to this view.

(b) *Pirate ships* are either ships which are entitled to sail under the flag of a recognised maritime power or they are not. In the former case, the flag State is estopped by the rule of international customary law which grants to all maritime powers an extraordinary jurisdiction over pirates, from giving diplomatic protection to either the ship or her crew.[63] In the latter case, the position is the same as in the case of a ship sailing under the flag of a non-existing State. The pirate ship lacks even a subject of international law which, if it were not estopped, would be entitled to exercise the right of diplomatic protection.[64]

(c) *The Bed of the Sea and the Continental Shelf.* The principle of the freedom of the seas applies to the waters of the high seas and the air space above the high seas. It does not, however, extend to the bed of the sea nor the subsoil. These may be appropriated by effective occupation provided that this does not interfere with legitimate users of the sea. In relation to the subsoil of the sea-bed, the mines off the Cornish, Kent and Northumberland coasts of England which are worked from land to points beyond the territorial sea illustrate this point. Exclusive rights regarding sedentary fisheries can hardly be exercised without interfering with the freedom of the seas. Rights in this category which are recognised in State practice and do not rest on treaties appear to be based on acquiescence rather than occupation. The Bahrein and Ceylon pearl fisheries

---

[63] See above, p. 88.
[64] See below, p. 162 *et seq.*

are famous examples, cited already in Vattel's *Droit des Gens* (1758).

In recent years, a number of countries have claimed exclusive jurisdiction over the sea-bed and subsoil of the continental shelf. The geological meaning of the term covers the land below the sea which gradually slopes down from the coast to a depth of, normally, 100 fathoms or 200 metres before a sudden drop to the bed of the ocean.

To the extent to which such claims purport to amount to the appropriation of, or exercise of exclusive jurisdiction over, the waters above the shelf, they run counter to the rules governing the principle of the freedom of the seas. By way of consent, acquiescence, recognition or, perhaps even on a *tu quoque* basis gradually leading to an estoppel, initially illegal claims may, however, be transformed into valid titles.

In the Geneva Convention on the Continental Shelf of 1958, the meaning of the term " continental shelf " has been considerably enlarged. It includes the sea-bed and subsoil of the submarine areas adjacent to the coast but outside the area of the territorial sea, to a depth of 200 metres or, beyond that limit, up to any point where the depth of the superjacent waters permits the exploitation of the natural resources of these submarine areas. It also covers the sea-bed and subsoil of similar submarine areas adjacent to the coasts of islands. The right of exclusive appropriation by the coastal State of these areas is recognised but, by and large, the legal status of the superjacent waters as high seas, and that of the air space above these waters, is preserved.[65]

III—INDIVIDUALS AND CORPORATIONS

Individuals and corporations are bearers of rights and duties under municipal law. Since, on the level of international customary law, they are mere objects, the problem, from the early days of medieval international law, was how to ascertain whether an individual was entitled to the benefits of a particular treaty of commerce. Passports provided the answer. In other words, it was left with the national authorities of the merchant

[65] See above, p. 122.

concerned to testify that the individual was under the protection of their sovereign.[66]

When, in the course of the nineteenth-century expansion of western industrialism and capitalism, private corporations came to operate on a large scale overseas, again the need made itself felt to establish criteria by which the connection of a corporation with a particular State could be tested. In time of war, trading with the enemy legislation posed similar problems.[67]

A. Individuals

Factors which link individuals to international persons are many. States exercise territorial jurisdictions over all individuals within their territory because of the presence therein of such individuals,[68] and personal jurisdiction over their nationals on the ground of the allegiance they owe, wherever they happen to be.[69]

Both nationality and domicile have much to recommend themselves as connecting factors. The test of nationality has won the day. Yet, the fact that, in Anglo-Saxon nationality law, *jus soli* (nationality determined by the place of birth) ranks equal with *jus sanguinis* [66] (nationality determined by parentage) proves that, though eclipsed, the principle of territoriality has left its imprint on its successful rival.

1. *The Significance of Nationality*

Nationality has come to provide the accepted link under international customary law between individuals and the subject of international law which may claim these objects as its own. Thus, nationality gives a State the requisite legal interest in protecting an individual against, for instance, a breach by another State of the minimum standard in favour of foreigners.[70] The existence of such legal interest is one of the constituent elements in any international claim which is based on damage suffered by an individual.[71] Similarly, in treaties, such as peace treaties or treaties of commerce and navigation,[72] the contracting

---

[66] See below, p. 541 *et seq.*
[68] See above, p. 86 *et seq.*
[70] See above, p. 99.
[72] See above, p. 103 *et seq.*

[67] See below, pp. 182 and 589.
[69] See above, p. 86 *et seq.*
[71] See below, p. 164 *et seq.*

parties have traditionally adopted nationality as the chief test in determining the beneficiaries of such treaties.

2. *The Impact of International Law on Nationality*

In principle, international law leaves each territorial sovereign to decide to which of his inhabitants he wishes to grant nationality. Thus, primarily, the topic is governed by the rules underlying the principle of sovereignty.[73] On a basis of reciprocity, other territorial sovereigns tend to recognise typical links employed in the municipal nationality laws of civilised nations such as the place of birth or parentage.[74]

For purposes of his own municipal law, a territorial sovereign may deny to groups of inhabitants, such as aborigines or gipsies, all or most rights of citizenship, yet still consider himself entitled to protect them in relation to other subjects of international law. If, as is likely, other States accept this claim, the meaning of nationality in international law and municipal law need not be identical.

If a territorial sovereign claims as his national an individual who, prima facie, appears more closely connected with another subject of international law, difficulties arise. For instance, a State which has made the cult of the moon goddess its State religion may grant its nationality to the adherents of this faith wherever they may happen to dwell. Then, while, under the municipal law of that State, any devotee of this creed is entitled to the privileges of citizenship, other subjects of international law need not recognise this nationality.

Further discrepancies between nationality on the levels of municipal law and international law may be the result of an estoppel on the ground of consent, acquiescence or recognition. For instance, under municipal law, citizens of a colonial or international protectorate may not be entitled to the nationality of the protecting power. By recognition of the protectorate as a colonial or international dependency of the protecting State, third parties may, however, have precluded themselves from contesting the claim of the protecting power to represent such

[73] See above, p. 57 *et seq*.
[74] See above, p. 129.

individuals on the international plane.[75] This is the meaning of the term *British-protected persons*. They are not British subjects, but, for international purposes, they are British nationals.

Similarly, on a basis of consent, acquiescence or recognition, mandatory and administering powers are entitled to exercise international protection over the inhabitants of mandated and trust territories, although these do not form part of their own dominions.

3. *Implications*

Three particular issues require attention: dual nationality, statelessness and naturalisation.

(a) *Dual Nationality*. So long as *jus soli* and *jus sanguinis* co-exist [76] as generally recognised methods of conferring nationality, cases of dual nationality are bound to arise. Some States take the view that, in relation to the other State who may also claim one of their nationals as his own, they refuse to exercise the right of diplomatic protection. Another possibility which finds some support in international judicial practice is, in each particular case, to make protection dependent on the over-riding or active nationality of an indivdual. This is the nationality which, at least for most purposes, he actually uses.

(b) *Statelessness*. The causes which lead to dual nationality [77] may also produce statelessness. Moreover, within the limits within which States are free to bestow their nationality, they are also free to take it away. If this happens while a national is abroad, such action may well amount to a breach of the duty owed by the home State to the State of sojourn to receive back its own national and, then, constitutes an international tort.[78] This is not, however, the main issue.

The real problems arise from a twofold hesitation on the part of States where refugees or displaced persons live. For humanitarian reasons, States of sojourn are disinclined to return such exiles against their will to the countries from which they have

---

75 See above, p. 54.
76 See above, p. 129.
77 See below, p. 544.
78 See below, p. 162 *et seq.*

escaped. At the same time, they are not prepared to naturalise individuals whom they may find difficult to incorporate into their body politic. By means of conventions, attempts have been made to alleviate the position of refugees and stateless persons. Otherwise, they are objects of international law for whom no subject of international law is internationally responsible—a notable twentieth century contribution to the category of *res nullius*.[79]

(c) *Naturalisation*. If, under its own municipal law, a State grants its nationality to the citizen of another State, such a naturalisation need not necessarily be accepted by third States. The test in each case is whether, as compared with any competing nationality,[80] a sufficiently close link between the naturalising State and the naturalised individual exists.

In some cases, the automatic extension of nationality, such as that of the husband's nationality to a foreign-born wife, or of the husband's naturalisation to his wife and children under age, is generally accepted as compatible with international law. In others, a sufficiently close link may exist, but the grant of naturalisation may run counter to the minimum standard of international law.[81] This applies to the compulsory naturalisation of resident foreigners. The exception to this rule is the right of a cessionary State to impose its nationality on all nationals of the ceding State domiciled in the ceded territory.[82]

4. *Tests other than Nationality*

These rest on consent or acquiescence. Thus, nothing prevents States from granting rights under a treaty not merely to one another's nationals, but to their respective inhabitants at large. Similarly, it may be implied in a treaty—as it is in the Charter of the United Nations—that an international institution may extend functional protection to agents who have suffered injury or to persons entitled through such agents.[83] If non-member States recognise, or acquiesce in, the assumption of such jurisdiction, this consensual test tends to acquire an increasingly absolute validity.[84]

---

[79] See above, p. 113, and below, p. 546.
[81] See above, p. 99.
[83] See below, p. 165 *et seq.*

[80] See below, p. 541.
[82] See above, p. 81.
[84] See below, p. 565 *et seq.*

B. Corporations

Corporate bodies with legal personality under municipal law are generally regarded as capable of having a nationality. In the first place, this nationality depends upon the system of municipal law under which the company has been created. Secondly, the test chosen must conform to the general practice of States. This makes recognition of a company's nationality dependent on the existence of a genuine link between the company and a particular State. The location of the head office (*siège social*), the domicile of the corporation, the country of incorporation, the control test, the test of beneficial interest and combinations of these tests have been widely applied and accepted by other States.

As States are free to decide on whether they wish to grant any international protection to their nationals, they may consider it advisable to limit intervention in favour of corporations which are wholly or, at least, effectively controlled by their nationals or interpose only to the extent of the beneficial interest of their nationals in a company.

To rely on the test of beneficial interest means to pierce the corporate veil. This may become necessary when nationals of a State have beneficial interests in a foreign company, and this company suffers from interference by the State of incorporation or by third States. Then, the home State of such shareholders may intervene diplomatically with the foreign State concerned, but only to the extent to which such beneficial interests are involved. All the more does this apply if, in fact or in law, the corporation has been deprived of its corporate existence or is in a state of liquidation.

In time of peace, States are generally disposed to recognise such tests of nationality as *siège social*, domicile, incorporation or control. Yet, if, as for instance in time of war, they have a special interest in ascertaining the identity of the beneficial owners or of the persons in actual control,[85] they tend to insist on the application of one of the various forms of the control test (nationality of the management, board of directors or key-shareholders).

Business enterprises which lack legal personality under their

[85] See below, p. 181 *et seq.* and p. 588.

municipal law, such as a partnership under the law of some countries, cannot have a nationality of their own.

IV—SHIPS AND AIRCRAFT

Ships in international law are under the protection of the State the flag of which they are entitled to fly. They possess the nationality of their flag-State. While the flag flown by a ship establishes a prima facie presumption in favour of the ship's true nationality, the ship's papers alone constitute real evidence of such nationality.

As with individuals,[86] it is for each sovereign State to lay down the conditions on which it grants to ships the right to fly its flag. In British practice, this right is limited to vessels owned by British subjects and British registered companies which have their principal place of business in one of Her Majesty's dominions. Moreover, unless exempted, the ship must be registered in accordance with the provisions of the Merchant Shipping Act, 1894.

Some controversy has been aroused by the practice of certain States, notably Panama, Honduras and Liberia—nicknamed the PanHonLib countries—of granting the right to fly their flags upon somewhat liberal terms. Their flags have thus come to be used by nationals of other States as flags of convenience in order to avoid burdens, such as taxation, social legislation, and safety regulations, which they would have to bear had they registered their ships under the flags of their own States. In accordance with the Geneva Convention on the High Seas of 1958, there must be a genuine link between the flag-State and a ship, and the flag-State must effectively exercise its jurisdiction and control in administrative, technical and social matters over ships flying its flag.

By way of treaty, the doubtful right of landlocked States to a maritime flag has been clarified.[87] Similarly, it has been doubted whether international institutions are entitled to let ships sail under their flags. Such difficulties as might arise from the lack of maritime codes and courts regarding the exercise of

---

[86] See above, p. 130.
[87] See above, p. 127.

effective jurisdiction by such institutions over ships sailing under their flags could be overcome. The only issue which would remain would be the attitude taken by non-member States. But, in the case of a near-universal organisation such as the United Nations, this aspect of the matter need not be unduly magnified.

The nationality of aircraft still rests entirely on a treaty basis. In the Paris Convention on the Regulation of Aerial Navigation of 1919, the test of registration was adopted. It is reaffirmed in the Chicago Convention on International Civil Aviation of 1944.

According to the Convention, no aircraft can be validly registered in more than one State, but its registration may be changed from one State to another. Parties to bilateral air transport agreements normally wish to avoid the possibility that an airline designated by one of the parties but in fact owned by nationals of another State, may claim the benefit of such agreements. It is the purpose of the substantial ownership clause to cope with this contingency.

CHAPTER 6

INTERNATIONAL TRANSACTIONS

" The Powers recognise that it is an essential principle of the law of nations that none of them can liberate itself from the engagements of a Treaty, nor modify the stipulations thereof, unless with the consent of the contracting parties by means of an amicable understanding " (Earl Granville at the Conference of London—1871).

" It is a principle of international law, and even a general concept of law, that any breach of an engagement involves an obligation to make reparation " (*Chorzów Factory* case—The Permanent Court of International Justice—1928).

INTERNATIONAL transactions of a legal character [1] are regulated primarily by the rules governing three of the fundamental principles of international law: good faith, consent and international responsibility. Others, such as the rules underlying the principles of sovereignty,[2] recognition,[3] freedom of the seas [4] and self-defence,[5] are also relevant but, in this context, of lesser significance.

As in systems of municipal law, legal bonds are created between subjects of international law either because they wish to establish such relations or because the law establishes such links between them irrespective of their wishes. Treaties and unilateral declarations are the means of creating voluntary obligations. By way of contrast, any breach of international law gives rise to duties of an involuntary character.

In an increasingly organised international society, the rules governing the principle of good faith tend to pervade all international transactions, both voluntary and involuntary. While the principle of consent in its widest sense, including that of recognition, governs voluntary transactions, that of international responsibility determines obligations of an involuntary character.

---

[1] See above, p. 2.
[2] See above, p. 57 *et seq.*
[3] See above, p. 61 *et seq.*
[4] See above, p. 122 *et seq.*
[5] See below, p. 172 *et seq.*

I—THE PRINCIPLE OF GOOD FAITH

The historical process of the infiltration of considerations of reasonableness and good faith into international customary law through a prolonged treaty practice, and the tendency to transform this body of law from *jus strictum* into *jus aequum*, has already been described.[6] The suggestion to establish duties of good faith and reasonableness short of treaty obligations to this effect by way of a general principle of law postulating the prohibition of the abuse of rights is tempting. The available evidence does not, however, appear to bear out this hypothesis.[7]

Thus, it is necessary to set out the relevant rules of international customary law which can be inductively substantiated, and which justify the abstraction from them of good faith as one of the seven fundamental principles of international law:

(1) a) Parties to consensual engagements must interpret and execute such engagements in good faith.[8]

b) Within the limits of their binding character, the same duties arise in the case of duly communicated unilateral acts.[9]

c) If a consensual engagement which is subject to ratification is actually ratified, good faith regulates the rights and duties of the contracting parties during the interval between signature and ratification and, sometimes, even further back.[10]

d) In the absence of provisions of a more specialised character, acts contrary to good faith on the part of an international institution, which itself derives its authority from a consensual engagement, are void.[11]

(2) Within limits to be ascertained from the actual contents of each particular rule, such rules of international customary law as form part of *jus aequum* must be interpreted as relative rights.[12]

(3) Other rules of international customary law are to be interpreted as absolute rights or *jus strictum* or in accordance with the ethical minimum standards laid down specifically in

---

6 See above, p. 25.   7 See above, pp. 30 and 99, and below, p. 412.
8 See below, p. 149.
9 See below, p. 160.
10 See below, p. 144.
11 See below, p. 245.
12 See above, pp. 25 and 100, and below, p. 168.

such rules.[13]   Their arbitrary or unreasonable exercise is not illegal, but amounts to an unfriendly act.[14]

(4) On the international judicial level, absolute rights tend to be transformed into relative rights in the course of a balancing process in which considerations of good faith and reasonableness play a prominent part.[15]

II—THE PRINCIPLE OF CONSENT

The rules underlying the principle of consent make possible—at least between the parties [16]—the modification and supplementation of rules of international customary law and general principles of law recognised by civilised nations.   In other words, they constitute the most potent law-creating process of international law.[17]

In the historical evolution of international law some of these rules were either incorporated in actual treaties or, more often, taken for granted.   For a considerable time now, the less controversial among these rules have become incorporated into international customary law.[18]   They can be stated under seven headings:

(1) Sovereign States have full capacity to enter into any kind of consensual engagement.[19]   The power of international persons of limited capacity, such as dependent States or international institutions, to undertake consensual engagements under international law is co-extensive with the scope of their international personality.[20]

(2) In the absence of a contrary intention, consensual engagements between subjects of international law are governed by international law.[21] Consensual engagements between subjects and objects, or between objects, of international law are outside the pale of international law.[22]

(3) In the absence of prior obligations to the contrary, as, for instance, may be contained in a *pactum de contrahendo*, that is

---

13 See below, p. 185 *et seq.*
15 See below, p. 233 *et seq.*
17 See above, p. 26 *et seq.*
19 See above, p. 60.
21 See above, p. 3.

14 See below, p. 173.
16 See below, p. 149 *et seq.*
18 See above, p. 28.
20 See above, p. 54.
22 See above, p. 40.

to say, an undertaking to negotiate or conclude another agreement, the entry into consensual engagements is purely optional.[23]

(4) Without prejudice to the rights of non-parties, a consensual engagement may cover issues of any kind and override international customary law and general principles of law recognised by civilised nations.[24]

(5) International customary law does not prescribe any particular form for consensual engagements.[25]

(6) In the absence of an intention of the parties not to create legal obligations, the effect of consent given in accordance with the requirements of international law is to create legal rights and duties between the contracting parties.[26]

(7) In the absence of an express or implied intention of the parties to the contrary, the suspension, revision and termination of consensual engagements depend on the consent or acquiescence of each of the contracting parties.[27]

Some of the facets of these rules call for further elucidation and will subsequently be discussed in their application to individual consensual engagements (*treaties*, if bilateral or multilateral, and *unilateral declarations*, if they become effective on communication to the addressee). One issue must, however, be raised at this point. It is whether, and if so how, the above rules differ from the rules embodied in individual consensual engagements.

The rules governing the principle of consent endow individual undertakings with binding character and determine their legal validity and effects. In other words, if individual agreements comply with these rules, they are in accordance with the governing rules of international customary law. It is also possible to state this proposition with emphasis on its complementary negative aspect. The breach of any consensual agreement brings into operation another rule of international customary law, *viz.*, that the breach of international engagements involves international responsibility.[28] In a more hallowed but, perhaps, unnecessarily conceptualist terminology, international engagements are binding because their violation entitles the injured party to apply

---

[23] See above, p. 58.
[25] See below, p. 143.
[27] See below, p. 157 *et seq.*

[24] See above, p. 26.
[26] See below, p. 149.
[28] See below, p. 162 *et seq.*

sanctions under international law. Admittedly, this does not, and cannot, explain why, ultimately, the rules of international customary law supporting individual consensual engagements are binding. The answer to this question can be found only on the meta-legal plane.[29]

It will be the burden of the two following Sections to deal with the more detailed rules that apply to individual treaties and unilateral declarations.

III—TREATIES

Treaties, conventions, agreements, protocols, exchanges of notes or other synonyms all mean the same thing: consensual engagements under international law. All of these are governed by the same rules.

A. The Meaning and Functions of Treaties

Every treaty has four constituent elements. *First*, it presupposes capacity of the parties to conclude treaties under international law or, in other words, their international personality.[30] *Secondly*, the parties must have intended to act under international law. In relations between subjects of international law, this may be presumed.[31] This excludes from the category of international treaties contracts which international persons have concluded with one another or with objects of international law under any system of municipal law.[32] *Thirdly*, there must be a meeting of wills between the parties: *consensus ad idem*. This distinguishes treaties from unilateral acts, which become effective upon communication to the addressee.[33] *Fourthly*, the parties must have the intention to create legal obligations. This distinguishes treaties from declarations of policy, such as the Atlantic Charter, or so-called gentlemen's agreements by which it is intended to create purely moral obligations.[34]

The functions fulfilled by treaties in accordance with more or less articulate intentions of individual contracting parties are

[29] See above, p. 26.
[31] See above, p. 3.
[33] See below, p. 161.

[30] See above, p. 47 *et seq.*
[32] See above, p. 1.
[34] See below, p. 551.

threefold. In the first place, treaties enable parties to settle finally actual and potential conflicts. Secondly, they make it possible for parties to modify and supplement the rules of international customary law by means of optional principles and standards.[35] Thirdly, they may lead to a transformation of unorganised international society into one which may be organised on any chosen level of social integration.[36]

Multilateral treaties in particular serve frequently as substitutes for the lack of an international legislature on the national pattern. They have, therefore, been described as law-making treaties. This terminology has its uses, so long as it is understood that any treaty which is more than declaratory of international customary law is entitled to this description, and no treaty can impose legal obligations on non-parties without their consent.[37] It underlines the special position of the great peace settlements of Westphalia (1648), Vienna and Paris (1815) and Versailles, St. Germain, Trianon and Neuilly (1919), as well as of treaties embodying basic changes such as the Kellogg Pact of 1928 and the Charter of the United Nations.[38] At least between the parties—and other powers which recognise or acquiesce in such rules of international constitutional law—treaties of this calibre amount to an international quasi-order.[39] They do not constitute a law " higher " than any other treaties. By the greater weight and number of their contracting parties, however, they are at least relatively more immune than bilateral political treaties from being disregarded altogether.[40]

Finally, a function, unintended by individual parties, has been fulfilled by treaties across the centuries. The rules laid down in such treaties have frequently provided the humus for the growth of rules of international customary law.[41]

B. The Compatibility of Treaties with the Principles of Sovereignty and Equality of States

Any treaty by which a sovereign State limits its own jurisdiction in favour of another subject of international law restricts the

---

[35] See above, pp. 39 and 103.
[36] See above, p. 21, and below, p. 373 *et seq.*
[37] See below, p. 149. [38] See above, p. 27, and below, p. 257.
[39] See above, pp. 26 and 102. [40] See below, p. 557.
[41] See above, p. 5.

exercise of its own sovereignty.[42] Independent States are, however, free under international customary law to transform themselves into dependent States or extinguish their sovereignty in favour of other subjects of international law.[43] Thus, any such limitation of the exercise of domestic jurisdiction is fully compatible with international law. Actually, it is one of the purposes served by treaties in an increasingly stratified world society to disguise, in the garbs of consent and formally reciprocal rights and duties, the growing relativity of sovereignty of all but the hegemonial powers in each of the world camps.[44]

It cannot be taken for granted or lightly assumed that sovereign States, being equal in law,[45] are prepared to subject themselves to the will of another sovereign State. This is the explanation of the presumption that treaties between subjects of international law are governed by international law.[46] Nothing prevents, however, sovereign States, if they are so minded, from providing expressly for such a contingency or the construction of a treaty in accordance with the municipal law of a third State.

C. Public Contracts

While treaties are transactions between subjects of international law, public contracts are consensual engagements between subjects of international law and objects of international law. Thus, the presumption is in favour of such contracts being governed by municipal law. It then depends on the intention of the parties whether the municipal law of the State concerned, that of any other State or an abstraction from municipal law such as the general principles of law recognised by civilised nations [47] should be considered as the law of the contract. The issue is one of Private International Law.

If the parties have expressly stipulated for the application of international law, this may mean one of two things. Either the subject of international law concerned has intended to bestow on the other party international personality for purposes of

---

[42] See above, p. 58 *et seq.*
[43] See above, p. 54.
[44] See above, p. 58, and below, p. 176.
[45] See above, p. 58.
[46] See above, p. 3.
[47] See above, p. 29.

particular contractual relations or, short of this, the parties have agreed to apply to the contract international law by way of analogy.[48]

D. The Conclusion of Treaties

Under this head, a number of problems call for examination: the treaty-making power in international law; the form of treaties; the significance of signature and ratification; the meaning and admissibility of reservations; the registration of treaties; the problems arising from defects in the formation of the joint will; and, finally, the question of treaty languages.

1. *Treaty-Making Power*

The rules of international law on international representation regulate the scope of the power of the organs of the subjects of international law to conclude treaties with one another.[49]

Heads of State and foreign ministers have full powers to commit their countries by means of treaties. Other diplomatic representatives require authorisation by means of instruments from their head of State, stating the precise extent of their powers.

These letters patent are termed full powers. They are exhibited for verification at the commencement of the transaction in question and, if there is no exchange of the actual documents, the other side is entitled to a certified copy. Whether for the purposes of negotiation, signature or ratification of a treaty, foreign States are entitled to rely on the ostensible authority of the agents concerned, without having to examine whether the representatives of other States are acting in accordance with their own municipal laws or their instructions. However, if the home State can prove that a diplomatic representative other than a head of State or foreign minister has acted contrary to instructions, it is entitled to denounce the unauthorised act of its agent.[50]

2. *Form*

International customary law does not prescribe any particular form to make a treaty binding. A treaty may be a formal

---

[48] See above, p. 73, and below, p. 558.　　　　[49] See above, p. 77.
[50] See below, p. 453 *et seq.*

agreement between heads of States; a less formal document signed
by foreign ministers or plenipotentiaries; a final act of a conference
setting out the various items agreed upon; a joint declaration;
an exchange of notes; or be couched in any other form expressing mutual consent. Thus, a treaty may even be verbal, although
this is neither usual nor advisable.

3. *Signature and Ratification*

International customary law does not know of any specific
procedure for obtaining consent to a treaty on the part of a
subject of international law. All that matters is that it has
been given.

The entirely optional procedure of initialling an agreement
(*ne varietur*) serves only to confirm the authenticity of a text.
In the absence of such a separate stage of verification, signature
of a treaty fulfils this function. If the treaty is not subject to
ratification, the signature necessarily also serves the additional
purpose of expressing the consent of the parties to be bound by
the treaty.

In the case of a treaty which is subject to ratification, this
act, which is absolutely discretionary, makes the treaty definitely
binding. Thus, until ratification, the signature of a treaty still
leaves the contracting parties free to choose between acceptance
and rejection of the text as it stands.[51] Once, however, the treaty
has been ratified, the date of signature may become retrospectively
important for purposes of interpreting the temporal effects of
the treaty.[52]

Whether a treaty requires ratification depends entirely on the
intention of the parties. This applies also to the time when a
treaty is to come into force: on signature; upon the exchange of
ratifications; provisionally, on signature and, definitively, with
the exchange of ratifications; or when a given number of parties
have signed or deposited their instruments of ratification.

Ratification of a treaty under international law must be distinguished from the approval which, under the municipal laws
of the contracting parties, may have to be given by specified
constitutional organs, such as a parliament or senate, before the

---

[51] See below, p. 553.
[52] See below. p. 149.

executive may proceed to ratification of the treaty on the international level.

The procedure of ratification in international law—like any other aspect of treaty-making power in the relations between subjects of international law—is governed exclusively by the relevant rules on international representation.[53] Thus, the Charter of the United Nations provides for its ratification by the signatory States in accordance with their respective constitutional processes (Article 110).[54] It is a matter of argument whether a clause on these lines means that, by the treaty, this matter has been expressly transferred to the exclusively domestic jurisdiction of each contracting party, or whether the inclusion of the subject has made it a matter of international concern. The former view appears to be more in keeping with the rules on international representation. This interpretation may also claim to be in the interest of the certainty of the law.

In the case of a multilateral treaty open to acceptance or accession, consent is given by depositing the instrument of acceptance or accession in accordance with the procedure laid down in the treaty. States may use in whichever way they wish their freedom under international customary law to invent any other forms of treaty-making procedure. Thus, members of the International Labour Organisation are bound to submit draft conventions, adopted by the General Conference with a two-thirds majority of the votes cast, to their respective legislatures within eighteen months at the latest and, upon their consent, to " ratify " such labour conventions. Ratification in this meaning of the term does not require any prior signature. It means notification of acceptance.[55]

4. *Reservations*

These unilateral acts are means by which parties attempt to qualify an outright signature or ratification of a treaty. Since a treaty is a meeting of wills, a qualified signature or ratification is a rejection of the offer made, coupled with a counter-offer to conclude the agreement as modified by the reservation. In the

[53] See above, p. 75.
[54] See below, p. 724.
[55] See below, p. 261.

case of a bilateral treaty, the refusal of the other contracting party to accept a reservation means that no agreement has been reached.

In principle, the position is the same in the case of a multilateral treaty which does not provide expressly for the admissibility of reservations. Unless all parties acquiesce in reservations added to a signature or ratification, two possibilities exist. It may have been the intention of the parties that the State insisting on such a reservation should not become a party to the convention, or that the reservation should be valid only in relation to parties other than those objecting to the reservation.

This fairly clear state of the law has been somewhat obscured by the Advisory Opinion of the International Court of Justice on *Reservations to the Genocide Convention* (1951). The Court confirmed that, in principle, States cannot be bound without their consent and, therefore, no reservation to a treaty can be effective against any party without its approval or acquiescence. Yet, in relation to agreements of a purely humanitarian character such as the Genocide Convention of 1948,[56] the Court held it to be the intention of the parties that such treaties should have the widest possible application. The majority of the Court, therefore, found that a State was entitled to rank as a party to such a treaty, even though reservations made by it were not accepted by all the other contracting parties. The Court added the rider that this concession applied only to reservations compatible with the aims and purposes of the treaty.

This opinion is open to serious theoretical and practical objections. It jeopardises certainty on a fundamental aspect of the law of treaties: the identity of the parties. The practical inconveniences of this innovation are hardly less pronounced. This reading of the law permits each contracting State to decide for itself whether it recognises a State which has made a reservation as a party to such a humanitarian convention. The General Assembly of the United Nations has made confusion worse confounded by instructing the Secretary-General to apply the Court's ruling to all multilateral treaties of which he is the depository.[57]

---

[56] See above, p. 74, and below, p. 438.
[57] See below, p. 307.

5. *Registration of Treaties*

States are free to invent any number of additional conditions which are to govern the treaty-making procedure. Thus, under Article 18 of the Covenant, members of the League of Nations were bound to register their treaties with the League Secretariat and, prior to registration, such treaties were not binding. The optimistic idea behind the drafting of this Article was that a clause of this kind would make an effective contribution to the abolition of secret diplomacy.

Article 102 of the Charter of the United Nations has maintained the system of registration of treaties to which United Nations members are parties. Prior to registration, no party to such an agreement may invoke a treaty before an organ of the United Nations.[58] Otherwise, however, the treaty remains valid. As with the League of Nations, treaties registered with the United Nations are published by the Secretariat.

6. *Defects in the Formation of the Joint Will*

Parties must carry out their treaty obligations in good faith.[59] Thus, a party which by its *fraud* has induced another party to enter a treaty is estopped from invoking the treaty.

The effect of *duress* or *compulsion* exercised by one of the parties during the conclusion of a treaty differs in international customary law according to the object of such pressure. If duress has been employed against the actual negotiators, as it was in the case of the German-Czech Treaty of March, 1939, the State whose negotiators have been so treated is not bound by the treaty. When presented with the treaty, it is still free to repudiate or ratify the tainted engagement.

If the pressure, whether political, economic or military, is exercised against the State as such, the consent so obtained is valid. Otherwise any peace treaty would be open to the objection that it was concluded under duress. The reason for this harsh rule of international customary law is that, unless it existed, every war would have to be fought to the finish.[60] Under the international quasi-orders of the Kellogg Pact and the United

[58] See below, p. 722.
[59] See above, p. 137.
[60] See below, p. 203.

Nations, treaties concluded under the threat of force, or by use of force in contravention of these Treaties, are at least voidable at the instance of the party acting under duress.[61]

It remains to consider *mistake*. If a contracting party has not contributed to the mistake of the other—the distinguishing mark between *unilateral* mistake and fraud—the rules on good faith do not appear to demand that such a mistake should in any way affect the validity of the consent given. If the mistake is *mutual*, that is to say, the parties are mistaken regarding each other's intentions and disagree on the object of their consent—as, for instance, the identity of two places with the same name—it depends on the circumstances of each case whether the treaty must, in good faith, be treated as void. If the parties have made a *common* mistake on an essential of the treaty, for instance, by concluding an agreement for the cession of an island which, at the time of the conclusion of the treaty, but unknown to both parties, had already ceased to exist, this amounts to dissent, and the treaty is void. By way of contrast, parties may have merely mis-described an object on the identity of which they are fully in agreement. In this case, the common mistake can be ignored (*falsa demonstratio non nocet*). Mistake of *law*, if relating to international law, is irrelevant and does not impair the validity of a treaty. If, on the international level, municipal law is considered merely as a legally relevant set of facts,[62] a mistake regarding municipal law is probably as relevant as any other mistake of fact.

7. *Treaty Languages*

French has lost its once dominant position as *the* diplomatic language and, since 1919, English has become at least as important. If the precedent of the United Nations Charter should be followed in other multilateral treaties, Russian, Chinese and Spanish are well on the way to acquiring a similar status. In bilateral treaties between countries whose languages differ, it is customary to prepare versions of the treaty in both languages and, possibly, also in a third language, such as English or

[61] See above, p. 63, and below, pp. 184 and 584.
[62] See above, p. 42.

French. In case of doubt, for purposes of interpretation,[63] equal weight attaches to each text.

E. Legal Effects of Treaties

Three aspects of the legal effects of treaties call for discussion: the effects in relation to the contracting parties; the effects in relation to non-parties or third parties, and issues arising from conflicts between treaties.

1. *Effects between the Contracting Parties*

These are regulated by the interaction of two rules underlying the principles of consent and good faith which have been set out in a previous Section. The first rule ordains that consent validly given creates legal rights and duties.[64] The second is the *jus aequum* rule which demands reasonableness and good faith in the application and interpretation of treaties.[65]

In this way, the temporal effects of treaties can be determined. Whether a treaty which is subject to ratification has a retroactive effect to the time of signature, or even further back, must be decided in each individual case by reference to the *jus aequum* rule.

Similarly, the question whether some of the effects of a treaty continue beyond the duration of the treaty can be settled only in this way. In a conceptualist terminology, the purely " contractual " clauses of a treaty do not survive it, but " dispositive " clauses are final. Yet, in deciding which clauses are contractual and which are dispositive, international law has no other criteria to offer than those of reasonableness and good faith.

2. *Effects on Non-Parties*

The negative and complementary aspect of the principle of consent is that, without its concurrence, no sovereign State may be bound by a treaty. Treaties confer no legal rights and impose no legal duties on non-parties (*pacta tertiis nec nocent nec prosunt*). It is, however, perfectly compatible with the

---

[63] See below, p. 152.
[64] See above, p. 139.
[65] See above, p. 137.

position of non-parties as sovereign and co-equal entities to be offered the opportunity to accede to the treaty. So long as non-parties remain free to accept or refuse such an offer, treaty provisions to this effect do not run counter to any of the prohibitory rules of international customary law.

Treaties which are otherwise completely unrelated may also be linked with one another by means of most-favoured-nation clauses.[66] The promisor of most-favoured-nation treatment is bound towards the beneficiary to grant him all advantages in the same field (*ejusdem generis* rule) which he has granted or may grant to third States. The rights of the beneficiary are, however, based solely on his own treaty with the promisor. Thus, the most-favoured-nation standard keeps squarely within the bounds of the rules on consent. The treaties between the promisor and third parties determine merely the contents of the legal obligations undertaken by the promisor towards the beneficiary.

According to paragraph 6 of Article 2 of the Charter, the United Nations shall ensure that non-member States act in accordance with the Principles of the Charter so far as may be necessary for the maintenance of international peace and security.[67] So long as the United Nations does not purport to impose its will on any non-member State which is unwilling to co-operate with it, this clause is fully compatible with the pertinent rules of international customary law. Should the Organisation trespass beyond this line, this would constitute a breach of international law, however morally justifiable such action would be.

3. *The Conflict of Treaties*

On the level of international customary law, any rules of an international public order by which the absolute freedom of contract of individual parties is limited are lacking.[68] Thus, in international customary law the legality of conflicting treaty obligations cannot be tested by reference to overriding principles

---

[66] See above, p. 103.
[67] See below, pp. 308 and 700.
[68] See above, pp. 26 and 101.

of public policy or *jus cogens*. Issues arising from conflicting obligations of parties to different treaties are dealt with in other ways. It is necessary to distinguish between four situations:

(a) *Situation 1*: *Identity of Parties*. In this case the parties (A and B) to two conflicting treaties (I and II) are identical. As both parties are bound to interpret and apply each treaty in good faith, the identity of the parties to both treaties permits the fusion of two separate equitable relations into one equitable nexus. Thus, problems arising from a conflict between the two treaties are regulated by the *jus aequum* rule.[69]

(b) *Situation 2*: *One Common Party to Two Conflicting Treaties*. Treaty I between A and B conflicts with Treaty II between A and C. A alone is a party to both treaties. Short of any act, such as recognition, which creates an estoppel,[70] mere knowledge of the existence and contents of the other treaty does not affect the position of either B or C. Each is entitled to claim from A fulfilment of its own treaty, but neither may invoke the conflicting treaty against A, for this would mean to purport to derive rights from a treaty to which it is not a party.

(c) *Situation 3*: *Several Common Parties*. Finally, a conflict may exist between two multilateral treaties (Treaty I between A, B and C, and Treaty II between A, B and D). In this case, it is necessary to distinguish between two different types of relations: the *inter se* relations between the two common parties to both treaties (A and B) and the relations between either of them (A or B) and a party to only one of the two conflicting treaties (C or D). While the *inter se* relations between A and B are identical with *Situation 1*, those between A (or B) and C (or D) are identical with *Situation 2*. Thus, *Situation 3* is a compound of *Situations 1* and *2*.

(d) *Situation 4*: *Complete Non-Identity of Parties*. All parties are different. Treaty I has been concluded between A, B and C, and Treaty II between X, Y and Z. No conflict of duties can arise.

[69] See above, pp. 25 and 149.
[70] See above, p. 64.

4. *The Conflict of Treaties on the Level of Organised International Society*

By the use of the rules governing consent, parties to a treaty may impose self-denying ordinances on themselves to invalidate existing treaties or not to conclude in the future treaties which run counter to accepted principles. The effectiveness of such a contractual international quasi-order increases in proportion to its universality. The greater the number of the parties, the more issues are likely to arise that will reproduce *Situation 1* rather than *Situation 2* and allow for the application of the *jus aequum* rule.[71]

This technique has been employed in the constituent documents of a great many international institutions and made possible the development of an international constitutional law.[72] Thus, it is provided in Article 103 of the Charter of the United Nations that, in the event of a conflict between the obligations of member States under the Charter and their obligations under any other international agreement, their obligations under the Charter shall prevail.[73] This rule of the international quasi-order of the United Nations rests on a fairly safe foundation. This is not an imaginary quality of the Charter as a " higher " law in comparison with other treaties, but the state of near-universality attained by the United Nations.

F. The Interpretation of Treaties

The interpretation of a treaty presupposes a validly concluded treaty.[74] While the revision of a treaty has as its object the change, for the future, of a text that may be perfectly clear,[75] treaty interpretation aims at the establishment of the true meaning of a treaty at the time when it was concluded.

As most words have more than one meaning, it is wellnigh impossible to establish the " objective " meaning of any treaty. The most that is feasible is to find a pragmatically plausible interpretation which corresponds as closely as possible to the

---

[71] See above, p. 25.
[72] See above, p. 101, and below, p. 227.
[73] See above, p. 141.
[74] See above, p. 143.
[75] See below, p. 155 *et seq*.

text of the treaty, the functions it is meant to serve and the actual intentions, if ascertainable, of the parties. As it is the duty of the parties to interpret and apply the treaty in good faith,[76] any international organ to which they may decide to delegate this task should not attempt to do more. All it can attempt is to apply considerations of reasonableness and good faith or, in other words, the *jus aequum* rule. In each case, the result of interpretation is, therefore, necessarily the outcome of a balancing process between conflicting equities.

International courts and tribunals fight shy of laying bare the equitable and common-sense reasons on which, in fact, their interpretative work is based. They tend to express these considerations in semi-technical and quasi-logical terminologies of a somewhat tautological character. Actually, all these can prove is that a court or tribunal has preferred one to another or a number of other possible interpretations. Yet, as a rule, these reasonings fail to explain *why* one interpretation has been chosen rather than another.

Seven techniques of treaty interpretation serve to give what is still widely thought to be greater professional respectability than a frank avowal of the exercise of what, at its best, is an equitable jurisdiction:

1. *Summary Interpretation*

If an organ holds that a text is " clear " or has an apparently self-evident " natural " or " ordinary " meaning, this means in fact that it avoids any articulate technique of interpretation. It relies on its intuitive powers and its immunity from criticism in a strongly hierarchical profession.

2. *Literal Interpretation*

In this form of interpretation, which includes grammatical interpretation, the emphasis is on the meaning of words in isolation and in the syntax of the sentence to which they belong.

3. *Systematic Interpretation*

If, rather than to the meaning of words in isolation and the context of the syntax, significance is primarily attached to their

---

[76] See above, p. 137.

meaning in the wider context of the paragraphs, articles and the treaty as a whole, literal interpretation is replaced by systematic interpretation.

4. *Logical Interpretation*

Its object is to eliminate self-contradictions, inconsistencies and absurdities in the interpretation of treaties by means of, at least on the surface, logically conclusive reasoning.

5. *Historical Interpretation*

In this approach, the meaning of an obscure text is clarified by reference to the drafting history or the preparatory work (*travaux préparatoires*) of the treaty.

6. *Functional Interpretation*

This technique, also known as the teleological method, serves to explain the meaning of an article by reference to the functions which, in regulating the legal relations between the parties, the particular clause or the treaty as a whole is intended to fulfil.

7. *Authoritative Interpretation*

Authoritative interpretation of a legal document, in the sense of joint interpretation by the parties, may take the form of preparatory material or lead to the insertion of interpretative clauses in a treaty. So long as these are not themselves in dispute, they are of the highest probative value. Otherwise, they are neither more nor less authoritative than any other disputed preparatory material or controversial treaty clause.

The application of one or more of these techniques of treaty interpretation may well lead to results which are identical with the straightforward application of the *jus aequum* rule. Yet, if international judicial organs fail to divulge why they favour one combination rather than another of these methods, they necessarily invite speculation on the reasons behind the reasons of their decisions.

In almost every case before the World Court involving the interpretation of treaties, there have been conflicting majority and minority opinions. Such diametrically opposed conclusions spring necessarily from the different techniques of treaty interpretation chosen by both majority and minority members of the Court. Disquisitions on the consequences of the adoption of some or other techniques do not, however, explain by themselves why some have been preferred to others which would have produced the opposite result. What must be expected from judicial international institutions is that, as they are bound to do,[77] they should disclose the *operative* reasons in the exercise of their judicial discretion.

G. The Revision of Treaties

In case of doubt, a treaty which does not contain a time-limit or entitle a party to denounce it, is of a permanent character. Thus, the Pact of Paris for the Renunciation of War of 1928, commonly known as the Kellogg Pact after the United States Secretary of State at the time of its conclusion, does not contain any clause which limits its duration. It is clear from its Preamble that no such intention on the part of the signatories can be implied, although the Pact has been broken only too often. It cannot, therefore, be lawfully changed except with the consent of all the original parties and those powers which have subsequently adhered to it.

Such rigidity may put a considerable strain on the good intentions of the contracting parties. They may be seriously inconvenienced by a treaty for reasons which are not always discernible at the time of its conclusion and, in practice, the possibility of achieving desired changes by the consent of all the parties may not always exist. This makes it desirable to provide for the revision of treaties.

If parties to treaties wish to avoid being irrevocably bound for ever, they are free to conclude short-term agreements with or without provisions for automatic renewal. Another possibility is for the parties to incorporate in a treaty which they intend to be of a permanent character provisions for periodical review and, if necessary, revision.

Thus, the Charter of the United Nations provides for its own revision in Chapter XVIII. Amendments to the Charter come into force for all members of the United Nations when they have

[77] See below, p. 736.

been adopted by a vote of two-thirds of the members of the General Assembly and ratified by two-thirds of the members of the United Nations, including all the permanent members of the Security Council. In contrast to the solution which had been adopted in the Covenant of the League of Nations, members of the United Nations who have voted against, and refuse to ratify, an amendment, do not automatically cease to be members of the United Nations, but are bound by such an amendment. In accordance with a Declaration of Interpretation adopted at the San Francisco Conference of 1945, in such a case a member State may, however, withdraw from the United Nations.[78]

Finally, the revision of a treaty may be left in the hands of an organ of a collective system such as the League of Nations or the United Nations. Article 19 of the League Covenant was a shy attempt in this direction, and the Charter of the United Nations hardly carries matters any further.[79]

De facto revision of a treaty differs from *de jure* revision in two respects. In the first place, it is the result of a gradual and inarticulate process of departure from consensual engagements without overt objection from other contracting parties. Secondly, it is a matter of interpretation in each individual case whether the process has stopped short of *de jure* revision by tacit consent and merely amounts to a waiver of past and present breaches of the treaty.

A significant illustration of *de facto* revision is the treatment of Paragraph 3 of Article 27 of the Charter of the United Nations in the practice of the Security Council. Notwithstanding the express stipulation that decisions of the Security Council on all matters other than procedure shall be made by an affirmative vote of seven members, it is now well established that abstention by a permanent member is not an impediment to a decision being taken by the Security Council.[80] Similarly, the Memorandum of Understanding regarding the Free Territory of Trieste between Italy, the United Kingdom, the United States and Yugoslavia of October 5, 1954, is a remarkable instance of a *de facto* revision of the Peace Treaty with Italy of 1947 by way of an express understanding among four of the parties to the Treaty.

[78] See below, p. 268.
[80] See below, p. 274.

[79] See below, p. 311.

H. The Suspension and Termination of Treaties

The right to suspend or terminate a treaty may be asserted on any one of six different grounds: consent, desuetude, retaliation, impossibility of performance, *clausula rebus sic stantibus* and war.

1. *Consent*

The parties to a treaty are always at liberty to agree to the modalities of its suspension and termination, either by express provisions in the treaty to this effect or by subsequent agreement.

2. *Desuetude*

This is tacit consent to, or acquiescence in, the permanent non-fulfilment of treaty obligations. It differs from a *waiver* of particular breaches of a treaty by the implied admission that the other party is legally entitled to disregard the treaty. Mere *non-user* of a right conferred by a treaty suffices even less to establish desuetude.

3. *Retaliation*

A party to a treaty may suspend compliance with it or treat it as abrogated on the ground that the other contracting party has failed to fulfil its obligations under the same treaty. If other means of redress are not available, this act derives its justification from the legality of reprisals in international customary law.[81] Like any other exercise of rights in a treaty nexus, this form of retaliation remains governed by the *jus aequum* rule.[82]

4. *Impossibility of Performance*

This may be objective or subjective. The extinction of a party to a treaty or the destruction of its object are illustrations of objective impossibility. The one situation is governed by the rules on the continuity and discontinuity of international

---

[81] See below, p. 173 *et seq.*
[82] See above, p. 25.

persons,[83] and the other by those on common mistake [84] and the *clausula rebus sic stantibus.*[85]

Subjective impossibility is peculiar to the parties to a treaty. It may be absolute or relative. If, on grounds which would exclude international responsibility even under *jus strictum,*[86] a party has the right to suspend or terminate its treaty obligations, the impossibility is absolute. The destruction of all whales by radio-active waste deposited in the high seas by a third State would amount to *force majeure* [87] and release a State from any treaty obligation to supply another State with whale meat. If, in reliance on *jus aequum,* a party asserts impossibility of performance, such impossibility is merely relative. Thus, a severe economic crisis may offer a good ground for the suspension of a treaty obligation.

5. *Clausula rebus sic stantibus*

Basic changes in circumstances which had been taken for granted by *all* the contracting parties at the conclusion of a treaty may also entitle the party against whom the change operates to suspend or denounce the treaty.

In more recent times, Russia (1870), Austria-Hungary (1908), Persia (1927), Nazi Germany (1936 and 1939) and the United States of America (1941) have invoked this doctrine, which is known by the abbreviation of the maxim *Omnis conventio intelligitur rebus sic stantibus.* Yet, in all but two of the cases mentioned, all that had changed was the relative power position and the greater freedom of action of the parties onerously affected by these treaties.

In the case of Persia, there was perhaps some justification to treat the extraterritoriality treaties as antiquated.[88] Yet, it is hard to accept that the only governing rule—the *jus aequum* rule—should have justified a unilateral denunciation of these treaties at somewhat short notice rather than a request for a negotiated modification or termination of these treaties. The invocation of the doctrine by the United States in 1941 is

---

[83] See above, p. 80 *et seq.*
[85] See below, p. 562.
[87] See below, p. 570.
[88] See above, pp. 6 and 12.

[84] See above, p. 148.
[86] See below, p. 168 *et seq.*

probably the strongest of these cases. The purpose of this step was to justify the temporary suspension of the International Load Line Convention of 1930 in the interest of the war effort. Actually it could well have been argued that, like other conventions in the field of international economic law, this Convention was intended to be applied only in peacetime conditions.[89] Thus, it would be difficult to argue that this measure was either contrary to reasonableness or good faith. In other words, it complied with the *jus aequum* rule.

In a swiftly changing world, the dynamic principle underlying the *clausula* has much to recommend itself. Yet, in the absence of an automatic decision by an impartial organ on all the issues involved, the *clausula* is open to abuse as a handy means of evading compliance with burdensome treaty obligations.[90]

6. *War*

It remains to discuss the effect of war on treaties. In exceptional cases only will a war in which none of the contracting parties is directly involved entitle any such party to claim the suspension or termination of the treaty. If one of two contracting parties becomes a belligerent while the other remains neutral, the state of war may entitle the former to plead a temporary impossibility of performance and the latter to argue that, during the war, the performance of its treaty obligations must give way to fulfilment of its duties as a neutral power.[91]

In the case of treaties between States which, subsequently, become enemies, it depends on the intentions of the parties whether war between them affects the treaty in question. Some treaties, such as conventions regarding the treatment of prisoners of war, are concluded for the very purpose of being applied in the contingency of war.[92] In other cases, the question whether the treaty continues in operation, is suspended or terminated by war can be decided only by reference to the nature of the obligations incurred in each concrete case by the contracting parties and by an interpretation of their intentions in accordance with

[89] See above, pp. 36 and 102.
[90] See below, p. 562 *et seq.*
[91] See below, p. 208 *et seq.*
[92] See below, p. 204 *et seq.*

reasonableness and good faith. In practice, the matter is usually settled retrospectively in the peace treaty.[93]

IV—UNILATERAL ACTS

The chief division is that between unilateral acts which produce legal effects in accordance with their intent and others which may produce legal effects contrary to their intent. The latter are illegal acts in breach of treaties, rules of international customary law and general principles of law recognised by civilised nations. They constitute international torts.[94] The former, together with closely related parallel and collective acts, are the concern of this Section.

A. Types of Unilateral Acts

Some types of unilateral acts, such as recognition[95] and reservation,[96] have already been discussed. Others of hardly less general significance are the following:

(1) *Notification.* This is information on steps taken, such as the assumption of territorial jurisdiction,[97] or declarations of war,[98] neutrality[99] and blockade.[1] The object of notification is to obtain clarification of the position taken towards the issue by the notified power.

(2) *Acquiescence.* Tacit consent cannot be presumed.[2] Thus, acquiescence may be inferred only if, in good faith, any other interpretation of silence is impossible.

(3) *Renunciation.* The waiver of a right may take the form of an express declaration. If coupled with an *Admission*, another type of unilateral act, it becomes a form of recognition.[3]

(4) *Protest.* Dissent expressed in this way precludes any inference of tacit recognition or acquiescence.

(5) *Unilateral Acts as Part of a wider Consensual Nexus.* The offer of a treaty and its acceptance are unilateral acts which form constituent elements of any bilateral treaty. A declaration under

---

[93] See below, p. 203 *et seq.*
[95] See above, p. 62 *et seq.*
[97] See above, p. 86.
[99] See below, p. 206.
[2] See above, p. 8.

[94] See below, p. 162 *et seq.*
[96] See above, p. 62 *et seq.*
[98] See below, p. 180.
[1] See below, p. 225.
[3] See above, p. 62.

Article 36 (the Optional Clause) of the Statute of the World Court is a unilateral act by which a State makes an offer at large to eligible parties.[4]

B. Legal Characteristics and Effects of Unilateral Acts

The legal characteristics of unilateral acts on the level of international customary law have already been elaborated in relation to recognition and are equally applicable to all unilateral acts.[5] They may be express or implied. While express unilateral acts become effective on communication to the addressee, the moment when implied unilateral acts become effective is necessarily a matter of inference. Unless they interfere with the rights of existing subjects of international law and, then, become illegal acts,[6] they are discretionary.

By consent or any other act creating an estoppel, subjects of international law may, however, limit their freedom in this, as in any other, respect.[7]

The governing rules are those on good faith, in particular the *jus aequum* rule.[8] The declared or inferred intent must be interpreted in accordance with good faith and reasonableness.

C. Parallel and Collective Acts

Parallel acts may be illustrated by declarations made by parties to a dispute before the Security Council.[9] Similarly, a vote taken by the organ of an international institution, as, for instance, the General Assembly of the United Nations on the admission of a new member, constitutes a collective act.[10]

In each case, the legal effects of such acts must be judged in the light of the *jus aequum* rule. Thus, disputing States may participate in passing a recommendation, as distinct from a binding decision, of the Security Council. It may well be that, in reason and good faith and according to the circumstances of

---

[4] See below, p. 239.
[5] See above, p. 62.
[6] See above, p. 59, and below, p. 164 *et seq.*
[7] See above, pp. 82 and 138.
[8] See above, pp. 25 and 137.
[9] See below, p. 283 *et seq.*
[10] See below, p. 267 *et seq.*

the case, this may amount to a consensual engagement between the two parties.

V—The Principle of International Responsibility

The rules underlying the principle of international responsibility are the complement of all other rules of international law. They transform otherwise declaratory precepts into legal norms and, in this sense, may also be described—albeit with little gain [1]—as the sanctions of international law. It is the function of these rules to determine the legal consequences of the breach of any of the other rules of international law, be they those of treaties, international customary law or general principles of law recognised by civilised nations.

The rules on international responsibility can be reduced to two propositions:

(1) The breach of any international obligation constitutes an *illegal act* or *international tort*.

(2) The commission of an international tort involves the duty to make reparation.

These rules are rules of international customary law. This means, *first*, that they arise independent of the will of any particular subject of international law and, *secondly*, that they may be modified by consent and acquiescence.

Thus, by consent, the rule on reparation can be transformed into rules providing for penalties corresponding to those in municipal criminal law.[2] Similarly, by consent or acquiescence, an international claim in tort may be waived and, in this way, the breach of any international obligation be healed. Although not differing in any respect from other forms of acquiescence,[3] this type of acquiescence is widely known as *extinctive prescription*.

Five aspects of the law relating to international torts require closer examination: the meaning of breach of an international obligation; the legal interest of the claimant; the identity of the tortfeasor; the requirement of fault and, finally, the forms of reparation.

---

[1] See above, p. 38 *et seq.*, and below, p. 173 *et seq.*
[2] See above, p. 108.   [3] See above, p. 8.

A. The Breach of an International Obligation

Terms such as *international illegal act* or *international tort* are merely synonyms for the breach of an international obligation.

To constitute such a breach, four conditions must be fulfilled:

(1) The breach must be against the will of the complainant (*ad invitum*). As with all rules of international *jus dispositivum*,[4] prior consent rules out, and condonation or acquiescence heals, the breach of any international obligation.

(2) The breach must not be justifiable as, for instance, by the exercise of the rights of self-defence [5] and reprisal.[6]

(3) The breach must be attributable or imputable to a subject of international law.[7]

(4) The breach must be voluntary.[8]

Thus, a breach of an international obligation—an international illegal act or an international tort—may be defined as an act or omission which is unjustified, uncondoned, attributable to a subject of international law and voluntary.

In some cases, it may be doubtful whether an obligation under international law has been broken. Thus, it is still uncertain whether agency of necessity (*negotiorum gestio*) and unjustified enrichment have been received into the body of the rules of international law.

Adapted to international law, *agency of necessity* means action in the interest of, but without consultation with, another subject of international law in circumstances which make immediate action imperative, as, for instance, emergency assistance to nationals of a friendly country in a third State. This institution runs counter both to the principles of sovereignty [9] and of consent.[10] Nevertheless, reasonableness and good faith may require that obligations arising from such unasked assistance should be met. At this point, the borderline between a moral duty and a legal duty postulated by the *jus aequum* rule becomes very thin. Yet, whether *negotiorum gestio* is in the one or the

---

[4] See above, p. 60.
[6] See below, p. 173.
[8] See below, p. 168.
[10] See above, p. 138 *et seq.*

[5] See below, p. 172.
[7] See below, p. 166.
[9] See above, p. 58 *et seq.*

other sphere is entirely a question of evidence. It is in the nature of claims of this kind that States tend to meet their obligations without raising such technical issues.

There is somewhat stronger evidence for acceptance of the principle of unjustified enrichment, if not as a rule of international customary law, at least as a general principle of law recognised by civilised nations. Again, a sense of honour is likely to prompt subjects of international law to settle such issues *ex gratia* rather than on the basis of strict law.

B. The Legal Interest of the Claimant

International customary law lacks any compulsory judicial organisation and, therefore, does not know of the distinction between procedural and substantive law.[11] Thus, on this level, the question of the legal interest that a claimant must be able to show to be allowed to present an international claim is necessarily one of substantive law. On the level of organised international society, the optional character of the jurisdiction of international judicial institutions calls for a threefold distinction. It is between matters of procedure, jurisdiction and substance. While some of the issues concerned with the existence of a legal interest arise as questions of procedure because they are concerned with the admissibility of an application, others affect the jurisdiction of international judicial institutions.[12]

If an international tort has been committed *directly* against a subject of international law as, for instance, by the invasion of the territory of another State, it is not necessary for the claimant to prove the infliction of actual damage. The illegal act itself—and even any real threat of such action—constitutes a sufficient legal interest.

If the tort has been committed against an object of international law—individuals, corporations, ships or aircraft [13]—such acts are prima facie outside the purview of international law. To transform such an act into an international tort, international customary law postulates a legal interest of a stringent character: nationality of the object in question.[14]

---

[11] See below, p. 238 *et seq.*
[13] See above, p. 129 *et seq.*

[12] See below, p. 237 *et seq.*
[14] See above, p. 129 *et seq.*

International judicial practice interprets this test so strictly as to demand the continuity of nationality from the time of the injury (*dies a quo*) until the date of judgment (*dies ad quem*). If protection of the individual were the *ratio legis* behind the rule on the continuity of nationality, the hardships resulting from this rule would lay it open to serious objections. For instance, if, before the award is delivered, the claimant dies and his heirs have a different nationality, the claim lapses. Yet, in fact, the rule serves a completely different purpose. It is to limit intervention in the domestic affairs of other States even if, in marginal cases, this object can be attained only at the price of considerable hardship to the individual. Exceptions to the nationality rule rest on consent, acquiescence or recognition. Recent illustrations are the functional protection by the United Nations granted to its officials and relevant provisions in the European Convention on Human Rights of 1950. Under this Convention, the European Commission of Human Rights and also contracting parties other than the home State of the national injured may bring alleged infractions of the Convention before the European Court of Human Rights.[15] The only proviso is that all the contracting parties concerned must have accepted the Court's jurisdiction.

Even if, in principle, the claimant's legal interest has been proved, the presentation of a claim on the international level may be premature. The local remedies rule determines *when* a claim of a national may be adopted as its own by a subject of international law.

Under the rule on the minimum standard of international law, States must provide an adequate judicial and administrative machinery and means for the effective redress of grievances suffered by foreign nationals.[16] If a State complies with this duty, it has done all that, by international law, it is required to do. If not, it is liable because its own organisation falls below this minimum standard. Thus, if superior organs exist which are competent to correct, for instance, a delay or denial of justice,[17] a foreign national must exhaust all local remedies before

[15] See above, p. 107, and below, p. 338.
[16] See above, p. 99.
[17] See below, p. 167.

his home State is entitled to take up the case on the international level.

If a State lacks effective local remedies, this amounts to a breach of the minimum standard. This omission itself constitutes an international tort and, in good faith, precludes the tortfeasor from invoking the local remedy rule. The defendant State always remains free to waive the benefit of the local remedies rule.

In this context, the Calvo Clause deserves to be mentioned. Its object is to limit or exclude the appeal by a foreign national to his home State for protection. To this end, ingenious clauses have been incorporated in public contracts. These have taken the form of stipulations that all disputes between the parties are to be settled exclusively by reference to municipal law; that a foreigner or foreign company consents to be treated as a national of the contracting State or that international reclamations of any kind are altogether excluded.

If this clause purports to affect the right of the home State to put forward an international claim in the interest of its national, it is completely ineffective. In international customary law, the national is a mere object and cannot dispose of the rights of any subject of international law. In the relations between subjects of international law, any claim in tort is a claim of a State or any other subject of international law concerned, and not of an individual or corporation. If, however, the clause is merely intended to prevent frivolous requests by foreigners for support from their home State, it is redundant, for it is the purpose of the local remedy rule to stop the prosecution of any premature international claim.

C. Identity of the Tortfeasor

To constitute an international tort, the act or omission must be attributable to a subject of international law.[18]

A sovereign State is responsible for all its organs, but only for its own organs. It is not responsible for spontaneous acts of individuals. Thus, a boycott of foreign goods organised by individuals or private organisations in a democratic State without

---

[18] See above, p. 47.

connivance by the government does not amount to a breach of a treaty of commerce with the country whose exports are subjected to the boycott. If, however, the government encouraged or promoted the boycott, it would commit a breach of treaty.

A State is equally responsible for its governmental, legislative, executive (including administrative) and judicial organs. Yet, in order to live up to the minimum standard of international law,[19] a State is also expected to grant to the judiciary a maximum of independence from the executive. It would, therefore, be unreasonable to hold a State, which complies with the principle of immunity of the judiciary from governmental direction, responsible for acts of the judiciary within the legitimate scope of their judicial duties. Thus, any act of the judiciary which does not amount to a delay or denial of justice cannot constitute an international tort.[20]

It also stands to reason that the higher the State organ that has committed the offence in question, the more serious is the responsibility of the State itself. In the case of acts of subordinate officials, reproof, dismissal or punishment of the officials concerned, coupled with a commensurate indemnity, is likely to constitute adequate reparation.

In the case of dependent States [21] or member States of a federation,[22] the protecting power or the federation is responsible for the tort of the subordinate unit to the extent to which the latter's international personality has ceased to exist. Similarly, a State is responsible for the tortious acts of self-governing units like municipalities if the tort is committed by those bodies in the exercise of their public functions. Were this otherwise, States could evade some of their international obligations by shielding behind divisions, artificially created under their own public law.[23]

The position is different in the case of revolutionaries. Offences committed by them against foreign nationals are acts of *force majeure* in so far as they concern the government against which the revolutionary movement is directed. Yet, not every case of riot and civil disorder is a revolution. Foreigners and

---

[19] See above, p. 99.
[21] See above, p. 54.
[23] See above, p. 40.

[20] See above, p. 162.
[22] See above, p. 50.

their home State can expect a certain minimum of efficiency on the part of the police of another country. A State, therefore, commits an international tort if it fails to comply with this minimum requirement. Should, however, the revolutionaries be successful and take over control of the State machinery, it would be contrary to good faith if they could deny their responsibility on the ground that, at the time of the commission of the tort, they did not yet bear any responsibility for the government of their State. Even if the revolutionaries are unsuccessful, the government may have to accept responsibility for routine acts of local administration in areas under the temporary control of revolutionaries.

D. The Requirement of Fault

General agreement exists that to constitute an international tort an act or omission must be voluntary. Even, then, in relations governed by *jus aequum*, necessity may excuse, but cannot justify—as do self-defence [24] and reprisals [25]—actions contrary to international law. It must, however, be emphasised that necessity presupposes an absolute impossibility of taking any course other than the one amounting to a breach of an international obligation. It is not a synonym for convenience. Thus, Germany's invasion of Belgium in 1914 contrary to her treaty obligations to respect the neutralisation of Belgium [26] was strategically advantageous. It was not, however, as the German Chancellor alleged, a necessity.

Necessity is a device of *jus aequum*. At the most, it excuses actions, but, by the same token, it may involve the duty to make compensation for the invasion of the right of another subject of international law. It is doubtful whether, beyond this, international customary law postulates any subjective element, such as wrongful intent, negligence or, at least, knowledge of the tortiously relevant facts. International arbitral practice is inconclusive. While the older awards show a certain predisposition towards the *culpa* doctrine, those of the post-1919 period tend, on balance, to favour that of objective responsibility.

[24] See above, p. 163, and below, p. 172 *et seq*.
[25] See below, p. 173.
[26] See above, p. 53.

Until the *Corfu Channel* (*Merits*) case (1949), the World Court's position had been unequivocal. It never paid any attention to guilty intent or negligence as a constituent element of international torts. Yet the *Corfu Channel* case is less conclusively in support of a general *culpa* doctrine than may appear on the surface. It is only concerned with an unlawful omission. A subject of international law is responsible only for its *own* unlawful omissions. These presuppose a duty to act. Whether this exists depends on the concrete circumstances of each case. Thus, in cases of omission, knowledge of the circumstances is indispensable and, to this extent, it is reasonable to insist on evidence of this subjective element.

Actually, attempts at hard and fast distinctions between objective and subjective responsibility are little more than doctrinal overgeneralisation. At least in international judicial practice, the relativity of any such distinction is apparent. The available international case law does not appear to support more than the proposition that the subject is governed by considerations of reasonableness and good faith, that is to say, the *jus aequum* rule.

E. Reparation

In international law, the duty to make reparation means the obligation to re-establish, as far as possible, the state of affairs as it would probably have existed had the international tort not been committed. The particular function of this rule is to assist in the restoration of the legal equilibrium which has been disturbed by the commission of an international tort.

Thus, in the first place, reparation takes the form of *restitution* in kind. If this is not possible, two subsidiary forms of reparation are available: *satisfaction* and *compensation*. Satisfaction is any non-monetary form of reparation which falls short of restitution in kind. A formal apology or condemnation of an act by an international tribunal illustrates this type of reparation. For the rest, there is only monetary compensation as a substitute for the impossible restoration of the *status quo ante*.

CHAPTER 7

LEGAL AND ILLEGAL USES OF FORCE

" The nature of Warre, consisteth not in actual fighting; but in
the known disposition thereto, during all the time there is no
assurance to the contrary. All other time is Peace." (Hobbes'
Leviathan—1651)

IF the rules of international customary law were limited to those
which, so far, have been discussed under the headings of six
fundamental principles, international law would constitute a self-
executing system of law. This type of international law would
be indistinguishable from international morality.[1] It would have
to rely on two major assumptions.

The first of these premises would be that the auto-interpretation of its rights and duties by each subject of international law
would more or less coincide with that of any other with which
it happened to be involved in a controversy. Preferably, this
concord should exist when the issue still turns on the rules
governing the principles of sovereignty,[2] recognition,[3] good
faith,[4] consent,[5] and freedom of the seas.[6] If such agreement
cannot be reached at this stage, it would have to be attained, at
the latest, when a breach of an international obligation has
taken place, and the matter is still governed by the rules on
international responsibility.[7] The second assumption would be
that the subjects of international law were not only willing to
agree on the nature and extent of their mutual legal obligations,
but also capable and willing to carry them out.

Actually, throughout the centuries, neither of these assumptions has been true over any prolonged period. Powers, great
and small alike, have fiercely disagreed with one another on
their respective legal rights. They have employed international
law to put forward legal claims which merely served to cover
their desires for greater gain and wider expansion.[8] They have

---

[1] See above, p. 2.
[3] See above, p. 62.
[5] See above, p. 138.
[7] See above, p. 162.

[2] See above, p. 58.
[4] See above, p. 137.
[6] See above, p. 122.
[8] See above, p. 8.

proved somewhat reluctant to submit major political issues with potential enemies to procedures of peaceful settlement.[9]   While this generalisation does not do justice to the self-denying ordinances imposed on themselves by some States at one time or another, these honourable exceptions to the rule do not appear to affect the overall picture.   In a hitherto always hierarchical international society, the tone is set by the great powers, and those among them with the lowest standard have tended to impose theirs on others who, if they could, might perhaps have acted differently.[10]   Yet, even if States had been less obsessed with the pursuit of real or imagined interests of their own, the strain on any legal system that lacks adequate institutions for peaceful change would still have been considerable.[11]

In fact, classical international law did not rest on such sanguine assumptions.   If anything, its rules on the legality of resort to force were so liberal, if not vague, as to open the door wide to international anarchy.[12]   In a state of practically un-inhibited auto-interpretation of legal obligations,[13] assertion necessarily stood against assertion.   As international customary law provided, if anything, too ample scope for the exercise of the right of self-defence [14] and the right to apply forcible reprisals,[15] it was impossible to settle with any legal finality which of the parties had acted in self-defence or in the exercise of a right of self-help.   Thus, probably inevitably, the Doctrine of international law resigned itself to treating war of any kind as legal.[16]

This situation made it impossible to conceive international law as a consistent legal system.   If a State was free to wage even aggressive warfare, there was little point in attempting to refine the law relating to the use of force in the exercise of either the right of self-defence or that of self-help.   It was then perhaps forgivable to cloak the impotence of international law in this sphere in an all-embracing doctrine of a " right " of self-preservation.[17]

In law, if not in fact, this position has been fundamentally changed by the Kellogg Pact of 1928 and, even more so, by the

---

[9] See below, p. 310 *et seq.*
[11] See below, pp. 311 and 374.
[13] See below, p. 234.
[15] See below, p. 173.
[17] See below, p. 175.

[10] See above, p. 9 *et seq.*
[12] See above, p. 61.
[14] See below, p. 172.
[16] See below, p. 584 *et seq.*

Charter of the United Nations.[18]   Under this combined quasi-order, international law has gained a greater systematic unity than it ever had before.   Although the means of authoritative verification of any claim to the right to use force are still woefully incomplete,[19] it certainly is no longer a vain effort to attempt to define the limits of lawful resort to compulsory measures short of war and to consider possible differences between the effects of legal and illegal war.[20]

I—The Principle of Self-Defence

The celebrated Note of April 24, 1841, from Secretary of State Webster to Mr. Fox in the British – United States controversies over the *Caroline* (1837) and *McLeod* (1840) incidents [21] contains a number of the constituent elements of the rules on self-defence. The formulation of self-defence in this Note has also received the approval of the International Military Tribunals of Nuremberg (1946) and Tokyo (1948).[22]   In the *Corfu Channel* (*Merits*) case (1949), the International Court of Justice further contributed to the elucidation of these rules.[23]

The position under international customary law [24] can be summarised under three heads:

(1) Measures of self-defence may be taken against

    (a) illegal acts or omissions which are attributable to another subject of international law;

    (b) acts of individuals, ships or aircraft which disentitle their home State from the grant of diplomatic protection, or any other subject of international law from the grant of functional protection;

    (c) similar acts of individuals, ships or aircraft without a subject of international law entitled to grant diplomatic [25] or functional [26] protection.

(2) The need for self-defence must be compelling and instant.

(3) Measures of self-defence comprise any action, including hot pursuit from territorial waters into the high seas, which is

---

[18] See below, p. 183.   [19] See below, pp. 183 and 309.
[20] See below, p. 183.   [21] See below, p. 582.
[22] See below, p. 582.   [23] See below, p. 582.
[24] See below, p. 581.   [25] See below, p. 129.
[26] See below, p. 132.

necessary to repel any imminent or present invasion of the rights of a subject of international law.

II—Measures of Self-Help

International law leaves its subjects free to retaliate against one another's unfriendly, but lawful, acts with unfriendly acts which also keep within the law. This possibility of *retorsion* fulfils the beneficial function of reducing to reasonableness any too rigorous exercise of absolute rights.[27] Thus, if, on principle, one State refuses to admit to its territory citizens of another State,[28] the latter may reply in kind, or refuse to grant other privileges which, in law, it is free to give or deny. It may, for instance, decide to break off diplomatic relations.[29]

If a subject of international law, which has committed an international tort, refuses to comply with its duty to make reparation,[30] the other party is not limited to measures of retorsion. It is entitled, under international customary law, to take *reprisals*. Such acts are in themselves illegal. They receive, however, their justification from being acts of retaliation against a *preceding* illegal act by the party against which reprisals are applied. In the predominant view, such reprisals must be more or less proportionate. It goes without saying that, in the case of non-identical reprisals, their proportionate character is somewhat difficult to establish.

If, for instance, State A imprisons citizens of State B without cause or trial and refuses to release them, State B has, under international customary law, a wide choice of political, economic and military counter-measures. It may decide to establish a blockade of State A's ports in the territorial sea of State A and seize a reasonable number of ships flying the flag of State A. The blockade must not, however, disturb in any way the ingress or egress of ships of the nationality of third powers. In this lies the difference between so-called peaceful and wartime blockades.[31]

Like any other right under international customary law,[32] the right of self-help may be limited or excluded by way of

---

[27] See above, p. 25.
[29] See above, p. 68.
[31] See below, p. 224.

[28] See below, p. 483 *et seq.*
[30] See above, p. 169.
[32] See above, p. 27.

treaty. By Hague Convention II of 1907, the so-called Porter
Convention, the right to employ forcible reprisals for the recovery
of contract debts which States have incurred towards foreign
nationals, has been limited.[33] Paragraph 4 of Article 2 of the
Charter of the United Nations is of even more far-reaching
significance. It prohibits the threat and application of any type
of forcible reprisal.[34]

III—The Three States of International Law

The place of compulsory measures short of war in classical
international law was always ambiguous. It became accepted
that States against which reprisals were applied had the choice
of either submitting to such interference or treating measures of
this kind as hostile acts which were incompatible with a state of
peace. Similarly, third parties were considered free to define
their own attitudes towards such measures. They could either
continue to apply in their relations with the disputants the
ordinary rules of the law of peace or substitute for these the law
of neutrality.[35]

A situation which the parties as well as third States may
treat at will either as a state of peace or as a state of war, differs
intrinsically from a clear-cut state of either peace or war. It
forms a distinct state of intermediacy (*status mixtus*) of its own.
The specific characteristic of this state is the option it gives to
the victim of reprisals to treat forcible reprisals either as
compatible with a state of peace or as amounting to a state of
war, as well as to third powers to put the whole or parts of the
law of neutrality into operation in relation to both sides.[36] In
practice, this may mean that, in the relations between the
contestants, for some purposes the law of peace remains in
operation, while for others, as, for instance, regarding the treatment of prisoners, the relevant rules of warfare apply.[37]

The combined effect of the Kellogg Pact and the Charter of
the United Nations (Articles 2 (4) and 51) [38] has been to resolve
the dilemma arising from the co-existence of a limited right to
apply forcible reprisals and of an unlimited right to resort to

[33] See below, p. 579.
[35] See below, p. 206 *et seq.*
[37] See below, p. 190 *et seq.*

[34] See below, p. 700.
[36] See below, p. 208 *et seq.*
[38] See below, pp. 309, 700 and 710

war. Under this international quasi-order, forcible reprisals have become illegal. At the same time, any other threat, or use of force save in self-defence against armed attack, has been prohibited. As befits a collective system for the maintenance of world peace and security,[39] a reservation is made in Article 51 of the Charter not only in favour of individual self-defence, but also in the interest of collective defence, albeit under the misnomer collective self-defence. International law under the prevailing international quasi-order certainly no longer justifies an all-embracing right of self-preservation.[40] The only rights which are still recognised are the specific rights of self-defence and reprisals falling short of the threat, or use, of force as well as a narrowly construed excuse of action on grounds of necessity.[41]

In the state of near-universality attained by the United Nations, the question of the survival of the rules of international customary law on reprisals and the unlimited right to resort to war may be thought to be somewhat hypothetical. Would it not, therefore, be timely to substitute for the distinction between the three states of international law the simpler division between legal and illegal uses of force under the quasi-order of the United Nations and the Kellogg Pact? As yet, this appears premature.

In the first place, non-member States may consider themselves free to ignore the Charter of the United Nations.[42] Even if parties to the Kellogg Pact, they may argue that this Treaty applies only to war in the technical sense, but not to compulsory measures short of war.[43] Secondly, in strained relations between a member of the United Nations and a non-member State, the latter may claim to remain unaffected by the Charter.[44] Thirdly, even in a dispute between member States, the Security Council may be unable to reach a decision under Chapter Seven of the Charter.[45] Finally, under the reservation of Article 107 of the Charter, members of the United Nations may take unilateral action against ex-enemy States in the Second World War.[46] So long as these contingencies cannot be ruled out, it would be inadvisable to throw the three states of international law to the winds.

[39] See below, p. 308 *et seq.*
[40] See above, p. 171, and below, p. 309.
[42] See above, p. 73.
[44] See above, p. 73.
[46] See below, p. 276.

[41] See below, p. 309.
[43] See below, p. 177.
[45] See below, p. 309.

IV—COLLECTIVE SECURITY

Renunciation of resort to force as a means of redress and policy cannot be attained in isolation. The use of force may be uncivilised or, in the nuclear age, downright suicidal. Still, in the past, it has fulfilled functions which, in a turbulent and dynamic environment, must be discharged in one way or another. It is the purpose of comprehensive international organisations, such as confederations,[47] or more closely knit associations, such as territorial or functional federations,[48] to institutionalise the legitimate use of force. If this object is to be attained, the rights of individual self-defence and of assistance to a victim of aggression by allies, as distinct from action under the control of the collective system, must be reduced to emergency and interim rights.

On the still relatively loose level of the confederate collective systems of the League of Nations and United Nations type,[49] collective security represents the institutionalised form of the legitimate use of force. It rests on two basic ideas. *First,* the member States band together against outsiders or the unknown power among themselves which may stray from the path of collective rectitude. *Secondly,* the member States agree in advance not to adopt policies of neutrality[50] between the member State which has used force illegally (the aggressor) and its victim, but to assist the latter to the limit of their capacity.

Since the days of the Perpetual League of 1291 between the Swiss Forest Communities, the Union of Utrecht of 1579, the Confederation of the United States of 1777, the Germanic Confederation of 1820 and the League of Nations of 1919—not to speak of even earlier attempts on similar lines in ancient Greece—groups of States have organised themselves in associations based on the principle of collective security by collective defence.

As far as collective security on the confederate level goes, the scheme laid down in the Charter of the United Nations contains all the essentials. Under Chapter Seven of the Charter, the Security Council may recommend or decide what diplomatic, economic or military measures member States should take in cases of threats to international peace, breaches of the peace

---

[47] See above, p. 50.
[48] See above, p. 50, and below, p. 381.
[49] See above, p. 50, and below, p. 265 *et seq.* [50] See below, p. 185.

and acts of aggression.[51] Where appropriate, the Security Council is enjoined to utilise regional arrangements or agencies for enforcement action under its authority. In contrast to the merely advisory power of the Council of the League of Nations, decisions of the Security Council under Chapter Seven of the Charter are binding upon member States.[52]

If, on the authority of the Security Council, member States take military measures, this constitutes a lawful use of force. In accordance with Paragraph 5 of Article 2 of the Charter, member States are bound to give the United Nations every assistance in any such action and must refrain from giving assistance to any State against which the United Nations is taking preventive or enforcement action. Moreover, at least between member States, their obligations under the Charter override conflicting obligations under any other agreement.[53]

The legality of collective measures adopted against non-member States which have not accepted the jurisdiction of the United Nations can always be justified on one of two grounds. If the non-member State, against which collective action is taken, is a party to the Kellogg Pact, such measures are justifiable on grounds of reprisals, self-defence or collective defence. If not, the non-member State can rely only on international customary law, and this leaves States free to go to war on any ground.[54] In relation to such a non-member State, members of the United Nations would not even be precluded from such action by the estoppel which has possibly been created by the Resolution of the General Assembly of 1946 affirming the Nuremberg Principles.[55]

The security system of the United Nations is based on the unstated but vital assumption that, if world peace is threatened or has actually been broken, the permanent members of the Security Council will act in unison. Exceptions apart, such as unanimity on the Korean incident in the Security Council during the temporary absence of the Soviet Union,[56] this condition of Chapter Seven of the Charter becoming operative has proved wanting. On the contrary, by the use of the reservations in the

[51] See below, p. 284.
[53] See below, p. 722.
[55] See below, p. 200.

[52] See below, p. 284.
[54] See above, p. 171.
[56] See below, p. 288.

Charter on collective defence and freedom of action regarding ex-enemy States,[56a] member States have arraigned themselves in two major antagonistic alignments. Behind the shields of their defensive alliances—on the one hand, the North Atlantic Pact, CENTO Pact, South-East Asia Pact and a host of bilateral treaties, and, on the other, the Warsaw Pact and the Sino-Russian alliance [57]—the two world camps face each other across an unstable world frontier.

In this impasse, attempts have been made to let the General Assembly, as the secondary organ in the field of collective security, fill the gap created by the self-exclusion of the Security Council. Yet, with the exception of its control of the purse strings of the Organisation by the exercise of its budgetary powers, the General Assembly is limited to the passing of recommendations on matters of collective security.[58] While the General Assembly, by the Uniting for Peace Resolution it adopted in 1950, has enabled itself to speed up its own proceedings, this Resolution can add nothing to its powers—or lack of powers—under the Charter.[59] Thus, this organ of the United Nations must be content to rely on the highly unpredictable element of spontaneous co-operation in each individual case on the part of member States.[60] On occasion, as with the establishment of the United Nations Emergency Force (UNEF) during the Suez crisis of 1956,[61] this condition is fulfilled. Then, an *ad hoc* system of collective security appears to spring into existence and take the place of that envisaged in the Charter of the United Nations.

If this element is lacking, each member State is thrown back upon itself. As a party to a treaty which has been broken by one side or the other, it must decide for itself the identity of the aggressor. It is then entitled, but not bound, to discriminate against the aggressor by way of reprisals and participate in the collective defence of the victim of aggression.[62] Yet, it may also decide to adopt the alternative pattern of strict neutrality in accordance with classical international law.[63]

These shortcomings of the quasi-order of the United Nations are not deficiencies of legal rules such as those on self-defence

---

56a See below, p. 276.
58 See below, p. 279.
60 See below, p. 288.
62 See above, pp. 176 and 177.

57 See below, p. 355.
59 See below, p. 287 *et seq.*
61 See below, p. 289.
63 See below, p. 208 *et seq.*

or on crimes against peace as war crimes on a treaty basis.[64] On the surface they are of an organisational character but, ultimately, they are symptoms of a deeper seated malaise: a lacking unity of purpose.

V—STATE AND EFFECTS OF WAR

In systems of power politics, and power politics in disguise,[65] the borderline between the three states of international law is necessarily fluid. While in a state of peace, subjects of international law are free to apply political and economic forms of pressure against one another, they may apply a limited degree of forcible pressure against one another in a state of intermediacy [66] and, subject to prohibitive rules of warfare,[67] all forms of pressure in time of war.

Whether a state of intermediacy or war exists depends on the views taken of the situation by the parties directly involved as well as third powers. From 1937 onwards, China and Japan were involved in hostilities of increasing scope and intensity. Yet, until 1941, Japan as well as China denied any intention of being involved in war with one another (*animus belligerendi*) and even played the farce of maintaining diplomatic relations with each other. Similarly, for pragmatic reasons of their own, other Powers were content to treat this situation as a state of peace. Again, in 1956, the United Kingdom and France denied that their armed conflict with Egypt amounted to war. Egypt, however, announced that she would treat British and French citizens as enemy nationals.[68]

A. State of War

In traditional terminology, war is supposed to produce a state of war, and all the legal effects of war are then deduced from this state of war. Actually, this form of presentation of the issue is as much a reversal of the true position as the derivation of legal rules from legal principles.[69] If a state of war does not mean merely war in its legal aspects, but is identical with the sum total of the legal consequences of war, it is merely an abstraction

---

[64] See below, p. 199.
[66] See above, p. 174.
[68] See below, p. 202.

[65] See above, p. 36.
[67] See below, p. 185 *et seq*.
[69] See above, p. 37 *et seq*.

from the rules governing three types of wartime relations: those between subjects of international law, between subjects and objects of international law and between objects of international law. Thus, the only legitimate use of this term is to treat it as a comprehensive abbreviation for these three sets of relations.

If there is a declaration of war, the commencement of war can be readily determined. A previous and reasoned declaration of war or an ultimatum with a conditional declaration of war is incumbent on parties to Hague Convention III of 1907 on the Opening of Hostilities. Under the Convention, the state of war must also be notified to neutral powers. International customary law does not require such a prior warning or notification of a state of war to neutral States. It depends on the circumstances of each case whether an ultimatum under Hague Convention III constitutes an illegal threat of force under Article 2 (4) of the United Nations Charter.

In the absence of a declaration of war, the actual date of the outbreak of war is necessarily a question of inference. It must then be determined by reference to any observable legal consequences of this elusive phenomenon. If, in their relations, States apply the laws of war and neutrality [70] or subject individuals and corporations in enemy and neutral countries to their trading with the enemy legislations,[71] these are fair indications that States are at war with one another. In other words, war can frequently be inferred only from a state of war.

Similarly, the end of war is conveniently marked by a peace treaty.[72] Yet, again, States are not bound to terminate war in so formal a manner. Then, the termination of war may also have to be inferred from the discontinuance of a state of war.

B. Effects of War

In international law, the legal effects of war manifest themselves on the three levels: in the relations between belligerent States as well as between belligerent States and neutral powers, between belligerent States and enemy nationals and, finally, between enemy nationals.[73]

[70] See below, p. 181 *et seq.*
[71] See below, p. 182.
[72] See below, p. 203.
[73] See below, p. 182.

1. *Relations between States*

In the relations between belligerent States, the rules of warfare replace those of the law of peace unless belligerents desire to continue to apply some of the rules of the law of peace.

Thus, if belligerents conclude with one another wartime treaties such as capitulation or armistice conventions,[74] they can do so only on the assumption that, for these purposes at least, the rules of international customary law on consent and good faith still apply in their relations. It is also entirely a matter of the intent of belligerents which of their pre-war treaties are maintained in force, suspended for the duration or terminated by the outbreak of war.[75]

While, in the relations between belligerents, the less stringent prohibitions of the laws of war replace those of the law of peace,[76] the changes in the relations between belligerent and non-belligerent powers are less drastic. In principle, the law of peace continues to govern their relations. It is modified, however, by the law of neutrality: a set of enabling rules which give greater freedom to belligerent States and impose considerable duties of abstention on non-belligerent powers.[77] In the case of treaties between States which, subsequently, change into belligerent and neutral powers, the typical intention of parties is that such treaties, especially those in the field of international economic law,[78] should continue to apply, but subject to any overriding interests which arise from the position of the contracting parties as belligerent and neutral States.

2. *Relations between Belligerent States and Enemy Nationals*

The relations between belligerent States and enemy nationals in the territories of the former, as distinct from occupied territories,[79] are chiefly governed by municipal law, that is to say, the rules underlying the principle of sovereignty.[80] Thus, civilians of enemy nationality may be interned or subjected to other restrictions in the interest of public policy, and their property may be sequestrated. Any arbitrary treatment of enemy nationals

---

[74] See below, p. 204.
[76] See below, p. 185 *et seq.*
[78] See above, pp. 102 and 159.
[80] See above, p. 58.

[75] See above, p. 159.
[77] See below, p. 208 *et seq.*
[79] See below, p. 192.

runs counter to the minimum requirements of the standard of civilisation and is prohibited.[81] The prohibitive rules in Section I of Part III of the Geneva Civilians Convention of 1949 (Convention IV) may be taken to be merely declaratory of the minimum standard to be observed, *e.g.*, prohibition of disregard of honour and family rights, of inhumane treatment, physical or moral coercion, policies of extermination, collective punishment, and pillage. The other Articles of the Convention relating to enemy nationals in the territory of a belligerent State aim at improvements in the lot of enemy civilians above this minimum and are binding only on parties to the Convention.[82]

If victorious powers desire to treat confiscation, as distinct from sequestration, of enemy property as contrary to the minimum standard, but, for instance, in view of acts of aggression committed by their enemies or, for other reasons, wish to keep the sequestrated property of defeated enemy nationals, the pattern adopted in the Peace Treaties of 1919 provides the answer. All the victors need do is to stipulate restitution of the private property of their own nationals which has been sequestrated by the enemy and credit the enemy's reparation account with the value of the property they themselves have confiscated or propose to treat in this way. A further refinement is, in the peace treaty, to impose on the defeated enemy an obligation to grant compensation to his own nationals for losses suffered by such confiscation of their assets.[83]

3. *Private Relations*

Relations between individuals or corporations under the territorial control of States which are at war with one another are necessarily governed by some system of municipal law.[84] International customary law leaves it with each belligerent to determine the effects of the outbreak of war on relations of this type, and this is usually done by way of trading with the enemy legislation.

This freedom extends even to the classifying as enemies nationals of neutral States who do not actually reside in enemy

---

[81] See above, p. 12.
[82] See below, p. 192.
[83] See below, p. 623.
[84] See above, p. 40.

territory, but maintain close political or economic links with enemy States. In Hague Convention V of 1907 on the Rights and Duties of Neutral Powers and Persons in War on Land, a not very impressive attempt has been made to define the status of neutral nationals and to single out acts falling short of, or leading to, their identification with the enemy. Neither the members of the British Commonwealth nor the Soviet Union are bound by this Convention.

Through clauses in peace treaties, issues such as the survival of pre-war contracts and quasi-contractual relations during the war between enemy nationals may become relevant from the point of view of international law. The adjustment of such relations is then frequently entrusted to clearing offices and mixed arbitral tribunals.[85]

4. *The Effects of Illegal War*

Under the consensual quasi-orders of the United Nations and the Kellogg Pact, the moral distinction between just and unjust wars, evolved by canonical and naturalist jurists,[86] has been transformed into one between legal and illegal war.

Illegal resort to war is certainly a breach of treaty[87] and, possibly, amounts also to the commission of a war crime.[88] The question, therefore, arises whether, and if so to what extent, lack of *jus ad bellum* impairs *jus in bello*, that is to say, protection of an aggressor State, its armed forces and civilian population by the laws of war and conventions intended to come into operation in time of war. As the prohibition of illegal war rests on two complementary treaties, *viz.*, the Charter of the United Nations and the Kellogg Pact, the question is essentially one of treaty interpretation.[89]

The Judgments of the International Military Tribunals of Nuremberg (1946) and Tokyo (1948) as well as a host of national war crimes trials in the wake of the Second World War are a pointer to a balanced view of the matter. The accused were tried not only for having committed crimes against peace and

---

[85] See above, p. 45.
[86] See above, p. 17, and below, p. 584.
[87] See above, p. 162.
[88] See below, p. 199.
[89] See above, p. 175.

humanity, but also for having committed war crimes in the technical sense, that is to say, violations of the laws and usages of war.[90] It is worth mentioning, however, that, in the British Royal Warrant of June 14, 1945, regulating the trial of war criminals, crimes against peace and humanity are totally ignored.[91]

This case law provides a powerful argument for the view that aggressive war as such does not free belligerents—especially not aggressors—from the obligation to abide by the accepted rules of warfare. The opposite opinion would amount to sanctioning a state of affairs in which the ordinary horrors of warfare would be greatly increased for those whose criminal responsibility may be nil, but who are more directly involved in the actual fighting than those responsible for any particular act of aggression. This view of the matter is strengthened by the existence of a number of contingencies in which, even in future, it may still be impossible to state with any degree of certainty which of the parties has engaged in illegal warfare.[92]

There is some substance in the view that collective action taken by the United Nations under Chapter Seven or Article 106 of the Charter[93] does not amount to war and, therefore, the question of the application of *jus in bello* does not arise. Yet, commonsense and concern for those who would suffer most from this purity of reasoning appear to forbid pressing this somewhat formalistic view to its logical conclusion. At least, this hesitation must carry weight in relation to the rules of warfare in the strict sense. Even more does it apply to conventions such as the Geneva Red Cross Conventions of 1949 which are intended to be applied in *all* circumstances.[94]

These inhibitions do not necessarily apply with the same strength or at all in spheres more remote from those of personal status. Thus, on grounds of reprisals against a breach of treaty committed by illegal resort to war, a belligerent may well refuse to recognise acquisition of title to property by an aggressor State which, otherwise, could not be challenged under the laws of war.

---

[90] See below, pp. 198 and 607.
[91] See below, p. 608.
[92] See above, p. 177.
[93] See below, pp. 708 and 722.
[94] See below, p. 203.

This applies both to property acquired by an enemy under the law of belligerent occupation or as the result of a prize court decision.[95]

Similarly, parties to the Kellogg Pact which remain at peace with the aggressor are entitled, by way of reprisal, to depart from the observance of strict neutrality between the Pact-breaker and his victim and to discriminate against the aggressor. The Destroyer Deal of 1940 between the United States and Great Britain and the United States " Aid Britain " Act of 1941 are famous illustrations of this proposition.[96] As with members of the United Nations (Article 2 (5) of the Charter [97]), parties to treaties may even be under a legal duty to discriminate against an aggressor State.

VI—FUNCTIONS AND FOUNDATIONS OF THE LAWS OF WAR

The intrinsic object of war is to impose the will of a belligerent State on the enemy by force. Thus, if the laws of war impose any real restraints on belligerents, they present a paradox that calls for explanation.

A. Functions of the Laws of War

It is the purpose of the laws of war to determine the permissible forms, areas and objects of the exercise of physical pressure by belligerents against each other. This is, however, a merely formal definition of the functions fulfilled by the laws of war. To comprehend the substantive tasks performed by this branch of international law, it is necessary to examine its evolution and to find the relevant criteria for the distinction between some very different types of rules in this field.

In historical perspective, the whole of the law of peace is the result of a development in the course of which war has been reduced to one of the three states of international law.[98] The teachings of Christianity, the writings of medieval moralists and Renaissance humanists, and considerations of chivalry all helped in imposing restraints on the Leviathans at war by awakening

[95] See below, pp. 192 and 219.
[96] See below, p. 610 *et seq.*
[97] See above, p. 176, and below, p. 700.
[98] See above, p. 174 *et seq.*

public opinion to the truth of the insight that, from the point of view of civilisation, resort to force is always a retrograde step.[99] If organised social groups employ force against each other, it depends on the relative size and number of the contestants and the potency of the means of destruction at their disposal whether armed conflicts between them seriously endanger the material bases of a civilisation and the values for which it stands. In particular, if the chain reaction of negative reciprocity is set in motion,[1] the risk of relapse into pristine savagery grows by leaps and bounds.

It is the function of the rules of warfare to ensure the operation of the principle of reciprocity in a positive direction and, in this way, to assure, however inadequately, the continuity of civilised life.[2] In serving this object, the rules of warfare, like any other rules of international law, impose limitations on the sovereignty of belligerent States and the pursuit of the strategic object of war: the imposition of the victor's will on the enemy. This strategic object, and the tactical means by which it is sought to be attained, are frequently expressed in the semi-legal jargon of military necessities or necessities of war. In fact, these necessities are nothing but a circumlocution for wartime sovereignty. The rules of warfare are the result of a continuous tug-of-war between these two formative agencies : the standard of civilisation and the necessities of war. Their dialectic relationship produces four different types of the laws of war.

First, some of the rules of warfare prohibit acts which contravene the standard of civilisation, but serve no military purpose whatsoever, such as sadistic acts of cruelty or wanton destruction of property by the soldiery.

Secondly, other rules, like those proscribing the use of poison and poisonous weapons, subordinate possible tactical advantages to the overriding demands of civilisation.[3]

Thirdly, there are rules which seek to attain a real compromise between the standard of civilisation and the necessities of war. An illustration of this type of rule is that which permits a damaged man-of-war to put into a neutral harbour for the

---

[99] See above, p. 171 *et seq.*
[1] See above, p. 10 *et seq.*
[2] See above, p. 12 *et seq.*
[3] See below, p. 189.

minimum period necessary to effect emergency repairs, provided that these repairs do not increase her fighting power.[4]

Fourthly, a last type of rule requires to be observed merely " as far as possible " or, in other words, subject to overriding necessities of war. The function of this type of purely *admonitory* rule is to cover up the impossibility or unwillingness of belligerents to subordinate the necessities of war to binding legal obligations in the interest of the standard of civilisation, or to strike a true compromise between these conflicting objects. The Hague Conventions of 1899 and 1907 contain a number of such emasculated articles.[5] The technique used to similar ends in the Geneva Red Cross Conventions of 1949 is to reduce provisions to purely *optional* rules by making their operation dependent on agreements on the subject to be concluded at a future date between the belligerents concerned.[6]

The rules of warfare are the only legal restraints on the most ruthless exercise of wartime sovereignty. In this field, international law is still nearest to pristine and prelegal sovereignty.[7] This also explains why, if rules of warfare are to be more than a pious fraud, they must be protected by exceptionally strong sanctions. Therefore, until peace is established, and breaches of the rules of warfare can again be treated as international torts calling for reparation,[8] belligerents may assume an extraordinary jurisdiction over enemy nationals who fall into their power and are accused of having contravened the laws and customs of war.[9]

B. Foundations of the Laws of War

In preambles of conventions relating to the laws of war, diplomatic correspondence and judicial *dicta*, numerous references to the laws of humanity, the requirements of civilisation and the conscience of mankind will be found. These allusions to the functions fulfilled by the rules of warfare must not be mistaken for evidence of an independent law-creating process.[10] In this respect, no difference exists between the rules of warfare and other rules of international law.

---

4 See below, p. 214.
6 See below, p. 197.
8 See above, p. 169.
10 See above, p. 24.

5 See below, p. 198.
7 See above, p. 58.
9 See above, p. 88, and below, p. 198.

The laws of war are essentially the products of international customary law and treaties. The general principles of law recognised by civilised nations hardly come into the picture. Yet, compared with the law of peace, some significant differences in emphasis exist. The laws and customs of war are less the remains of past treaty practice.[11] They are the common denominator of roughly parallel municipal articles of war and *règlements*, which the leading military nations had enacted as standards of conduct for their own guidance and largely copied from one another. The Ordinance issued in 1386 by Richard II of England for the government of his army is an early illustration of such regulations.

The United States Field Instructions of 1863, the work of Francis Lieber, initiated the next phase: the exposition of governmental views on land warfare in the form of manuals. The first British *Manual of Military Law* was published in 1884. While the Articles of War phase was the formative period of the customs of war (*usus in bello*), the Manual phase belongs to a subsequent period when a good many of the customs of war had hardened into rules of international customary law and became gradually codified in international conventions.

In the following Sections, the impact of the continuous interplay of the standard of civilisation and the necessities of war will be examined in relation to the rules of land, sea and air warfare. It may, however, be advisable to point out expressly that it is not enough to vindicate in any particular case the requirements of either the standard of civilisation or of the necessities of war to prove the existence or non-existence of a rule of warfare. In each case, it must be shown that the demands of this standard have led to the creation of an actual rule in accordance with one of the recognised law-creating processes.[12] Conversely, if any particular rule of warfare exists, its non-observance cannot be justified on grounds of alleged necessities of war.

VII—The Law of Land Warfare

In the field of the law of land warfare in the narrower sense—as distinct from the law of belligerent occupation and matters

---

[11] See above, p. 28. [12] See above, p. 24.

covered by the Red Cross Conventions of 1929 and 1949 [13]—the Hague Conventions of 1899 and 1907 constitute probably the furthest advance yet made in restricting wartime sovereignty in the interest of the standard of civilisation. The impact of the standard of civilisation on the rules of land warfare has led to a differentiation between lawful and unlawful objects of warfare *ratione loci, instrumenti vel personae.*

A. Limitations Ratione Loci

In a terminology which goes back to Oppenheim, areas where war actually takes place are *theatres of war,* and areas where hostilities may be lawfully prepared and conducted are *regions of war.* Thus, the territory of a neutral State may become a theatre of war but, at least in relation to the belligerent guilty of a breach of neutrality, it is not a region of war.[14] Beyond this, even in regions of war, undefended places must not be attacked or bombarded. Churches and hospitals not used by the enemy for military purposes, as well as cultural property in places covered by the Hague Convention of 1954, are likewise exempted.

B. Limitations Ratione Instrumenti

The use of particular devices or means of destruction may be incompatible with the standard of civilisation. This may be due to a glaring incongruity between means and ends which shocks public conscience, for instance, expanding bullets; excessive inhumanity, such as the use of poison or poisonous weapons; or the treacherous character of some stratagems, such as the improper use of flags of truce or enemy uniforms.

The affirmation in the Geneva Protocol of 1925 of the prohibition of the diffusion of " asphyxiating, poisonous or other gases, and of all analogous liquids, materials or devices " and of " bacteriological methods of warfare " is probably merely declaratory of international customary law and covers also the use of nuclear weapons.[15] In the case of the latter, their radiation effects are hardly less significant than their explosive power,

13 See below, p. 190 *et seq.*
14 See below, p. 211 *et seq.*
15 See below, p. 593.

and it appears impossible to ignore this aspect of the matter because of its supposed " collateral " character.

C. Limitations Ratione Personae

Within limits which must not be overlooked, the rules of warfare reflect two distinctions which overlap but serve very different purposes. The one is between *combatants* and *non-combatants* and applies during actual hostilities. The other is between *members of armed forces* and *civilians*. It becomes operative only if an individual falls into enemy hands or, for other reasons, happens to be in enemy territory.

1. *Combatants and Non-Combatants*

While hostilities last, this distinction serves to draw a line between legal and illegal objects of land warfare. Non-combatants must not be made intentional objects of warfare.[16] This is the rationale of the prohibitions to refuse to give quarter to enemy soldiers willing to surrender and of killing or wounding prisoners after surrender.

2. *Members of Armed Forces and Civilians*

To settle questions which only arise when individuals fall into the hands of the enemy, the distinction between combatants and non-combatants has to be supplemented by that between members of armed forces and civilians. In particular, the question whether an individual is protected by the laws and customs of war or by the Geneva Red Cross Conventions of 1929 and 1949 depends on these combined tests.

For these purposes, armed forces of a belligerent include not only the regular forces but also militia or volunteer corps, like the Home Guard in the United Kingdom during the Second World War. The protection also extends to any other volunteer corps or organised resistance movement, which, for instance, operates behind the enemy's lines, provided that four conditions are fulfilled. They must be commanded by responsible officers, have a fixed distinctive sign recognisable at a distance, carry

---

[16] See below, p. 590 *et seq.*

arms openly and, finally, conduct their operations in accordance with the laws and customs of war.

Inhabitants of a non-occupied territory who, on the approach of the enemy, spontaneously take up arms to resist the invader (*levée en masse*), without having time to form themselves into regular armed units, are in the same privileged position. They must, however, comply with two tests. They must carry arms openly and respect the laws and customs of war. Otherwise, they are not entitled to the protection of the Geneva Red Cross Conventions of 1929 and 1949 or of the laws and customs of war and, within the limits of the standard of civilisation, the enemy may deal with them at his discretion.

3. *Wounded and Sick Soldiers*

Members of armed forces in the categories enumerated above who fall into enemy hands are protected both by the laws and customs of war and special Geneva Red Cross Conventions of 1929 and 1949. They must be treated humanely and cared for without discrimination of any kind.

4. *Prisoners of War*

Are no longer captives of either individual captors or the military units of their captors, but of the detaining power which thus becomes internationally responsible for their treatment.

The detaining power must maintain prisoners of war adequately and treat them in a humane manner. Under the Geneva Prisoners of War Conventions of 1929 and 1949, measures of reprisals against prisoners of war are expressly prohibited. Officers and unfit prisoners may not be compelled to work. Prisoners must not be assigned to work of a military, dangerous, unhealthy or humiliating character. Neutral States which have been appointed as protecting powers are charged with the task of watching over the application of these Conventions by belligerents. In spite of its exemplary initiative and record, the International Committee of the Red Cross—a private international organisation, composed of Swiss citizens—has not been entrusted with this task. Only with the consent of the parties to a conflict is the Committee permitted to work for the protection and relief of prisoners of war.

5. *Belligerent Occupation*

The two basic rules of the law of belligerent occupation are the prohibition of wartime annexation and the limitation of its territorial scope to enemy territory outside the actual fighting zones of land warfare.

The first rule makes it impossible for the occupying power, while the war lasts, to annex or otherwise dispose of the occupied territory.[17] The second rule limits the body of law which is codified in the Hague Conventions on Land Warfare of 1899 and 1907 and in the Geneva Civilians Convention of 1949 to those parts of the enemy territory which the invader has effectively occupied.

Thus, the civilian population of enemy-occupied territories can expect compliance with the standard of civilisation to a greater extent than can civilians living in actual fighting zones. At the same time, occupied territories are contiguous to the fighting zones. The rules of the law of belligerent occupation, therefore, constitute a true compromise between the exigencies of the standard of civilisation and the necessities of war.[18] On balance, the rules relating to the government and treatment of the inhabitants and property of occupied territories make considerable concessions to the needs of the standard of civilisation. Together with the law relating to wounded and sick soldiers and prisoners of war, this body of law constitutes probably the least hypothetical part of the laws of land warfare.

VIII—THE LAW OF MARITIME WARFARE

The object of warfare at sea is auxiliary to land warfare. It consists in the control of the high seas in order to cut off communications between the enemy and the outside world and, thus, makes its contribution to breaking the enemy's will to resist.

In contrast to land warfare as conceived in classical international law,[19] sea warfare is as much directed against enemy civilians and their property as against the navy of the enemy, at least in the sense that it aims at the destruction of the enemy's

---

[17] See above, p. 80.
[18] See above, p. 186.
[19] See above, p. 188 *et seq.*

wealth. In naval warfare, the element of economic war is preponderant. Therefore, enemy property, including ships and cargoes, encountered on the high seas, in the territorial waters of either belligerent, on inland and land-locked seas and on a belligerent's own ships is liable to seizure and capture.[20]

A belligerent man-of-war is entitled, if necessary, to destroy enemy merchant vessels.[21] This, however, is only permissible if passengers and crew can be taken on board the man-of-war or have a reasonable chance of saving themselves. The attacking ship has also to safeguard the papers of the ship to be destroyed. These rules apply to both surface men-of-war and submarines. They are embodied in the Treaty regarding Naval Disarmament of 1930 between France, Great Britain, Italy, Japan and the United States of America and in the Protocol of November 6, 1936, to which nearly fifty Powers had adhered before the outbreak of the Second World War.

Aircraft engaged in sea warfare must observe these rules as much as naval craft. Any other view would amount to the inadmissible contention that " a prohibition ceases to be binding whenever a new instrument for doing the prohibited act is invented or discovered " (J. W. Garner). Actually, the *ratio legis* is the same in the case of surface men-of-war, submarines and aircraft: the protection of non-combatants. The departure from these rules by even some of the United Nations during the Second World War can be justified only within the limits of reprisals against the totalitarian aggressors for their persistent and indiscriminate acts of international lawlessness.[22] In fields in which, as in air warfare, relevant rules are fewer, it may be impossible to attain a corresponding degree of protection for non-combatants.[23] The decisive difference in the law of maritime warfare is that such rules exist and, therefore, must be observed.

Hospital ships are immune from attack and capture by the enemy within the limits of Hague Convention X of 1907 and Geneva Red Cross Convention II of 1949. Owing to the relative insignificance for war purposes of bona fide coastal fishing vessels and small boats engaged in local trade, vessels in these categories are exempted from capture. The same applies to ships engaged

[20] See below, p. 588.
[21] See below, p. 195.
[22] See above, p. 67.
[23] See below, p. 197.

in scientific, religious or philanthropic missions. Hague Convention XI, which embodies these exceptions, provides also for the immunity of postal correspondence. As this privilege does not extend to contraband, but only to genuine correspondence, Great Britain has maintained in both world wars that a belligerent is entitled to examine mail-bags and their contents in order to find out whether they contain articles of a " noxious " character.

If neutrals were free to ignore the existence of war between other States, the objects of maritime warfare could be easily defeated.[24] Thus, in a development which has extended over centuries, an equilibrium between the rights of neutrals and belligerents has been established.[25] In this context, it is necessary to refer at least to the basic rules. These demand absolute abstention and impartiality by neutral powers and renunciation on their part of any claim, against belligerents, to protect from identification with the enemy any of their nationals who put themselves or their property at the disposal of any belligerent. General acceptance of these duties by neutral powers has made it feasible for maritime belligerents to exercise effective control of the sea routes between their enemies and the rest of the world.

Until the nineteenth century, no sharp distinction between navies and merchant fleets corresponding to the distinction between armed forces and civilians existed. It required the wealth of the modern State to enable it to rely primarily on a standing navy. Moreover, in former days, the high seas were so infested by pirates that even a bona fide merchant ship had to be armed for purposes of self-defence. Thus, it appeared natural that, in case of need, a sovereign should be entitled to commission merchant ships for purposes of warfare. This practice was called privateering. In the Declaration of Paris of 1856, privateering was abolished between the signatories. By the beginning of the twentieth century it had fallen into complete desuetude.

It does not follow from this that States renounce the services of their merchant navies in modern sea warfare for purposes of combatant duties. It merely means that a ship cannot have simultaneously the status of a merchantman and a man-of-war. As is made evident by Hague Convention VII of 1907, belligerents

---

24 See below, p. 212.
25 See above, p. 181.

remain free to convert merchant ships into warships. Yet, the apparent conciseness of the Convention hides far-reaching disagreement between land and sea powers on questions such as whether a vessel may be converted into a warship on the high seas or only in a port of her own country and whether, in the course of the same war, she can be reconverted into a merchant ship.[26]

Owing to the methods of submarine warfare practised by Germany in both world wars, the problem arose whether defensively armed merchantmen should be regarded as men-of-war or as merchant vessels. The majority of neutrals decided in favour of the second alternative. In the case of auxiliary vessels, such as colliers or tankers in the service of belligerent fleets, the exclusive use at the critical time of such vessels in the interest of fighting ships determines their character as warships.

The same applies in the case of neutral ships which take a direct part in hostilities or are under enemy control, in the exclusive employment of the enemy government or engaged in the transport of enemy troops or the transmission of intelligence in the interest of the enemy. Prize Courts of belligerents and international tribunals have both elaborated the principle that the status of such ships does not depend on any formalities. It turns on a functional test, that is to say, whether such vessels are under the control of a belligerent and used for purposes of warfare.[27]

In the case of neutral vessels that sail in the convoy of a belligerent, special problems arise. Such ships cannot expect to be exempted from hostile attack. Their vicinity to belligerent men-of-war assimilates them to enemy vessels. It has even been held by a Greco-German Mixed Arbitral Tribunal that their subordination to the orders of the officer in command of the convoy makes them akin to belligerent men-of-war.

The ancient right of belligerents to take prisoner the crew of captured enemy merchant vessels is limited by Hague Convention XI of 1907. The exemption from captivity of nationals of neutral States, and of enemy crews who give the required promise not to undertake any service connected with the operations of

---

[26] See below, p. 601.
[27] See below, p. 601 *et seq.*

the war, does not apply to crews of ships which have taken part in hostilities.

A borderline problem between land and sea warfare is raised by the bombardment of land targets by naval forces. In accordance with Hague Convention IX of 1907, the bombardment by naval forces of undefended ports, towns or buildings is prohibited. There was, however, no agreement among the signatories whether a harbour off which automatic submarine contact mines were anchored was to be considered as undefended.

The principle laid down in Article 1 of the Convention is weakened by exceptions regarding the legality of the bombardment of military objectives in undefended places and of the bombardment of even undefended places in the case of refusal on the part of local authorities to comply with demands for requisitions. Article 6 of the Convention provides that " if the military situation permits, the commander of the attacking naval force, before commencing the bombardment, must do his utmost to warn the authorities." This article is a typical instance of the drafting methods used at the Hague Peace Conferences. A humanitarian principle is laid down, but reduced to meaninglessness by a reservation which makes compliance with the principle dependent on the circumstances of each individual case.[28]

In warfare at sea, as in land warfare,[29] ruses of war, but not treacherous stratagems, are permitted. Flag abuse in land warfare is dealt with in Article 23 (f) of the Hague Regulations on Land Warfare of 1899 and 1907. The *improper* use of a flag of truce, of the national flag or of the military insignia and uniform of the enemy, as well as Red Cross badges, is prohibited. No agreement exists, however, on the occasions when the use of enemy flags and uniforms is proper. In sea warfare, the situations in which the use of false flags is advantageous are less varied. Thus, a clear rule has grown up in accordance with which the use of false flags for the purpose of deceiving the enemy is a permissible war ruse. A man-of-war must, however, hoist her own colours before opening fire. According to British practice, a merchantman may also use false colours in order to escape capture or destruction by the enemy.[30]

[28] See above, p. 187.
[29] See above, p. 189.
[30] See above, p. 189.

IX—THE LAW OF AIR WARFARE

Air warfare in any of its forms, whether in support of land or sea warfare or termed " independent," is but another tactical means towards the strategic end of all warfare, which is to break the enemy's will to resist.[31] Like other branches of the laws of war, even the embryonic law of air warfare provides examples of each of the four types of the rules of war.[32]

The Geneva Red Cross Conventions of 1949 prohibit intentional attacks on military and civilian hospitals so long as they are used for their appointed purposes. These rules apply to all forms of warfare and, therefore, also to air warfare. They assert unequivocally the demands of the standard of civilisation. As is characteristic of Type One rules, they relate only to situations in which this standard does not come into collision with the necessities of war.

The rules prohibiting the use of particular means of warfare, such as gas, poison, bacteriological, biological and nuclear weapons,[33] extend to warfare in any of the three dimensions and represent Type Two of the rules of warfare.

Type Three is exemplified by Article 25 of Hague Convention IV of 1907 : " The attack or bombardment, *by whatever means,* of towns, villages, dwellings or buildings which are undefended is prohibited." It constitutes a genuine compromise between the two contending principles. Rightly or wrongly, the test chosen for distinguishing between legal or illegal objects of attack or bombardment is whether a place is defended.

The italicised words were added at the Second Hague Peace Conference so as to include air warfare. *Undefended* places are, therefore, no longer identical with *open* places in land warfare, that is to say, undefended places in the fighting zone which a belligerent is able to occupy without the use of force. Nor does this comprehensive formulation permit any distinction between auxiliary air warfare, when the prohibition applies, and independent or " strategic " air warfare, when it is supposed not to apply.[34] A place which is defended by anti-aircraft guns, fighter

---

[31] See above, p. 185 *et seq.*
[32] See above, p. 186.
[33] See above, p. 189, and below, p. 593.
[34] See below, p. 604.

aircraft or ground-to-air missiles, is, however, no longer an undefended place for purposes of air warfare.

The purely optional Articles in the Geneva Red Cross Conventions of 1949 on the immunity of medical aircraft from attack, illustrate rules of Type Four. In particular, the provisions on hospital and safety zones in the Civilians Convention are characteristic of wartime sovereignty triumphant in the guise of purely admonitory rules of warfare.

In the Hague draft Rules on Aerial Warfare of 1923, an attempt is made to limit aerial bombardment to military objectives. They are defined as " objects of which the destruction or injury would constitute a distinct military advantage to the belligerent." The significance of this and subsequent draft rules consists in furnishing indirect but authoritative evidence of the unwillingness of the major powers to limit the " freedom " of the air for purposes of mutual destruction, if not co-extermination. These draft conventions are also sadly indicative of a continuous process of shrinkage of the meaning of civilian population in the minds of those in charge of the legal experts at conferences on the codification of the laws of war.

Thus, these drafts underline the overall trend towards total war in contemporary warfare, when, with short-range, medium-range and intercontinental missiles, the idea of air warfare as a distinct form of warfare becomes somewhat dated. If this development were ever allowed to reach its culmination, the laws of war would cease to fulfil the limited regulative function that, in the past, they were allowed to exercise. At this point, an age of mechanised barbarism would sink back into a state of amorphous and pristine slaughter.

X—Breaches of the Rules of Warfare

The breach of any of the rules and customs of war and of conventions relating to the laws of war constitutes an international tort and involves the duty of reparation.[35] Beyond this, belligerent States are entitled to assume an extraordinary jurisdiction over members of enemy forces and civilians who fall into their hands and are charged with war crimes.[36]

[35] See above, p. 169.
[36] See above, pp. 88 and 183.

Espionage, that is to say, the collection or transmission of intelligence in the interest of the enemy inside territory under the jurisdiction of a belligerent by civilians or members of enemy forces not in their own uniform, is not a war crime under international law. Yet, because of the danger it presents to national security, belligerents are entitled to punish spies as they see fit.[37] This discretion is limited only in the interest of the standard of civilisation. Even a spy is entitled to a trial, and this right must also not be denied to war criminals.

Beyond this, the standard of civilisation, as received into the laws and customs of war, forbids any barbarous form of punishment. Otherwise, belligerents are free to impose any condign punishment on war criminals. They are, therefore, free to refuse to accept the defence of superior orders or to take it into account only in mitigation of punishment. The position of an individual as head of State or holder of any other exalted office does not create immunity from trial and punishment for war crimes.

In the Geneva Red Cross Conventions of 1949, some of the most serious war crimes are classified as *grave breaches* of these Conventions. They include such acts as biological experiments on prisoners of war and civilian internees; compelling a prisoner of war to serve in the enemy forces; unlawful deportation of civilians from enemy-occupied territories; the taking of hostages and wanton appropriation or destruction of property. Parties to the Convention must either try before their own courts persons, regardless of nationality, who are accused of having committed or ordered such acts or, on presentation of a prima facie case, hand them over for trial to another contracting party concerned.

The Charters of the International Military Tribunals of Nuremberg and Tokyo cover not only war crimes in the strict sense, that is to say, breaches of the laws of warfare (*jus in bello*), but also crimes against peace (*jus ad bellum*) and crimes against humanity. The breaches by Germany and Japan of the Kellogg Pact were treated not only as treaty violations, but also as war crimes in this extended sense. Crimes against humanity were interpreted as limited to inhuman acts which had been committed in connection with war crimes in the strict sense and crimes against peace.[38]

[37] See above, p. 88.   [38] See below, p. 607.

The jurisdiction of the Nuremberg Tribunal rested on Germany's *debellatio* and the *co-imperium* exercised by the Occupying Powers over Germany.[39] That of the Tokyo Tribunal was based on Japan's unconditional surrender, that is to say, the consent of the defeated enemy power. Thus, irrespective of whether, at the time of these trials, crimes against peace or humanity formed part of general international law, the legality of these trials is not open to challenge.

In a Resolution adopted unanimously by the General Assembly of the United Nations (1946), the member States of the United Nations " affirmed " the principles embodied in the Charter of the Nuremberg Tribunal and its Judgment. It is possible to consider such a resolution as merely a non-binding recommendation.[40] It is equally arguable that, by voting for the Resolution, the members of the United Nations have estopped themselves from denying that crimes against peace and humanity are based on rules of international customary law. It is even possible to include in this estoppel States which, subsequently, joined the United Nations or non-member States which, like Germany, accepted the principles of the United Nations Charter by way of a treaty commitment. All these States took these steps in full knowledge of the *lex societatis* of the United Nations.

It is, however, significant that when, in 1953, the Korean Armistice was concluded, both sides tacitly agreed not to insist on the institution of trials even for traditional war crimes. Similarly, in striking contrast to the United States Army Field Manual on *The Law of Land Warfare* (1956), the studious omission of any reference to crimes against peace and humanity in both the list of Russian military crimes (RSFSR Criminal Code, 1952) and the latest edition of Part Three of the *British Manual of Military Law* (1958) emphasises the as yet precarious character of these additions to war crimes in the classical sense.[41]

XI—ARMED CONFLICTS NOT OF AN INTERNATIONAL CHARACTER

Three types of armed conflict call for consideration : colonial war, civil war and international conflicts which, in relation to

---

[39] See above, p. 116.
[40] See below, p. 279.
[41] See above, p. 198.

some of the participants, are conflicts of a non-international character.

A. Colonial Wars

Strictly speaking such laws and customs of war as apply in warfare between subjects of international law do not apply in armed conflicts with, or between, groups outside the pale of international law. Thus, in the colonial wars in the western hemisphere, Africa and Asia, the colonial powers, their trading companies and the white settlers treated such rules of warfare as they did apply—frequently without receiving reciprocal treatment—merely as self-denying ordinances, due rather to their own sense of the dignity of man than to their more primitive enemies.

B. Civil War

From the point of view of a government in power, a rebellion or revolution may appear as a heinous crime, to be repressed by all the means at the disposal of the forces of law and order. Yet, if a revolt develops into a prolonged civil war, and revolutionaries establish effective control over large areas of a country, such a state of affairs is, for all practical purposes, indistinguishable from war. In particular, this is how third States tend to view the situation.

If the recognised government no longer exercises any effective control over portions of its territory, and the revolutionaries are able and willing to abide by the laws of war, the latter qualify sooner or later for recognition as insurgents or belligerents.[42] Even the legitimate government itself may find it advisable to recognise its rebels as belligerents. If it grants such recognition, it is then entitled to exercise, in relation to third States and their nationals, all the rights of a belligerent in its own territory and on the high seas. It may also wish to save itself the embarrassment of having to treat the captured rebels as traitors. Last, but not necessarily least, it may take this step for humanitarian reasons.

If a legitimate government does recognise its rebels as belligerents, it must then, in all its relations with the rebels, apply the laws of war. Similarly, third States which have recognised

[42] See above, p. 69 *et seq.*

revolutionaries as belligerents must conform in all respects with the law of neutrality in relation to both parties to the civil war. If third States limit their recognition of revolutionaries to one of insurgency, their typical intention is to deny such insurgents the exercise of belligerent rights on, or above, the high seas.[43]

C. Co-Belligerency

Belligerents may grant to armed forces recruited from enemy deserters or enemy nationals living abroad an international status and may even put them under the jurisdiction of a government-in-exile.

Thus, in the course of the First World War, some of the Allied and Associated Powers recognised Czechoslovak and Polish armies as co-belligerents. The status and immunities of such forces depend exclusively on the agreements in question and can be claimed only from States which have recognised such co-belligerency. The belligerents against whom such forces take the field are not committed in any way by such arrangements.

The " co-belligerency " assumed by Italy in 1939 and that granted to her by the wartime United Nations in 1943 have entirely different meanings. Mussolini understood by " co-belligerency " that, short of entry into the war, Fascist Italy would flout in favour of Nazi Germany as many rules of the law of neutrality as she could with impunity. The " co-belligerency " granted to Italy after Mussolini's overthrow meant something different. The term was intended to convey that, while parts of her territory had to remain under Allied wartime administration, Italy was accepted as an ally, but with a status falling short of that of one of the wartime United Nations.

D. The Impact of the Geneva Red Cross Conventions of 1949

If one or both parties to an armed conflict do not treat it as an international conflict, they are still free to conduct hostilities in accordance with the laws of war. This was what happened in the Korean War, which neither the North nor South Korean Governments, nor their respective allies, treated as an international conflict, and in the armed conflict between Egypt and the interventionist Powers in 1956.[44]

---

[43] See above, p. 70, and below, p. 617.   [44] See above, p. 179.

This situation has been changed, at least to some extent, in the relations between parties to the Geneva Red Cross Conventions of 1949. In the case of *any* armed conflict occurring in one of their territories, they have undertaken to treat humanely and without any discrimination non-combatants, including members of armed forces who have laid down their arms or are *hors de combat*. In particular, the taking of hostages is prohibited, and so is the passing of sentences and the carrying out of executions without a proper trial. The application of these provisions does not, however, imply any recognition of a state of insurgency or belligerency and, therefore, leaves governments free to treat rebels as traitors under their municipal law.

XII—Termination of War

War may end with one side utterly defeated and completely overrun by the other (*debellatio*),[45] as happened with Germany in the Second World War. In such a case, the victor has a three-fold choice. He may annex the territory of the vanquished, abandon it as *territorium nullius*, a mere derelict object of international law, or establish a new international person, dependent or independent, in place of that which has ceased to exist.

States may also, without any formality, slip back from a state of war into a state of peace, as happened in 1716 in the war between Sweden and Poland. One or both belligerents may also be content to make formal declarations to this effect under their own municipal law, as was done in 1951 by a Proclamation made by the President of the United States terminating the war with Germany. In the same year, the United Kingdom terminated its state of war with Germany by a notice published in the *London Gazette* and information to this effect addressed to the Federal Government of Germany.

Finally, there remains the most usual form of establishing peace, that is to say, the conclusion of a peace treaty. It enables belligerents clearly to determine to what extent they wish to leave matters as they are when hostilities cease (*status quo post bellum*) or as they had been before the war (*status quo ante bellum*).

[45] See above, p. 116.

In contrast to a peace treaty, a truce or an armistice has merely the effect of temporarily suspending active hostilities, whether for the removal of the wounded and sick or pending the negotiation of surrender. When formal peace negotiations prove impossible, an armistice may also serve to establish a *de facto* peace. In this case, the border-line between a suspension and termination of war becomes blurred, as has proved the case with the armistice agreements, concluded under the auspices of the United Nations, for the termination of hostilities between Israel and her Arab neighbours.

While a *local* armistice may be concluded by military commanders, governments or commanders-in-chief alone are competent to authorise the conclusion of a *general* armistice. An armistice comprehends all the units under the command of the officer on whose behalf it is made.

As distinct from an armistice, which is an agreement, an instrument of unconditional surrender is a unilateral act of a defeated enemy, signed in the presence of representatives of the victorious side. On May 8, 1945, hostilities with Germany were terminated in this way by an instrument signed at Rheims on behalf of the German High Command. An unconditional surrender is based on the assumption that if the defeated side complies with all the orders given by the victor—but keeping within the limits imposed by the standard of civilisation—hostilities will not be resumed. Conventions which remain in force in *all* circumstances, such as the Geneva Red Cross Conventions of 1949,[46] are not affected by an unconditional surrender.

At the latest from the coming into force of a peace treaty, the law of war is replaced between former belligerents by the law of peace. Similarly, in the relations between the former belligerents and third States, the ordinary law of peace is again substituted for the law of neutrality. Thus, while under the Prisoners of War Convention of 1929 repatriation of prisoners of war was to be effected as soon as possible after the conclusion of peace, that of 1949 prescribes repatriation already on cessation of active hostilities, that is to say, when, in good faith, neither side expects a resumption of hostilities.

---

[46] See above, p. 184.

As in the case of other treaties,[47] the date from which a peace treaty comes into operation depends entirely on the intention of the parties. If the peace treaty is subject to ratification, the normal intention is to bring it into force as from the date of the exchange of ratifications.[48]

---

[47] See above, p. 144, and below, p. 553.
[48] See above, p. 144.

CHAPTER 8

THE LAW OF NEUTRALITY

" His Highness is knit in league and amity with either of the said
Princes, not intending without honest and just occasions to violate
the same, but so to order and direct himself and his subjects in
all his proceedings . . . that always he may declare himself in this
poynt of neutrality upright and indifferent." (First English
Proclamation of Neutrality by King Henry VIII—1536.)

THE essence of neutrality is that States not involved in war take
an attitude of impartial abstention towards belligerents, and, in
their turn, the latter respect the territorial integrity of neutral
States.

I—NEUTRALITY IN HISTORICAL PERSPECTIVE

The origins of the law of neutrality both in land and maritime
warfare can be traced right back to medieval international law.
This is not surprising, for the sociological conditions of neutrality
were pre-eminently fulfilled in medieval politics.[1]

A political system consisting of a sufficient number of *de jure*
and *de facto* sovereign States was in existence. While some of
these were linked together in networks of alliances, others preferred to remain friends with both camps or to wait for the
highest bidder. If non-committed States were not to be driven
into the enemy camp, a belligerent would be well advised to treat
such a power with becoming respect. In exchange, he might
expect that the neutral power would not show exclusive favours
to his enemy.

It merely required one further step—a common conviction that
both belligerent and neutral powers were under a legal obligation
to act in this way [2]—to transform neutrality from a pattern of
discretionary behaviour into a legal institution. Even so, until
the eighteenth century, States considered themselves entitled to
practise imperfect, that is to say, discriminatory, neutrality on
one of two grounds. This was considered legal if such discrimination was due to prior treaty engagements or to sympathy with the

[1] See above, p. 4.   [2] See above, p. 27.

just cause of one of the belligerents. By the nineteenth century, however, it became accepted that imperfect neutrality amounted to a breach of neutrality.

In an age which accepted the legality of resort to war whatever the reason for it, perfect neutrality was the logical counterpart to legal unconcern with *jus ad bellum*.[3] Yet, when, within the framework of international quasi-orders, the distinction between legal and illegal use of force was established,[4] the pendulum again swung the other way. Neutrality was viewed as a negation of collective security.[5]

Yet, both the collective systems of the League of Nations and the United Nations still allow for contingencies in which even member States—let alone non-member States—remain free to decide for themselves on their attitude to armed conflicts.[6] Moreover, in armed conflicts within a country, third States, by their recognition of revolutionaries as belligerents, may still become obliged to apply the law of neutrality.[7] Finally, there are States, such as Switzerland, which, even now, are under an international obligation to remain permanently neutral[8] and, only recently, Austria has chosen to base her own foreign policy on the principle of neutrality.[9] Thus, the law of neutrality appears to be far from dated.

It is, however, frequently thought that, in the conditions of an increasingly integrated world society, present-day warfare makes neutrality impossible. Admittedly, it is easier to maintain neutrality in the duel type of war, such as the Franco-German War of 1870–1871 or the Russo-Japanese War of 1904–1905, than in a world war. Yet, even in the Second World War, countries like Switzerland, Sweden and Spain succeeded better than might have been expected in preserving their neutrality.

The real paradox is that the more the world powers prepare for their co-extermination by way of push-button warfare with intercontinental missiles, the more attractive the pattern of neutrality becomes to an increasing number of non-committed countries and to others which would wish nothing better, in such

---

[3] See above, p. 183.
[5] See above, p. 176.
[7] See above, p. 70.
[8] See above, p. 53, and below, p. 209.
[9] See above, p. 53.

[4] See above, p. 183.
[6] See above, p. 177.

an eventuality, than to be spectators in a fight to the finish between the giant powers.

II—THE BASIC RULES

The rights and duties of neutral powers under international customary law can be summarised in three propositions:

First, a neutral State must abstain from taking sides in the war and from assisting either belligerent.

Secondly, a neutral State has both the right and duty to prevent its territory from being used by either belligerent as a base for hostile operations.

Thirdly, a neutral State must acquiesce in certain restrictions which belligerents are entitled to impose on peaceful intercourse between its citizens and their enemies, in particular, limitations of the freedom of the seas.[10]

The duties of neutrality, like those of State responsibility in general,[11] are limited to acts and omissions of the neutral State itself. They do not extend to spontaneous unneutral activities on the part of its citizens or corporations entitled to its nationality.[12] These may, at their own risk assist either belligerent. At this point, the law of neutrality considerably relaxes the ordinary law of peace in favour of belligerents.[13] Although, by international law, unneutral activities on the part of neutral nationals are not illegal, they are subject to the wartime jurisdiction of each belligerent. Within the limits imposed by the standard of civilisation, a belligerent is entitled to make such acts offences under his own municipal law. As, by the law of neutrality, these matters have been transferred to the sphere of exclusive wartime jurisdiction of belligerent powers, a neutral State is precluded from intervening on behalf of its nationals so long as belligerents keep within the limits drawn by international law.

Neutral States are free to impose more stringent duties of abstention on their nationals. Municipal enactments of this type, such as Foreign Enlistment Acts, must, however, be applied with strict impartiality in relation to all belligerents.

[10] See above, p. 122 *et seq.*
[11] See above, p. 162.
[12] See above, pp. 129 and 133.
[13] See above, p. 181.

All over the world, and not only in countries with socialist and communist régimes, the State has increasingly encroached on spheres formerly the exclusive concern of private enterprise. This expansion of the public, at the expense of the private, sector of national economies does not make it impossible to work the traditional law of neutrality. It merely means that the emphasis is changing from the rules governing the activities of neutral nationals to those calling for State abstention and impartiality. As in the law of State responsibility,[14] the different pace in the growth of State planning does not appear materially to affect the substantive reciprocity of rights and duties on which this branch of international law is based.

III—PERMANENT NEUTRALITY AND NEUTRALISATION

Under international customary law, a neutral power remains free to exchange at will its state of neutrality for one of belligerency. Even in systems of undisguised power politics, major powers which wish to decide for themselves on the issue of peace and war may be anxious to increase international stability by not having to fight over small countries in geographical key-positions. They may, therefore, be willing to underwrite the permanent neutrality of such countries or even themselves take the initiative in their neutralisation.[15]

A State which has undertaken to remain permanently neutral or is neutralised by a treaty to which it is a party commits a breach of treaty [16] if it resorts to war otherwise than in self-defence.[17] It depends on the treaty in question whether such a State is still free to conclude a defensive alliance or take part in any system of collective security.[18] If parties to a treaty which have undertaken to respect or guarantee the neutrality of a State fail to do so, they also become guilty of a breach of treaty.

The classical illustration of permanent neutrality or neutralisation—opinions differ on this point [19]—is that of Switzerland under the Eight-Power Declaration of March 20, 1815, and accepted by the Swiss Confederation on May 27 of the same year. This

---

[14] See above, p. 162.
[16] See above, p. 162.
[18] See above, p. 176.

[15] See above, p. 52.
[17] See above, p. 172.
[19] See above, p. 207.

collective guarantee of perpetual neutrality was confirmed in an Act of November 20, 1815, signed by Austria, France, Great Britain, Prussia and Russia, characteristically termed the Protecting Powers.

In 1920, Switzerland joined the League of Nations on the understanding that she would have to participate in economic and financial, but not military sanctions under Article 16 of the Covenant.[20] In 1938, when, after the failure of the half-hearted sanctions experiment against Italy, the *de facto* revision of the Covenant was in full swing,[21] Switzerland obtained her release even from the duty to apply economic and financial sanctions. While Switzerland co-operates with the United Nations and the Specialised Agencies in matters not impinging on her neutrality, she has considered it advisable not to become a member of the United Nations. As already mentioned, Austria has chosen a different course.[22]

The term neutralisation is also used in a less stringent sense. Neutralisation as applied to international waterways such as the Suez, Panama or Kiel Canals merely means that such waterways are assimilated to natural straits. Then, even the passage of belligerent men-of-war does not compromise the neutrality of the State in the territory of which a canal is situated.[23] The exact scope of the duties of the State through whose territory the waterway passes must in each case be ascertained by reference to the treaty in question.

IV—Rights and Duties of Neutral States

The key to the understanding of the law of neutrality is that the rules governing neutrality confer rights, and impose duties, both on belligerent and neutral States. Any breach of these duties constitutes an international tort [24] and, if the duties are embodied in a convention, also a breach of treaty.[25]

It is advisable to treat the rights and duties of neutral powers in relation to land, sea and air warfare separately.

20 See above, pp. 53 and 176 *et seq.*
21 See above, p. 156.
22 See above, p. 54.
23 See below, p. 491 *et seq.*
24 See above, p. 162 *et seq.*
25 See above, p. 162 *et seq.*

A. Neutrality in Land Warfare

The rights and duties of neutral powers in land warfare are set out in some detail in Hague Convention V of 1907 and, on the whole, are of a declaratory character. The United Kingdom is not a party to this Convention, as some of the provisions on non-identification of neutral nationals with belligerents were considered to impose undue limitations on belligerents. The less controversial rules which are codified in the Convention merely spell out in more detail the basic rules on the duties of abstention and impartiality which are incumbent on neutral powers and on the inviolability of neutral territory.[26] They can be summarised under six headings:

1. *Troop Movements*

As the neutral territory is inviolable, it must not be used for war purposes by either belligerent and, in particular, not for the movement of troops across it. If a neutral State resists, if necessary by force, an invasion of its territory, it acts in justified defence of its neutrality and does not commit a hostile act. If it fails to safeguard its territorial integrity, the other belligerent is entitled, by way of reprisal, to institute military operations against enemy forces which have established themselves in the neutral territory.[27]

2. *Supplies*

Belligerents must not move convoys of military supplies across neutral territory. They are, however, free to purchase war material through ordinary commercial channels, and neutral States are under no duty to prohibit its export.

3. *Transmission of Information*

Belligerents may not erect wireless stations or other apparatus in neutral territory for the purpose of communicating with their armed forces. They may also not use such installations which, prior to the war, they have established there for purely military purposes, and without opening them generally to the public.

[26] See above, p. 208.
[27] See above, p. 208.

4. *Recruiting*

Belligerents must not open recruiting agencies in neutral territory or use such territory for the formation and organisation of hostile expeditions.

5. *Asylum*

A neutral State may, but need not, give refuge to units of belligerent forces. If it does so, it must disarm and intern them. It must treat in the same way organised bodies of deserters seeking to join the enemy. It may, however, permit individual deserters to depart for the enemy country and need not detain escaped prisoners of war.

6. *Passage of Sick and Wounded*

A neutral State may, but is under no obligation to, permit the passage through its territory of sick and wounded members of belligerent forces. If, however, the belligerent concerned hands them over to the neutral power, the sick and wounded soldiers must be interned. The same applies if a belligerent brings sick and wounded prisoners of war belonging to the enemy forces into the neutral territory.

B. Neutrality in Maritime Warfare

The classical dispute in this field is the *Alabama* case which, during the American Civil War, had arisen between Great Britain and the United States of America and was settled in 1872 by arbitration. The fundamental issue was whether, after both governments had recognised the Confederate States as belligerents,[28] Great Britain, as a neutral power, had allowed her territory to be abused as a base for hostile operations. Several ships had been built in British shipyards for the use of the Confederate Navy. Before the vessels set out on their career as commerce raiders, they were fitted with guns and other naval equipment outside territorial waters.

The decision on the issue of liability depended on the standard of international responsibility that was to be chosen: requirements of British municipal law or possible tests of international law

---

[28] See above, p. 70.

such as the means at the disposal of a neutral power to prevent breaches of its neutrality or a still more exacting standard of due diligence.[29] As Great Britain was determined to purchase United States good will at any reasonable price, and the United States maintained a bold front, the latter handsomely won this contest in brinkmanship. Accordingly, in the *compromis* of 1871, by which it was agreed to submit the issue to arbitration, the dice were heavily loaded in favour of the United States by the so-called Three Rules of Washington. As these demanded compliance with the standard of due diligence, that is to say, the absence of negligence in the circumstances,[30] a decision of the tribunal under the Treaty in favour of the United States on the main question could be expected with reasonable certainty, and so matters turned out.

It is significant that, although the United States and Great Britain agreed to abide in future by the Three Rules of Washington and to invite other maritime nations to follow their lead, the standard of liability postulated in these Rules was found too exacting at the Hague Peace Conference of 1907. In Convention XIII on the Rights and Duties of Neutral Powers in Naval War, the duty of surveillance was reduced to the means at the disposal of a neutral power.

The United Kingdom is not a party to this Convention. The Articles on the revictualling of belligerent men-of-war in, and on the entry of prizes into, neutral ports[31] were thought to tilt the balance of naval power too much in favour of weak naval powers. The rest of the Convention, however, is chiefly declaratory of international customary law. In these Articles, the duties of abstention and impartiality of neutral powers in maritime war are merely elaborated in greater detail.

1. *Use of Neutral Territory*

Maritime belligerents must respect the status of the territory and territorial sea of neutral powers.[32] They may not commit hostile acts in the territory or territorial sea of a neutral power nor use these areas as bases for hostile operations. Thus, prizes

[29] See above, p. 208.
[30] See below, p. 611.
[31] See above, p. 186.
[32] See above, p. 208.

captured therein must be released and the prize crews interned. Similarly, the establishment by belligerents of prize courts either in neutral territory or on a ship inside the neutral territorial sea would amount to an abuse of neutral territory for belligerent purposes.

2. *Passage through the Territorial Sea*

The mere passage through the territorial sea of a belligerent man-of-war or a ship taken as prize does not compromise the neutrality of the littoral State. A belligerent ship must not, however, so arrange her passage as to assimilate a neutral territorial area to an operational area. This was what happened in the case of the *Altmark* (1940), a German fleet auxiliary carrying British prisoners of war along the Norwegian coast until her interception by the British destroyer *Cossack*.[33]

3. *War Supplies and Arming for Hostile Purposes*

A neutral power may not supply, directly or indirectly, ammunition or other war material to belligerent men-of-war. It must also employ the means at its disposal [34] to prevent the fitting out or arming of any ship in its jurisdiction which it has reason to believe is intended to engage in hostile operations against shipping of another power. If, nevertheless, a ship has been adapted for war purposes in a port under the jurisdiction of the neutral State, the latter must use all means at its disposal to prevent her departure.

4. *Temporary Stay of Belligerent Men-of-War*

Belligerent warships may be permitted to enter neutral waters and ports for purposes of obtaining emergency supplies and carrying out such urgent repairs as are absolutely necessary to render them seaworthy and do not add to their fighting power prior to such entry.

Normally, the maximum time-limit for such a stay is twenty-four hours. The twenty-four hour rule does not apply to belligerent men-of-war which are devoted entirely to humanitarian,

---

[33] See below, p. 611.
[34] See above, p. 213.

scientific or religious purposes. A belligerent man-of-war held up by damage or stress of weather may also prolong her stay in a neutral port. If the ship is damaged, it is for the neutral power to decide on the repairs necessary to make her seaworthy and the time required for this purpose. If the man-of-war does not depart within the time allowed, ship and crew must be interned.

Under the Havana Convention on Maritime Neutrality of 1928 and the United States Neutrality Regulations of 1939, damage caused by enemy fire may not be made good in neutral ports. Beyond this, neutral States may impose any further restrictions they consider advisable upon the entry and stay of belligerent men-of-war in neutral waters and ports, provided that they apply such regulations with strict impartiality.

C. Neutrality in Air Warfare

A neutral power must use the means at its disposal to deny to belligerent aircraft the use of its air space above its territory and its territorial sea.[35] Military aircraft of belligerents, their crews and passengers who land, or are forced to land, in neutral territory must be interned.

Under the Geneva Red Cross Conventions of 1949, exceptions apply in favour of medical aircraft of belligerents. They may overfly the territory of a neutral State and land there in case of necessity, but only after prior notice of passage, and with the consent of the neutral power concerned.

V—Neutral Nationals and Property in War on Land

The rights and duties of belligerents in relation to neutral nationals and property in land warfare differ according to their presence in a belligerent's own country, in enemy-occupied territory or in enemy territory.

A. Presence in a Belligerent's Own Territory

Neutral nationals in the territory of belligerents still enjoy the protection of the minimum standard of international law,[36] but

---

[35] See above, p. 112.
[36] See above, p. 99.

are exposed to the same hazards as the belligerent's own
nationals. So long as a neutral State maintains diplomatic
relations with a belligerent, its nationals in the territory of the
belligerent concerned are not protected by Geneva Red Cross
Convention IV (the Civilians Convention) of 1949.[37]

Since ancient times, belligerents have considered themselves
entitled to exercise in their own, and also in occupied, territories
the right of *angary*. This meant originally the requisition of
urgently required land and sea transport.

The right of angary has come to be extended to any kind of
neutral property under the jurisdiction of a belligerent. If this
right is exercised, full compensation must be paid. Normally,
no need exists for a belligerent to invoke this right. His peacetime powers of expropriation cover such situations in his own
territory,[38] and an occupying power has adequate powers of
seizure and requisition under the law of belligerent occupation.[39]
Some British judicial authority, however, exists for the view
that neutral property which is only temporarily, or against the
will of the neutral owner, in territories under the control of a
belligerent, is not subject to seizure or expropriation otherwise
than under the right of angary.[40]

B. Presence in Occupied Territory

Neutral nationals and property in enemy-occupied territories,
unless they are there for purely temporary purposes, are treated
in the same way as the enemy population. In other words, they
are under the protection of the law of belligerent occupation and
the applicable Articles of Geneva Red Cross Convention IV (the
Civilians Convention) of 1949.[41] Under this Convention, neutral
nationals enjoy one privilege of their own. Unless this is contrary
to the national interest of the Occupying Power, they are entitled
to leave the occupied territory.

C. Presence in Enemy Territory

By their voluntary residence in the territory of a belligerent
neutral nationals and their property become sufficiently identified

---

[37] See above, p. 182.
[39] See above, p. 192.
[41] See above, p. 192.

[38] See above, p. 99.
[40] See below, p. 678.

with the local population to entitle the other belligerent to attribute enemy character to such neutral nationals, whether individuals or corporations.

VI—Neutral Nationals and Property in War at Sea

The law in this field, as applied in the pre-1914 period, was settled in broad outlines by the Declaration of Paris of 1856.[42] Disagreement between land and sea powers continued to exist, however, on a great many questions not settled in the Declaration. Moreover, the views of States, while neutral, varied considerably from those held with equal strength when belligerent.

One of the major assumptions in the Declaration of Paris was the freedom of innocent merchants to trade with belligerents at their own risk. Innocence in this context meant trade between private merchants of neutral nationality and private merchants in belligerent countries with the common object of making profit. Yet, corresponding to the extension of State control over import and export trade in neutral as well as in belligerent countries,[43] the sector of genuine private enterprise considerably contracted. This trend widened the scope of the complementary sphere of State abstention on the part of neutrals and narrowed the number of recipients of consignments in enemy countries whose imports were exempted from hostile interference.

These changes in emphasis were intensified by novel restrictive measures on the part of maritime belligerents which neutral powers had perforce to accept: the extension of the lists of absolute contraband,[44] disappearance for all practical purposes of the distinction between absolute and conditional contraband,[45] extensive interpretation of the rule of ultimate destination,[46] and adaptation of contraband control [47] and wartime blockades [48] to modern requirements.

The net result of this development is that, in present-day warfare at sea, belligerents, who are strong enough to do so, will endeavour to cut off the exports as well as the imports of their

---

[42] See above, p. 194, and below, p. 222.
[44] See below, p. 221.
[46] See below, p. 222.
[48] See below, p. 224.

[43] See above, p. 182.
[45] See below, p. 220.
[47] See below, p. 221.

enemies.   Moreover, they will attempt to ration neutral powers in such a way as to prevent them from assisting their enemies to conduct their foreign trade through neutral channels.

A. The Right of Visit and Search

Compared with the freedom of the seas in time of peace,[49] in time of war the rights of neutral shipping on the high seas are seriously curtailed.   While a neutral State must abstain from assisting either belligerent, it is under no duty to prevent its nationals from performing services for, rendering assistance to, or trading with, either belligerent.   Neutral nationals do so, however, at their own risk.

Belligerents may not interfere with these forms of private enterprise if they are carried on inside neutral territory.   They are, however, entitled to assume a type of extraordinary jurisdiction over neutral ships on the high seas by exercising the right of visit and search.[50]   Otherwise, they would be unable to find out whether a neutral vessel was carrying contraband,[51] engaged in unneutral service,[52] or attempting to break a blockade.[53]

During the First World War, it became controversial between the Allied Powers and the United States, while the latter was neutral, whether the right of visit and search had to be exercised on the high seas.   In the opinion of the Allied Powers it was permissible to divert the suspected ship for the purpose of search to one of their ports.   Apart from the dangers resulting for both the visiting and visited ships from submarines—in both World Wars, German submarines ignored the rules which were applicable to them as much as to surface ships [54]—the greatly increased size of modern merchant vessels rules out, for all practical purposes, a thorough search of such ships on the high seas.   Furthermore, in the intricate conditions of modern commerce, a merchant ship is no longer arrested primarily on the basis of damning evidence found on board the visited vessel or admissions made by the master or members of the crew. Suspicion is usually based on evidence produced by economic

---

[49] See above, p. 122.
[51] See below, p. 220.
[53] See below, p. 224.
[54] See above, p. 193, and below, p. 602.

[50] See above, pp. 126 and 194.
[52] See below, p. 223.

intelligence departments. Thus, visit in the traditional sense of the word has become an outmoded formality.

If neutrals are willing to co-operate with belligerents who are in control of the high seas, the issue of navicerts—first practised by England in 1590 and applied on a large scale by the Allied Powers in the First and Second World Wars—provides a convenient solution. They serve as safe-conducts for ships which submit to voluntary inspection in the port of departure by officials of a belligerent or to other conditions laid down by belligerents. Such ships are then issued with papers which are recognised by the naval authorities in charge of contraband control.

B. Seizure, Destruction and Adjudication of Neutral Prize

Enemy men-of-war and other public enemy ships, enemy and neutral ships taking part in hostilities, and fleet auxiliaries, such as colliers or prison ships, are subject to *capture*.[55] Title vests immediately in the belligerent State. International law does not require any subsequent prize court proceedings. With private enemy ships and neutral ships the position is different. *Seizure* by an intercepting man-of-war is merely provisional and makes the prize (*prisa* or captured thing) liable to prize court proceedings. On condemnation of the prize, the seizure becomes *capture* and title is transferred by the judgment from the owner to the belligerent State.

Observance of the rule that the intercepting ship must bring the prize into a port of the belligerent for purposes of adjudication may clash with overriding necessities of naval warfare. Yet, these necessities are recognised in the law of maritime neutrality only in two cases. If observance of this rule would endanger the safety of the intercepting man-of-war or the success of the operation in which she is engaged, the prize may be destroyed. Two conditions must, however, be fulfilled. The intercepting ship must be able to ensure the safety of all persons on board the prize and safeguard her papers. Moreover, subsequent prize court proceedings remain obligatory.

States are free to organise their prize courts as they see fit. In spite of the fact that, in most countries, prize courts are free,

---

[55] See above, p. 193 *et seq.*

within limits, to apply international law, they are municipal courts. British prize courts administer " the course of Admiralty and the law of nations." Like other municipal courts, they are, however, bound to apply statutes, as distinct from Orders-in-Council or other forms of subordinate legislation, irrespective of the compatibility of such enactments with international law.[56] However ill-founded individual judgments of prize courts may be, the international validity of the titles which they constitute is generally admitted. The reason is the common interest in the certainty of law for third persons who acquire title in prize. In the case of illegal resort to war, an exception to this rule is arguable.[57] The remedy against abuse of jurisdiction in prize lies in the tortious responsibility of belligerents for their prize courts as for other judicial State organs falling below the standards postulated by international law.[58]

C. Contraband

In the widest sense, the term *contraband* covers any goods the transport of which to, or from, an enemy country is prohibited by a belligerent. The classical concept of contraband, which crystallised between 1856 and 1914, is however, more limited. In the first place, only goods destined *for* an enemy country may be declared contraband.[59] Thus, prima facie, exports by private individuals *from* enemy countries are not contraband. Secondly, contraband goods must be at least potentially useful for war purposes.

1. *Types of Contraband*

It is left to belligerents to determine in detail what goods they consider to be contraband. Since the seventeenth century, a distinction was increasingly made between *absolute* and *conditional* contraband.

Cargo which is necessarily useful for purposes of war is absolute contraband. Once, therefore, the enemy destination of arms and ammunition is established, they are liable to confiscation.

---

[56] See above, p. 42.
[58] See above, p. 99.

[57] See above, p. 183.
[59] See below, p. 222.

Goods which are equally useful for civilian and military purposes are conditional contraband. In addition to enemy destination, it is necessary to prove that such goods are actually intended for the use of the government or the armed forces of the enemy.

This distinction is embodied in the unratified Declaration of London (1909), but is largely obsolete. Already for reasons of shortage of foreign currency, all imports into belligerent countries tend to become government-controlled. Moreover, with the possible exception of ostrich feathers, practically everything is potentially useful for purposes of war and is, therefore, conditional contraband. Raw cotton, treated in the Declaration of London as non-contraband and subsequently one of the most important ingredients in the manufacture of explosives, illustrates this proposition. Even plum-stones, left over after making jam, are used in the making of jet engines.

2. *Evolution of the Law of Contraband*

Under the rules of maritime warfare, enemy goods carried on enemy ships, whether public or private, whether carried to or from enemy territory, are liable to seizure on the high seas [60] and to confiscation. Difficulties arise with neutral goods on enemy ships and enemy goods on neutral ships. Their treatment underwent considerable changes in the course of the history of international maritime law.

British practice followed the rules laid down in the *Consolato del Mare*, a fourteenth century codification of customs of the sea observed by Mediterranean sea powers. According to this customary law, belligerents were entitled to seize all enemy property in neutral ships irrespective of whether it was import into, or export from, the enemy country. Neutral property in enemy ships, however, except contraband in the narrower sense of the term,[61] remained unmolested.

France applied a different rule. According to her practice, the neutral or enemy character of the ship determined the character of the goods on board. In the Armed Neutralities, sponsored by Russia in 1780 and 1800, attempts were made to

[60] See above, p. 193.
[61] See above, p. 220.

force Great Britain to accept this principle of " Free ships, free goods." The British attitude remained unchanged until, in the course of the Crimean War, Great Britain and France became allies in their war against Russia, and it became imperative that they should co-ordinate their prize laws.

The result was a compromise to the advantage of neutrals. The neutral flag was to cover enemy goods, with the exception of contraband. Conversely, and subject to the same exception, neutral goods under the enemy flag were not to be liable to capture. This rule was first agreed upon only for the duration of the war. Subsequently, it was included in the Declaration of Paris of 1856 and gradually came to be accepted by other maritime powers as declaratory of international customary law.

The issue was, however, reopened in the First World War when Germany used submarines in violation of the accepted principles of maritime warfare and neutrality. By way of reprisals, the Allied and Associated Powers seized all goods of either enemy origin or enemy destination, even if nominally owned by neutral nationals and irrespective of the flag under which they were carried.

D. The Doctrine of Continuous Voyage

Attempts by the enemy to import contraband through a neutral country are governed by the so-called doctrine of continuous voyage or, more accurately, the rule of ultimate destination. Contraband does not cease to be contraband because it is apparently destined for a neutral country. What matters is the real and ultimate *enemy* destination of the cargo. In the complex conditions of modern commerce, it requires the assistance of economic intelligence departments and of statistics to ascertain whether goods are meant to form part of the common stock of a neutral country or are merely part of a maritime trade which is enemy trade in disguise.[62]

During the First and the Second World Wars, this rule was extended by the Allied Powers to goods of enemy origin. It is irrelevant that, in form, a neutral appears as a vendor trading in a neutral country if, in fact, he is merely an intermediary

---

[62] See above, p. 220.

between a vendor, whether an enemy or neutral national, operating in enemy territory and purchasers in third States. The test is whether the first neutral purchaser has bought the goods in good faith for his own account and is, therefore, free to dispose of them as he wishes.

E. Unneutral Services

A neutral merchant ship may be used in ways which make her indistinguishable from an enemy merchant ship.[63] Such a ship may also be engaged in services other than carrying contraband which, in the eyes of belligerents, may identify her just as much with the enemy. A case mentioned in the unratified Declaration of London is that of a voyage specially undertaken by a neutral ship for the purpose of transporting passengers who are members of armed forces of the enemy.

Since the First World War, British practice has included among individuals incorporated in the armed forces reservists and persons who are under an obligation to serve and are on their way home to do so. Similarly, transmission of intelligence in the interest of the enemy falls under the category of unneutral services. In each case, the voluntary character of the service and the actual, and not merely intended, assistance to the enemy have to be proved in order to justify condemnation of the ship in prize. Even if there is no ground for the seizure of the vessel, enemy nationals in the categories mentioned above may, in accordance with British practice, be removed from neutral ships on the high seas.[64]

F. Submarine Cables and Wireless Telegraphy

On grounds of necessities of war, belligerents may cut international cables connecting belligerent countries or belligerent with neutral countries, but only on the high seas or in enemy waters. Neutral States are not entitled to indemnity for the losses thus sustained.

In accordance with the Recommendations of the Commission of Jurists of 1923 [65] which, on this point, correspond to State

[63] See above, p. 193.
[64] See below, p. 616.
[65] See above, p. 198.

practice, the transmission by radio of military intelligence for the immediate use of a belligerent by a neutral ship or aircraft on, or over, the high seas is a hostile act. The ship or aircraft becomes liable to be fired upon and to be captured. A belligerent may also order such ships or aircraft to alter their course or to refrain temporarily from making use of their radio-transmitting apparatus while in the vicinity of his forces.

G. The Rule of the War of 1756

During the Seven Years' War, France found herself unable, owing to British naval superiority, to carry on her colonial trade exclusively by means of French merchant ships, to which, in time of peace, it had been reserved. In 1756, therefore, France allowed Dutch ships to participate in this trade. Great Britain then issued fleet instructions for such neutral ships and cargoes to be seized as prize as if they were enemy ships.

British prize courts, which, already before this date, had applied this rule, elaborated the doctrine, which became known as the Rule of the War of 1756, that neutral ships taking over in time of war a trade closed to them in time of peace thereby acquire enemy character. The Rule applies both to coastwise trade and to trade between the metropolitan and colonial territories. It makes no difference—and this is the connection between the Rule of 1756 and that of continuous voyage [66]—whether such neutral ships first call at a neutral intermediate port before continuing their journey to enemy territory.

H. Blockade

A belligerent may establish a blockade of the coast of his enemy. The purpose of a blockade is the complete isolation of the blockaded area from all its sea communications.

In accordance with a rule of international customary law, so-called paper blockades are prohibited. In other words, a blockade must be effective. This rule was incorporated in the Declaration of Paris of 1856. The blockade must be maintained by a force sufficient to prevent access to, and egress from, enemy ports and may be enforced by aircraft as well as by ships.

[66] See above, p. 222.

Moreover, a blockade must be limited to the ports of the enemy and not include neutral ports. By the British Order in Council of July 7, 1916, this rule was given a more extensive interpretation. The contraband doctrine of ultimate destination was extended to blockades.[67] This meant that, if a neutral ship merely pretended to be destined for a neutral port, but, in fact, after calling there, was meant to continue her journey to the blockaded area, she was still guilty of attempted breach of blockade.

In addition, a blockade must be applied impartially against ships of all countries, and, finally, it must be declared in advance and notified to neutral powers.[68] Ships seized for breach of blockade are, together with their cargoes, liable to condemnation as good and lawful prize.

I. Defence Areas, War Zones and Mines

Due to more recent developments in sea warfare, especially the use of submarines, the traditional form of blockade has lost much of the significance which it had before the First World War.

Belligerents have found it necessary to limit the freedom of the seas beyond the enforcement of visit and search of neutral shipping and of blockades by the establishment of defence areas and war zones. Thus, in the Russo-Japanese War of 1904-1905, Japan resorted to the device of controlling neutral shipping in notified areas which extended up to ten miles from land. In November 1914, the British Admiralty announced that, owing to mines and other measures taken by the British naval authorities, a specified area in the North Sea had become unsafe for neutral shipping. At the same time, neutrals were informed of routes which, in so far as Great Britain was concerned, they could safely take. Germany proclaimed similar war zones from which neutral shipping was excluded on pain of destruction without warning.

Both sides justified their departures from the traditional rules of international maritime law as reprisals.[69] In this case, British reprisals were based on German mine-laying which did not discriminate between men-of-war and merchant ships. Yet Hague

---

[67] See above, p. 222.
[68] See above, p. 160.
[69] See above, p. 173, and below, p. 226.

Convention VIII of 1907 which purported to lay down governing rules, in effect did more harm than good, for, by its Article 6, it tended to give all the rules codified in it a purely admonitory character.[70]

Considered against the general background of the rules of sea warfare, mines, like any other weapons, must be considered illegal if their use is not possible without discrimination between combatants and non-combatants, and between belligerents and neutrals.[71] Thus, the use of unanchored mines which do not become harmless within a very short period after their release is prohibited. Anchored mines are admittedly useful for the delineation and protection of defence areas and war zones. Their use is, however, only legal if they become automatically harmless as soon as they break away from their moorings.

K. Scope and Limits of Maritime Reprisals

Reprisals are in themselves illegal acts. It is, therefore, logical to argue that they may be applied in sea warfare, as in any other field, against the wrongdoer alone.[72] Their legality is not in question if they merely affect neutrals in an incidental way, as in the case of a retaliatory naval bombardment of an enemy town in which neutrals happen to be resident.[73] Yet, in sea warfare, some reprisals against the enemy, such as extensive war zones and defence areas, tend to hit neutrals equally hard, although neutrals are not responsible for the wrong against which retaliatory measures are directed.

It has been held by British Prize Courts that such reprisals may be considered as legal in relation to neutrals only if they do not inflict on them inconveniences greater than must, under the circumstances, be considered reasonable.

---

[70] See above, p. 187.
[71] See above, p. 192 *et seq.*
[72] See above, p. 173.
[73] See above, p. 196.

CHAPTER 9

THE LAW OF INTERNATIONAL INSTITUTIONS:
I. NON-COMPREHENSIVE INSTITUTIONS

" To me it has always appeared that our problem is to project into international life the institutions of which we have had experience in national life " (J. Lorimer, *The Institutes of the Law of Nations*, 1884).

To present international law in the mid-twentieth century without paying full attention to the emergence of international institutions would be to draw a somewhat lop-sided picture.[1] On the basis, and frequently in derogation, of the rules of international customary law, a complex superstructure of international organisation has been erected. By consent,[2] expressed in the constitutions of these institutions and frequently also by implication in subsequent practice,[3] member States have made significant departures from the rules on unanimity and equality of votes[4] and, thus, considerably limited the exercise of their independence.[5] They have done so in order to make possible the achievement of common objectives which, without collective efforts, could not have been obtained at all, except in more cumbersome ways.

I—TYPES OF INTERNATIONAL INSTITUTIONS

For purposes of international constitutional law, five classifications of international institutions appear helpful:

First, according to their intended duration: *ad hoc, provisional* and *permanent* institutions.

Secondly, according to the nature of their powers: *judicial, conciliatory, governmental, administrative, co-ordinative* and *legislative* institutions. If an institution has organs endowed with all or most of these powers, the institution is *comprehensive.* Otherwise, it is *non-comprehensive.*

[1] See above, p. 101.
[2] See above, p. 138 *et seq.*
[3] See below, p. 254.
[4] See above, p. 58.
[5] See above, p. 101 *et seq.*

Thirdly, according to the homogeneous or heterogeneous character of their objectives, *single-purpose* and *multi-purpose* institutions, and according to the substantive character of their objectives, *political* and *functional,* that is to say, economic, social and humanitarian, institutions.

Fourthly, according to their scope of jurisdiction,

(a) *personal* scope (*ratione personae*): *universal, universalist,* and *sectional.* If the institution aims at universality, but still falls short of this object, this state of affairs is indicated by the term *universalist.* If the test of membership is extrinsic as, in the case of institutions built around antagonistic alignments, they are *sectional* groupings.

(b) *geographical* scope (*ratione loci*): *global, regional, local.*

(c) *substantive* scope (*ratione materiae*): *general* and *limited.*

(d) *temporal* scope (*ratione temporis*). For instance, the jurisdiction of a judicial international institution may be limited to disputes which have arisen after a certain date.

Fifthly, according to the degree of *integration*: *international* and *supra-national* institutions.[6]

In order to emphasise the historical continuity in the evolution of international institutions and of international constitutional law, the second of the five classifications, that is to say, that between comprehensive and non-comprehensive international institutions, has been selected as the primary classification. If and when appropriate, others are employed as subsidiary classifications. In particular, when dealing with the hypertrophy of international institutions in the post-1945 period, it will become necessary to set out in some detail the constitutional and legal implications of *hybrid* institutions.[7] They are institutions which represent significant variations of the more traditional types in the realm of international organisation.

At least one legal rule and three presumptions apply to any type of international institution.

First, international institutions are the products of treaties. In principle, therefore, they establish rights and duties only between the parties.[8] Non-parties can be committed only by way

---

[6] See above, p. 45.
[7] See below, p. 315 *et seq.*
[8] See above, p. 149.

of consent,[9] acquiescence,[10] recognition [11] or estoppel created in any other way by their own behaviour.[12]

Secondly, in case of doubt, any international institution is competent to determine its own jurisdiction.

Thirdly, in case of doubt, the intention of parties, which have granted jurisdictional rights to an international institution, is to transfer to the institution in question an exclusive jurisdiction. In other words, they renounce any claim to take individual action on matters within the jurisdiction of the institution.

Fourthly, in case of doubt, member States have granted to an international institution such implied powers as are indispensable for the proper fulfilment of its appointed functions.[13]

II—JUDICIAL INTERNATIONAL INSTITUTIONS

Diplomatic conferences apart,[14] international judicial institutions deserve pride of place on three grounds alone. Treaties providing for *ad hoc* arbitration between States go back to the earliest stages of international law.[15] Furthermore, tendencies which appear to be common to social institutions, such as trends to develop *ad hoc* institutions into permanent institutions and to widen the scope of their activities, manifested themselves in this field earlier than in any other.[16] Finally, significant rules such as that on the right of international institutions to determine for themselves the scope of their jurisdiction,[17] or the majority rule,[18] were first developed by international tribunals.

A. Patterns for the Peaceful Settlement of International Disputes

Techniques for the pacific settlement of international disputes include negotiation, good offices, mediation, conciliation, inquiry, arbitration and judicial settlement. *Negotiation* means direct discussion of a dispute between the parties. *Good offices* share with *mediation* the element of friendly intervention by a third party. Yet, while good offices by a third party merely serve to bring the parties to a dispute together, a mediating third party

---

9 See above, p. 138.
11 See above, p. 62.
13 See above, p. 165.
15 See below, p. 230 *et seq.*
17 See below, p. 239.

10 See above, p. 117.
12 See above, p. 121.
14 See below, p. 257.
16 See below, p. 230.
18 See below, p. 254.

actually takes part in the discussion in order to assist in the solution of the dispute. *Conciliation* covers the efforts of an international institution in bringing about a friendly settlement of a dispute, without, however, imposing any particular solution on the parties.

An *inquiry* conducted by an international institution serves to elicit the facts of a dispute and, occasionally, also the law applicable thereto. It thus provides a detached basis for settling a dispute rather than its authoritative solution. Compared with the limited or general jurisdiction of judicial international institutions,[19] commissions of inquiry constitute an attack on sovereignty along the line of least resistance. Thus, the value of this type of international institution was, if anything, considerably overstated by both Hague Peace Conferences. In the Hague Conventions on the Pacific Settlement of International Disputes of 1899 and 1907, provision was made for the establishment of international commissions of inquiry and the creation of the Permanent Court of Arbitration.[20]

In both Conventions the object of *arbitration* is defined as the settlement of disputes between States by judges of their own choice, and on the basis of respect for law. Arbitration differs from mediation and conciliation in the duty incumbent on parties to arbitral proceedings to accept and carry out the award in good faith.[21] The only difference between arbitration and *judicial settlement* lies in the method of selecting the members of these judicial organs. While, in arbitration proceedings, this is done by agreement between the parties, judicial settlement presupposes the existence of a standing tribunal with its own bench of judges [22] and its own rules of procedure which parties to a dispute must accept.[23]

B. Arbitration in Historical Perspective

The institution of arbitration was known to the Greek City-States, but, even in the settlement of their inter-city disputes, did not play any significant role. In the medieval phase of international law, the place of arbitration was also relatively subordinate. The settlement of a dispute might be entrusted to the Pope, to a king

---

[19] See below, p. 237.
[21] See above, p. 137.
[23] See below, p. 242.

[20] See below, p. 232.
[22] See below, p. 235.

in amity with both disputants, to an equal number of arbitrators appointed by each side or to the ambassadors of the contestants, with a possible reference, in case of disagreement between the ambassadors, to umpires selected by neutral princes. Thus, the arbitration treaty concluded in 1176 between the Kings of Castile and Navarre provided for arbitration of their disputes by King Henry II of England, father-in-law of the King of Castile and nephew of the King of Navarre.

The cycle of modern bilateral arbitrations commenced with the Jay Treaty of Arbitration of 1794 between Great Britain and the United States.[24] It received some further impetus from the success of the *Alabama* Arbitration (1872)[25] and, on the face of it, was carried yet a step further with the establishment of the Permanent Court of Arbitration.[26] It reached its zenith with the numerous mixed arbitral tribunals set up by the Peace Treaties of 1919 to 1923 in the wake of the First World War.[27] During the inter-war period, the volume of *ad hoc* arbitration was still appreciable, but has since noticeably declined. The texts of these awards are being made conveniently available by the United Nations Secretariat in a series of *Reports of International Arbitral Awards*.

Since the establishment of the Permanent Court of International Justice in 1922, the use of bilateral tribunals has visibly declined. Nonetheless, treaties still frequently contain a *clause compromissoire*, that is to say, an arbitration clause by which contracting parties undertake to submit to special tribunals, created as a rule in accordance with the treaty, any disputes regarding its application or interpretation. Thus, in the Peace Treaties of 1947 with Italy and the satellites of the European Axis—Bulgaria, Hungary, Rumania and Finland—provision is made for such tribunals, misnamed conciliation commissions, and some of these, in particular the Italo-United States Commission, have delivered decisions of some general interest.[28]

The World Court, a convenient, although perhaps unduly euphemistic abbreviation for the Permanent Court of International Justice and its successor, the International Court of

---

[24] See below, p. 239.
[25] See above, p. 212, and below, p. 611.
[26] See above, p. 230, and below, p. 232.
[27] See above, p. 45.

[28] See below, p. 623 *et seq.*

Justice, forms the last link in this long chain of international judicial institutions. It is the first that is truly permanent. The so-called Permanent Court of Arbitration,[29] which still exists side by side with the World Court and is organically linked with it in the procedure for the election of judges of the World Court,[30] is in fact neither permanent nor a court. All that is permanent about it are a permanent council, a standing bureau and a panel of names from which, by agreement, parties to a dispute may select their own arbitrators. Its awards prior to the Second World War are easily accessible in the two volumes of Scott's *Hague Court Reports.*

In the post-1945 period, the growth of international institutions has led to a remarkable development in the field of quasi-international judicial institutions. On the model of the League of Nations Administrative Tribunal, the Administrative Tribunals of the United Nations and of the International Labour Organisation adjudicate on disputes connected with employment between international civil servants and the United Nations or specialised agencies.[31]

These tribunals are quasi-international, for the law applied is not international law, but the internal law of each organisation which itself is based on its constitution, that is to say, an international treaty. Thus, in fact, this law is internationally authorised or postulated municipal law. It is of a public, rather than private, character.

Similarly, the European Coal and Steel Community, the European Economic Community and the European Atomic Energy Community have consolidated into a joint Court the Court established originally by the first-mentioned organisation.[32] The Court is open not only to member States, but also to corporations and individuals directly affected by rulings of organs of these supra-national institutions. Its constitution offers telling evidence of the transition which is taking place in " Little Europe " from international law to municipal law by way of functional federation.[33] Again, the International Military Tribunals of Nuremberg and Tokyo, established after the Second

---

[29] See below, p. 371.
[31] See below, p. 305.
[33] See below, p. 353.
[30] See below, p. 235.
[32] See below, p. 348.

World War, were, in all but name, joint municipal military courts rather than international courts.

Starting from the other end, relations between powerful international enterprises as, for instance, oil companies and the rulers of backward countries are so much on a footing of *de facto* equality, and the local law is so primitive that, in arbitration cases between them, some form of quasi-international law constitutes probably the most equitable basis for awards. The tribunal in the *Abu Dhabi* arbitration (1951) illustrates this marginal type of institution between international public and private arbitration.[34]

As the World Court constitutes the most advanced form yet reached in the sphere of judicial international institutions, the problems arising in connection with them will be discussed primarily with reference to this Court.

C. Functions

The International Court of Justice is the principal judicial organ of the United Nations.[35] The Statute, which forms an integral part of the Charter,[36] is its governing instrument. In accordance with Article 38 of the Statute, the Court's function is to decide in accordance with international law such disputes as are submitted to it.[37] If the practice of its predecessor, the Permanent Court of International Justice, is any guide, this reference to international law is not intended to preclude the Court from dealing with issues submitted to it in accordance with its Statute which turn primarily or exclusively on points of municipal law.[38]

In any event, the definition of the Court's function in Article 38 of its Statute is too narrow as the Court exercises also an advisory function.[39] Moreover, by the same Article the Court is authorised to decide cases *ex aequo et bono* if the parties agree thereto.[40] The consent of the parties in such an event is not directed to the application by the Court of equitable considerations within the framework of existing international law, such as the application of the *jus aequum* rule.[41] For this, no special

---

[34] See above, p. 1 and p. 40.
[36] See below, p. 720.
[38] See above, p. 44.
[40] See below, p. 239.

[35] See below, p. 720.
[37] See below, p. 733.
[39] See below, p. 240.
[41] See above, p. 25 and p. 153.

authorisation would be required. The purpose of this clause is to permit the Court to apply corrective equity, if necessary, in modification or supersession of the law (*contra legem*). In other words, the parties grant the Court an *ad hoc* legislative power to seek an equitable and practical solution to their dispute, even though such a settlement may not be in conformity with the strictly legal rights and duties of the parties.

The choice which is open to the parties under the Court's Statute to have a dispute decided either on the basis of international law or by reference to equitable considerations assists in comprehending more clearly the true character of international conflicts. The issue whether a dispute is legal or political, and justiciable or non-justiciable, does not depend on any inherent characteristic of the dispute, but on the attitude taken towards it by the parties. If they are willing to put the emphasis on the legal aspects of the dispute, it is legal and justiciable. If not, it is political and non-justiciable. Whether it is treated as one or the other is, as is well shown by the *Alabama* case,[42] a political decision.

It is implicit in this proposition that in international law, as created by the three law-creating processes mentioned in Article 38 of the Court's Statute,[43] no gaps or *lacunae* exist. The practice of the World Court has shown that in international law the problem of *non liquet*—*i.e.*, that, because of the inadequacy or obscurity of the existing law a decision on the basis of law is not possible—is illusory. In the absence of any other applicable rule, it is always possible to decide a case in favour of the defendant, that is to say, on the presumption in favour of the freedom of States under international law.[44]

A dispute is political or non-justiciable so long as one or both of the parties do not wish it to be solved on the basis of international law. This may be prompted by a desire either to seek a revision of the existing law [45] or to benefit from the anarchy of the application of international law in a state of auto-interpretation.[46]

[42] See above, p. 231.
[43] See above, p. 23.
[44] See above, p. 58.
[45] See above, p. 58, and below, p. 247.
[46] See above, p. 8.

D. Organisation

It is provided in Article 92 of the Charter of the United Nations that the International Court of Justice shall function in accordance with its Statute. It is also expressly mentioned that this Statute is based upon that of the Permanent Court of International Justice. At the same time, the International Court is one of the principal organs of the United Nations and its Statute forms an integral part of the Charter. By way of contrast, the Statute of the Permanent Court was a separate agreement and did not form part of the Covenant of the League of Nations.[47]

The World Court is the first truly permanent judicial international institution. It is served by a well-staffed and efficient Registry. The full Court consists of fifteen judges, who must be elected by both the General Assembly and the Security Council of the United Nations. In the interest of continuity, the terms of office of the members of the Court are so staggered that, every three years, one-third of the seats become vacant.

The electors are enjoined to pay due regard to the fact that the Court as a whole ought to represent the main forms of civilisation and the principal legal systems of the world. Candidates for election are to be nominated from persons of " high moral character." They must be either persons " who possess the qualifications required in their respective countries for appointment to the highest judicial offices " or " jurisconsults of recognised competence in international law." [48] Thus, at least under the Statute, expertise in international law is not a *sine qua non* of membership of the Court.

Various provisions in the Statute serve as guarantees of the judicial independence of the members of the Court. That they constitute a body of " independent " judges is expressly postulated.[49] Candidates are nominated by the various national groups on the panel of arbitrators of the Permanent Court of Arbitration,[50] or equivalent groups in States not represented on the Permanent Court of Arbitration, rather than by governments. It was, however, admitted at the time the Charter of

---

[47] See below, p. 720.   [48] See below, p. 725.
[49] See below, p. 725.
[50] See above, p. 232.

the United Nations was drafted, that, during the inter-war period, this self-denying ordinance had functioned only somewhat nominally. As is probably inevitable with candidatures which have to be acceptable to both the General Assembly and the Security Council, the trend towards manipulation and deals has, if anything, become even more pronounced in the post-1945 era. Judges are elected for nine years and are eligible for re-election. Every judge, before taking up his duties, has to make a solemn declaration in open Court that he will " impartially and conscientiously " exercise his powers. A member of the Court can be dismissed only by the unanimous decision of all the other members. While engaged on the business of the Court, the judges enjoy diplomatic privileges and immunities.

Furthermore, in the interest of judicial independence, the financial emoluments of the judges are on a rather generous scale, and a variety of incompatibilities has been established. No member may exercise any political or administrative function, or engage in any other occupation of a professional nature. Still less is any member entitled to act as agent, counsel, or advocate in any case before any other judicial body. A member may not sit in any case in which he has previously taken part either as agent, counsel, or advocate for one of the parties before the Court or as a member of another court or of a commission of enquiry, or in any other capacity. Finally, if the President of the Court becomes aware of any special reason why a member of the Court should not sit in a particular case, it is his duty to act on this information. In case of disagreement, the Court decides.

For instance, during the hearing of the *Anglo-Iranian Oil Co. Case* (*Preliminary Objection*—1952), the Acting President of the Court announced that Judge Sir Benegal Rao, who, in the previous year, had represented India on the Security Council when it dealt with the United Kingdom's complaint against Iran for failure to comply with the interim measures indicated by the Court, had, in agreement with the Court, considered it his duty not to sit.

The Court is permanently in session, except during the judicial vacations. Normally the full Court shall sit, nine members forming a quorum. Parties may, however, submit their disputes to any one or more of the chambers, composed of three or more judges as determined by the Court, which are established to deal with particular categories of cases, such as labour or transport cases, or to the chamber of summary procedure composed of five judges. Judgments given by any of these chambers are considered as rendered by the Court. So far, however, only the chamber of summary procedure has ever been called upon to function, and that only once in the early days of the Permanent Court of International Justice.[51]

A characteristic feature of the World Court is the inclusion of national judges. Accordingly, judges of the nationality of the parties continue to sit in cases before the Court in which their own countries are involved. If the Court includes a judge of the nationality of only one of the parties, the other party may appoint an *ad hoc* judge. If the Court does not include any judge of the nationality of the parties, each of the parties may designate an *ad hoc* judge. An *ad hoc* judge need not possess the nationality of the party which appoints him. Thus, in the various stages of the *Corfu Channel* case (1948/9),[52] Albania nominated two different Czechoslovak judges. The purpose of this rule is to increase the confidence of the parties in the Court by giving them this additional guarantee that all essential aspects of the matter will be duly weighed in the Court's private sittings.

E. Jurisdiction

The jurisdiction of the International Court of Justice is twofold: contentious and advisory.

1. *Contentious Jurisdiction*

In contentious proceedings, the Court is open only to States. Members of the United Nations are *ipso facto* parties to the Statute and have access to the Court. A State which is not a member of the United Nations may become a party to the Statute and thereby eligible to appear before the Court on conditions to be determined in each case by the General Assembly upon the recommendation of the Security Council.[53] Under the

---

[51] See below, p. 729.
[52] See below, p. 627.
[53] See below, p. 732.

Court's Statute, the conditions under which the Court shall be open to States not parties to the Statute are to be laid down by the Security Council.[54]

On the recommendation of the Security Council, the General Assembly has accepted three non-member States as parties to the Statute: Switzerland, Liechtenstein and San Marino. The Security Council also adopted in 1946 a general resolution governing the admission to the Court of States not parties to the Statute. A number of States have availed themselves of this Resolution either in specific cases (Albania and Italy), or in general (Cambodia, Ceylon, Finland, the Federal Republic of Germany, Italy, Japan, Laos and Viet Nam), although all except the Federal Republic of Germany and Viet Nam have since become members of the United Nations.

The fact that the Court is open to States does not necessarily mean that it has jurisdiction to adjudicate disputes between them. Such jurisdiction of any judicial international institution depends entirely on the consent of the parties concerned. The distinction, therefore, between " voluntary " and " compulsory " arbitration or judicial settlement of international disputes is somewhat misleading.

As a matter of fact, jurisdiction is *ad hoc*, of a limited or general character. In the first case, the jurisdiction of a judicial international institution is created by an international treaty (*compromis*) for the decision of a single case or a group of cases. *Limited* jurisdiction may be created, for instance, by a *clause compromissoire*, that is to say, an arbitration clause by which contracting parties agree to submit to arbitration differences on the application or interpretation of particular treaties or by an optional clause like that in Article 36 of the Statute of the International Court of Justice.[55] General jurisdiction of the Court in the meaning of jurisdiction over any type of dispute between members of the United Nations is not excluded by the scheme of the Charter. As is shown, however, by the machinery for the settlement of disputes which are likely to endanger the maintenance of international peace and security, such an eventuality is not considered to be typical.[56]

---

[54] See below, p. 732.
[56] See below, p. 308.

[55] See below, p. 732.

The Optional Clause in the Statute of the International Court of Justice calls for closer attention. Under Article 36, parties to the Statute may at any time declare that in relation to any other State accepting the same obligation, they submit, without any further special agreement, to the jurisdiction of the Court regarding certain types of disputes. These declarations may be made in conditional or unconditional form. They are deposited with the Secretary-General of the United Nations and reproduced in the *Yearbooks* published by the Court. If declarations are subject to reciprocity, according to the Court's practice, the Court's jurisdiction is limited to the narrower of two declarations made by parties to a dispute before the Court.

Article 36 (6) of the Statute reiterates a rule which, since the arbitrations under the Jay Treaty of 1794,[57] judicial international institutions have consistently applied. It is that, in the event of a dispute as to whether the Court has jurisdiction, the matter shall be settled by the decision of the Court. This rule renders doubtful the validity of some of the reservations made by States in their declarations whereby they arrogate to themselves the power to determine whether certain matters are within the scope of their declarations.

In the Court's view, a reservation of this type is valid. In a *jurisprudence constante* of his own, Judge Sir Hersch Lauterpacht has equally consistently held that such reservations invalidate the entire declaration.[58] Yet, a perhaps more constructive view of the matter which could rely on the rule of interpretation of legal instruments so as to make them effective rather than ineffective,[59] appears possible. Invalidity would then be limited to the reservations incompatible with the Court's Statute.

A declaration under the Optional Clause may be withdrawn at any time except when the Court has already been seized of a case coming within that declaration by an application from another party to the Statute.

The jurisdiction of the Court *ex aequo et bono* [60] in contentious matters is subject to the same rules as those mentioned above, except that, in addition, the consent of the parties to this course must also be clearly established. For this reason,

---

[57] See above, p. 231.
[59] See above, p. 152.
[58] See below, p. 629.
[60] See above, p. 233.

the Court lacks jurisdiction if one of the parties to a dispute makes a declaration accepting jurisdiction *ex aequo et bono*, while the other party is prepared to accept merely the ordinary jurisdiction of the Court.

2. *Advisory Jurisdiction*

Under the Charter of the United Nations, the General Assembly and the Security Council are entitled to request the International Court of Justice to give an advisory opinion on any legal question.[61] Moreover, the General Assembly may at any time authorise other organs of the United Nations and specialised agencies to ask the Court for advisory opinions on any legal question within the scope of their activities.

The General Assembly has given such permission to two other principal organs of the United Nations, that is to say, the Economic and Social Council[62] and the Trusteeship Council,[63] but not to the Secretariat.[64] In addition, it has granted such authority to two of its own auxiliary organs, the Interim Committee and the Committee on Applications for Review of Administrative Tribunal Judgments, better known as the " Screening Committee," and to a number of specialised agencies.[65]

The specialised agencies so authorised are the International Labour Organisation, the United Nations Educational, Scientific and Cultural Organisation, the Food and Agriculture Organisation, the International Civil Aviation Organisation, the International Bank for Reconstruction and Development, the International Monetary Fund, the International Telecommunication Union, the World Health Organisation, the Intergovernmental Maritime Consultative Organisation, the World Meteorological Organisation, the International Finance Corporation, assimilated in this respect to a specialised agency, and the International Atomic Energy Agency.

In accordance with a complementary Article in its Statute,[66] the International Court of Justice may give an advisory opinion on any legal question at the request of any body authorised by,

---

[61] See below, p. 720.
[63] See below, p. 298 *et seq.*
[65] See below, p. 328.

[62] See below, p. 291 *et seq.*
[64] See below, p. 303 *et seq.*
[66] See below, p. 737.

or in accordance with, the Charter of the United Nations to make such a request.

While, under the Charter and the Court's Statute, States alone may be parties to contentious proceedings before the Court,[67] only international institutions or organs of such institutions may request advisory opinions. In practice, the distinction is less rigid than might, at first sight, appear. The applicant in contentious proceedings may ask the Court for a declaratory, as distinct from a mandatory, judgment.[68] This, then, differs from an advisory opinion merely in being formally binding on the parties, whereas an advisory opinion lacks this quality.[69] Conversely, as is proved by the practice of the World Court as well as by its own Rules of Court, an advisory opinion may well constitute in substance, if not in form, a settlement of a legal dispute pending between States.

If, as is provided in the Convention on the Privileges and Immunities of the United Nations of 1946,[70] differences between the United Nations and a member State on the interpretation or application of the Convention are settled by way of a request for an advisory opinion, and both sides undertake in advance to accept the opinion as " decisive," such a " binding " opinion becomes even more closely assimilated to a judgment. Similarly, in relation to judgments of the Administrative Tribunals of the United Nations and the International Labour Organisation,[71] the World Court exercises, in fact, a revisory jurisdiction over these Tribunals by way of advisory opinions.[72] Differing in this from an appellate jurisdiction which is concerned with the merits of the decision in question, revisory jurisdiction is limited to a review of observance by the inferior tribunal of the essentials of judicial process, including questions of jurisdiction.[73]

The Court's power to give advisory opinions is discretionary. Ever since the World Court's refusal to give an advisory opinion in the *Eastern Carelia* case (1923), the Court has exercised this discretion in accordance with two governing rules. It has refused to give the requested opinion, first of all, if the subject-matter falls outside the jurisdiction of the requesting institution

[67] See above, p. 237.
[69] See below, p. 247.
[71] See below, p. 651.
[73] See above, p. 240, and below, p. 652.

[68] See below, p. 244.
[70] See below, p. 277.
[72] See below, p. 305.

or organ and, secondly, if compliance with the request would involve the Court in departing from the essential obligations resulting from its judicial function as, for instance, substantive equality of the " parties." [74]

The wide sweep of the jurisdiction of the General Assembly [75] and of the Security Council [76]—not to mention the potential issues covered by the jurisdiction of all the specialised agencies authorised to make requests [77]—shows that there are few questions on which it would be impossible to seek an advisory opinion of the Court. Yet, so far, international institutions have scarcely been more forthcoming in seeking legal guidance from the International Court of Justice by way of advisory opinions than individual States in the form of binding judgments.

F. Procedure

In the Statute of the World Court, merely the broad outlines of the procedure to be followed before the Court are laid down. In contentious cases, an action may be brought either by notification of a special agreement between the parties or by a unilateral application from one of the parties. In the latter case, however, the consent of the other party to the jurisdiction of the Court must either have been given in advance, or is given to the Court itself. Otherwise, the Court lacks jurisdiction to enter into the merits of the case. If the consent of one of the parties is implied, the jurisdiction so established is also occasionally termed *forum prorogatum*. Provided that the Court possesses jurisdiction to hear the case, it has power to act in the event of default by one of the parties.

The procedure is divided into two parts: written and oral. When the Court considers it appropriate, it may, on its own initiative or upon application, indicate interim measures which ought to be taken to preserve the respective rights of either party pending the Court's judgment. [78] Unless the parties have specifically consented to be bound, [79] the effect of such an interlocutory order is moral rather than legal. If, subsequently, the Court finds that it lacks jurisdiction over the case, the order

---

[74] See below, p. 732.
[76] See below, p. 284.
[78] See below, p. 632.

[75] See below, p. 278.
[77] See above, p. 240.
[79] See below, p. 734.

becomes completely irrelevant. For the rest, as enjoined by its Statute,[80] the Court has formulated its own rules of procedure in its Rules of Court.

In the exercise of its advisory function, the Court is directed by the Statute to be guided by the provisions applicable in contentious cases to the extent to which the Court regards these appropriate in advisory proceedings. The Rules of Court apply with similar modifications.

Even when the constituent instruments remain silent on questions of procedure, no real difficulties arise. The implied intention of the parties in any such consensual nexus must be that the organ created is able properly to fulfil its appointed functions.[81] Any international institution must, therefore, be presumed to be authorised to devise its own rules of procedure.

In the case of judicial international institutions, an additional basis for procedural law exists. The World Court is enjoined by its Statute to apply, *inter alia*, the general principles of law recognised by civilised nations.[82] International tribunals also have increasingly taken it for granted that the arbitration treaties from which they derive their jurisdiction authorise them to rely on this law-creating process.[83]

Thus, in addition to the *jus aequum* rule,[84] judicial international law may draw on general legal principles in judicial organisation accepted by civilised, as distinct from savage and barbarous, nations.[85] For instance, a court must give a fair hearing to both sides (*audiatur et altera pars*). Actually, in this particular case, it would be equally appropriate to base this rule on the implied intention of equals before the law who, on no other footing, can be assumed to have accepted the always voluntary jurisdiction of a court of their own choice.[86]

Similarly, in the absence of express agreement to the contrary between the parties on the evaluation or exclusion of evidence— an agreement which, under its Statute, the Court would have to apply[87]—both good faith and general principles of procedural law as applied in civilised countries demand that a judicial organ

---

[80] See below, p. 730.
[82] See below, p. 732.
[84] See above, pp. 25 and 153.
[86] See above, p. 58.

[81] See above, p. 227.
[83] See above, p. 29.
[85] See above, p. 12.
[87] See below, p. 733.

should have full discretion in evaluating the evidence and in applying the law to the facts thus established.

G. Judgments and Advisory Opinions

It remains to discuss the types, effects and execution of judgments and the differences between judgments and advisory opinions.

1. *Types of Judgments*

The two most important distinctions are between judgments on *preliminary objections*, as, for instance, when the court's jurisdiction is challenged, and judgments on the *merits* of a case, and between *declaratory* and *mandatory* judgments.

In international law, the second distinction is less important than in municipal law. As a rule, States, in proportion to their place in the hierarchy of power, appear hesitant to submit themselves to the jurisdiction of others. If, however, they have decided to do so—perhaps, because of the friendliness of their relations with the other party, the relative insignificance of the issue or even their desire to set an example of virtuous behaviour —their own moral credit requires that they should keep their word and carry out the judgment in good faith.

It is, therefore, a minor matter whether an issue is formulated as related to, for instance, the interpretation of a treaty—and thus calling for a declaratory judgment—or as asking the court to condemn the other party to do or not to do something, as is the case with a mandatory judgment.

2. *Effects*

The legal effects of an international judgment consist in its finality and in its binding force between the parties to a dispute (*res judicata*). In the case of a judgment on preliminary objections, the binding character of the judgment does not extend to matters of substance which are merely dealt with incidentally in the judgment.

Decisions of international courts or tribunals do not have the effect of precedents in the technical sense of English law (*stare decisis*). Neither the court nor the parties are bound in future cases by the legal rules on which the decision is based. Such authority as international decisions may claim is entirely persuasive. In particular in so far as the World Court is concerned, it rests on its prominent position in the hierarchy of law-determining agencies. At the same time, any such judgment is the product of fallible human beings who are merely an *element* of their own law-determining agency and, therefore, can never be accepted as authoritative without sympathetic, but critical scrutiny.[88]

If an international tribunal or court has manifestly exceeded its jurisdiction, it has stepped beyond the consensual basis on which it is founded. Its judgment is, therefore, null and void. Similarly, the equitable nexus in which a judicial international institution operates [89] entails that the corruption of judges by one of the parties, or a patent and substantial error in the award or judgment, also involves its nullity.

International awards and judgments are final.[90] In the absence of express authority to that effect, international courts and tribunals are, therefore, not entitled to interpret or revise their decisions. In the case of fraud by a party, as, for instance, the production of forged documents or bribery of witnesses, tribunals, while still functioning, have considered themselves entitled in equity to reopen proceedings and, if necessary, to annul a tainted award. Nor is there any appeal from one international tribunal to another, unless the parties to arbitral or judicial proceedings have agreed specifically on such a course.[91]

The Statute of the International Court of Justice permits the *interpretation* of a judgment by the Court at the request of a party in the event of a dispute as to the meaning and scope of the judgment. Within narrow limits, *revision* of a judgment of the International Court of Justice is also possible. Subsequent to the delivery of the judgment, decisive facts, such as important new documents or fraud practised by the other party, must have been discovered which had been previously unknown to the Court and to the party claiming revision. Moreover, such ignorance must not have been due to negligence. Revisory proceedings

[88] See above, p. 32 and 233 *et seq.*
[89] See above, p. 233.
[90] See above, p. 241.
[91] See below, p. 246.

are opened by a judgment of the Court, declaring the application admissible.

In the Rules of the World Court provision is also made for the procedure to be followed in the case of an appeal to the Court against the decision of another court or tribunal.[92] Such proceedings presuppose, however, that parties to the arbitral or judicial settlement of an issue before another judicial international institution have unequivocally agreed on establishing the appellate jurisdiction of the World Court.[93]

3. *Execution*

The duty to carry out awards and judgments in good faith is an implied duty which follows from the basic agreement to submit a case to arbitral or judicial settlement.

In the Charter of the United Nations, provision is made for complaints about non-execution of a judgment of the World Court to be submitted to the Security Council.[94] It is then for the Security Council to make recommendations or decisions to give effect to the judgment. Although it is controversial, the better view appears to be that a decision of the Security Council under Article 94 is a decision on a substantive matter and, therefore, subject to the veto power of the permanent members.[95] Yet, even if the view were taken that it was a procedural matter, a permanent member of the Security Council would always be free, by the exercise of the double veto,[96] to turn any such issue into one of substance. Thus, in the absence of a willingness on the part of all permanent members to forgo the veto in matters affecting the quasi-order of the United Nations,[97] this attempt to institutionalise the execution of judgments does not appear to have carried matters much further.

In the *Corfu Channel* case, Albania refused to carry out the final Judgment (1949) of the World Court, which had awarded substantial damages to the United Kingdom. It is significant that the latter tried all conceivable means of obtaining payment save submitting the issue to the Security Council under Article 94 of the Charter of the United Nations.[98]

---

[92] See above, p. 245.
[94] See below, p. 720.
[96] See below, p. 274.
[98] See below, p. 720.

[93] See above, p. 241.
[95] See below, p. 273.
[97] See above, p. 147.

4. *Advisory Opinions*

As the name indicates, advisory opinions of the World Court merely convey counsel. They are not binding, if only for the reason that there are no parties to the proceedings. Moreover, they are addressed to the requesting organ. Thus, they cannot formally affect the legal position of subjects of international law whose rights and duties may, in fact, have been the subject of the Court's scrutiny.

The General Assembly of the United Nations has broken the long established tradition of the League of Nations by not giving full effect to the advisory opinion it received from the World Court on the *Effect of Awards of the United Nations Administrative Tribunal* (1954).[99] Similarly, the Union of South Africa has declined to give effect to any of the advisory opinions on South-West Africa,[1] and Bulgaria, Hungary and Rumania have ignored the Court's opinions on the *Interpretation of Peace Treaties* (1950).[2]

H. An Evanescent Mystique

Some of the prestige which attached to judicial international institutions in the pre-1914 and inter-war periods, was the result of touching but somewhat naive views on the structure and dynamics of international society. Successive generations of well-meaning international lawyers considered that the arbitral and judicial settlement of international disputes on the basis of respect for law constituted a practical short cut to world peace through world law,[3] and drew comfort from the reassuring reflection that any international dispute was potentially a legal dispute. Those who knew better too often refrained from stating the obvious that, if this was so, every legal dispute was also potentially a political dispute.[4]

Growing hesitation on the part of members of the United Nations to sign declarations under the Optional Clause [5]—less than half of the present member States are committed in this way—and an increasing number of sweeping reservations to the Declarations made under the Clause are telling evidence of the real views held by legal advisers and governments on judicial

---

[99] See below, p. 635.
[2] See below, p. 635.
[4] See above, p. 234.

[1] See below, p. 635.
[3] See below, p. 380.
[5] See below, p. 629.

international institutions.[6] If anything, the somewhat erratic character of the jurisprudence of the International Court of Justice has sharpened such doubts, even if, out of a mistaken sense of loyalty to a supposed " cause " of international law, they are not usually voiced.[7]

The crux of the matter is that relatively few rules of international law are clearly established. Even those which are fairly settled permit considerable divergence of views on the points where they come into conflict with one another or with more controversial rules of international law. Thus, without undue mental gymnastics, any international arbitrator or judge can arrive from unstated major premises at practically any conclusion which he wishes to reach. At best, this choice, which need not be consciously made, is governed by undisclosed and inarticulate considerations of reasonableness and good faith.[8] Yet, while tribunals and courts are bound to give the reasons on which their awards and judgments are based,[9] it is not common practice to disclose the operative reasons which lead to a preference for one of more optional courses of consequential argument. To some extent, these difficulties are inseparable from the judicial process in any environment. Yet, in international society, they arise to a degree unparalleled in more stable and closely knit communities.

In this situation, the problem-in-chief for governments is not whether a particular dispute should be treated as legal or political, for with some change in emphasis, the amalgam of pragmatic, equitable and legal arguments is present in all phases of an international dispute.[10] The crucial issue is whether the parties consider it advisable to maintain direct control over the dispute or hand it over to settlement by a body of detached, wise and distinguished, but somewhat unpredictable world Solomons. If deeds, and not words, are the test, the prevailing trend is that the more powerful disputants are, the more likely they are to become potential enemies, or the more vital the dispute is, the less is its chance of being submitted to international adjudication.

---

6 See below, p. 629 *et seq.*
7 See below, p. 629 *et seq.*
8 See above, pp. 25 and 153.
9 See below, p. 736.
10 See above, p. 233 *et seq.*

III—Governmental International Institutions

International government comparable to national government is still highly exceptional. In a world in which, behind the principles of sovereign equality and interdependence in the Charter of the United Nations,[11] hegemonial dependencies and antagonistic alignments of world camps loom as large as ever,[12] this is hardly surprising.

Still, instances of international government of a sort are not entirely wanting. On the level of international, as distinct from supra-national, institutions [13] the available material falls into three categories:

First, an approximation to international government may be attained in time of war. Allied wartime organisations in the First and Second World Wars illustrate this type of governmental international institution.[14]

Secondly, some kind of international government may be unavoidable if two or more sovereign States exercise *co-imperium* over an entity with a distinct international personality or *condominium* over a territory lacking this status. The Allied governments in Germany and Austria in the wake of the Second World War exemplify the first variant,[15] and joint exercise of sovereignty over colonial territories, such as the New Hebrides,[16] bears witness to the existence of the second.

Thirdly, exceptional situations—some on the colonial fringe and others the result of compromises in peace settlements—give rise to the exercise of governmental powers in forms akin to international government. The Free State of Cracow (1815–1846), the Saar Territory (1919–1935), the Free City of Danzig (1919–1939),[19] the International City of Tangier (1923–1956) [20] and the still-born experiment of the Free City of Trieste under the Peace Treaty with Italy of 1947 [21] offer relevant illustrations.

With the exception of the two still extant cases of colonial *condominium* and the still not yet exorcised ghost of Allied *co-imperium* over Germany as a whole and Berlin for purposes of

---

11 See above, p. 58 *et seq.*
13 See below, p. 343.
15 See above, p. 52, and below, p. 426.
19 See below, p. 639.
21 See below, p. 431.

12 See above, pp. 58 and 176.
14 See below, p. 381.
16 See above, p. 52.
20 See below, p. 442.

West-East relations, none of these experiments have survived into the present. This fact underlines the exceptional character of ventures in international government.

IV—ADMINISTRATIVE INTERNATIONAL INSTITUTIONS

Government and administration almost imperceptibly shade off into one another. The difference is merely one of degree between matters of primary and subordinate significance. In systems which are motivated primarily by power, the subordinate character of an activity does not reflect on its functional significance from a community point of view.[22] It merely means that, in the light of power, the activity concerned is somewhat peripheral or irrelevant.

Thus, in the spheres of international communications, economic and social matters, health or the co-ordination of scientific efforts, international institutions have been allowed to develop on an increasing scale. The International River Commissions under the Peace Treaties of Paris (1814) and Vienna (1815), the European Danube Commission established in 1856 on a temporary basis and reconstituted in 1865 as a permanent institution,[23] the Geodetic Union (1864) and the Universal Postal Union (1874)[25] are prototypes of administrative international institutions.

In particular, a comparison between the histories of the Telegraphic Union (1865)[26] and the Universal Postal Union is instructive. Foreign offices and ministries of war showed a lively interest in the former, but not the latter. Thus, until its absorption in the Telecommunications Union (1934), the Telegraphic Union never quite outgrew its congenital anaemia. By way of contrast, the Universal Postal Union greatly benefited from being found insignificant in the eyes of the high and mighty. It laid down a pattern for functional federation[27] or supra-national institutions[28] in the international field. Albeit only for the reciprocal

---

22 See above, p. 9.
23 See below, p. 497.
25 See below, p. 655.
26 See below, p. 655.
27 See above, p. 232, and below, p. 381.
28 See above, p. 232, and below, p. 349.

exchange of correspondence, the territories of the member States form a single world territory.

A. Functions

Corresponding to the increasing scope of State activities within the State,[29] administrative international institutions have spread from the spheres of communications, health and science to those of labour, relief, education, development, economics and finance.[30]

In each of these fields it is the purpose of the administration, organisation, union or international corporation concerned to initiate, stimulate and co-ordinate activities on an inter-State level. As with administration within the State, the essence of international administration is freedom of action and the exercise of discretion within such limits as are prescribed to each of these institutions by its constitution.

Some of these activities are carried out *exclusively* by the administrative international institution in question. Thus, the European Danube Commission had sole responsibility for navigation on the maritime Danube.[31] In other cases, there may be a *division* of labour, as in the case of the international organisation of railway transport. The Central Office for International Railway Transport (1890), for instance, fulfils primarily functions of administrative co-ordination and also acts as a clearing centre for settling accounts between the national railway administrations.[32]

Finally, the actual task of administration may be *delegated* to an individual power or group of powers, as is the case with trust territories under the Charter of the United Nations. Then, the function of a body like the Trusteeship Council becomes limited to the examination of reports which are submitted to it by the administering power and to the fulfilment of other supervisory functions.[33]

B. Organisation

The main problems in the organisational field relate to organs, legal capacity, methods of voting and co-ordination of activities between different agencies in related fields.

[29] See above, p. 488 *et seq.*
[31] See above, p. 250.
[33] See below, p. 301.

[30] See below, p. 654.
[32] See above, p. 103.

1. *Organs*

As a rule, an administrative international institution has a plenary organ on which all member States are represented. This may be known as the Assembly, General Conference, or, as in the case of the General Agreement on Tariffs and Trade, the Contracting Parties.[34] This body determines the policy of the institution, approves its budget and exercises any other powers conferred upon it by the constitution of the organisation.

The executive centre of administrative international institutions is known as a bureau (especially in pre-1914 public unions), central office or secretariat. There, the routine work of the organisation is carried on.

The expansion of international institutions during the last half-century has led to the creation of a new type of bureaucracy, an international civil service. In order to enable these officials to fulfil the international tasks entrusted to them without interference by their home States or other sectional interests, they are accorded extensive immunities and privileges. Member States are enjoined to respect the international character of the administration, and the civil servants themselves must undertake not to accept outside instructions.[35]

It varies whether such executive power as it may claim is entrusted to the administrative centre itself, frequently headed by a Director or Secretary-General, or to an executive committee which itself controls the secretariat. According to the significance which member States attach to an institution, corresponding importance is attached to their representation by government delegates on the executive organ.[36] Especially in an age with a rapidly developing technology, power has other than political and military aspects. World and middle powers, therefore, are just as keenly interested in fields such as economics or communications. As the major powers normally also provide for the greater portion of the finances, they tend to be strongly represented even on executive organs of primarily functional institutions.

Thus, the Council of the International Civil Aviation Organisation consists of twenty-one members. In electing the

[34] See below, p. 323.   [35] See above, p. 95, and below, p. 637.
[36] See above, p. 78.

members of the Council, the Assembly is enjoined by the Constitution to give adequate representation to, first, the States of chief importance in air transport, secondly, the States not otherwise included which make the largest contribution to the provision of facilities for international civil air navigation and, thirdly, the States not otherwise included whose designation will insure that all the major geographic areas of the world are represented on the Council.[37]

Similarly, the Maritime Safety Committee of the Inter-Governmental Maritime Consultative Organisation consists of fourteen members chosen from member States with an important interest in maritime safety, of which no less than eight must represent the largest ship-owning nations. The remainder is reserved to other interests in maritime safety, such as the States whose nationals furnish large contingents of crews or passengers.

Finally, the constitutions of the International Monetary Fund and the International Bank for Reconstruction and Development are instructive. Five of the twelve Executive Directors are appointed by the members having the largest quotas (IMF) or the largest number of shares (International Bank).[38]

2. *Legal Capacity*

The more closely the activities of an administrative international institution relate to everyday life, the more likely it is that the institution may be involved in transactions with States, corporations or individuals. At this point, the legal status of the institutions and its organs becomes a matter of some moment.

When, for instance, the Bank for International Settlements was created in 1930, it was denied personality in international law but granted full and parallel legal personality in each of the member States. The Bank was constituted as a limited company with its seat at Basle, and the central banks of the States establishing the Bank became its members. In addition, it was given, in all member States, far-reaching immunities from taxation and guarantees against expropriation.[39]

In the constitutions of the International Monetary Fund and the International Bank for Reconstruction and Development,

---

[37] See below, p. 654.
[39] See below, p. 349.

[38] See below, p. 654.

the problem is solved in a more elastic manner. It is merely stipulated that the Fund and the Bank shall possess full legal personality, in particular capacity to enter into contracts, acquire, and dispose of, immovable and movable property, and institute legal proceedings.[40]   Similarly, in the case of the International Civil Aviation Organisation the problem is approached from a functional point of view. The Organisation enjoys in the territory of each contracting party such legal capacity as may be necessary for the performance of its functions, but subject to the rider that full legal personality is compatible with the constitution and laws of the State concerned.[41]

3. *Voting*

Unless the constitution of an international institution provides otherwise, all members are entitled to equal voting rights, and decisions of any institutional organ require unanimity.   This follows from the treaty character of international institutions and the presumptions in favour of the sovereignty and equality of parties to consensual engagements.[42]   An exception applies in favour of judicial international institutions. Ever since the Jay Treaty of 1794,[43] it has been accepted as the typical intention of parties, on which international tribunals consider themselves entitled to act, that judicial awards are based on majority decisions.

If States wish to submit to majority decisions or weighted voting, they do not hesitate to make express provision to this effect. Thus, the majority principle is applied in the congresses of the Universal Postal Union.[44]   Similarly, in the constitutions of the International Monetary Fund and the International Bank for Reconstruction and Development, the system of weighted votes has been adopted.[45]   Even if there is no open differentiation, great powers may, in practice, be granted automatic representation in committees from which other members are excluded.   In particular, if major powers are asked to shoulder increased burdens, they tend to insist on responsibility marching with power.[46]

---

[40] See below, p. 240.   [41] See below, p. 263.
[42] See above, pp. 58 and 138.   [43] See above, p. 231.
[44] See above, p. 250.   [45] See below, p. 327.
[46] See below, p. 284.

Discrimination in voting rights can also be used for the purpose of creating a kind of associate membership for entities not otherwise acceptable to an international institution. Thus, if a politically dependent territory is autonomous in certain fields, such as health, telecommunications or metereological services, its acceptance to limited membership—excluding voting rights on matters reserved to sovereign States—provides a possible answer. This pattern has been adopted, for instance, in the Constitutions of the International Telecommunications Union [47] and the World Meteorological Organisation.[48]

Since the days of the UNRRA (United Nations Relief and Rehabilitation Administration) Agreement of 1943 [49] and the Bretton Woods Agreements of 1944 on the International Fund and the International Bank for Reconstruction and Development,[50] a marked trend from the unanimity rule to the majority rule in administrative international institutions can be observed. It is, however, accompanied by a less advertised and even more significant development which alone has made this change in emphasis possible: reservation of special veto powers or weighted votes to the world powers as the price of their co-operation.[51] A hardly more attractive alternative has been a strict, if not niggardly, circumscription of the powers of such institutions.

In this context, the majority principle is hardly evidence of a growing internationalism. It appears rather to reflect the increasing irrelevance of the many, as distinct from the select few.[52] As yet, however, this practice does not appear to have displaced the presumptions of classical international law in favour of the sovereignty and equality of the subjects of international law.[53] Both the majority rule and any differential voting rights must still be expressly stipulated. They cannot be attained by stealth.

C. Co-ordination of Efforts

During the era of the League of Nations, some hesitant efforts were made to co-ordinate the haphazard sprawl of administrative international institutions. When the Charter of the United

---

47 See below, p. 320.
49 See below, pp. 316 and 458.
51 See below, p. 284.
53 See above, p. 59.

48 See below, p. 320.
50 See below, pp. 324, 559 and 654.
52 See above, p. 5.

Nations was drafted, it was considered that the United Nations, as the overall organisation of world society, should be made primarily responsible for reduction of duplication and overlapping in the work of international institutions and for the effective co-ordination of their activities. Under the Charter, responsibility for the discharge of these functions is vested in the General Assembly and, under its authority, in the Economic and Social Council.[54] In practice, a great deal of this responsibility has fallen on the Secretariat of the United Nations.

The basic scheme is that the economic, social, cultural, educational, health and related fields should be covered by international institutions with wide international responsibilities. These bodies should be brought into relationship with the United Nations and then function as its *specialised agencies*.[55]

Partly on the initiative of already existing organisations, such as the International Labour Organisation,[56] partly on that of the United Nations, such relations agreements were concluded or steps taken to create new specialised agencies as, for instance, the World Health Organisation[57] or the Inter-Governmental Maritime Consultative Organisation.[58] The relations agreements themselves contain provisions for the purpose of furthering co-ordination.

The Economic and Social Council gains the necessary information from consultation with, and reports submitted by, the specialised agencies and the exchange of representatives who, on a basis of reciprocity, participate in the deliberations of the Council and the agencies. In this way, the Council is enabled to make, if necessary, recommendations to the various specialised agencies, the General Assembly and the member States.[59]

In addition to the twelve specialised agencies which exist at present,[60] there are about sixty other, including regional, intergovernmental organisations and an even greater number of nongovernmental organisations concerned with matters within the competence of the Economic and Social Council.[61]

[54] See below, p. 296.
[56] See below, p. 260.
[58] See below, pp. 317 and 535.
[60] See below, p. 316 *et seq*.

[55] See below, p. 296.
[57] See below, pp. 320 and 654.
[59] See below, pp. 295 and 713.
[61] See below, p. 294.

Joint operational programmes promoted by the United Nations Secretariat are the latest and most constructive contributions yet made to the co-ordination of these institutional activities. The constitutions of the individual specialised agencies also contain provisions by which entry into effective working relations with other international organisations, inter- and non-governmental, is authorised and encouraged.

V—LEGISLATIVE INTERNATIONAL INSTITUTIONS

In this sphere it appears especially difficult to evaluate fairly the state of integration that has been attained in international society. Matters are not exactly helped by somewhat exaggerated claims advanced in the interest of some institutions with legislative or, rather, quasi-legislative jurisdiction. Yet, as with other topics of international law which are beclouded by passing fashions and ideologies,[62] a breakdown of the problem by reference to the various levels of international integration reached so far assists in maintaining a sense of proportion.[62]

A. The Classical Conference Pattern

In unorganised international society, any functional specialisation which would permit the equation of conferences with legislative international institutions is lacking. The more important of these conferences, in the past termed congresses, have fulfilled not only legislative, but also governmental, administrative and, on occasion, even quasi-judicial functions.

At the same time, it is probably true that the most important tasks performed by the great peace congresses and conferences of the last three centuries have been akin to those entrusted to constituent assemblies in national communities. At least for the subsequent inter-war period, each of the major peace settlements has provided a framework of a quasi-constitutional character.[63]

Specialised international conferences have contributed to the codification and development of international law in an even more decisive way.[64] Among these, the Hague Peace Conferences of

---

1899 and 1907, the Barcelona Conference on Navigable Waterways and Freedom of Transit (1921), the Warsaw Conference on the Unification of the Law relating to Carriage by Air (1929), the Geneva Conference on Narcotic Drugs (1931), the London Conference on the Protection of Industrial Property (1934), the Geneva Red Cross Conference (1949), the Geneva Copyright Conference (1952) and the Geneva Conference on the Law of the Sea (1958) may be singled out.

These conferences have served three different, but not mutually exclusive, purposes. In their various fields, some have concerned themselves with a restatement of existing international customary law. Others have tried to develop rules of international customary and treaty law or to formulate new rules of international law in spheres that, until then, had been in the exclusive jurisdiction of sovereign States.[65]

1. *The Law and Procedure of International Conferences*

In manuals on the practice and techniques of international conferences, a number of usages, such as the election of the head of the host State or of a person designated by him as president of a conference, or rules regarding the precedence of participating States, are recorded. Yet they lack the legally binding character which is the test of rules of international customary law.[66]

The only two rules which measure up to this requirement are those on unanimity and equality of votes at international conferences. Actually, it would probably be more accurate to describe them as presumptions which are based on the rules governing the principles of sovereignty and equality of States.[67] If nothing to the contrary has been agreed, it cannot be assumed that subjects of international law, which are sovereign and equal in status, would take part on any other footing in an international conference.

In practice, the unanimity rule has been limited to votes in the plenum, as distinct from committees of a conference, for a rigid application of the unanimity rule would have reduced even the deliberative stages of conferences to chaos. Beyond this, at

---

[65] See above, p. 89 *et seq.*
[66] See above, p. 27 *et seq.*
[67] See above, p. 58 *et seq.*

the Hague Peace Conferences of 1899 and 1907, proposals which had attained support only from the great majority of delegations were assimilated, with the acquiescence of dissenting minorities, to unanimous decisions by means of the fiction of near-unanimity.[68]

2. *Evaluation*

Legislation in municipal law means the enactment of rules by a law-making organ for the community as a whole in a manner which effectively overrules dissent. Excepting the notorious *liberum veto* which frustrated the Polish Diet for two centuries until the partition of the Kingdom of Poland, the analogy between municipal legislation and conference diplomacy breaks down already over the unanimity rule.

Moreover, participating States remain free to refuse to sign the Final or General Act, which sums up the conclusions reached, and to which the draft conventions agreed on at the conference are frequently attached. These draft conventions may require both signature and ratification. In this case, States which have participated at the conference are still free agents regarding the signature or ratification of such conventions.[69] Furthermore, the law-making effort of an international conference is limited to participating States and others who, on invitation, are willing to accede subsequently to the treaty.[70] Finally, they may, by means of reservations to their signatures or acts of ratification, take back a great deal of what they may be thought to have given away in becoming parties to conventions adopted at the conference.[71]

If words are to retain some exact meaning and not to become blurred merely for the sake of facile exercises in make-belief and self-deception, it must be admitted that this type of law-making by consent falls short of legislation in the usual sense of the term. At most, this type of international activity deserves to be called quasi-legislative. This is where matters stand on the level of unorganised international society. Law-making stops short at the point of quasi-legislative international institutions.

[68] See below, p. 636 *et seq.*
[69] See above, p. 144 *et seq.*
[70] See above, p. 145.
[71] See above, p. 145.

B. Legislation and Quasi-Legislation
in Organised International Society

On the surface, remarkable changes have taken place. The number of international institutions endowed with some semblance of legislative powers has increased by leaps and bounds. Moreover, if numbers of institutions were the decisive point, the majority rule in voting procedures would appear to have become the rule in the legislative sphere no less than in that of administration.[72] Any such presentation of the picture would, however, be slightly misleading. It would ignore the limitation of the powers actually entrusted to some of these seemingly imposing bodies as well as safety devices built in the constitutions of others, such as, for instance, overt or concealed contracting-out clauses.[73]

Actually, both legislation and quasi-legislation exist in present-day international society, but on different levels. On that of universalist institutions, the emphasis is still on the prefix rather than on the noun. Inside supranational institutions, however, truly legislative organs have made their appearance.[74]

The International Labour Organisation, a product of the Peace Treaties of 1919 and of a then widespread anxiety to create a mild antidote to the lures of Communism, illustrates the possibility of perceptive and original innovations in the field of international institutions.

1. *Representation of Horizontal Interests*

The vertical division of the world into apparently impenetrable monads of sovereign States can be softened by taking account of horizontal stratifications of sectional interests. This can be attained, for instance, by adding to government representatives in international institutions delegates representing relevant and complementary social cross-sections.

In the field of labour, this has meant the addition of delegates representing both employers and workers. It has given the International Labour Organisation its characteristic tripartite

---

[72] See above, p. 254.
[73] See above, p. 175, and below, pp. 275 and 314.
[74] See below, p. 352.

structure. At least, this is true of two of its three main organs, the General Conference and the Governing Body. In the nature of things, the Organisation's administrative centre, the International Labour Office, cannot easily be organised on this basis.

Some of the difficulties into which the Organisation has run result from the membership of authoritarian and totalitarian States in which the reality of independent employers' and workers' delegates, that is to say, delegates who are not government-instructed, becomes rather hypothetical.[75] This is probably one, but not the only, reason why none of the other specialised agencies of the United Nations has attempted to follow, at least in this respect, in the footsteps of the International Labour Organisation. To some extent, however, this idea has been resuscitated on the supranational level.[76]

2. *Quasi-Legislative Techniques*

Recommendations and draft conventions, euphemistically termed conventions in the Constitution of the International Labour Organisation, may be adopted by the General Conference with a two-thirds majority of the votes cast by the delegates present at the meeting. Although, like the government delegates, the non-government delegates are nominated by the governments of member States after consultation with the national organisations of employers and workers, all delegates in the General Conference are entitled to vote individually, that is to say, they need not vote as national *blocs*.

Within eighteen months from the closing of the Session of the Conference, each member State must bring draft conventions before the competent national authorities for the enactment of legislation or other action. If the member State obtains the consent of its legislative authorities to the draft convention, no signature is required, but merely notification of acceptance. In the Constitution, this procedure is described in a somewhat confusing manner as ratification.[77]

Similarly, member States are obliged, within eighteen months of the closing of the Session of the Conference, to bring recommendations before the relevant national authorities and to inform

[75] See below, p. 639.   [76] See below, p. 347.
[77] See above, p. 145.

the Director-General of the International Labour Office of action, if any, that has been taken. In addition, member States have undertaken to report, at appropriate intervals as requested by the Governing Body, on the position of the law and practice in their country on matters dealt with in such recommendations and on the extent to which effect has been given, or is proposed to be given, to these recommendations.

A number of the member States of the International Labour Organisation are federal States.[78] Thus, issues within the purview of the Organisation may fall within the jurisdiction of the constituent States, provinces or cantons, as distinct from that of federal authorities. In such cases, the duties of member States are still further relaxed. Federal members have fulfilled their duties if, in accordance with their constitutions, they arrange for draft conventions and recommendations to be brought before the competent federal, state, provincial or cantonal authorities within eighteen months and to arrange for periodical consultation between federal and local authorities on co-ordinating action to give effect to such draft conventions or recommendations.

The legislative efforts of the International Labour Organisation are consolidated from time to time in impressive, but slightly deceptive International Labour Codes. Thus, unless anything to the contrary is stipulated in any particular labour convention, a convention which has been ratified by only one member State is under the Constitution of the International Labour Organisation technically in force, even though binding only upon that member.

Moreover, member States which, to judge by the state of their own municipal law, are most in need of accepting a particular convention are frequently not found among those which have done so. Finally, on the basis of a calculation made inside the International Labour Office, the figure of actual acceptances is no more than between one-fifth and one-quarter of the possible maximum. While the unflagging efforts which have been required to attain even this modest result must be fully acknowledged, it does not belittle these endeavours to admit that these low yields appear symptomatic of the limits of functional quasi-legislation in contemporary world society.[79]

[78] See above, p. 50.
[79] See below, p. 639 *et seq.*

This technique of quasi-legislation has been adopted with minor modifications by three other specialised agencies of the United Nations: the United Nations Educational, Scientific and Cultural Organisation, the Food and Agriculture Organisation, and the World Health Organisation.[80]

Within narrowly defined limits, the World Health Organisation has given an additional quasi-legislative power to its Assembly. It may, by a majority of members present and voting, adopt regulations regarding, for instance, sanitary and quarantine requirements, nomenclature of diseases and causes of death, and standards regarding the safety, purity and potency of pharmaceutical products. By adding, with the same majority, any of these matters to the existing categories of "important questions," the Health Assembly may make the adoption of any such regulations dependent on support by a two-thirds majority of the members present and voting. Provided that the Health Assembly has given due notice to the member States of the adoption of any particular health regulations, these come into force except for such members as may notify the Director-General of rejection or reservations within the period stated in the notice.[81] The powers of the Congress of the World Meteorological Organisation to adopt technical regulations covering meteorological practices and procedures are of a comparable character.

Similarly, the Council of the International Civil Aviation Organisation is authorised to adopt, by a two-thirds majority, international standards on matters concerned with air navigation. Again a procedure is provided which enables member States to contract out of such obligations which, otherwise, are binding.[82]

On a regional level, the legislative activities of the Council of Europe deserve mention. Under its Statute, one of the duties of the Committee of Ministers is to further, on the recommendation of the Consultative Assembly or on its own initiative, the conclusion of conventions between its member States. Commencing with the European Convention on Human Rights of 1950, a considerable number of conventions in the social, cultural and educational fields have been concluded on the Council's initiative.[83] The fact that, in this relatively homogeneous

[80] See below, p. 328.
[82] See below, p. 654.

[81] See below, p. 654.
[83] See below, p. 337.

environment, more traditional forms of international law-making have been so successfully employed is a pointer to what, for the success of such ventures, is more important than advances in quasi-legislative techniques : an underlying unity of purpose.

If, on rare occasions, this condition was fulfilled, it was not found unduly difficult even before the First World War to endow international institutions, in particular river commissions, with truly legislative functions regarding the regulation of river navigation. In this respect, the jurisdiction exercised by the European Commission of the Danube over the maritime portion of this river was more comprehensive than that of any other international river organisation.[84]

Another swallow which failed to herald the summer of international legislation was the International Commission for Air Navigation, established under the Paris Convention of 1919 [85] on this subject. The Commission consisted of all the parties to the Convention and had power to revise with binding effect for all parties most of the technical regulations contained in annexes to the Convention. The control thus exercised by this body over what constitutes the first international code of air navigation went considerably further that what, in 1944, proved attainable in the inter-continental framework of the International Civil Aviation Organisation.[86]

The wider significance of the Paris experiment in regional and functional federation is that it foreshadows subsequent attempts along the same road between States which, in a telling Americanism, have ceased to be " viable " in isolation.[84]

---

[84] See above, p. 250, and below, p. 497.
[85] See below, p. 512.
[86] See above, p. 109.

CHAPTER 10

THE LAW OF INTERNATIONAL INSTITUTIONS: II. COMPREHENSIVE INSTITUTIONS

" In order to render this Security as complete as possible, it seems necessary, at the period of a General Pacification, to form a Treaty to which all the principal Powers of Europe should be Parties, by which their respective Rights and Possessions, as they then have been established, shall be fixed and recognised, and they should all bind themselves mutually to protect and support each other, against any attempt to infringe them " (Pitt's Memorandum on the Deliverance and Security of Europe—1805).

LIKE the League of Nations, which it replaces, the United Nations is an attempt to provide a permanent institutional framework for international society. Both experiments have in common that they do not aspire to attain international integration on the level of a world State. They represent confederations of the type which existed in the United States of America before 1787, in Switzerland before 1848 or in the Germanic Confederation from 1815 to 1866.[1]

The common feature of such confederations is that the member States undertake to limit the exercise of their sovereignty in accordance with the constituent covenant or charter. They do not, however, as a rule permit any direct contact between the organs of the union and their own subjects. Confederate organs fall short of being endowed with legislative or governmental jurisdiction. Member States, especially the more powerful among them, tend to limit their political freedom less than appears on the surface and, to this end, employ devices such as the veto power and carefully worded contracting-out clauses.[2] What distinguishes such confederations from other international institutions is their comprehensive character. They are served by quasi-governmental, quasi-legislative, administrative and judicial organs.

I—FUNCTIONS

The primary purpose of the United Nations, as it was with the League of Nations, is to maintain international peace and

---

[1] See above, p. 50.   [2] See below, p. 273 *et seq.*

security.[3] The other objects outlined in the Charter—furtherance of international co-operation in so-called non-political, especially in economic and social, fields and encouragement of respect for human rights and fundamental freedoms—are auxiliary to this main purpose. But the economic conditions of peace are second in importance only to the political foundations of any true world order. Bitter experience has also taught the lesson that disregard of human rights and fundamental freedoms breeds totalitarianism, and totalitarianism accentuates the tendencies towards war immanent in any system of power politics.[4]

The Charter of the United Nations, like the Covenant of the League of Nations and the Kellogg Pact, does not rely merely on limitation of the right to wage war. In both, peace is conceived as an equilibrium between international stability and change, and armaments are seen as symptoms of the lack of such harmony. To ensure it, a variety of methods for the pacific settlement of international disputes is offered to member States, and even some machinery for peaceful change is provided. Provision is also made for powerful sanctions to be applied should peace be broken. Members of the United Nations are encouraged to limit their armaments. Finally, the care bestowed by the San Francisco Conference on methods of economic and social co-operation indicates the awareness of the draftsmen of the Charter of the need to conceive peace in other than purely negative terms.

II—MEMBERSHIP

In contemporary world society all-out wars between the world powers are necessarily world wars. Thus, the principle of universality is inherent in any organisation which, in this global environment, aims at the maintenance of international peace.

The Covenant of the League of Nations was based on the principle of homogeneous universality. Membership was to be limited to *self-governing*, that is to say, democratic communities. In a futile quest for universality at any price, this term received a very different meaning in the practice of the League. It came to be interpreted as equivalent to external self-government or

---

[3] See below, p. 308 *et seq*.
[4] See above, p. 179.

sovereignty. In effect, the tests of membership in the Charter of the United Nations amount to little more.

A. Classes and Conditions of Membership

The original members of the United Nations are those which, having participated in the San Francisco Conference of 1945 or having previously signed the United Nations Declaration of 1942, have signed and ratified the Charter.[5] Other States are eligible for membership if they satisfy four conditions. They must be peace-loving, accept the obligations of the Charter and be able and willing to carry out these obligations.[6]

When Switzerland became a member of the League of Nations in 1920, it was expressly agreed that her obligations of membership should be so restricted as not to compromise her status as a permanently neutral State.[7] When Austria joined the United Nations, no express decision of a similar kind was taken.[8] Neither was Japan's membership made dependent on any clarification of those articles of her constitution which possibly prevent her from participation in the application of military sanctions.

The admission of new members to the United Nations is effected by a decision of the General Assembly on the recommendation of the Security Council.[10] Admission is a joint act by both organs. Thus, the recommendation by the Security Council must be positive in character. While the General Assembly is able to prevent the admission of a candidate State whose application has the support of the Security Council, it may not admit a State in the absence of a recommendation to this effect from the Security Council.

In theory, each candidature must be decided on its own merits and, in its advisory opinion on *Membership in the United Nations* (1948),[11] the World Court has held that it is contrary to the Charter to add conditions of membership over and above those laid down in the Charter. In the practice of the United Nations, however, a certain amount of inter-camp trading has become unavoidable. Its purpose is to secure the admission of

---

[5] See above, p. 145.
[7] See above, p. 210.
[10] See below, p. 701.
[11] See below, p. 635.

[6] See below, p. 701.
[8] See above, p. 210.

States which the Soviet Union considers to be associated with the Western camp in exchange for the simultaneous admission of other States which the Western Powers regard as camp-followers of the Soviet Union.[12] In the case of non-committed States, however, both camps vie with each other in easing the path of newcomers even if it is somewhat doubtful whether they can fulfil all of the four conditions laid down in the Charter.[13]

Another innovation introduced in United Nations practice is that, in fact, decisions bearing on membership are taken by the Secretariat on its own authority. Thus, when, in 1947, India and Pakistan attained their independence, the Secretariat decided that the Dominion of India remained an original member of the United Nations while Pakistan was treated as a new State which had to apply for admission to membership. Similarly, when, in 1956, the United Arab Republic was established by the union between Egypt and Syria, the Secretariat of the United Nations ceased to treat Syria as a member of the United Nations because a State of that name no longer existed, and accepted the new credentials of the former Egyptian delegate as the delegate of the United Arab Republic. In both cases, the principal organs of the United Nations charged by the Charter with responsibility for membership questions acquiesced in these exercises by the Secretariat in " nominalist " philosophy.

B. Suspension, Withdrawal and Expulsion of Members

In cases laid down in the Charter, membership may be suspended, and members may be expelled from the United Nations.[14] In the Covenant of the League of Nations the right to withdraw from the Organisation was expressly reserved to member States. In the Dumbarton Oaks Proposals, which formed the basis of the discussions at the San Francisco Conference, a clause to this effect was intentionally omitted. The intention was to underline in this way the permanent and universal character of the United Nations. At San Francisco, however, the right of withdrawal was reintroduced through a back door. The Conference approved in plenary session the report of one of its committees in which the

---

12 See below, p. 634 *et seq.*
13 See above, p. 267.
14 See below, p. 701.

right of members to withdraw in exceptional circumstances was affirmed.

It is arguable that even if no such approval had been given, the right to withdraw would still have existed. As with other implied treaty obligations, the interpretation of the intentions of the parties tends to be somewhat speculative.[15] It is, therefore, possible to put the emphasis on the presumption against any limitation of sovereignty[16] and so to arrive at this conclusion. It is, however, also feasible to hold the opposite view and to justify it by putting the emphasis on the preparatory material and the purposes of the United Nations.[17]

C. Control over Non-Member States

Under the Charter, the United Nations is to ensure, in the interest of international peace and security, that non-member States act in accordance with the Principles of the Charter.[18] Unless, however, the non-member concerned consents to, or acquiesces in, such action, it would be difficult to reconcile any United Nations action to this effect with existing international law.[19]

D. Mandates and Trust Territories

In Article 22 of the Covenant, the League of Nations recognised the existence of communities which were " not yet able to stand by themselves under the strenuous conditions of the modern world." Ex-enemy territories of this type were subjected to a tutelary régime under the ultimate responsibility of the League of Nations.[20]

Under the Charter of the United Nations, the principle of trusteeship may be applied not only to territories detached from enemy States as a result of the Second World War, but also to former mandates if agreements to this effect have been concluded between the former mandatories and the United Nations, and to territories which colonial powers voluntarily place under the trusteeship system.[21]

Such trust territories cannot be members of the United

---

[15] See above, p. 152.
[17] See above, p. 154, and below, p. 636.
[19] See above, p. 73.
[21] See above, p. 57, and below, p. 298 *et seq.*

[16] See above, p. 58.
[18] See below, p. 700.
[20] See above, p. 55.

Nations. This would be incompatible with the principle of " sovereign equality " of the members of the United Nations.[22] Yet the well-being of the inhabitants of these territories, and especially the development of self-government, is declared to be a " sacred trust " incumbent upon the member States which administer trust territories.[23]

E. Non-Self-Governing Territories

In the Charter of the United Nations, non-self-governing territories means dependent territories other than trust territories which do not form part of metropolitan territories of member States. Regarding these territories, member States have undertaken international obligations which, although set out under the heading of a Declaration,[24] are as binding as those embodied in any other chapter of the Charter.

The reports submitted by administering members are scrutinised in three bodies: the General Assembly, its Fourth Committee and a Committee on Information from Non-Self-Governing Territories, elected by the Fourth Committee and consisting in equal parts of representatives of administering and non-administering members.[25] In a process of trial and error, these bodies have gradually improvised a still controversial machinery for the scrutiny of the reports submitted by administering members.

In 1953, the General Assembly adopted a Resolution, in which the main factors in deciding whether a territory falls, or has ceased to fall, into this category, are set out. To judge by the result, their authors appear to have aimed at a cross between national self-determination [26] and self-government as originally understood in the Covenant as a qualification for League membership.[27]

III—Sovereignty and Equality in the United Nations

It is twice affirmed in the Charter that the United Nations is based on the principle of the sovereign equality of all its members.[28]

---

[22] See above, p. 58, and below, p. 700.
[24] See below, p. 715.
[26] See above, p. 67.
[28] See above, p. 58.

[23] See below, p. 715.
[25] See below, p. 299.
[27] See above, p. 266.

A. Sovereignty

Under Paragraph 8 of Article 15 of the Covenant of the League of Nations, a member State was allowed to challenge the jurisdiction of the Council—and of the Assembly—to settle a dispute on the ground that it arose out of a matter which " by international law is solely within the domestic jurisdiction of that party." It was then for the Council to find on the correctness of this submission and, even for purposes of a unanimous report, the concurring votes of the parties were not required.[29]

In the Charter of the United Nations, the reservation in favour of the sovereignty of member States has been considerably strengthened. Under Paragraph 7 of Article 2, save for enforcement measures under Chapter VII, " nothing contained in the present Charter shall authorise the United Nations to intervene in matters which are essentially within the domestic jurisdiction of any State or shall require the Members to submit such matters to settlement under the present Charter." [30]

The word " essentially " has been substituted for " solely." The measuring rod of international law, contained both in the League Covenant and the Dumbarton Oaks Proposals, has been shelved. What had been an exception to the jurisdiction of the League Council and, in a subsidiary way, also of the Assembly, as organs of international conciliation is transformed into one of seven Principles enumerated in Article 2 of the Charter, in accordance with which both the Organisation and member States are bound to act.[31] Finally, as distinct from the Covenant, it is no longer a matter within the exclusive jurisdiction of the international organ concerned to find whether the exception clause applies. Thus, in each case, it is equally possible to rely on one of two conflicting presumptions in the interpretation of consensual international obligations. While, in accordance with the one, each international institution decides for itself on its own jurisdiction,[32] by virtue of the other, implied restrictions of sovereignty must not be presumed.[33]

[29] See below, pp. 275 and 649.
[30] See below, pp. 278 and 700.
[31] See below, p. 700.
[32] See above, p. 229.
[33] See above, p. 58.

It has been argued that the severity of this exception clause can be mitigated by a strict interpretation of the word " intervene." Yet, intervention in the technical sense, that is to say, under international customary law, means interference with matters within the exclusive jurisdiction of a subject of international law and, unless justified by a specific rule to the opposite effect, constitutes an illegal act.[34] If the intervention in Paragraph 7 of Article 2 of the Charter had this meaning, it would amount to the somewhat self-evident proposition that the United Nations should refrain from acting in a manner which would involve the commission of an international tort. It would not, however, settle whether the discussion of, and recommendations on, matters in the sphere of essentially domestic jurisdiction are outside the competence of organs of the United Nations.[35]

In the light of the preparatory material, little doubt is possible on the intention of the States represented at the San Francisco Conference. It was that, in a generalised form, Paragraph 7 of Article 2 of the Charter should fulfil functions corresponding to those of Paragraph 8 of Article 15 in the Covenant. The United Nations was not to concern itself with matters essentially within the domestic jurisdiction of member and non-member States alike. Yet, the scope of such *ultra vires* matters was not intended to be settled once and for all. It was to be worked out empirically in a process of trial and error.

In theory, authoritative guidance on questions in this category can always be obtained by means of an advisory opinion from the World Court.[36] Yet, when this issue arose in practice, as, for instance, over the treatment of Indians in South Africa (1946) in the General Assembly and over the Indonesian Question (1947) in the Security Council, both these organs of the United Nations voted down the attempts made to consult the Court. The General Assembly in particular has a tendency to encroach on matters which, on a primarily legal interpretation, may well be inside the exception clause of Article 2 (7).[37]

In one field, however, reliance on uncontrolled *ad hoc* interpretation of the scope of reserved jurisdiction does not work.

[34] See above, pp. 59 and 162.
[35] See below, p. 278.
[36] See above, p. 240 *et seq.*
[37] See below, p. 700.

As distinct from other international institutions which can merely rely on a rebuttable presumption in favour of their right to determine their own jurisdiction,[38] this presumption has become so strong in the case of judicial international institutions that parties must expect this to happen.[39] This accounts for the United States type of reservation to the Optional Clause of the Statute of the World Court. It is so phrased as to leave the State which accepts the jurisdiction of the World Court the sole arbiter of whether a matter is essentially within its own domestic jurisdiction.[40]

As with other international institutions, any departure from the principle of unanimity in the non-judicial organs of the United Nations had to be expressly stipulated in the Charter. Thus, it is provided that the simple majority rule applies in the General Assembly to all questions save those declared important by the Charter or the General Assembly, in which case a two-thirds majority is required. The Assembly decides on the inclusion of any subject in the category of important matters by simple majority of the members present and voting.[41]

It is not easy to generalise from the practice of the General Assembly what matters it considers as important in this sense, for so many of its resolutions are adopted by very large majorities. It is, however, probably safe to state that, by and large, simple majorities are considered sufficient only in matters relating to organisation, the conduct of business and other procedural matters. In the Economic and Social Council and the Trusteeship Council the rule of simple majority applies without exception.[42]

In the case of the Security Council, a distinction is made in the Charter between procedural and other matters. For procedural matters, the majority must include seven out of the eleven votes. With three exceptions, the majority of seven on matters of substance must, according to Article 27 of the Charter,[43] include the concurring votes of the five permanent

---

[38] See above, p. 229.
[39] See above, p. 239 *et seq.*
[40] See above, pp. 239 and 247, and below, p. 629.
[41] See below, p. 704.
[42] See below, pp. 714 and 719.
[43] See below, p. 706.

members. In practice, however, the abstention or absence of a permanent member does not invalidate a vote. The first two exceptions are that, in decisions under Chapter VI [44] and under Paragraph 3 of Article 52,[45] a party to a dispute must abstain from voting. The third exception is that an absolute majority of votes, without distinction between permanent and non-permanent members, suffices for the election of judges of the World Court.

The scope of the veto power is explained in a Statement on Voting Procedure in the Security Council issued on June 7, 1945, by the four Governments sponsoring the San Francisco Conference—the permanent members of the Security Council, except France, who subsequently associated herself with the Statement. While this interpretation is not binding on any other members of the United Nations, each of the parties to this Instrument can expect that action in accordance with it will be respected by the other parties.

In an attempt to limit the exercise of the veto, the General Assembly, by a large majority, adopted in 1949 a resolution on the subject of voting in the Security Council. Its purpose was to set out in detail matters which, without undue sacrifice, any permanent member might well be content to treat as procedural. Yet, the most that compliance with such counsels of self-restraint can achieve is a less mechanical use of the veto than was the practice of the Soviet Union during the Stalinist era.

Actually, the preliminary decision on whether an issue is procedural or substantive requires a vote of seven members, including those of the permanent members. In other words, the question, whether an issue is subject to the veto, is itself subject to the veto. This refinement is known as the double veto. But, if the President for the month in question is prepared to use the Rules of Procedure of the Security Council for this purpose, the double veto may be avoided by a so-called Presidential Ruling. This means that the President rules a matter to be procedural. In this case, this ruling stands unless overruled by a vote of seven members of the Security Council.

The view has been expressed that, minor exceptions apart,

[44] See below, p. 707.
[45] See below, p. 711.

every member of the League Council had a veto and, that, therefore, the limitation of the veto to five powers constitutes a considerable advance in international organisation. It appears,
however, more realistic to view this selectiveness rather as the
acknowledgment of a trend towards centralisation by which the
number of the bearers of political, as distinct from legal,
sovereignty has actually been reduced to probably fewer States
than those entitled to the veto.[46]

The veto is the legal expression of the reserve power, denied
to the many, to bring the security machinery of the United
Nations to a standstill if this should be demanded by what a
veto-State considers to be an overriding interest of its own.
Combined with the other reservations of a similar calibre—the
right of individual and collective self-defence [47] and preservation
of freedom of action against ex-enemy States [48]—the grant of this
reserve power makes the international order of the United Nations
dependent on the good sense of the super-powers and is one of
the major factors in reducing it to a mere quasi-order.[49]

The ineffectiveness of the vetoes exercised by France and the
United Kingdom in the face of joint resistance by the United
States and the Soviet Union over the Suez intervention of 1956
has thrown into relief the *de facto* hierarchies which exist even
between permanent members of the Security Council. As in
corresponding fields of municipal constitutional law, so at this
point of international constitutional law, an exposition of the law
can afford to ignore these legally relevant facts of international
life only at the price of liability to mistakes of this calibre.

B. Equality

In principle, equality of status and before the law, which is all
that equality in international customary law means,[47] is respected
in the Charter of the United Nations. The privileged position in
the United Nations of the permanent members of the Security
Council, which is not limited to *ex officio* membership of the
Council and the veto power,[48] but also applies, for instance, to

[46] See above, p. 58, and below, p. 363.
[47] See above, p. 176.
[48] See below, pp. 276 and 723.
[49] See above, p. 147 *et seq.*

the procedures for the revision of the Charter,[50] is the first departure from this rule. It rests, however, on consent and is, therefore,
in conformity with international law.[49]   The plurality of votes
granted, in fact, in the General Assembly to the Soviet Union
by admission to separate membership of the Ukraine and Byelo-
russia may be considered as a further deviation from the principle of equality, but, again, is sanctioned by consent.

An intriguing problem is presented by Article 107 of the
Charter.[51]   The Charter is based on the principle of sovereign
equality. Yet, member States have reserved to themselves complete freedom of action against ex-enemy States which is
taken or authorised as a result of the Second World War.[52]

It is possible to argue that the rationale of this Article is
to be applied only during a transitional period while the ex-enemy
States would not yet be members of the United Nations and
still be in need of readjustment to the standards laid down by
the United Nations.   Once, however, an ex-enemy State is
admitted to membership of the United Nations, the existing
members have attested to such a new member its peace-loving
character, this being one of the decisive qualifications for
membership.[53]   Then, this Article cannot possibly apply any
longer to ex-enemy member States. In this view, any other interpretation would seriously impair the position of ex-enemy States
as sovereign and equal members of the United Nations and would
be contrary to the rule of treaty interpretation that apparently
conflicting treaty clauses should be harmoniously construed and
not lead to avoidable contradictions.[54]

It is, however, also possible to read Article 107 in a more
literal manner and to emphasise that it does not distinguish in
any way between ex-enemy States which are, and those which
are not, members of the United Nations.   Thus, by applying
for membership of an international institution which, for all to
see, contains a number of articles departing from the principle
of the equality of States, and being accepted as members on this
footing, ex-enemy States have freely consented to accept some

---

50 See above, p. 155, and below, p. 723.
51 See below, p. 723.
52 See below, p. 314.
53 See above, p. 267.
54 See above, p. 154.

discrimination that serves merely as a precautionary measure against any relapse into their past aggressiveness.

IV—THE INTERNATIONAL STATUS OF THE UNITED NATIONS

As with more recent administrative international institutions,[55] the Organisation has not been granted international personality in so many words. It is merely provided in the Charter that the Organisation shall enjoy in the territory of each of the member States such legal capacity, privileges and immunities as are necessary for the exercise of its functions and the fulfilment of its purposes.[56] In a similar formulation, provision has been made for the diplomatic immunity of representatives of member States and officials of the United Nations.[57]

In this respect, the position of the United Nations is comparable to that of the League of Nations. At least after the conclusion of the mandate treaties between the League and the various mandatories[58] and the agreements between the League of Nations and Switzerland, it was clear that the members of the League of Nations had intended to endow this international confederation with international personality.

The trusteeship agreements between the United Nations and the various administering authorities, the General Convention on the Privileges and Immunities of the United Nations of 1946, and the United Nations Headquarters Agreement of 1947 between the United Nations and the United States provide corresponding evidence regarding the international personality of the United Nations.

Although the World Court appears to have overshot the mark in ascribing to the Organisation an objective international personality—valid even in relation to non-member States which refuse to recognise the United Nations[59]—it is valuable that, in its advisory opinion on *Injuries Suffered in the Service of the United Nations* (1949), the Court has expressly affirmed the international personality of the United Nations.

---

[55] See above, p. 253.
[56] See below, p. 722.
[57] See below, p. 721.
[58] See above, p. 56.
[59] See above, p. 73.

V—ORGANISATION

In the Charter, six organs are singled out as the principal organs of the United Nations: the General Assembly, the Security Council, the Economic and Social Council, the Trusteeship Council, the International Court of Justice and the Secretariat. Actually, two of these, the Economic and Social Council and the Trusteeship Council, are auxiliary bodies. Within their respective spheres, it is their function to advise and assist, primarily, the General Assembly and, to a lesser extent, the Security Council.

A. The General Assembly

The complex character of the General Assembly has encouraged somewhat subjective assessments of this key organ of the United Nations. Descriptions vary from a slightly condescending portrait of the Assembly as a world forum or the world's town meeting to wishful adumbrations in terms of an embryonic world parliament.[60]

If the evaluation of the functions fulfilled by the General Assembly is to be rationally verifiable, the relevant tests applied in any such classification must be made articulate beyond doubt. For purposes of the law of international institutions, three criteria appear to be of primary significance. They are, *first*, the scope of the Assembly's jurisdiction, *secondly*, the nature of its powers and, *thirdly*, the techniques applied in the conduct of its business.

1. *Scope of Jurisdiction*

In addition to more specific competences set out in other Articles of the Charter, it is provided in Article 10—known as the omnibus Article—that the General Assembly may discuss any question or matter within the scope of the Charter.[61]

The range of this jurisdiction is subject to only one proviso. Like other organs of the United Nations, the General Assembly may not intervene in matters essentially within the domestic jurisdiction of States.[62] Yet, under Article 14 of the Charter,[63]

---

60 See below, p. 380.
61 See below, p. 702.
62 See above, p. 271.
63 See below, p. 703.

it may concern itself with this otherwise reserved field for the purpose of the peaceful adjustment of any situation, " regardless of origin," which it deems likely to impair the " general welfare or friendly relations among nations." This includes situations resulting from a violation of Articles 1 and 2 of the Charter, in which the Purposes and Principles of the United Nations are set out. Some of these, as, for instance, the principle of " equal rights and self-determination of peoples " [64] and respect for human rights and fundamental freedoms,[65] cover so wide a field as, for all practical purposes, to cancel most of the domestic jurisdiction exception.

2. *Nature of Powers*

The General Assembly has the right to *discuss* any of the matters within its jurisdiction. Save in relation to disputes or situations of which the Security Council is seised,[66] the General Assembly may also make *recommendations*. In the practice of the General Assembly, these have been addressed to other organs of the United Nations, to the member States at large or to individual member States, to non-member States, to non-governmental organisations and even to individuals.

Whatever political or moral force the recommendations of the General Assembly may claim, as such they are not legally binding. They may acquire a legally binding character in other ways as, for instance, by consent, acquiescence or estoppel. Thus, parties to a dispute may accept in advance the obligation to carry out a particular recommendation.[67] This was what happened when the United States, France, the United Kingdom, and the Soviet Union failed to reach agreement on the fate of the Italian colonies. They agreed that if, within one year from the entry into force of the Peace Treaty with Italy, they could not settle the matter, it would be referred to the General Assembly of the United Nations, and that they would accept the Assembly's recommendation as binding. Similarly, by voting for a declaratory resolution, member States may estop themselves from subsequently contesting the truth of a statement embodied in the resolution.[68]

---

[64] See above, p. 67.
[66] See below, pp. 286 and 702.
[68] See above, p. 160.

[65] See below, p. 642 *et seq.*
[67] See above, p. 161.

Only in internal affairs of the United Nations has the Assembly a right of *decision* in the substantive meaning of the term. The admission of new members,[69] the exercise of its budgetary powers [70] and the approval of trusteeship agreements, other than those relating to strategic areas,[71] are relevant illustrations.

3. *Techniques*

Five major factors appear to condition the procedures followed in the conduct of the business of the General Assembly as the members' meeting of the United Nations : its permanency, its size, the wide range of its jurisdiction, the public character of its meetings and, finally, the procedural object-in-chief of its debates : resolutions.

The General Assembly is a permanent body and, special sessions apart, meets at regular annual intervals.[72] Beyond this, a number of circumstances tend to give it an element of corporate existence. An increasing number of member States have established permanent delegations which are accredited to United Nations headquarters.[73] Moreover, key members of these permanent as well as *ad hoc* delegations represent their countries in the Assembly over prolonged periods. Finally, the elected officers of the Assembly and its committees are gently, but firmly, guided by a body of competent and well co-ordinated United Nations officials.

The United Nations has over eighty members, and each of these is entitled to be represented by a maximum of five delegates present at the same time. Thus, more than four hundred delegates have a right to be present at meetings of the General Assembly.

An organ of this size can be kept in order only if it subjects itself to the discipline of necessarily technical rules of procedure. Moreover, debates in the plenum of the Assembly must be well prepared. It is, therefore, wisely provided in the Rules of Procedure of the General Assembly that, in the absence of a decision to the contrary, the Assembly shall not make any final decision—in the wider sense of this term, that is to say, including

[69] See above, p. 267, and below, p. 701.
[70] See below, p. 703.
[71] See above, p. 57, and below, p. 301.
[72] See below, p. 704.
[73] See above, p. 78.

recommendations [74]—upon any item on the Agenda until it has received the report of a committee on the subject.

Considering the wide range of the jurisdiction exercised by the General Assembly, this means that the Assembly must rely on an elaborate structure of committees and subsidiary organs. At least an idea of the structure of the General Assembly will be conveyed by listing some of these.

The General Assembly is served by seven main Committees: the Political and Security Committee, the Economic and Financial Committee, the Social, Humanitarian and Cultural Committee, the Trusteeship Committee, the Administrative and Budgetary Committee, the Legal Committee and the Special Political Committee. In addition, there are two Procedural Committees: the General and Credentials Committees, and two Standing Committees: the Advisory Committee on Administrative and Budgetary Questions and the Committee on Contributions.

Finally, prolific permanent, semi-permanent and *ad hoc* committees and agencies have been created by the General Assembly. Among these figure prominently the Interim Committee of the General Assembly, the Peace Observation Commission, the Collective Measures Committee, the International Law Commission, the United Nations Children's Fund (UNICEF), the Office of the United Nations High Commissioner for Refugees, the United Nations Administrative Tribunal and the United Nations Emergency Force (UNEF).

In principle, the meetings of the General Assembly, its committees and sub-committees, take place in public and their work is chiefly directed towards the adoption of resolutions, which will ultimately be adopted in the plenum by majority vote.[75] As has been rightly stressed by Professor Jessup, the impact of these two factors on the procedure of the General Assembly must not be minimised.

4. *Evaluation*

The application in isolation of each of these three tests—scope of jurisdiction, nature of powers and characteristics of the procedure—would lead to different results in assessing the place

---

[74] See above, p. 279.
[75] See above, p. 273.

of the General Assembly in the scheme of the Charter and the practice of the United Nations. The real task, however, is to view this organ in a commensurate perspective. It then becomes evident that all these three facets must be treated as inter-related.

The wide scope of the jurisdiction exercised by the General Assembly involves the fulfilment by one and the same organ of a variety of functions which, on lower levels of international integration, are entrusted to different one-purpose institutions.[76]

Thus, for instance, in promoting the development of international law and its codification,[77] the General Assembly continues in the tradition of quasi-legislative international institutions.[78] If the Assembly concerns itself with the settlement of international disputes,[79] it fulfils the functions of an international conciliation commission.[80] In assuming responsibility for executive action, as in the highly exceptional circumstances of the Korean and Suez incidents,[81] it conjures up the picture of a supreme organ of outraged world conscience. Finally, when the General Assembly exercises its powers of decision in a technical sense,[82] it fulfils functions of a truly directory and supervisory character. Thus, more than any other organ of the United Nations, the General Assembly reflects in its own composite character that of the Organisation as a comprehensive and multi-purpose institution of a universalist character.

Yet, the scope of jurisdiction, the size of the organ or other peculiarities which prescribe to the General Assembly its techniques and give it a quasi-parliamentarian flavour appear less significant than the uniform limitation of its powers in other than purely organisational and internal matters. In this respect, the General Assembly is typical of the restrictions imposed on organs with a wide sweep of jurisdiction on the confederate level. Their power to act stands in an inverse ratio to the scope of their jurisdiction.

This innocuousness from the point of view of State sovereignty also accounts for the liberality with which the world powers have permitted the General Assembly to become endowed with the right to adopt resolutions by a majority vote[83] and to indulge

[76] See above, p. 227 *et seq*
[78] See above, p. 257 *et seq.*
[80] See above, p. 230.
[82] See above, p. 280.

[77] See below, pp. 365 and 661.
[79] See below, p. 310 *et seq.*
[81] See above, pp. 177 and 275.
[83] See above, p. 273 *et seq.*

in proceedings of a quasi-parliamentary character.[84] These, however, are chiefly trappings. From the point of view of international constitutional law, what matters more than the play-acting and self-hypnosis inseparable from the atmosphere of these international beehives, is the legally binding or non-binding character of the products of such prodigious efforts.

B. The Security Council

The fathers of the League of Nations were not prepared to grant to the League Council even the appearance of an executive organ. They, therefore, defined the functions of the Assembly and the Council in identical terms. It was left to the practice of the League of Nations to establish empirically that a relatively compact organ, which can be convened at short notice, is able to meet frequently and is prepared to withdraw into the seclusion of private meetings, has the advantage every time over a necessarily more cumbersome plenary meeting of members.

The Security Council of the United Nations is conceived in more ambitious terms.

1. *Composition*

The Security Council consists of eleven members. Five of these are permanent members—the so-called Big Five: the United States, the Soviet Union, China, France and the United Kingdom—and six are non-permanent members elected by the General Assembly for a term of two years.[85] In accordance with a gentlemen's agreement believed to have been reached in 1946 between the Big Five, but not always observed during the " Cold War," the non-permanent members should represent five, largely regional, groups: Western and Eastern Europe, the Near East, Latin America and the British Commonwealth. The position regarding South Asia, South-East Asia and the Pacific was left somewhat vague. As with other agreements of this kind, they are not legally binding even on the parties to such arrangements, but are meant to assist in keeping the wheels turning.[86]

---

[84] See above, p. 260 *et seq.*
[85] See below, p. 705.
[86] See above, p. 140.

2. *Powers*

The Security Council is charged with primary responsibility for the maintenance of international peace and security.[87] If the Council makes recommendations under Chapter VI of the Charter in the interest of the pacific settlement of international disputes or under Article 39, its resolutions are not binding on the parties.[88]

The position is different in the case of decisions under Chapter VII with respect to any threat to the peace, breach of the peace or act of aggression. Such decisions are binding on the parties and other members of the United Nations. Moreover, under this head, the Security Council may take enforcement action of one of two kinds. If a party does not comply with provisional measures indicated by the Security Council or other decisions of the Council under Chapter VII, the Security Council may either call upon the member States to apply non-military sanctions, or direct the application of military sanctions against parties to a dispute.[89]

3. *Structure*

To be able to fulfil its responsibilities, the Security Council must be so organised as to be able to function continuously. Each member is bound to be represented at all times at the seat of the United Nations.

Moreover, in matters affecting international peace and security, the members of the United Nations have undertaken to treat the Security Council as their agent and to accept and carry out its decisions " in accordance with the present Charter." [90] Thus, by all appearances, the Security Council may be described as an international executive organ and has all the potentialities of a world directorate.

This is, however, true only if the Security Council is able to comply with the safety devices which are intended to keep it firmly inside the confederate pattern. This is the purpose of the veto power. It means that a member which has this right is able

[87] See below, p. 308.
[88] See below, p. 707.
[89] See below, p. 708.
[90] See above, p. 78, and below, p. 705.

on its own to frustrate the collective will of the organ concerned. Any of the permanent members of the Security Council may exercise this right at will in relation to questions other than those of a procedural character. As has been explained, the veto does not apply if the permanent member concerned is itself a party to a dispute.[91] On questions of procedure, a permanent member is still able to get its own way by the exercise of the double veto.[92] On questions of substance, it must rely on the good services of another " friendly " permanent member, but when enforcement measures are involved it is again able to exercise its veto without any limitations. Even if a permanent member is not able to exercise the veto by proxy—from the point of view of the Soviet Union, this is a significant result of Communist China not being represented in the Security Council—a permanent member against whom the Security Council decides to apply sanctions under Chapter VII is still free to veto such action single-handed.

Actually, a situation in which the Security Council may have to call upon member States to apply military sanctions in the form envisaged in the Charter cannot easily arise. The Military Staff Committee, which is supposed to advise and assist the Security Council on matters relating to enforcement action, has been moribund from the start.[93] Yet, with a zeal hardly surpassed in the history of international institutions, it still goes through the motions of regular meetings. Similarly, the special agreements on the armed forces, assistance and facilities which each of the member States is to make available to the Security Council are still to be negotiated " as soon as possible." [94]

Provision for transitional security arrangements is made in the Charter. As these are operative until the special agreements between the Security Council and the member States come into force, the potentialities of this provision are still not yet exhausted.[95] Under this Article, the five permanent members of the Security Council shall consult with one another and, as occasion requires, with other members of the United Nations on joint action on behalf of the United Nations for the purpose of

---

[91] See above, p. 274, and below, p. 706.
[92] See above, p. 274.
[93] See below, p. 709.
[94] See below, p. 709.
[95] See below, p. 722.

maintaining international peace and security. Yet, so long as the Security Council is hamstrung by the division of the permanent members into antagonistic camps, this Article cannot offer any way out of the impasse in which the Security Council finds itself.

4. *The Security Council and the General Assembly*

The equilibrium contemplated in the Charter between the two main organs of the United Nations has been considerably disturbed in the constitutional practice of the United Nations during the " Cold War."

(a) *The Scheme of the Charter.* Under Article 24 (1) of the Charter, the Security Council is entrusted with " primary " responsibility for the maintenance of international peace and security.[96] This formulation invites a search for organs which, in this sphere, may have to fulfil secondary functions.

Express provision is made in Article 106 of the Charter [97] for the fulfilment of the enforcement functions of the Security Council during the transitional period; that is to say, until the entry into force of the special agreements between the United Nations and the member States under Article 43 of the Charter.[98] During this interval, the enforcement functions of the Security Council are entrusted to the permanent members of the Security Council.

Two other provisions of the Charter are intended to forestall encroachments by the General Assembly on the prerogatives of the Security Council. The General Assembly is precluded from making recommendations, on its own initiative, to the Security Council on disputes or situations regarding which the latter is " exercising " its appointed functions.[99] It is a matter for argument whether the fact that an item is on the agenda of the Security Council means that the Council is exercising its jurisdiction in the matter. In addition, the General Assembly must refer any question on which " action " is required to the Security Council " before or after discussion." [1] Finally, in contrast to

---

96 See below, p. 705.
97 See below, p. 722.
98 See above, p. 285, and below, p. 709.
99 See below, p. 702.
1 See above, p. 279, and below, p. 702.

the General Assembly, which, in principle, is to meet only at yearly intervals,[2] the Security Council is meant to function continuously.[3]

There are, however, other Articles in the Charter which, to some extent, redress the balance in favour of the General Assembly. The Security Council must submit annual and special reports to the General Assembly. These must include an " account " of the measures that the Security Council has decided upon or taken to maintain international peace and security.[4] The wide scope of the jurisdiction granted to the General Assembly by Articles 10 and 14 of the Charter may also be recalled in this context.[5] Lastly, the General Assembly, as the organ in control of the budget, is entitled to use this power to review critically the activities of other organs of the United Nations, including the Security Council.[6] Admittedly, this does not help very much if another organ is merely intent on remaining inactive.

(b) *Division of Functions in Practice.* The failure of the Security Council to carry out its appointed tasks on all but rare occasions has led to determined attempts to fill the gap thus created in the machinery of the United Nations.

In the first place, the General Assembly has made itself more readily available than had been originally considered necessary. It has considerably extended the duration of its sessions and, in 1947, created an Interim Committee, more generally known as the " Little Assembly." This subsidiary organ of the General Assembly has been entrusted with a limited jurisdiction which is intended to enable it to hold the fort while the Assembly is not in session.

By the Uniting for Peace Resolution, which the Assembly adopted in 1950, the procedure for convening special sessions of the General Assembly at short notice has been considerably streamlined. On the same occasion, the General Assembly established two further subsidiary bodies: the Peace Observation Commission and the Collective Measures Committee. The task

---

2 See above, p. 280, and below, p. 704.
3 See above, p. 284, and below, p. 706.
4 See below, p. 705.
5 See above, p. 278 *et seq.*
6 See above, p. 280, and below, p. 703.

of the Peace Observation Commission is to observe and report on international tensions the continuance of which is likely to endanger international peace and security. That of the Collective Measures Committee is to report on measures to maintain and strengthen international peace and security. In the same Resolution, the General Assembly recommended to the member States to maintain units within their national armed forces which, on the recommendation of the Security Council or the General Assembly, can be promptly made available for service as United Nations units.

The Uniting for Peace Resolution can be fully understood only in the context in which it was adopted. During the temporary absence of the Soviet Union in protest against the non-representation of Communist China on the Security Council, the Council adopted a number of resolutions regarding the Korean conflict. Although open to different interpretations, in these resolutions the Security Council recommended the collective defence of Korea, meaning thereby the South Korean Government, which was the only Korean government recognised by the United Nations.[7]

Moreover, the Security Council authorised the action taken by the United States, the South Korean Government and, in the end, sixteen other member States, to be designated a United Nations action. The unified United Nations Command was also permitted to use the United Nations flag concurrently with those of the participating nations. When the Russian representative returned to the Security Council, his exercise of the veto power threw the Council back into its former state of near-paralysis.

Armed with the Uniting for Peace Resolution, the General Assembly proceeded on its course of making the United Nations work. In 1951, it requested the members of the Collective Measures Committee to act as a Committee to consider additional measures to meet the aggression in Korea (Additional Measures Committee). On the recommendation of this Committee, the General Assembly, in the same year, recommended to member States the application of an embargo on the export of arms and strategic materials to Communist China.

In 1956, the exercise of the British and French vetoes in the

[7] See above, pp, 177 and 282.

Security Council again condemned the Council to manifest its constitutional weakness. Then, even the Soviet Union recognised the value of the Uniting for Peace Resolution and, with somewhat Platonic reservations, co-operated with fervour in the task of stirring the General Assembly into action. The result of the pressure exercised by the General Assembly was the withdrawal of the interventionist forces from Egypt in accordance with agreed timetables and in close co-operation with the newly created United Nations Emergency Force (UNEF). In sponsoring the creation and operation of an international force interposed between parties to an armed conflict, the General Assembly has made its most ambitious intrusion yet into the sphere of active participation in the restoration and maintenance of international peace and security.

(c) *Evaluation.* The Articles of the Charter referred to above are sufficiently elastic to lend themselves to very different interpretations. They may legitimately be used both to prove and disprove the constitutional character of the jurisdiction assumed by the General Assembly. Whether these arguments lead one way or another is predetermined by the major premise selected and, on occasion, this depends on the location of the inquirer's spiritual home.

Each of the operative major premises, which lead to diametrically opposite conclusions, may be chosen in accordance with impeccable canons of treaty interpretation.[8] According to both, the object is to find out what was the intention of the contracting parties at the time when the Charter came into force, that is to say, on October 24, 1945.[9] At this point, however, the ways of the two reasonings part.

In the first interpretation, what matters is the division of functions between the Security Council and the General Assembly as it was established on the creation of the United Nations. Any subsequent departure from this scheme which falls short of a formal revision of the Charter[10] can then be plausibly dismissed as illegal. Such a " conservative " interpretation of the Charter can be ably supported by reliance on *travaux préparatoires*

[8] See above, p. 152 *et seq.*
[9] See below, p. 724.
[10] See above, p. 155, and below, p. 723.

S.M.

19

and techniques of literal and systematic treaty interpretation.[11] It produces results strangely similar to the Russian arguments in the Security Council and the General Assembly on the illegality of the Uniting for Peace Resolution.

In a more " liberal " or " progressive " view of the matter, the intention of the parties was to provide a general framework within which the Organisation was to fulfil, as best it could, its allotted tasks in an as yet uncharted future. If, by clinging to the text of the Charter, the United Nations would be merely frustrated, an " interpretation for survival "—to choose Professor McDougal's suggestive formulation—must be adopted. A slightly impressionist reading of the text of the Charter, coupled with a fair dose of teleological treaty interpretation,[12] will then lead to conclusions which bear more than a faint resemblance to those prevalent in Western countries and the United Nations Secretariat.

It is not surprising that, in view of this wide choice between available major premises,[13] the Eastern bloc did not press to have the constitutional character of the intrusion by the General Assembly into the preserve of the Security Council tested in an advisory opinion of the World Court. A fairly simple mathematical calculation must have told them the majority by which the opinion was likely to go against their own interpretation. What is more intriguing is why their Western counterparts should have failed to take advantage of techniques of prognostication with which the " realist " school in American jurisprudence should have made them familiar.

It would mean overshooting the mark to describe the assimilation of the jurisdiction of the General Assembly to that of the Security Council—very much a return to the pattern of the League Covenant [14]—as a *de jure* revision of the Charter by desuetude.[15] This process still lacks the requisite subjective element of *convictio juris sive necessitatis* that distinguishes a practice acceptable to a considerable majority of member States from a legally binding new rule.[16]

Yet, even assuming that the policy initiated by the great

---

[11] See above, p. 153.
[13] See above, pp. 154–155.
[15] See above, p. 156, and below, p. 649.

[12] See above, p. 154.
[14] See above, p. 177.
[16] See above, p. 27.

majority of members more than a decade ago was illegal, dissenting members can do little about it. If they refuse to test their view in the World Court—and there may be excellent reasons for this—they are limited to an unenviable choice. It is between leaving the Organisation or voicing repetitive, and increasingly ineffectual, protests. If, when the occasion offers itself, they fall for the temptation of using such practices for their own ends, they weaken their position even further. As has already been mentioned,[17] this happened when, in 1956, the Soviet Union voted in favour of a resolution of the Security Council invoking the Uniting for Peace Resolution. At this point, the legality of a constitutional practice becomes a somewhat hypothetical issue. What then comes to matter is its gradually more relevant continuity.

So far, this process of change still falls short of a *de jure* revision of the Charter. It has, however, passed beyond the point when the issue is merely one of conformity with, or breach of, a legally binding rule. The dynamics of events have led to an in-between state of *de facto* revision.[18] In form, the United Nations repeats in this respect an experience familiar from the history of the League of Nations. In substance, there is, however, a decisive difference. Then, the trend of the *de facto* revision was towards a whittling down of the collective system. Now, it is towards its activation.

C. The Economic and Social Council

The incongruities surrounding the Economic and Social Council are striking. The nomenclature " Council " suggests a place in the top ranks of the institutional hierarchy of the United Nations. At the same time, the Economic and Social Council has been firmly subordinated to the General Assembly.[19] It shares both these features with the Trusteeship Council,[20] and for similar reasons. The status of both organs was somewhat inflated to provide the medium and small States with some compensation for the privileges exacted by the Big Five. Moreover, the draftsmen at the Dumbarton Oaks and San Francisco Conferences were

---

[17] See above, p. 289.   [18] See above, p. 156, and below, p. 649.
[19] See above, p. 278 *et seq.*, and below, p. 712.
[20] See below, p. 298 *et seq.*

aware of the Bruce Report of 1939 in which a drastic reorganisation of the technical services of the League of Nations had been recommended.

The responsibilities of the League of Nations in the economic, financial and social fields were, to say the least, expressed incompletely in the Covenant. The International Labour Organisation was established as an autonomous organisation within the League. Its constitution was, however, embodied in a separate part of the Peace Treaties of 1919, and it increasingly dissociated itself from its parent body.[21] With the advantages of publicity accruing to it from its tripartite organisation and direct contacts with member States, it soon began to overshadow all other international organs in the economic and social field. Pretentious, but, on the whole, somewhat inconclusive economic *ad hoc* conferences, which were convened under the auspices of the League of Nations, merely strengthened an overall impression of failure.

Yet a number of expert committees did at least some valuable ground work. Two committees—the Economic and Financial Committees—deserve to be singled out. Their members were appointed by the League Council. These Committees were responsible to the Council and were able to rely on the assistance of highly competent specialised sections of the League Secretariat. What they lacked was sufficient contact with the League Assembly and, even more, with the member States.

Compared with this modest organisation, the structure of the Economic and Social Council was to be very much grander. Yet the member States were resolved on retaining a final say in the matters which were to come under the Council's jurisdiction. Thus, a certain amount of window-dressing proved unavoidable. This will become apparent from a closer examination of the constitutional aspects of the Economic and Social Council.

1. *Composition*

The Economic and Social Council consists of eighteen members. Each year, six of these are elected for three-year terms by the General Assembly with a two-thirds majority of the members present and voting. Retiring members are eligible for re-election. Each member is entitled to one representative.[22]

---

[21] See above, p. 260, and below, p. 639.   [22] See below, p. 713.

Although, in law, the permanent members of the Security Council have no privileged position regarding their representation in the Economic and Social Council, in fact, they have been continuously re-elected since the Council's establishment. Similarly, the frequent re-election of such States as Canada, India and Yugoslavia indicates a desire by the General Assembly to emphasise the need both for continuity and for worldwide representation in the Economic and Social Council.

2. *Structure*

To visualise the Economic and Social Council merely as an auxiliary body of the General Assembly would give a highly distorted impression. The Assembly is already so overburdened that, for the less controversial issues among the matters within the jurisdiction of the Economic and Social Council,[23] the Council tends to become the Assembly. Moreover, it is itself the centre of a complicated structure of related and subordinate commissions and committees.

These are of five types: *functional* commissions, including the Transport and Communications Commission and the Commission on Human Rights; *regional* economic commissions for Europe, Asia and the Far East, Latin America and Africa; *standing* committees as, for instance, the Technical Assistance Committee; *special* bodies, such as the Permanent Central Opium Board and the United Nations Children's Fund as well as *sessional* and *ad hoc* committees.

Finally, as part of the task of the Economic and Social Council to co-ordinate the activities of the specialised agencies of the United Nations, machinery has been established to maintain contact with each of these institutions and to organise joint operational programmes.[24]

3. *Scope of Jurisdiction*

The wide range of the subjects covered by the jurisdiction of the Economic and Social Council rests on five overlapping authorisations:

---

[23] See above, p. 256, and below, p. 713.
[24] See above, p. 256, and below, p. 713.

First, the General Assembly and, *secondly,* the Security Council may call on the Economic and Social Council for assistance. Thus, any matter within their jurisdiction which they assign to the Economic and Social Council is within its competence.[25]

Thirdly, in Article 62 of the Charter, the initiation of studies and reports on international economic, social, cultural, educational, health and related matters, as well as the making of recommendations for the purpose of promoting respect for, and observance of, human rights and freedoms, are enumerated as specific functions which are entrusted to the Economic and Social Council.[26]

Fourthly, under the authority of the General Assembly, responsibility for the discharge of the Organisation's functions under Chapter IX of the Charter on International Economic and Social Co-operation is vested in the Economic and Social Council. In addition to the matters already enumerated, this Chapter includes promotion by the United Nations of higher standards of living, full employment, and conditions of economic and social progress and development.[27]

Fifthly, it is the duty of the Economic and Social Council to co-ordinate the policies and activities of the specialised agencies.[28]

Any matter the " promotion " of which the Charter makes the concern of the General Assembly and the Economic and Social Council, falls to this extent within the province of the United Nations. Moreover, by Article 56 of the Charter, the member States have pledged themselves expressly to take joint and separate action in co-operation with the Organisation for the achievement of these objects. Any other aspect of the matter remains in the sphere of the essentially domestic jurisdiction of members and is still covered by the reservation of Article 2 (7) of the Charter of the United Nations.[29]

4. *Nature of Powers*

It is provided in the Charter that each member of the Economic and Social Council shall have one vote, and that " decisions "

[25] See below, p. 714
[26] See below, p. 713.
[27] See below, p. 712.
[28] See below, p. 713.
[29] See below, p. 700.

of the Council are to be made by a majority of the members present and voting.[30] As in relation to the other organs of the United Nations,[31] the use of the term " decision " in the Charter is not necessarily indicative of the nature of these powers. Actually, they fall into five distinct categories.

First, the Economic and Social Council may undertake or initiate studies and reports on any issue within its province.[32]

Secondly, the Economic and Social Council may make recommendations to the General Assembly, to members of the United Nations and to specialised agencies.[33] In its practice, the Council has interpreted this power as entitling it to address recommendations not only to States at large but also to particular categories and groups of member States, to individual member States and even to non-member States. Moreover, it has delegated this power to its regional commissions.[34] Recommendations by the Economic and Social Council to the General Assembly may take the form of draft conventions on any matter falling within its competence.[35]

Thirdly, in accordance with rules prescribed by the General Assembly, the Economic and Social Council may call international conferences on matters within its jurisdiction. It must, however, be satisfied that the work to be done by the conference cannot be done satisfactorily by any organ of the United Nations or by any specialised agency.

Highly exceptional cases apart, all member States of the United Nations are invited to participate in such conferences. Discretion is, however, exercised regarding non-member States. This applies both to whether they should be invited at all and, if so, on what footing, that is to say, whether as observers or with full voting rights. Similarly, dependent territories, which are autonomous in the field covered by the terms of reference of the conference in question, have been invited after consultation with the member State responsible for the conduct of their foreign relations. On occasion, interested specialised agencies have also

[30] See below, p. 714.
[31] See above, pp. 274 and 280, and below, p. 302.
[32] See below, p. 713.
[33] See below, p. 713.
[34] See below, p. 714.
[35] See below, p. 713.

been asked to participate either as observers or with the rights they enjoy at sessions of the Economic and Social Council.

Fourthly, the Economic and Social Council has been granted the power to enter into agreements with inter-governmental institutions for the purpose of establishing such institutions as specialised agencies of the United Nations.[36] Such agreements are subject to the approval of the General Assembly.[37] They provide for varying degrees of supervision of the specialised agencies by, and consultation with, the Economic and Social Council.

In the chronological order of the agreements by which these institutions have become specialised agencies of the United Nations or, as the International Finance Corporation, have become assimilated to this status, they are the following: the International Labour Organisation (ILO—1946); the United Nations Educational, Scientific and Cultural Organisation (UNESCO—1946); the Food and Agriculture Organisation of the United Nations (FAO—1946); the International Civil Aviation Organisation (ICAO—1947); the International Bank for Reconstruction and Development (IBRD—1947); the International Monetary Fund (IMF—1947); the Universal Postal Union (UPU—1948); the World Health Organisation (WHO—1948); the International Telecommunication Union (ITU—1949); the World Meteorological Organisation (WMO—1951); the International Finance Corporation (IFC—1957); the International Atomic Energy Agency (IAEA—1957) and the Inter-Governmental Maritime Consultative Organisation (IMCO—1959).

The International Refugee Organisation (IRO—1948) was dissolved in 1952. Those of its activities as were continued were transferred to a subsidiary body of the General Assembly, the Office of the United Nations High Commissioner for Refugees. The General Agreement on Tariffs and Trade (GATT) is the interim organisation for a specialised agency which in this field is still to come into existence: the Organisation for Trade Co-operation (OTC). GATT, although working in close co-operation with the United Nations, is not linked with it by a relations agreement and, thus, is not a specialised agency.

[36] See above, p. 256.
[37] See below, p. 712.

In the exercise of its authority to make arrangements for consultation with non-governmental organisations concerned with matters within its competence, the Economic and Social Council has granted consultative status to over two hundred and fifty such international and national organisations. A few of these— that is to say, those in category A—are entitled to propose to the Committee of the Economic and Social Council on Non-Governmental Organisations the inclusion of items on the provisional agenda of the Council and, at the discretion of the Council or the committee concerned, make oral statements before it. However, any of these organisations may submit written statements for the consideration of the Council or its committees, subject, however, to stringent restrictions on length.

Fifthly, in the organisational field, the Economic and Social Council may make decisions in the sense that it takes at least some action as, for instance, the establishment of subordinate bodies or the dispatch of a commission of inquiry to a particular country, but always only at the request, or with the concurrence, of the government concerned.

It remains to point to some self-denying ordinances which, in its practice, the Economic and Social Council has imposed on itself. It has discouraged attempts made by some of its members to censure individual States for having fallen below the standards of attainment set out in Chapter IX of the Charter [38] and the— in any case not legally binding—Declaration of Human Rights.[39] Similarly, the Council has refused to become involved in concrete disputes between individual States on matters within its jurisdiction by assuming any conciliatory or quasi-judicial functions.

In further pursuance of this policy of self-abnegation, the Economic and Social Council has endorsed the view of its Human Rights Commission that it lacks the power to take action of any kind on complaints regarding alleged violations of human rights. By an arrangement with the International Labour Organisation, the Economic and Social Council has also divested itself largely of responsibility for dealing with allegations regarding infringements of trade union rights. The International Labour Organisation has established on behalf of the United Nations and itself

---

[38] See above, p. 294.
[39] See above, p. 74, and below, p. 640 *et seq*.

a Fact-Finding and Conciliation Commission on Freedom of Association. Yet, unless the issue turns on a labour convention ratified by the ILO member concerned,[40] complaints may be referred to the Commission only with the consent of the member State concerned. If the State concerned is not a member of the International Labour Organisation, it is for the Economic and Social Council to obtain such concurrence.

D. The Trusteeship Council

The Permanent Mandates Commission of the League of Nations was no more than a committee of the League Council. It was, however, a committee with a difference. Provision was made for it in the League Covenant.

Such success as the Mandates Commission attained was probably due to the happy coincidence of a number of circumstances. Not only was a fair percentage of the members of the Commission appointed as individuals, and not as government representatives, but they also had the rarer quality of being truly independent-minded. Moreover, the majority of them were nationals of non-mandatory powers and, in fact though not in law, the members of the Commission enjoyed a considerable security of tenure. Finally, although sessions of the Commission other than the opening meetings were held in private, the minutes of the Commission and its report to the League Council were published and received considerable publicity.[41]

All that the draftsmen of the Covenant had to say on the Mandates Commission was compressed into one paragraph of one Article. Their successors of San Francisco devoted a whole Chapter of the Charter to the Trusteeship Council. It is, however, more significant that, in spite of being one of the principal organs of the United Nations,[42] the Trusteeship Council is merely an auxiliary body of, primarily, the General Assembly and, in the second place, the Security Council. As such, it assists both these organs in the discharge of their functions in relation to trust territories.

If anything, the Trusteeship Council suffers from a surfeit of publicity. Unless the Council or any of its subsidiary bodies

40 See above, p. 145.   41 See above. pp. 56 and 269.
42 See above, p. 278.

decides otherwise, meetings are held in public. Yet, neither are the conditions of appointment comparable with those of members of the Mandates Commission nor are the administering powers limited to a minority rôle. Thus, the Trusteeship Council is a less formidable proposition than might appear at first sight.

1. *Composition*

Representation in the Trusteeship Council is based on a combination of three considerations. In the first place, each administering power is entitled to a seat on the Council. Furthermore, all permanent members of the Security Council must be represented. Finally, the non-administering powers are to balance the administering powers.

At present, seven members of the Council are there as administering powers, three of them being permanent members of the Security Council. Thus, two of the places allocated to non-administering powers are taken by the other two permanent members of the Security Council, leaving five seats for other non-administering powers. These are elected for three-year terms by the General Assembly by a two-thirds majority of the members present and voting. When Italy was made an administering power of the trust territory of Somaliland, she was given a seat on the Trusteeship Council, although then not yet a member of the United Nations.

Each member is represented on the Trusteeship Council by one delegate. In accordance with Article 86 (2) of the Charter,[43] he must be " specially " qualified. His choice is, however, left with the designating member State.

2. *Structure*

Compared with the spider web around the Economic and Social Council, the structure of the Trusteeship Council is sweet simplicity. The only subsidiary organs for which provision is made in the Charter are visiting missions to the trust territories.[44] Yet, even in this case, the power is one primarily granted to the General Assembly. In addition, the Trusteeship Council may

[43] See below, p. 719.
[44] See below. p. 719.

draw on assistance from the Economic and Social Council and the specialised agencies on matters within their competence.[45]

While, under the Charter, the Economic and Social Council is authorised to establish commissions for the performance of its functions,[46] there is no corresponding provision regarding the Trusteeship Council. Nevertheless, in its Rules of Procedure, the Council has considered itself authorised to set up such committees as it deems necessary, and has established two standing committees, one on Administrative Unions (1949) and the other on Petitions (1952).

The task of the Committee on Administrative Unions is to examine the compatibility with the Charter and with relevant trust agreements of administrative unions between trust territories and neighbouring colonies of administering authorities, and to advise the General Assembly on such issues. The function of the Committee on Petitions is the preliminary examination of petitions which, under Article 87 (b) of the Charter,[47] the General Assembly and, under its authority, the Trusteeship Council may accept and examine in consultation with the administering authority.[48] In both cases, the better view probably is that the Trusteeship Council has established these committees in the exercise of an implied authority to take such action as is necessary to carry out its appointed functions. The Trusteeship Council determines the composition of these subsidiary organs. It is, however, provided in its Rules of Procedure that the members of the Committee on Petitions shall be evenly divided between administering and non-administering members.

3. *Scope of Jurisdiction*

The basic division of functions between the United Nations and the administering authorities is that the former supervise, and the latter administer, the trust territories.[49] Under the Trusteeship Agreement for Somaliland of 1950, Italy consented to restrictions of her administrative freedom not to be found in other trusteeship agreements. She was to be aided and advised

[45] See below, p. 720.
[46] See below, p. 714.
[47] See below, p. 719.
[48] See below, pp. 703 and 719.
[49] See above, p. 57.

in her administration, which was to lead to independence within ten years of the approval of the Agreement by the General Assembly, by an Advisory Council composed of representatives of Colombia, Egypt and the Philippines.

The auxiliary character of the jurisdiction of the Trusteeship Council in relation to the General Assembly and the Security Council is strongly emphasised in the Charter of the United Nations. The formulation of a questionnaire which forms the basis of the annual reports submitted to the General Assembly by the administering authorities is the only task left by the Charter exclusively with the Trusteeship Council.[50] Otherwise, the whole of its supervisory jurisdiction over non-strategic trust territories is exercised under the authority of the General Assembly. With regard to trust territories designated as strategic areas, it plays a similar, but even more limited, rôle as an auxiliary organ of the Security Council.[51]

Thus, compared with the exceedingly wide scope and diffuse character of the jurisdiction of the Economic and Social Council —not to speak of that of the General Assembly itself—the jurisdiction of the Trusteeship Council is enviably compact and homogeneous.

4. *Nature of Powers*

The General Assembly and, in relation to strategic areas, the Security Council fulfil their supervisory functions in relation to trust territories in five different ways and operate by delegating, subject to review, the exercise of these powers to the Trusteeship Council:

First, approval of the terms of individual trusteeship agreements, including their amendment and termination.

Secondly, consideration of the reports submitted by the administering authorities. These are based on a detailed questionnaire prepared by the Trusteeship Council.[52]

Thirdly, examination, in consultation with the administering authority,[53] of petitions which, under the Rules of the Trusteeship Council, may be addressed directly to the Secretary-General

[50] See below, p. 719.
[51] See above, p. 57, and below, p. 719.
[52] See below, p. 719.
[53] See above, p. 57, and below, p. 719.

of the United Nations or transmitted to him through the administering authority. Under its Rules of Procedure, the Trusteeship Council may hear oral representations in support of written petitions and, in exceptional cases, receive oral petitions. Subject to instructions received from the Trusteeship Council, its representatives on visiting and other official missions may also receive oral representations or petitions. Finally, the Fourth Committee of the General Assembly—the Trusteeship Committee [54]—has established a still controversial practice of giving oral hearings to individuals and organisations in trust territories.

Fourthly, examination of the reports made by its own periodic visiting missions and of the observations thereon by the administering authority concerned.

Fifthly, action under further authority granted in individual trusteeship agreements. Thus, for instance, prior to the termination of the Trusteeship Agreement for Somaliland, the Trusteeship Council had to consider a plan for the orderly transfer of all the functions of government to a duly constituted independent government of Somalia.

The decisions of the Trusteeship Council are taken by a simple majority of the members present and voting. With the exception of decisions on purely organisational matters and on the formulation and modifications of the questionnaire to be answered by administering authorities,[55] the decisions of the Trusteeship Council are merely recommendations to the General Assembly.[56] They are embodied in comprehensive annual reports by the Council to the Assembly.

On this basis, the General Assembly and its Fourth Committee [57] exercise such powers of supervision as have been granted to the United Nations under the Charter and the trusteeship agreements. This raises the issue whether an administering authority is bound to accept recommendations made in its supervisory capacity by the General Assembly or the Trusteeship Council at the request, or with approval, of the Assembly. As

---

[54] See above, p. 281, and below, p. 704.
[55] See above, p. 301.
[56] See above, p. 278.
[57] See above, p. 281.

the administering authority has voluntarily accepted the status of a trustee on the clear understanding that the other contracting party, that is to say, the United Nations, has such powers, much is to be said on balance in favour of a positive answer. Qualifications of this view may be called for in some cases on the ground of more restrictive formulations in individual trusteeship agreements.

It is also possible to argue that the hierarchical relationship between the General Assembly and the Trusteeship Council entitles the former to issue binding instructions to the latter.[58] This view of the matter is not, however, conclusive. The members of the Trusteeship Council represent their governments.[59] The latter may not be prepared to accept the interpretation that, because the Trusteeship Council is an auxiliary body of the General Assembly, it is their bounden duty to make effective a resolution of the General Assembly by going as far as to instruct their delegates on the Council to vote in a particular manner.

As the Union of South Africa has refused to submit the mandated territory of South-West Africa to the trusteeship system,[60] the General Assembly established in 1949 an *ad hoc* committee which became in 1953 the Committee on South-West Africa. Its function is—as recommended in the advisory opinion of the World Court on the *International Status of South-West Africa* (1950)—to assist the Assembly in the exercise of its supervisory jurisdiction. As far as possible, this supervision is to keep within the limits of the functions formerly exercised by the League of Nations in relation to mandated territories. So far, however, the Union of South Africa has boycotted the Committee and in fact administers South-West Africa as if the mandate treaty were no longer in operation.[61]

E. The Secretariat

As the International Court of Justice has already been discussed in the context of judicial international institutions,[62] only the sixth

[58] See above, pp. 298 and 301.
[59] See above, pp. 78 and 299.
[60] See above, p. 56.
[61] See above, p. 56.
[62] See above, p. 233.

and last of the principal organs of the United Nations calls for attention.

It has been suggested that the Secretary-General, and not the Secretariat, constitutes the sixth principal organ of the United Nations. It is true that, in the Charter, some duties are imposed on the Secretary-General, and specific powers have been granted to him in person.[63] Yet, the Secretariat as such is also charged with duties of its own under the Charter.[64]

It is also difficult to see why the hierarchical structure of the Secretariat should militate against the view that the Secretariat, and not merely its head, is the organ in question. The difference between leadership in a bureaucratic organisation and equality in collegiate democracy is very much a question of degree, and to attempt to identify the Secretariat with the Secretary-General appears a misplaced form of hero-worship. Moreover, the view that the Secretariat as such is the principal organ can draw strong support from the Charter. While, in Article 7, the Secretariat is enumerated expressly as one of the principal organs,[65] in Article 97, the position of the Secretary-General as an integral part of the Secretariat is unequivocally affirmed.[66]

1. *Secretary-General and Secretariat*

While any tendency to sever the head from the body must be resisted in the best interest of both, the relation between the Secretary-General and the staff of the Secretariat is necessarily of a hierarchical character. It is a compromise between the directorial system, which subjects officials to the rule of despotism, however restrained and enlightened, and one which is reduced to inefficiency by undue regard for " acquired " rights of individual civil servants.[67]

The staff is appointed by the Secretary-General under staff regulations established by the General Assembly. Their purpose is to guarantee the international character, integrity and efficiency of the United Nations civil service. In matters of appointment, transfer, promotion and termination of appointment, termed in a becoming Americanism " separation from

---

[63] See below, pp. 306 and 721.   [64] See below, p. 721.
[65] See below, p. 701.   [66] See below, p. 721.
[67] See above, p. 302.

service," the Secretary-General exercises a considerable measure of discretionary power.

This discretion is tempered, in the first place, by a number of administrative safeguards in favour of staff members. Moreover, they are entitled to a judicial review by the United Nations Administrative Tribunal of their complaints regarding alleged non-observance of their terms of appointment. Subject to a revisory jurisdiction of the World Court, the judgments of the Tribunal are final.[68]

2. *The Office of the Secretary-General*

The Secretary-General is "appointed" by the General Assembly on the recommendation of the Security Council. For this purpose, an affirmative vote of seven members of the Security Council, including the concurring votes of the permanent members, is required.[69]

In the General Assembly, unless it decides otherwise, a simple majority of the members present and voting suffices for the purpose of making the appointment.[70] As with other Articles of the Charter which are based on the assumption of co-operation between the Security Council and the General Assembly,[71] the Assembly may proceed to the appointment only on a positive recommendation by the Security Council. In the Charter, this act is described as an appointment and not an election. Admittedly, the difference between the two is merely one of emphasis. If effect is to be given to the wording of the Charter, the vote of the Assembly must be understood as the means of establishing articulately the collective will of the General Assembly.

The length of the Secretary-General's term of office is not specified in the Charter. The original tenure of the first two holders of this office has been limited to five years by way of resolutions of the General Assembly. The appointment has, however, been treated as renewable for a further five-year term at the end of the first term of tenure. Under these Resolutions, the procedure prescribed for the original appointment must again

---

[68] See above, p. 241.
[69] See above, p. 273.
[70] See above, p. 273.
[71] See above, p. 267.

be complied with both in the Security Council and the General Assembly.

It proved impossible in 1950 to secure the necessary agreement in the Security Council on either the renewal of Mr. Trygve Lie's appointment or the nomination of any other candidate. The Assembly then proceeded, without a recommendation to this effect by the Security Council, to an extension of Mr. Trygve Lie's term of office for another three years. Whole batteries of arguments for, and against, the constitutional character of this measure have been advanced. While, on pragmatic grounds, something is to be said for the line taken by the General Assembly, it is hard to square it either with the text or spirit of Article 97 of the Charter. Yet, again, neither side was prepared to test its strongly voiced view by an advisory opinion of the World Court.[72]

3. *Nature and Scope of the Powers of the Secretary-General*

In the Charter, the Secretary-General is described as the chief administrative officer of the United Nations.[73] In this capacity he acts, either in person or through deputies, at meetings of the General Assembly, the Security Council, the Economic and Social Council and the Trusteeship Council, and any of these organs may entrust him with additional functions. Finally, under the Charter itself, he is charged with further responsibilities, in particular by Article 99.[74]

It would be unwise to attempt to assess the scope of the powers of the Secretary-General on this basis alone. Personal factors apart, the range of his jurisdiction depends decisively on a complex and highly variable factor: the vigour and cohesion of the other principal organs of the United Nations. Had the Security Council actually worked as had been contemplated at Dumbarton Oaks and San Francisco, the Secretary-General would probably have differed little from his forerunners in the League of Nations. Yet, as the constitutional practice of the United Nations has shaped, the General Assembly has taken on some of the duties of the Security Council.[75] But, owing to its

---

[72] See above, p. 290.
[73] See below, p. 721.
[74] See below, p. 721.
[75] See above, p. 286.

own structural peculiarities, the General Assembly is at a considerable disadvantage as a governing organ in comparison with the Security Council.[76] Moreover, its resolutions are frequently so vague as to leave plenty of scope for imaginative interpretation. Thus, provided that the Secretary-General maintains an attitude of strict neutrality towards the major sectional groupings, more tasks tend to be entrusted to him than Chapter XV of the Charter appears to suggest.

As the office has developed in the practice of the United Nations, the functions fulfilled by the Secretary-General fall into three chief categories. In the order of their importance, they are of a political, representative and administrative character.

(a) The *political* side of this work is illustrated by Mr. Trygve Lie's unobtrusive assistance in 1949 in ending the Russian blockade of Berlin, his successor's informal visit to Peking to secure the release of United States airmen and his continuous efforts at mediation in a number of the world's trouble spots, in particular the Near East.

On the surface at least, these activities are unrelated to the reserve powers granted to the Secretary-General under Article 99 of the Charter, to bring to the attention of the Security Council any matter which, in his opinion, may threaten the maintenance of international peace and security [77] and, under the Rules of Procedure of the General Assembly, to address the Assembly on any question it has under consideration.

(b) The *representative* functions fulfilled by the Secretary-General include the exercise, subject to the approval of the General Assembly,[78] of a treaty-making power on behalf of the United Nations and representation of the United Nations in legal proceedings before national courts, the United Nations Administrative Tribunal, arbitral tribunals and, in connection with requests for advisory opinions, the World Court.[79]

(c) The *administrative* tasks of the Secretary-General comprise a diffuse collection of activities. They extend from responsibility for the registration and publication of treaties [80] and the control

---

[76] See above, p. 278.
[78] See above, p. 279.
[80] See above, p. 146.

[77] See below, p. 308.
[79] See above, p. 77.

of expenditure [81] to the drawing up of the agenda of the General Assembly and other organs as well as the co-ordination and integration of the manifold efforts inside the United Nations.[82]

(d) *Evaluation.* In relation to some of these activities, especially in the political field, the significance of the personal contribution made by the Secretary-General is greater than in relation to others. However, most of the work that is done in his name is of necessity done by others, and his own personal contribution is primarily one of initiation, control and representation. Thus, to view the holder of the office of the Secretary-General of the United Nations otherwise than as the apex of a vast bureaucratic structure would mean to lack either realism or candour.

VI—JURISDICTION

At the beginning of this Chapter, the functions meant to be fulfilled by the United Nations have been summarily sketched.[83] In the context of the organisation of the United Nations, the nature and scope of the powers of each of its principal organs have been shortly explained.[84] It remains to explore the limitations imposed by its constitution on the United Nations *as a whole* in the pursuit of its objectives: maintenance of world order, functional international co-operation, promotion of respect for human rights and international trusteeship.

A. The Maintenance of World Order

To do justice to the efforts of the United Nations in the interest of world peace, it is necessary to obtain a conspectus of the various means employed on the confederate level towards this overriding object. As in the League of Nations and earlier collective systems on similar patterns,[85] a drastic limitation of the right to use force is merely the negative aspect of a more comprehensive programme.

To prevent the strain on these prohibitory rules from becoming intolerable, provision is made for the pacific settlement of international disputes and for the peaceful change of existing law

[81] See above, p. 280.   [82] See above, p. 306.
[83] See above, p. 265.   [84] See above, p. 278.
[85] See above, p. 176.

and rights in extreme cases. In a wider sense, even the objectives of the United Nations in the fields of functional co-operation, the protection of human rights and international trusteeship serve the same ultimate purpose.[86]

So that existing rights should not be at the mercy of brute force, and change take place only in an orderly manner and in accordance with generally accepted equitable principles, a strong system of collective security is to protect the international order against unilateral action. Finally, to subject even the most powerful States to the collective will, disarmament or, at least, a considerable limitation of armaments is an indispensable ingredient of the confederate blueprint.

The Charter of the United Nations bears evidence of attempts, some more hesitant than others, in all these directions.

1. *Limitation of the Resort to Force*

In this respect, the restrictions laid down in the Charter go further than corresponding Articles in the Covenant of the League of Nations and Kellogg Pact. The use of force, otherwise than in self-defence or collective defence, has been made illegal.[87] Automatic judicial verification of the legality of resort to force is, however, lacking.[88] Such binding authority as there is under the Charter to define " aggression "—that is to say, resort to force contrary to legal obligations to refrain from its use—is entrusted to political organs of the United Nations.

Under Article 39 of the Charter,[89] the Security Council may determine the existence of any threat to the peace, breach of the peace or act of aggression. The Council is, however, constitutionally incapable of exercising this power against the will of any of its permanent members.[90]

The most that the General Assembly may do under its improvised jurisdiction in this field is to adopt resolutions expressing its opinion on such issues. These may be of inestimable political and moral significance. However, they lack legally binding force. Even so, an overwhelming vote of the Assembly is likely

[86] See above, p. 266.
[87] See above, p. 174 *et seq.*
[88] See above, p. 183 *et seq.*, and below, p. 584.
[89] See below, p. 708.
[90] See above, pp. 273 and 284.

to confirm those who have in any case decided to act in self-defence or collective defence in the righteousness of their cause and to sway others to commit themselves to their side. Nonetheless, a view expressed by a majority of delegates in a political body amounts to a controversial auto-interpretation of the Charter as much as that of a dissenting minority. None of these government-appointed delegates are judges or even members of a parliament with overriding jurisdiction. Each represents his own state in an essentially deliberative and political body.[91]

2. *The Peaceful Settlement of International Disputes*

The United Nations offers the widest possible choice of legal and non-legal devices for the settlement of disputes.[92] In principle, it is for the parties to decide whether to avail themselves of these opportunities. Yet, if the continuance of a dispute is likely to endanger the maintenance of international peace and security, matters are no longer left exclusively to the parties.

The Security Council may call upon the parties to settle their dispute by one of the means enumerated in Article 33 of the Charter.[93] If the parties are unable to do so, they must refer the dispute to the Security Council.[94] The Council may also, on its own initiative, investigate any dispute or situation which might lead to international friction or give rise to a dispute, in order to determine whether its continuance is likely to endanger the maintenance of international peace and security.[95]

Provision is made for member States [96] and, within narrower limits, non-member States [97] as well as the Secretary-General [98] to bring to the attention of the Security Council matters which, in their opinion, threaten the maintenance of international peace and security. Yet, even if not one of the permanent members, who are not parties to the dispute, exercises its veto power,[99] all the action the Security Council is entitled to take under Chapter VI of the Charter is to make to the parties recommendations which

---

[91] See above, p. 78.
[93] See above, p. 284, and below, p. 707.
[94] See below, p. 708.
[96] See below, p. 707.
[98] See above, p. 307, and below, p. 721.
[99] See above, p. 274.

[92] See above, p. 229.

[95] See below, p. 707.
[97] See below, p. 707.

fall short of being legally binding.[1] If the question is referred to
the General Assembly by the Security Council or brought to its
attention by a member State or non-member State,[2] these procedures also lead to the same optimal result : recommendations.

3. *Peaceful Change*

If parties to a dispute desire its settlement *ex aequo et bono,*
they are free under the Statute of the World Court expressly to
authorise the Court to give a judgment based on equitable
considerations and, if necessary, to override rights otherwise
protected by international law.[3] Similarly, recommendations
made by the Security Council or Assembly under the conciliation
procedure of Chapter VI of the Charter may embody proposals
involving a modification in the existing *status quo.*

In the former case, the judgment of the World Court is
binding, and the Court's jurisdiction depends on the consent of
the parties. In the latter case, the jurisdiction of each of the two
United Nations conciliation organs may be invoked without the
consent of the parties, but their recommendations are not
binding. Only in the case of provisional measures resolved on
by the Security Council under Chapter VII [4] may the *status quo*
be incidentally modified. Any such measures are, however,
without prejudice to the rights, claims or position of the parties.[5]

By and large, this state of affairs reproduces the position
under the Covenant of the League of Nations. Then, too, an
ineffectual effort was made in Article 19 of the Covenant to
provide some machinery by which the League Assembly could
make recommendations for the revision of treaties which had
become " inapplicable " and consider international conditions
the continuance of which might endanger the peace of the world.[6]
Article 14 of the Charter is the counterpart to Article 19 of the
Covenant. Its chief value consists in enlarging the General
Assembly's scope of jurisdiction, if only for purposes of discussion
and recommendation.[7]

---

[1] See above, p. 284.
[3] See above, p. 239, and below, p. 783.
[4] See below, pp. 312 and 708.
[5] See below, p. 708.
[6] See above, p. 156.
[7] See above, p. 278.

[2] See below, p. 707.

4. Collective Security and Disarmament

The investigation of a dispute or situation under Chapter VI of the Charter by the Security Council may culminate in a finding that the dispute or situation is likely to endanger the maintenance of international peace and security. This evaluation may then provide the basis for recommendations or decisions of the Security Council under Article 39—that is to say, under Chapter VII of the Charter. It also entitles the Council to request the parties to comply with any provisional measures the Council may consider necessary or desirable.[8] It has, however, already been explained why the sanctions apparatus of the Charter can be expected to operate only in highly exceptional cases and, even then, hardly as contemplated in the Charter.[9]

The same centrifugal and disintegrating forces which have tended to reduce Chapter VII of the Charter to a memorial to the unity of wartime allies have also prevented a more than nominal implementation of Article 26 of the Charter.[10] This Article already is a retreat from the position on disarmament in the Covenant of the League of Nations. It is left with the Security Council to submit plans to the members of the United Nations for the " regulation " of armaments. A faint echo of disarmament, as it had been envisaged in the Covenant, is to be found only in Article 11 of the Charter.[11] This authorises the General Assembly to consider the principles governing disarmament and the regulation of armaments.

B. The Other Objectives

The jurisdiction of the United Nations in the fields of functional international co-operation [12] and the promotion of respect for human rights [13] is limited to the encouragement of voluntary efforts and programmes. This is not to disparage endeavour on this basis. It may well be thought that free and spontaneous co-operation is socially more valuable than action in dutiful compliance with legal obligations. Yet, for purposes of this

---

[8] See above, p. 311, and below, p. 708.
[9] See above, pp. 177 and 288.
[10] See below, p. 705.
[11] See below, p. 702.
[12] See above, pp. 266 and 292.
[13] See above, pp. 266 and 279.

inquiry, the crucial issue is to delimit the line where the realm of law ends and that of sovereign discretion begins.

Where member States have undertaken binding commitments, that is to say, in relation to trust territories and non-self-governing territories, the jurisdiction of the United Nations is limited, but, by and large, effectively exercised.[14] Beyond this, under the pressure of the General Assembly, the improvised machinery relating to non-political aspects of the administration of non-self-governing territories tends to assimilate colonial administration at large to internationally accountable colonial stewardship.[15]

C. Evaluation

If the maintenance of peace was to be the *raison d'être* of the United Nations, there was wisdom in casting the net widely in drafting its objectives. Yet, if co-operation to this end was to be established between democratic, authoritarian and totalitarian States, and between States whose economies were based on principles of *laissez-faire* and varying forms of capitalist, directionist and socialist planning, this basic decision settled another matter : a drastic limitation of the powers of the United Nations in all spheres affected by these political and economic divergencies.

Thus, a direct connection exists between the pattern of heterogeneous universality [16] and the limitation of the powers of the United Nations in matters of functional international co-operation and human rights. A comparison of the achievements in these spheres with those attained in more homogeneous environments confirms this diagnosis.[17]

On the assumption that this limitation of the powers of the United Nations in matters on the periphery of the main tasks to be performed by the organisation was the price to be paid for a strong world order, this self-denying ordinance was eminently reasonable. Yet was this international order to be made sufficiently strong as to deserve being so called? Doubts have already been voiced in earlier Chapters,[18] and it has been the

---

[14] See above, p. 298 *et seq.*
[15] See above, p. 270.
[16] See above, p. 266.
[17] See below, p. 329 *et seq.*
[18] See above, pp. 147 and 171.

burden of this Chapter to explain why the so-called international order of the United Nations is, at the most, an international quasi-order.

The veto power, the rights of practically unverifiable self-defence and collective defence and reserve powers in relation to former enemy States are all but different facets of the decisive aspect of the matter. The world powers have used the confederate pattern so as to remain free to contract out of their apparent submission to the rule of law under the Charter of the United Nations. In fact, their political sovereignty remains as untamed as ever.[19]

Nothing could, however, be more superficial than to blame the confederate pattern of international organisation for these shortcomings. The renewed choice in 1945 of this pattern is itself a symptom of the gulf that still yawns between the world as a single activity area and the, as yet, very much smaller sectional and competitive loyalty areas of the antagonistic blocs formed under the leadership of hegemonial powers.

Such modicum of international quasi-order and peace as, at present, exists does not rest primarily on the United Nations. The reverse proposition would be nearer to the truth. The United Nations rests on the precarious balance between the world camps which itself is the result of an uneasy nuclear stalemate. Yet, while this breathing space lasts, the framework of the United Nations can be used to give a more positive and constructive meaning to co-existence under fear of co-extermination.

In most ways, this situation differs less than might be thought from that of previous inter-war periods. Apparent progress in international law and organisation is but a reflex of a relatively stable balance of power, but is also as precarious as so unstable a foundation. The vital difference between past and present lies elsewhere : in the appalling price of failure to preserve this quasi-order in the **Nuclear Age**.

[19] See above, p. 271.

CHAPTER 11

THE LAW OF INTERNATIONAL INSTITUTIONS:
III. HYBRID INSTITUTIONS

" Acts are the test of words."
Jeremy Bentham, *Anti-Machiavel* (1789)

A BEWILDERING number and variety of recent institutions still call for consideration. Their existence certainly establishes one point: the uneven pace of integration in world society. The best way of reducing this creative chaos to some kind of order may be to inquire into the needs which they are intended to meet. For this purpose, it is helpful to distinguish between developments on three different levels.

In the Charter itself, provision is made for the efforts of the United Nations to be supplemented by a number of functional institutions on a world scale.[1] Similarly, in Chapter VIII of the Charter regional institutions of a political character are accepted as complementary to the global security system of the United Nations.[2] Moreover, centripetal trends within some regions have encouraged the creation of regional institutions of a functional character. Finally, the very weakness of the global security system of the United Nations has tended to create antagonistic groupings of member States and to consolidate these blocs in institutions of a sectional character.

Thus, the main divisions of the remaining institutions emerge. They fall into the classes of, *first*, functional institutions with universal aspirations, *secondly*, regional institutions, political as well as functional, and, *thirdly*, sectional institutions. They all have in common a hybrid character. In other words, they are best understood as combinations and variations of more basic forms of institutional co-operation.

Analysis in this Chapter will perforce be limited to permanent institutions. Yet, for purposes of more intensive study, some ephemeral institutions may still claim interest. Here it must

[1] See above, p. 256 *et seq.*
[2] See above, p. 178 *et seq.*, and below, p. 355.

315

suffice to recall at least the existence and demise of the most important of those institutions which assisted a war-torn world in finding its feet again.

On a global level, these were the United Nations Relief and Rehabilitation Administration (UNRRA) and the International Refugee Organisation (IRO).[3] For purposes of the comparative study of international institutions, non-permanent regional institutions, such as the Emergency Economic Committee for Europe, whose functions were taken over in 1947 by the Economic Commission for Europe, the European Coal Organisation and the European Central Inland Transport Organisation, also deserve to be remembered.

I—Universalist One-Purpose Institutions

This group consists of fourteen institutions : the twelve specialised agencies of the United Nations, the International Finance Corporation, which is affiliated to the International Bank for Reconstruction and Development, and the General Agreement on Tariffs and Trade (GATT).

A. Common Characteristics

These functional institutions have six features in common.

First, they all work in close contact with the United Nations. Only its character as an interim organisation prevents GATT from being a specialised agency in the formal meaning of the term.[4] All these institutions, except GATT, are linked with the United Nations by relations agreements.[5]

Secondly, each of these institutions is the product of a multilateral treaty. This is one of the features which distinguishes these agencies from functional organs of the United Nations such as the Technical Assistance Administration,[6] UNICEF,[7] or the United Nations Special Fund which are based on resolutions of the General Assembly.

Thirdly, like the United Nations, these institutions are of a comprehensive character, and their organs are entrusted with

---

[3] See above, p. 295.   [4] See above, p. 256.
[5] See above, p. 296.   [6] See above, p. 293.
[7] See above, p. 293.

powers borrowed from most or all types of non-comprehensive international institutions.[8]

Fourthly, differing from the United Nations, these institutions are one-purpose institutions. Admittedly, the objectives of some of these institutions, as, for instance, the International Labour Organisation, the World Health Organisation and UNESCO, are more diffuse than, for instance, those of GATT or the International Atomic Energy Agency. Nevertheless, the purposes served by these institutions are, at least relatively, more homogeneous than those of a multi-purpose institution on the United Nations pattern.

Fifthly, all these institutions aim at universality. This does not exclude that, within a potentially global framework, a number of these institutions, *e.g.*, the World Health Organisation, the International Labour Organisation and the Food and Agriculture Organisation, pay considerable attention to the regional side of their activities. Moreover, the meaning of universality varies with the purpose of each institution. In the case of the World Health Organisation, this must mean absolute universality. Yet, relative universality, extending to all, or the chief, maritime powers, may be all that is necessary to attain the objects of the Inter-Governmental Maritime Consultative Organisation.[9]

Sixthly, as distinct from the automatic membership in the International Labour Organisation of members of the League of Nations, membership in all these functional institutions is now entirely optional.

B. Membership

In most of the constitutions of these functional agencies, States as such are envisaged as members. In others, such as the International Bank, the Monetary Fund, the Finance Corporation and GATT, however, governments are so described. In the constitution of the Postal Union, members are referred to even more casually as " sovereign countries," in that of the Food and Agriculture Organisation as " nations," and in that of the International Telecommunication Union simply as " countries."

Some of these discrepancies in formulation are clearly the result of bad drafting. Yet, a studied understatement of the

[8] See above, p. 227 *et seq.*   [9] See above, p. 253.

contemplated status of an international institution may also assist governments such as the United States Administration in overcoming constitutional difficulties regarding ratification.[10] On occasion, such informality has also served as a reminder to the international civil service of its modest position as compared with that of powerful national bureaucracies. Whether such treaties are drafted as inter-State or inter-governmental agreements, the legal consequences are the same. In either case, the international entity as such is the member, and not the organ which always acts in a purely representative capacity.[11]

1. *Admission to Full Membership*

In all but the most recent institutions in this category, the conditions of original membership are now largely of historical interest. Thus, on this point, only the International Atomic Energy Agency, the Finance Corporation and the Maritime Consultative Organisation call for consideration.

The initial members of the International Atomic Energy Agency are the members of the United Nations or of any specialised agency which have signed the Statute of IAEA within a prescribed time and deposited instruments of ratification. The original members of the Finance Corporation are those members of the International Bank which have subscribed to the Corporation's capital stock, signed the Agreement before the closing date and deposited an instrument of acceptance of the Agreement.

A different method has been adopted in the constitution of the Maritime Consultative Organisation. It is between, first, members of the United Nations which, at any time, may become members of IMCO by signature or acceptance of the Convention; secondly, States not members of the United Nations, but invited to send representatives to the United Nations Maritime Conference of 1948 and entitled to membership on the same footing as the first category, and thirdly, other States not members of the United Nations. These can become parties to the Convention only if, on the recommendation of the IMCO Council, their application has been approved by two-thirds of the full members, and their admission has not been vetoed by the General Assembly of the United Nations.

[10] See above p. 145.   [11] See above, p. 78.

The conditions regulating the admission of ordinary members fall into three main groups. Half the agencies leave the decision to their plenary organs. While most of these require a two-thirds majority of either the total membership or, at least, of votes cast, a simple majority suffices for admission to the World Health Organisation and the Universal Postal Union.

In others, such as the International Atomic Energy Agency, the Maritime Consultative Organisation and UNESCO, the United Nations pattern, that is to say, decision on the application by the plenary meeting on a recommendation by the executive organ, has been chosen.[12] In the case of UNESCO, this procedure applies only to States not members of the United Nations. Members of the United Nations are entitled to become members of UNESCO at their unilateral request. Moreover, in the cases of IMCO[13] and UNESCO membership depends on the General Assembly of the United Nations refraining from exercising its veto power.

Finally, the Fund, the Bank and the Finance Corporation make admission dependent on terms prescribed in individual cases. One of the reasons for this indefiniteness is the need to settle by way of prior negotiation the quotas or shares to be allocated to new members.

2. *Associate Membership*

Only the Statute of the Atomic Energy Agency repeats the formulation of the Charter of the United Nations that the Agency is based on the principle of the sovereign equality of its members.[14] In fact, however, with the exception of the Postal Union, the other agencies apply the same rule and limit full membership to sovereign States. This exception is, however, more apparent than real. The Postal Union has accepted as full members a number of colonies specifically enumerated in its Constitution. Actually, this has meant giving plural votes to the colonial powers concerned while these territories were in a state of dependency.

---

[12] See above, p. 267.
[13] See above, p. 253.
[14] See above, p. 270.

Some of these institutions—the Maritime Consultative Organisation, the Telecommunication Union, the World Health Organisation and the World Meteorological Organisation—make provision for the associate membership of dependent territories. In each case, admission depends in the first place on a request to this effect from the colonial power concerned or, in the case of trust territories, the United Nations. The voting rights of associate members and their eligibility to representation in institutional organs are either excluded or severely limited.

3. *Suspension*

It is a moot point whether, in the absence of express provision to this effect, an international institution may suspend a member. As in all these cases, the conflicting arguments of treaty interpretation are based either on the exclusion of implied limitations of State sovereignty or on the assumption—and in this case, this is probably the preferable view—that the parties must have intended to give the organisation all the powers which are indispensable for the adequate fulfilment of its objectives and not incompatible with the intention expressed in the constituent document.[15] But, if a constitution, such as that of the Labour Organisation, permits suspension from voting rights alone and on specified grounds only, this suggests that suspension on any other ground would be contrary to the intention of the parties.

Nearly half of the institutions concerned have wisely settled the issue by expressly giving the necessary authority to their plenary organs. Suspension of a member from the United Nations leads, at the request of the United Nations, to suspension from UNESCO.[16]

In the Statute of the Atomic Energy Agency, a distinction is made between, in principle, automatic suspension of voting rights in the case of arrears with financial contributions and the case of persistent breaches of other membership obligations. In the latter case, the General Conference may suspend the member by a two-thirds majority of members present and voting, but only upon recommendation by the Board of Governors.

---

[15] See above, pp. 153 and 229.
[16] See above, p. 319.

4. *Expulsion*

It is more doubtful whether an international institution should be granted the power of expulsion, as distinct from suspension. It is, however, arguable that, irrespective of whether such powers are given to an international institution, persistent violations of membership obligations amount to a serious breach of treaty. This then entitles other members to retaliate by way of reprisal by excluding the defaulting member from the organisation.[17]

The constitutions of all three financial agencies—the Monetary Fund, the Bank and the Finance Corporation—provide for suspension procedures possibly leading to expulsion or, as it is termed in the Agreement on the Monetary Fund, a compulsory withdrawal from membership. If, within a specified period, a member of the Civil Aviation Organisation refuses to ratify an amendment to the Constitution which has come into force, the Assembly may decide that the non-ratifying State has ceased to be a member of the Organisation and a party to the Civil Aviation Convention. Expulsion from the United Nations leads to automatic expulsion from UNESCO. Similarly, a resolution of the General Assembly of the United Nations suffices to terminate automatically the membership of any State or territory in the Maritime Consultative Organisation.

5. *Withdrawal*

The World Health Organisation is the only one of the functional agencies under discussion which does not make provision for the voluntary withdrawal of a member. In the abstract, it is arguable that, in the absence of an express provision for withdrawal, the permanency of a treaty must be presumed.[18] Whether this inference is justified is, however, ultimately a question of the intention of the parties to a treaty. Since the implied right of members of the United Nations to withdraw from the Organisation for important reasons has been conceded,[19] it would be difficult without special reason to stretch to any greater length the presumption in favour of the permanency of consensual engagements in the case of other treaties of an institutional type.

---

[17] See above, pp. 157 and 173, and below, p. 636.
[18] See above, p. 155.
[19] See above, p. 268.

As the World Health Conference of 1946 granted a right of withdrawal to dissident members only in the case of the acceptance by the Organisation of a constitutional amendment, it may well be argued that, otherwise, no such implied right of withdrawal exists.

The concern of States for their economic and financial sovereignty has been met by the reservation of an instantaneous right of withdrawal from the Monetary Fund, Bank and Finance Corporation, subject to the settlement of all outstanding obligations. Similarly, in the case of GATT, the period of notice required for withdrawal is merely six months. Otherwise, as with the Universal Postal Union, the period of notice is as a rule one year or, as with the International Labour Organisation, two years.

A member of the Atomic Energy Agency may withdraw at any time after five years from the date of the Agency's Statute coming into operation, or whenever it finds an amendment to the Statute which has been adopted unacceptable.[20] Withdrawal of a member from the Monetary Fund leads to an automatic lapse of membership in the International Bank and Finance Corporation.

C. Organisation

The general scheme of organisation of these functional institutions is one of division of labour between three types of organs: the members' meeting, the executive committee and the secretariat, headed by a Director or Secretary-General. The constitutional structure of the Telecommunication Union is considerably more elaborate than that of most of the other functional agencies. Its principal organs are the *Plenipotentiary Conference*, which is the supreme organ of the Union and, normally, meets every five years, *Administrative Conferences* for more technical issues and meeting simultaneously with the Plenipotentiary Conference, as well as six *permanent* organs: the Administrative Council, the General Secretariat and four technical committees.

The World Meteorological Organisation must needs pay greater attention than other functional institutions of a universalist character to the regional aspects of its work. Thus, its

---

[20] See below, p. 329.

Regional Meteorological Organisations rank on the same footing as its other principal organs.

GATT, with its members' meeting—the sessions of the Contracting Parties—and a modest Secretariat, constitutes the other extreme.[21] The explanation is that GATT was meant to constitute merely a provisional skeleton organisation until the Charter adopted in 1948 at the Havana Conference on Trade and Employment and, with it, the International Trade Organisation came into operation. Due to the failure of the United States to ratify the Havana Convention and sustained opposition from a variety of powerful vested interests, it proved impossible to realise this comprehensive scheme. If and when the necessary number of acceptances has been received, GATT will be replaced by the Organisation for Trade Co-operation (OTC), a more limited undertaking with three principal organs conforming to type.

It will become apparent from a closer comparative analysis that, in spite of apparent similarities, considerable structural differences exist between the corresponding organs of some of those functional institutions.

1. *The Members' Meeting*

In each of these agencies, the plenary organ discharges four responsibilities. *First*, either alone, as in the ILO, or together with the executive committee, as in the Atomic Energy Agency, it is responsible for the election of new members. Only in the Postal Union—in this respect an anachronism—is admission of new members not made a duty of any Union organ, but remains the responsibility of the governments of the member States. Applications for admission are addressed to the Swiss Government and forwarded by the latter to the member States. The success of the application depends on approval by at least two-thirds of the member States.

Secondly, the plenary meeting elects the members of the executive committee other than those designated in some instances, as in the Monetary Fund and the International Bank, by individual members. *Thirdly*, the members' meeting has the chief control of the budget and, *fourthly*, it is the chief deliberating body of each of these institutions.

---

[21] See below, p. 654 *et seq.*

The functional interests most directly concerned and the specialised knowledge they represent obtain the maximum of open recognition they have so far received in the International Labour Organisation.[22] This tripartite pattern has not, however, been followed in the composition of the plenary meeting of any other of these institutions.[23] Actually, policy has been put in reverse. The prevailing view is expressed with unmistakable pointedness in the constitution of UNESCO : " The General Conference shall consist of the representatives of the States Members of the Organisation."

In a minor key, use has been made of the principle of functional representation in the creation of an Advisory Council attached to the International Bank. It is composed of at least seven representatives of banking, commercial, industrial, labour and agricultural interests, and they are selected by the Board of Governors, the plenary organ of the World Bank. The task of the Council is to advise the Bank on matters of general policy. In the Constitution of the Meteorological Organisation it is provided that the principal delegate of each member in the Congress is to be the director of its meteorological service.

The position of the plenary organ in relation to the executive committee varies considerably in these institutions. The supremacy of the members' meeting over all other organs is asserted unequivocally in the constitutions of the Monetary Fund, the International Bank, the World Meteorological Organisation and the Telecommunication Union. In the Constitution of the Civil Aviation Organisation, the same idea is expressed in the form of the delegation of powers by the Assembly to the Council which remains " responsible " to it. Moreover, the Assembly's jurisdiction over all residuary matters which are not expressly assigned to the Council is expressly reserved.

In institutions such as the Maritime Consultative Organisation, the position of the members' meeting is considerably weaker. Regular sessions of its Assembly take place only every two years and, between the sessions, the Council exercises all but the quasi-legislative functions of the Organisation. Half-way between are placed those functional institutions whose plenary

[22] See above, p. 260, and below, p. 639.
[23] See below, p. 347.

organs, like that of the Labour Organisation,[24] perform largely quasi-legislative tasks. They form a more vital part in the institutional life of their organisation than, for instance, the congresses of a largely administrative and co-ordinating body such as the Postal Union.

2. *The Executive Committee*

The major considerations in the representation of members in the executive committee are to ensure adequate representation of, first, the leading member States in the functional field concerned and, secondly, all relevant regions of the world.

Thus, half of the sixteen persons representing governments in the Governing Body of the Labour Organisation are appointed by the member States of chief industrial importance. Their identity is determined by the Governing Body in accordance with a procedure which is designed to ensure the application of relatively objective tests. Candidates for the other sixteen seats are elected respectively by the employers' and workers' delegates to the Conference. Two employers' and two workers' representatives must belong to non-European States.

The Board of Governors of the Atomic Energy Agency adopts a similar system for the selection of the members most advanced in the technology of atomic energy, including the production of source materials. The eight areas to be taken into account are North America, Latin America, Western Europe, Eastern Europe, Africa and the Middle East, South Asia, South East Asia and the Pacific and, finally, the Far East.

In some of these institutions, such as UNESCO, the Health Organisation and the Civil Aviation Organisation, all members of the executive committee are elected by the members' meeting. In others, such as the International Bank, each of the five members having the largest number of shares appoints his own nominee. The remaining seven are elected by all the Governors other than those of the five appointing members.

In some of the constitutions it is provided that, in electing members of the executive committee, the members' meeting should keep in mind the requisite professional qualifications of

[24] See above, p. 261.

candidates. Such an injunction is especially appropriate if, as in the cases of the Postal Union and Health Organisation, the meeting merely elects the member States to be represented on the executive committee and leaves it to each of these to designate its own representative.

Failing any express provision to the contrary, delegates in any international institution are representatives of their member States.[25] If members of an executive committee are to fulfil more independent functions, this must be expressly stipulated. Thus, it is stated in the Constitution of UNESCO, and similarly in that of the Meteorological Organisation, that the members of the Executive Board shall exercise the powers delegated to them by the General Conference " on behalf of the Conference as a whole and not as representatives of their respective governments."

The executive committees of some of these institutions, as, for instance, the Civil Aviation Organisation, are in permanent session. Moreover, during the intervals between the sessions of the members' meeting, some of these executive committees are authorised to exercise most of the powers of the organisation.[26]

3. *The Secretariat*

The frequency of the sessions of the members' meeting and the *de facto*, rather than *de jure*, permanency of the executive committee are two of the major factors which determine the degree of effective supervision of the secretariat. The identity of the organ appointing and controlling the head of the secretariat, the length of the appointment of the Director or Secretary-General and other terms of his contract of service, in particular the grounds for earlier termination of the appointment, are other decisive elements in this relationship. On the level of the constitution, the appointing and controlling bodies alone are normally determined. The other issues are left to be dealt with in the resolution passed on the appointment or in the contract.

In a number of agencies, for instance, the Food and Agriculture Organisation and Monetary Fund, the appointment of the Director or Secretary-General is exclusively in the hands

[25] See above, p. 78.
[26] See above, p. 322.

of the members' meeting. In others, such as the Health Organisation, the members' meeting acts on the recommendation of the executive committee. In the Atomic Energy Agency, the Board of Governors, with the approval of the General Conference, makes the appointment, and the term of office is fixed at four years in the Constitution. In institutions following the pattern of the Labour Organisation, the appointment of the Director-General is the exclusive responsibility of the executive committee.

Again, the identity of the supervisory body varies. While the Director of the Food and Agriculture Organisation is under the general supervision of the Conference and the Council, the President of the International Bank is under the control of the Executive Directors. Finally, the central office of the Postal Union works under the general supervision of the Swiss Postal Administration.

D. Jurisdiction and Powers

The scope of the jurisdiction of the fourteen agencies under discussion varies considerably, ranging from the Health and Labour Organisations to institutions such as the Monetary Fund and GATT, with considerably more compact functions.[27]

It still remains to examine five features of these organisations: voting rules, power to take action, procedures for the settlement of disputes, sanctions against defaulting members and, finally, the revision of the constituent instruments.

1. *Voting*

All but three of these institutions are based on the rule of one vote for each member.[28] Only the three monetary and financial institutions apply the rules of votes weighted according to the quota of gold and currency or the amount of capital contributed. All accept the majority rule. On routine questions, a simple majority usually suffices. For matters declared important by the constitution or the members' meeting, a qualified majority—as a rule a two-thirds majority of those present and voting—is required.

[27] See above, p. 252.
[28] See above, p. 254.

2. *Powers*

The nature of the powers of the fourteen functional agencies varies with the scope of their jurisdiction. The wider the jurisdiction of the institution, as with the Food and Agriculture Organisation, the Labour Organisation and UNESCO, the more its power tends to be limited to the promotion of voluntary co-ordination of efforts, recommendations and the initiation of draft conventions.

Conversely, the more concrete its tasks—as are those of the three monetary and financial institutions or the Atomic Energy Agency—the greater are the chances of the institution to escape from the frustrating atmosphere of permanent deliberation and peroration.

3. *Disputes*

A number of the functional agencies are entitled to request the World Court for advisory opinions on any legal question arising within the scope of their jurisdiction.[29] Issues concerning the mutual relations between the institution in question and the United Nations or other specialised agencies are, however, excluded from this authorisation.

Disputes between members and between members and the institution on the interpretation and application of the constitution must, as a rule, first be submitted to settlement inside the organisation. If the matter cannot be disposed of in this way, provision is normally made for a decision by an outside judicial organ such as the World Court or an arbitrator.

In the case of the three monetary and financial institutions, the decision of the members' meeting is, in principle, final. Provision for judicial settlement is made only in the case of disagreement during the state of liquidation of the institution or in connection with the withdrawal of a member.

4. *Sanctions*

In addition to the powers of expulsion and suspension,[30] two of these institutions—the Civil Aviation Organisation and the Labour Organisation—are authorised by their constitutions to

[29] See above, p. 240.
[30] See above, p. 321.

apply further sanctions against defaulting members. Such value as clauses of this type may claim lies chiefly in the prophylactic effect of their existence. The real guarantee of compliance by members with their obligations is the system of sanctions which is immanent in legal rules based on the principle of reciprocity.[31]

5. *Revision*

In nearly all these constitutions, the danger of absolute rigidity has been avoided and provision made for their amendment. Those of the three monetary and financial institutions are in this respect more conservative than those of the other functional agencies. Frequently, a two-thirds majority of all members or only those present and voting is required. In some institutions, as, for instance, UNESCO, an amendment so accepted becomes binding on all members. In the case of others, such as the Meteorological Organisation, the amendment is not binding on dissenting States if it imposes new obligations on members. In others again, such as the Civil Aviation Organisation, the dissenting member is not automatically bound, but may be excluded by the members' meeting, or, as in the Atomic Energy Agency, is bound by the amendment, but free to withdraw from the organisation. On the basis of a declaratory statement incorporated in the records of the World Health Conference of 1946, this is the position also in the World Health Organisation.

II—REGIONAL INSTITUTIONS

Regional institutions fall into three distinct groups: multi-purpose, one-purpose and supra-national institutions.

A. Multi-Purpose Institutions

A number of institutions belong to this group: the Organisation of American States (1948), the Council of Europe (1949), the Organisation of Central American States (Charter of San Salvador —1951), the Northern Council (1952), and the Benelux Inter-parliamentary Consultative Council (1955).[32] All these institutions are on the confederate level. From the institutional

---

[31] See above, p. 10.   [32] See below, p. 357.

point of view, two of these, the Organisation of American States (OAS) and the Council of Europe, may claim particular interest.

1. *The Organisation of American States*

This Organisation constitutes the culmination of attempts at regional co-operation which go back to the Commercial Bureau of the American Republics (1890), since 1910 called the Pan-American Union. Intensified collaboration in the Western Hemisphere during the Second World War led to the Act of Chapultepec of 1945. In a rudimentary form, this already contains some of the salient features of the Bogotá Charter of 1948, the constituent instrument of OAS.

The Act of Chapultepec antedated by several months the Charter of the United Nations. Its existence considerably affected the formulation of Chapter VIII of the United Nations Charter on Regional Arrangements.[33]

(a) The *objects* of OAS, as set out in its Charter, are to achieve peace and justice, promote the solidarity of the American States, strengthen their collaboration, and defend their sovereignty, territorial integrity and independence.

From the twelve principles re-affirmed in the Charter of OAS, the following may be singled out: " International law is the standard of conduct of States in their reciprocal relations "; " good faith shall govern the relations between States "; " victory does not give rights "; " social justice and social security are bases of lasting peace "; " the American States proclaim the fundamental rights of the individual without distinction as to race, nationality, creed and sex " and recognise the need for " close co-operation for the high purposes of civilisation." They also accept the principle of good neighbourliness, in particular as applied to their economic relations.

Beyond this, the Charter contains an extensive catalogue of fundamental rights and duties of States. Its emphasis on the principle of the equality of States[34] and the prohibition of intervention[35] is symptomatic of widespread anxieties in Latin

[33] See below, p. 711 *et seq.*
[34] See above, p. 58.
[35] See above, p. 59.

America and, probably, as much directed against the United States as outsiders.

This catalogue of rights and duties has a double significance. It shows how, beyond the point of a restatement of existing law, additional political, ethical and ideological postulates can be legitimately received into the body of international law.[36] Yet, it also offers telling evidence of the limited value of such declamations on the confederate level.[37]

(b) *Membership* is open to all American States which ratify the Charter of OAS and, with the exception of Canada, all American States have done so. The constitution does not provide for the suspension or exclusion of members. A member may, however, withdraw from the Organisation by written notice to the Secretariat.

(c) *Organisation*. The *Inter-American Conference* is the members' meeting of OAS and its supreme organ. It continues the traditions of the periodic conferences of the Pan-American Union. The Conference meets normally every five years and may consider any matter relating to friendly relations among American States.

The *Meeting of Consultation* consists of the ministers of foreign affairs of the member States or, exceptionally, special delegates representing them. It is a deliberative body for the consideration of urgent problems of common interest.

Any member State may request that a Meeting of Consultation be called. The Council of OAS decides on this request. In the case of an armed attack " within the territory of an American State " or " within the region of security delimited by treaties in force " the Meeting of Consultation is convened by the Chairman of the Council. The Meeting of Consultation is assisted by the *Inter-American Peace Committee* and an *Advisory Defence Committee*, both located in Washington, D.C.

The *Council* is the equivalent of the Governing Body of the Pan-American Union. It is subordinated to the Assembly and Meeting of Consultation, but, in fact, it is the permanent " executive " organ of OAS. Its primary duties are co-ordination of the activities of the Organisation, supervision of the Secretariat

---

[36] See above, p. 12.
[37] See above, p. 265.

and approval of the OAS budget. In emergencies, the Council may also act provisionally as the Organ of Consultation until the Foreign Ministers' Meeting of Consultation can take place.

The *Inter-American Economic and Social Council*, the *Inter-American Council of Jurists* and the *Inter-American Cultural Council* are advisory organs of the Council with " technical autonomy."

The former Pan-American Union has been made, under its old name, the *General Secretariat* of OAS and is situated in Washington, D.C. It is headed by a Secretary-General, who is elected by the Council for a ten-year term, but is not re-eligible. He also may not be succeeded by a person of the same nationality. The Secretary-General is the legal representative of the Union. The Constitution also makes provision for *Specialised Conferences* and *Specialised Organisations* of a functional character.

(d) *Scope of Jurisdiction.* The substantive scope of the jurisdiction of OAS is comparable to that of comprehensive and multi-purpose institutions of the United Nations type.

In the field of collective security, the OAS Charter refers back to the Inter-American Treaty of Reciprocal Assistance of 1947, known as the Rio Treaty. As collective regional action under Chapter VIII of the United Nations Charter requires *prior* authorisation by the Security Council,[38] the Rio Treaty is formulated primarily as a treaty of collective defence under Article 51 of the Charter of the United Nations.[39] On this basis, collective action may be continued *until* stopped by the Security Council. It is arguable that, for this purpose, a mere decision by the Security Council does not by itself suffice, but that it requires the taking of " measures necessary to maintain international peace and security."[40]

(e) *Powers.* The Inter-American Conference corresponds to the General Assembly of the United Nations and, like it, is essentially a deliberative organ. In accordance with the Charter, each member State has one vote. Otherwise, the rules of procedure for each session are prepared by the Council and submitted for consideration to the member States. Apart from

---

[38] See below, p. 711.
[39] See above, p. 175.
[40] See below, p. 708.

cases enumerated in the constitution in which a two-thirds majority is required, decisions may be taken by an absolute majority of members present at the meeting.

In other than procedural matters, for which a simple majority suffices, the Meeting of Consultation takes decisions by a two-thirds majority. In the case of decisions under the Rio Treaty, only members who have ratified the Treaty are entitled to vote. Directly interested parties are excluded from voting, but only if the dispute is one between American States. While such decisions, including those involving the application of diplomatic and economic sanctions, are binding on all members, no member is under any duty to employ armed force without its own consent.

The Council is entitled to formulate its own regulations. In matters concerned with the initiation of consultation and the fulfilment of liaison functions under the Rio Treaty, the Council acts by an absolute majority of the members entitled to vote. The same grounds of exclusion from voting apply as in the Meeting of Consultation.

Amendments to the Charter may be adopted only at an Inter-American Conference convened for this purpose. They enter into force on ratification by two-thirds of the member States, but only in relation to those which have done so. To work this system in practice calls for no mean measure of virtuosity.

(f) *Evaluation.* The over-organisation of OAS is striking. In particular, the three advisory Councils suffer from disparities between width of jurisdiction and dearth of powers not unknown in universalist institutions on the confederate level.[41]

If anything, the Inter-American Council of Jurists and the Inter-American Juridical Committee, its permanent technical commission, have outdone the International Law Commission in the production of draft conventions and reports.[42] Even on a regional level, the translation of such preparatory work into operative conventions is a painfully slow process. Nonetheless, over the years, quite a respectable body of inter-American treaty law has come into existence.[43]

Perhaps the least unreal part of the achievement of OAS is

[41] See above, p. 50.
[42] See above, p. 282.
[43] See above, p. 2.

its machinery for the peaceful settlement of inter-American disputes. It is unfortunate that this largely constructive record should have been marred by the treatment of the intervention by " unknown " powers in Guatemala (1954). In this case, under active leadership by the United States, the procedures of both OAS and the United Nations were ingeniously put in reverse so as to reduce to meaninglessness the prohibition of intervention " enshrined " in the Bogotá Charter.

2. *The Council of Europe*

Operating perhaps too unostentatiously from Strasbourg, the Council of Europe is the West European counterpart to the Organisation of American States. Like OAS, its Statute of 1949 has a strongly ideological flavour. Civilisation, individual freedom, political liberty, the rule of law and " genuine " democracy are its watchwords.

(a) *Membership.* Founding members are the Benelux countries, Denmark, Norway, Sweden, France, Ireland, Italy and the United Kingdom. Other European States may become members on being invited by the Committee of Ministers after consultation with the Assembly. An applicant must accept the principles of the rule of law and of the enjoyment by all persons within its jurisdiction of human rights and fundamental freedoms. In this way, Greece, Iceland, Turkey, the German Federal Republic and Austria have been admitted.

In special circumstances, a European country which is able and willing to comply with the ideological conditions of membership may be admitted as an associate member entitled to be represented only in the Consultative Assembly. Until her admission as a full member in 1951, the Federal Republic of Germany was an associate member, and so was the Saar before her reintegration into Germany.

The Committee of Ministers may suspend and exclude members. Withdrawal is by notice to the Secretary-General.

(b) *Organisation.* If democracy is one of the Council's ideals, its own organisation reflects a somewhat authoritarian variant of control from below. In contrast to the Charter of the Organisation of American States, the emphasis in the Statute is very much on the Committee of Ministers. It required an express amendment of the Statute to remove at least some of the apron strings by which the Committee of Ministers had intended to tie the Consultative Assembly.

The *Committee of Ministers* consists of the ministers of foreign affairs of the member States, or their alternates. Members take the chair in rotation for a session. To the extent to which the word is appropriate in this context,[44] the Committee of Ministers " acts " on behalf of the Council and, with a few reservations in favour of the Assembly, decides also all internal matters. In principle, the Council meets in private. The Committee of Ministers is served by the Committee of Ministers' Deputies, often consisting of permanent representatives of member States, and a number of expert committees.

The *Consultative Assembly*, composed of one hundred and thirty-five members, is the deliberative organ of the Council. Representation in the Assembly is weighted to give eighteen seats each to France, Germany, Italy and the United Kingdom, seventeen to the Benelux countries and the rest to the other members of the Council.[45]

Normally, the representatives of each member State are elected by its parliament or appointed as that parliament decides. Members of the Assembly may not at the same time be members of the Committee of Ministers. The Assembly elects its own President who controls its proceedings. As a rule, it meets once a year for a maximum period of one month, and meetings are held in public. Although with some difficulties, the Assembly has secured the consent of the Committee of Ministers for the Assembly's committees to meet also between its sessions.

Under rules of procedure drawn up by the Committee of Ministers in consultation with the Assembly, members of the Committee of Ministers may address the Assembly on behalf of the Committee or in their individual capacity. A *Joint Committee*, established in 1950 by a procedure falling short of a formal amendment of the Statute,[46] provides an additional channel of contact between the Committee of Ministers and the Assembly.

[44] See below, p. 336.
[45] See below, p. 657.
[46] See above, pp. 155 and 291.

The *Secretariat* serves both the Committee of Ministers and the Assembly. Its Secretary-General and Deputy Secretary-General are appointed by the Assembly on the recommendation of the Committee of Ministers which controls the Secretariat.

(c) *Jurisdiction and Powers.* With the exception of defence matters, the organs of the Council may concern themselves with any aspect of the promotion of greater unity between the member States. In practice, the Consultative Assembly has not always observed this limitation. By Article 1 of the Statute, the Council's jurisdiction covers " economic, social, cultural, scientific, legal and administrative matters " as well as human rights and fundamental freedoms. As one has come to expect on the confederate level, this width of jurisdiction is matched only by the paucity of powers entrusted to the Council.

Voting in the Committee of Ministers is normally by a two-thirds majority of its members. Each member has one vote. Procedural and minor decisions of a financial and administrative character may be taken by a simple majority of the members. Resolutions on matters classified as important—in a highly relative sense—must be passed unanimously by the representatives voting and include a majority of all the members.

Members of the Assembly are State representatives. In practice, however, no attempt is made to force national bloc votes, and members vote in their individual capacity. While recommendations by the Assembly to the Committee of Ministers require a two-thirds majority, other resolutions are adopted by a simple majority.

With the exception of decisions of a purely internal character, the powers of the Committee of Ministers and the Consultative Assembly do not extend beyond the expression of opinion or of recommendation.

(d) *Amendments* fall into three categories. Under the first procedure, amendments must be acceptable to the Committee of Ministers, which then makes its recommendations to the member States. If such amendments decisively affect the existing structure of the Council, recommendations require unanimity.[47] Otherwise a two-thirds majority suffices.[48] An

[47] See above, p. 254.
[48] See above, p. 254.

amending protocol comes into force when ratified by two-thirds of the member States. Under this procedure, the somewhat undignified position of the Consultative Assembly has been to some extent alleviated.[49]

Minor revisions concerning the Assembly and finance merely require approval by both principal organs. Finally, in 1951, the Committee of Ministers evolved a procedure of *de facto* revision by the adoption, and communication to the Assembly, of texts of a statutory character. They are rules of a constitutional character which supplement, but in no way contradict, the provisions of the Statute.[50]

(e) *Evaluation*. In forty-two Articles, the authors of the Statute succeeded in saving the Contracting Parties from tangible legal commitments towards the unification of Europe. However, in spite of the anxiety shown in particular by the representatives of the United Kingdom to avoid being pushed further by the dynamic events than they intended to become involved in this venture, the Council's record is better than might in the circumstances be expected.

Thanks to persistent prodding by the Consultative Assembly, the Council is building up a common law of Western Europe by means of multilateral conventions in the ideological, humanitarian, social and technical fields. So far, the European Convention on Human Rights of 1950 is the most important contribution made by the Council in this quasi-legislative capacity. Its object is to safeguard the rule of law in the Western meaning of the term and basic political freedoms of the individual, including his right to associate with others for political and economic purposes. Parties to the Convention may extend its application to their dependent territories wherever situated.

Machinery on the national and international levels for the observance of these standards is provided in the Convention. Unless parties expressly accept the right of petition by individuals,[51] the European Commission of Human Rights may concern itself only with alleged breaches of the Convention which are referred to it by a Contracting Party. Similarly, the jurisdiction

---

[49] See above, p. 335.
[50] See above, p. 155.
[51] See above, p. 302.

of the European Court of Human Rights is purely optional even
for parties to the Convention.[52]

B. Regional One-Purpose Institutions

Functional institutions of a regional character are of four
different types.   The United Nations has created in its commissions regional agencies with far-reaching autonomy on the
pattern of the Economic Commission for Europe.[53] Universalist
one-purpose institutions, such as the International Labour and
Meteorological Organisations [54] rely to varying degrees on
regional organs of their own.   In both these cases, the regional
agencies or organs operate within the framework of universalist
institutions and themselves lack distinct legal personality.

The regional multi-purpose organisation of the American
States also uses this type of dependent specialised regional
agency.[55]   In addition, however, it is surrounded by related one-
purpose institutions of a regional character, such as the Inter-
American Institute of Agricultural Sciences (1944), the Pan-
American Sanitary Organisation (1950) and the Inter-American
Development Bank (1959).

Finally, a number of independent one-purpose institutions
of a functional and regional character have sprung up all over
the world since the Second World War.   Leaving Europe aside
for the moment, there are in the Atlantic area the Postal Union
of the Americas and Spain (1946), the Caribbean Commission
(1946) and the International Commission for the Northwest
Atlantic Fisheries (1949).   A General Fisheries Council for the
Mediterranean (1949) has also been established.   Africa is represented by the Scientific Council for Africa South of the Sahara
(1951) and the Commission for Technical Co-operation in Africa
South of the Sahara (1954).

The International Islamic Economic Organisation (1949)
covers the Near and Middle East.   The radius of operation of
the Colombo Plan Organisation (1950) is fully described by its
official title: Council for Technical Co-operation in South and

---

52 See above, p. 165.
53 See above, p. 316.
54 See above, p. 316.
55 See above, p. 330

South-East Asia. Finally, the South Pacific Commission (1947) and the International North Pacific Fisheries Commission (1952) should be mentioned.

All these institutions constitute adaptations in a simplified form of patterns familiar from the classical types of permanent conferences, administrative institutions and the universalist variant of functional institutions.[56] Yet, among the corresponding institutions in Western Europe,[57] one at least has more significant features of its own: the Organisation for European Economic Co-operation (OEEC—1948).

1. *Objects*

OEEC was primarily created for the administration of United States aid under the Marshall Plan. From the beginning, however, its long-term objective was defined as nothing less than the achievement of a sound European economy through the economic co-operation of its members.

2. *Membership*

The original members are Austria, Benelux, the three Scandinavian countries, France, Greece, Iceland, Ireland, Italy, Portugal, Switzerland, Turkey, the United Kingdom and the Commanders-in-Chief of the three Western occupation zones of Germany.

With the assent of the Council of the Organisation, which requires unanimity,[58] other European countries may accede to the Convention for European Economic Co-operation. In this way, they become automatically members of OEEC. This opportunity was meant to be available to any European State, including the Communist States of Eastern Europe. This feature of OEEC, that is to say, that it is an " open " institution, distinguishes it from the " closed " organisations of a sectional character.[59] At least on the surface, the Council for Mutual Economic Aid (COMECON—1949), which is the Russian-sponsored retort to OEEC, is also an open organisation.

---

[56] See above, pp. 250, 257 and 316.
[57] See below, p. 656.
[58] See below, p. 341.
[59] See below, p. 355.

The Federal Republic of Germany succeeded the zonal representatives of the Occupation Powers in 1949 without formal admission. Also, in a manner not provided for in the constitution, the United States of America and Canada became Associate Members, and arrangements have been made for limited participation by Spain and Yugoslavia in the work of the Organisation. In 1959, Spain exchanged this status for full membership.

If a member State refuses to carry out its obligations under the Convention, the others may decide by mutual agreement to " continue their co-operation within the Organisation without that member," that is to say, to treat him as being no longer a party to the Convention [60] and, thus, as expelled from OEEC. Withdrawal is effected by twelve months' notice to the French Government.

3. *Organisation*

The *Council*, which is the members' meeting, is the principal organ of OEEC. Its routine meetings are attended by civil servants from the permanent delegations or ministries of member States. On more important occasions, representation is on a ministerial level.

The *Executive Committee*, consisting of seven members designated annually by the Council, works under " general and specific instructions " of the Council. It fulfils, in fact, the functions of a preparatory and scrutinising committee for the Council. At the head of the *Secretariat* is a Secretary-General appointed by, and responsible to, the Council.

The Council has made liberal use of its authority to establish subordinate organs for the performance of the Organisation's functions. It is advised by technical committees, composed of government representatives, and by boards, consisting of experts who are nominated by their governments, but serve in an individual capacity.

The most important of the Organisation's specialised organs, the European Payments Union, was established by a separate treaty (1950) for the purpose of making the currencies of members mutually transferable and, thus, to encourage multilateral trade. It has been superseded by the European Fund, operating under the European Monetary Agreement of 1955.

[60] See below, p. 657.

Similarly, the European Productivity Agency (1953), a largely autonomous body inside OEEC, serves to assist members in increasing the development of their production, above all the progressive modernisation of their equipment and techniques. Finally, the European Nuclear Energy Agency (1957) operates under the ultimate authority of the Council of OEEC for the promotion of co-operation between members in the use of nuclear energy for peaceful purposes. It must be distinguished both from the European Organisation for Nuclear Research (1953), sponsored by UNESCO, and from EURATOM, one of the three supranational organisations of " little Europe." [61]

All these specialised organs of OEEC operate within the framework of the Organisation, that is to say, they lack separate legal personality.

It is convenient to mention in this context also two European technical institutions outside OEEC, but closely linked with it. The one is the Customs Co-operation Council (1950), created as a complement to OEEC and with a predominantly European membership. The other is the Conference of Ministers of Transport (1953), which came into existence by the efforts of OEEC. By way of contrast, the idea of a European Civil Aviation Conference germinated in the Council of Europe, but the Conference is linked administratively with the International Civil Aviation Organisation.

4. *Jurisdiction and Powers*

In principle, OEEC is based on the unanimity rule. In particular, this applies to any revision of its objects and powers. Member States which do not wish to be committed in any particular case by the action of the Organisation, but do not want to stand in the way of others on matters which, in their own view, do not affect them, may declare themselves not interested in such issues. Then, their abstention does not impair the vote. Such a decision is, however, binding only on the members voting in favour of the proposal.

The Code of Liberalisation of Trade and Invisible Transactions adopted and revised by decisions of the Council is one of the outstanding instances of the process of strengthening the

[61] See below, p. 343.

multilateral framework of international economic law by way of decisions of the Council.

The Legal Adviser of OEEC has rightly drawn attention to interesting techniques employed in the constitutional practice of the Organisation to create further flexibility by the creation of categories of decisions with limited effect. This has been achieved by the acceptance of reservations, for instance, on the grounds of possible constitutional or policy objections of the home government of the delegate making such a reservation.[62] Frequently, the Council has also found that the exercise of the lesser power of recommendation suffices. If the parties are convinced of the need for joint action, they will take it irrespective of the label of the resolution. If not, the necessary unanimity for a decision would, in any case, be lacking.

In contrast to decisions of supra-national institutions,[63] the implementation of decisions of OEEC rests with each member State. The formal sanction of expulsion as an " ultimate weapon " has already been noted.[64] This is, however, hardly the clue to the creditable record of members in living up to their obligations to OEEC. The explanation lies in the character of the obligations undertaken in Part I of the Convention. In these Articles, the Parties have committed themselves to a co-ordinated development of their own economies by the greatest possible interchange of goods and services, the reduction of tariffs and other restrictions of imports, the maintenance of monetary stability and full employment.

These obligations differ in kind from those of classical international economic law. While the purpose of bilateral treaties on this footing is to secure compliance with primarily negative duties of abstention and non-interference,[65] the object of the OEEC Convention is to engender positive action on mutually agreed lines. In particular, to the extent to which these duties involve a greater intensity of effort towards a common goal, the legislative problem is not one of finding rigid measuring rods, but of finding elastic standards and tests of the degree of approximation to jointly fixed, and revised, targets. There are

---

[62] See below, p. 659.
[63] See below, p. 351.
[64] See above, p. 340.
[65] See above, p. 102 *et seq.*

unavoidable elements of variability and relativity in these assessments which call for the type of flexible, but firm institutional framework that OEEC provides.

C. Supra-National Institutions

The last category of regional institutions of a functional character is that of supra-national institutions. On the official level, this term was first used in Article 9 of the Treaty constituting the European Coal and Steel Community (ECSC—1951). This was to be followed by the European Defence Community. Owing to French uneasiness, however, over the integration of her own army into a European army, the Defence Community failed to materialise. In spite of this setback, two other institutions on the model of the Coal and Steel Community have been established: the European Economic Community (EEC—1957) and the European Atomic Energy Community (EURATOM—1957).

1. *Formative Factors*

To avoid the danger of overgeneralisation, it is necessary to explain the very special needs which gave rise to this form of functional centralisation on a regional basis.

An objective need existed to organise in the most efficient form the optimum area of monopolistic industries in Western Europe, such as coal and steel. As is shown by the proposals made since 1923 by German financial experts for a West European economic community and by the cartel agreements of the pre-1939 period, these and other industries had even then outgrown the confines of the national State. This development was fully in line with the ever increasing process of concentration in all types of contemporary economy. Some of the subjective needs sprang from the obstacles impeding the political federation of Western Europe and from the irritation caused on the Continent by apparently interminable vacillations in British policy towards European integration. Growing impatience, fostered by awareness in interested quarters of the potentialities of an exclusively Continental alignment, then became canalised into schemes for a " Little Europe," consisting of the Benelux countries, France, the Federal Republic of Germany and Italy. If, for the time being, the political federation of this area was beyond reach, functional federation might prove a circuitous, but perhaps even surer way towards this goal. Had not the German customs union (1834) paved the way for Bismarck's German federation ?

2. *Functional Federalism*

As political federalism removes the frontiers between member States for all purposes for which a federal power has been created, so functional federation makes frontiers meaningless in corresponding economic, social and other technical fields.

The test applied so far in distinguishing between *political* federation and confederation has been whether, in the exercise of its functions, any of the principal organs of the union has direct access to the citizens of the member States.[66] In dealing with *functional* federation, it may be advisable to make two additional propositions articulate. The one is that federal organs must exist which are not subject to direction by the member States as such. On the level of traditional international institutions, this is accepted only in relation to judicial institutions.[67] The other is that the organs in question must be endowed with competences of more than a merely deliberative and consultative character. If all these conditions, which come close to the criteria applied by Professor Reuter in defining supra-nationalism,[68] are fulfilled, the functional institution may be regarded as federal. It should, however, be realised that whether these, or any other tests, are chosen, they are merely terms of classification. All they can achieve is to clarify the sense in which words such as federation or confederation are employed.[69]

3. *Forerunners*

Highly centralised international institutions are the very antipodes of that almost metalegal experiment in devolution and, in a sense, also in supra-nationalism: the British Commonwealth of Nations.[70] They have also little in common with another

---

[66] See above, p. 50.
[67] See above, p. 235.
[68] See below, p. 349.
[69] See above, p. 50.
[70] See above, p. 51.

relevant type of union which is represented by the Union for the Protection of Industrial Property (patents, industrial designs, trade marks and repression of unfair competition—1883), the Union for the Protection of Literary and Artistic Works (1886) and the Inter-Governmental Committee established by the Universal Copyright Convention of 1952.

From a functional point of view these unions are relevant, for their common object is either to create uniform municipal law or, at least, to secure national treatment for citizens of other contracting parties.[71] From an institutional point of view, however, they are of little interest. Typical of the classical type of administrative union,[72] their bureaux are hardly more than centres of study and information on matters relating to the application and revision of these conventions.

A closer affinity exists between the three European Communities and the Universal Postal Union. In fact, the organs of the Universal Postal Union are as free as can be from governmental control by the member States and left to get on with their appointed tasks. With the reservation that its functional freedom is not constitutionally guaranteed, this union may well be described as a venture in functional federalism on a world scale.[73] Similarly, the Permanent Commission under the Brussels Sugar Convention of 1902 is relevant as an early international attempt to limit production of sugar under the supervision of a permanent executive organ, which was authorised to decide by majority.

Customs unions constitute another relevant link. They share an essential feature with the common markets of the European Communities. For their own particular purposes, they eliminate the previously existing customs frontiers between the members of such unions, replacing them by common customs frontiers. There is a direct line from the Prussian and Austrian customs unions of the mid-nineteenth century to the most immediately relevant forerunner of " Little Europe ": Benelux, the customs and economic union of Belgium, the Netherlands and Luxembourg, planned since 1944 and gradually put into operation since 1947.

[71] See above, p. 2.
[72] See above, p. 235.
[73] See above, p. 250.

4. *Objectives*

The purpose of the three supra-national institutions is to bring about the fusion of essential interests of the member States. In more concrete terms, the common markets these institutions assist in establishing and maintaining are the central theme of their constitutions.

As it is put in the ECSC Treaty, " limited direct intervention " on the part of the three Communities may be required. This extends to initiating and controlling the production of the commodities in question and the operation of their markets. The Communities may also be called upon to sponsor, or carry out, research in these fields.

5. *Organisation*

The basic structure of these Communities is fairly simple. In the constituent instruments, in which the term " constitution " is carefully avoided, the organs are described as " institutions." Each of the Communities has its own executive organ and an organ representing the governments of member States. All these Communities have, however, two other organs in common: the Assembly and the Court. There are differences in emphasis between the structure of ECSC on the one hand, and EEC and EURATOM on the other. They bear evidence of second thoughts and a tendency to adopt a slower pace on the road towards supra-nationalism.

(a) *The Executive Organ.* While both the High Authority of ECSC and the Commission of EEC consist of nine members, that of EURATOM is limited to five.

Eight of the members of the High Authority are designated by the governments of the member States by agreement among themselves, and the ninth is elected by these eight members. By way of contrast, all the members of the Commission of EEC and EURATOM are appointed by agreement between the member States. While in ECSC, the term of appointment is six years, in EEC and EURATOM it is four years. In each case, the appointments are renewable.

The members States of ECSC have undertaken to respect the " supra-national character " of the office of members of the High Authority, and the members of the High Authority are enjoined to refrain from any conduct likely to jeopardise their independence. Similar standards of incompatibility, without, however, any reference to the supra-national character of the office of the members of the Commissions, are laid down in the constitutions of EEC and EURATOM.

While the High Authority is the sole executive organ of ECSC, the Commissions of EEC and EURATOM have to share this power with the Councils of their organisations.

(b) *The Organ Representing the Member States.* The function of the Council of each of the three Communities is to provide adequate representation of the interests of individual member States. The Council consists of one representative from each member. The delegates must be members of the governments of the member States.

While the primary function of the Council of ECSC is to " harmonise " the actions of the High Authority and of the individual governments, those of the Councils of EEC and EURATOM are considerably more far-reaching. By and large, the Commissions are responsible for administration, and the Councils are the policy-making bodies.

(c) *Consultative Committees.* These purely advisory organs represent a modest concession to the principle of functional representation.[74] The Consultative Committee of ECSC consists of a minimum of thirty and a maximum of fifty-one members. Producers, workers, consumers and dealers must be included in equal numbers. Members serve in their individual capacity and are not bound by any mandate or instruction from the organisation which proposed them as candidates.

The Committee is attached to the High Authority. Consultation, unless prescribed by the constitution, is in the discretion of the High Authority. In EEC and EURATOM, both the Council and the Commission are " assisted " by Economic and Social Committees of a similarly subordinate character.

(d) *The European Parliament.* In the last stages of the drafting of the constitutions of EEC and EURATOM it was decided to reduce the number of contemplated parliamentary organs by the creation of a single Assembly for all three supra-national

[74] See above, p. 261, and below, p. 639.

institutions: the European Parliamentary Assembly. This salutary decision was the result of forceful intervention on behalf of two Assemblies already existing: the Council of Europe [75] and Western Union.[76]

The European Parliament consists of one hundred and forty-two delegates, thirty-six each from Germany, France and Italy and thirty-four from the Benelux countries. The members of the European Parliament are appointed by the national parliaments in accordance with procedures laid down by the member States. In respect of each Community, the European Parliament exercises the jurisdiction entrusted to the Assembly of that Community [77] by its own Constitution. Provision is also made for some co-ordination of efforts between the European Parliament and the Assembly of the Council of Europe.

(e) *The Court.* The judicial functions of all three Communities are exercised by a common Court of Justice consisting of seven members. The judges are appointed by agreement between the governments of the member States for renewable terms of six years.

An interesting feature of the Court's organisation is the office of Advocate-General. Similar to the *Commissaire du Gouvernement* in the French *Conseil d'Etat* and the Judge-Advocate in English military law, the Court is assisted by two Advocates-General or Court advocates, as they had been termed in the Constitution of ECSC. The Advocates-General of the Court of Justice are appointed in the same way as the judges, and their task consists in presenting publicly and with " complete impartiality and independence " oral reasoned arguments on the cases submitted to the Court.

(f) *Subsidiary Agencies.* The EEC Treaty makes provision for two subsidiary agencies: the European Social Fund and the European Investment Bank.

The purposes of the Social Fund are to promote employment facilities within the Community and create greater geographical and occupational mobility of workers. The administration is in the hands of the EEC Commission, assisted in this task by a

---

[75] See above, p. 335.
[77] See below, p. 352.

[76] See below, p. 356.

committee representing governments, trade unions and employers' associations.

While the Social Fund has no legal personality of its own, this has been granted to the Investment Bank on a footing similar to the Bank for International Settlements: the most extensive legal personality that, in each member State, is accorded to legal persons under their respective municipal law.[78]

The members of the Bank are the member States of EEC. The tasks of the Bank are to finance projects likely to contribute to a balanced and organic development of the common market of EEC. Like other international financial institutions of this type, the Bank enjoys extensive privileges and immunities in each of the member States of the Community.

In accordance with its constituent instrument, EURATOM is to establish an agency for the control of the supply of nuclear source materials. The Agency, which will operate under the direction of EURATOM, will have a separate legal personality and enjoy financial autonomy.

6. *The Meaning of Supra-Nationalism*

Does the term " supra-national " mean nothing more than an international institution with wider and stronger executive powers than those normally granted to such bodies in the past? Is it synonymous with functional federation? Does it signify a novel intermediate stage of international integration between these extremes?

Examination of the jurisdiction and powers of the chief organs of these three Communities in the light of the tests of functional federalism—transfer of significant competences, protection of the union organs against interference by member States and exercise of direct authority over individuals and business enterprises in member States [79]—should provide rationally verifiable answers to these questions.

(a) *Co-ordinating Powers.* A mere glance at the constitutions of the three Communities, in particular EEC, reveals the wide scope of jurisdiction granted to these institutions. Similarly, the key-position in contemporary economies of commodities such as coal, steel and nuclear energy does not require elaboration. In

---

[78] See above, p. 72.   [79] See above, p. 128.

contrast to the typical experience on the level of international institutional co-operation,[80] the wide scope of jurisdiction granted to the executive organs of the three Communities is matched by far-reaching powers of co-ordination.

These organs may issue *regulations* of a quasi-legislative character. This power varies from constitution to constitution, but is most pronounced in EEC. By implication, such regulations must be taken to override conflicting national legislation. They may also make administrative *decisions*, both general and particular, which are binding in every respect. Such decisions must be distinguished from *recommendations*, which are binding regarding objectives, but not regarding the means by which they are to be attained and, finally, from *opinions*, which are not binding.

Voting in the High Authority of ECSC and the Commissions of EEC and EURATOM is by absolute majority. The freedom of these organs from instructions by member States as such is constitutionally guaranteed.[81]

Admittedly, the Commissions of EEC and EURATOM may frequently act only in co-operation with their Councils. In some cases, even the whole executive power is reserved to the Councils, and these are entirely composed of representatives of the member States. Thus, on the surface, the generalisation appears permissible that, in each of these Communities, the last word is usually with the Council rather than the Commission. It is, however, made somewhat difficult for the Council to ignore recommendations of the Commissions in the frequent cases in which the constitutions of EEC and EURATOM require such recommendations.[82] Moreover, the composition of these Councils does not differ in kind from that of corresponding organs of political federations as, for instance, the Federal Councils of successive German constitutions. While these organs are composed of instructed delegates, they themselves are federal organs and part of the delicate balance between joint and several interests that must always exist in any federal system.[83]

The application by ECSC of enforcement measures against member States for non-compliance with their treaty obligations

---

80 See above, pp. 327 and 341.
82 See below, p. 348.

81 See above, p. 346.
83 See above, p. 348.

depends on concurrence by the Council in any action proposed by the High Authority. A two-thirds majority in the Council is required for such a decision.[84] In the constitutions of EEC and EURATOM no provision is made for any form of execution against member States.

Execution against bodies and persons other than member States for the non-fulfilment of financial obligations to the Communities is possible under all three Treaties. Such execution takes place in accordance with the municipal law of the member State concerned, and this State must be formally associated with it. The execution is, however, mandatory, and the organs of the member State act as mere agents of the Communities.

In the EURATOM Treaty, execution is not limited to pecuniary obligations. In matters of safety regulations, the Commission may send inspectors of its own to any places or persons subject to the Community's control. Penalties for the infringement of such regulations imposed by the Community include the temporary replacement of the administration of an enterprise and the withholding of supplies of fissionable material.

(b) *The Functions of the Councils.* The Councils fulfil a dual function. As has been pointed out, they play a vital part in the processes of maintaining and modifying the initially established balance between the competences of the Communities and those retained by the member States. The Councils are organs of control. Without their concurrence, the other organs of the Communities are unable to expand their own jurisdiction at the expense of the member States.

Their second function is to make allowances for differences in power between member States and, within limits acceptable to all member States, even to give legal expression to hegemonial claims of some of the members. Weighted votes and veto rights have been used for this purpose on the Continent since the days of the German federal Constitution of 1871.

In each Community, the admission of new members is limited to European States and requires a unanimous vote. Any revision of the constitution of ECSC on the proposal either of a member State or of the High Authority has to go through several stages

[84] See above, p. 350, and below, p. 352.

and, ultimately, depends on ratification by all member States. Yet, for the requisite conference of member States to be called at all, a two-thirds majority in the Council is required. In the two other Communities, a simple majority suffices for the purpose of calling a revision conference. Unless otherwise provided in the three constitutions, voting in the Council of ECSC requires an absolute majority and in those of the other two Communities a qualified majority on matters of substance.

The hegemonial element in ECSC finds expression in the provision that the majority must always include the vote of any State which produces at least twenty per cent. of the total value of coal and steel produced in the Community. So far, only France and the Federal Republic of Germany belong to this category.

In the other two constitutions, weighted votes apply wherever these treaties prescribe qualified majorities. In such cases, France, Germany and Italy have four votes each and the Benelux countries five votes together.

If voting in the Councils of EEC and EURATOM depends on a previous proposal by their Commission, twelve votes constitute a majority. In all other cases those twelve votes must include those of four members. This means that at least one Benelux country has concurred. In the former case, the fact that the proposal comes from a supra-national organ is some guarantee of its intrinsic desirability. In other cases inclusion of at least one Benelux country in the majority serves to protect the " Small Three " from being outvoted by the " Big Three."

(c) *The Functions of the Assembly.* The European Parliamentary Assembly is a single body common to all three Communities. Its powers in relation to each Community are, however, determined by the treaty establishing the Community in question.[85]

Such legislative powers as are granted to these predominantly co-ordinating and administrative institutions are not vested in the Assembly. The power to define unfair price practices or the meaning of control of an enterprise is vested in the High

---

[85] See above, p. 348.

Authority of ECSC. Similarly, the enactment of general regulations by EEC and EURATOM is the exclusive responsibility of their Councils or Commissions. Thus, beyond its general consultative status and its necessary co-operation in a subordinate form in minor revisions of the ECSC Treaty, the Assembly has no legislative powers in relation to any of the three Communities. The Assembly has, however, some features of a parliamentary institution. Although lacking budgetary powers, it may pass a vote of censure on the general report submitted to it by the High Authority of ECSC. If this has been passed by a two-thirds majority of the members present and voting and representing a majority of the total membership, the High Authority as a body must resign. The Assembly exercises a corresponding control over the Commissions of the two other Communities. As, however, the functions of these Commissions are more restricted than those of the High Authority, these powers of the Assembly should not be unduly magnified. Their significance lies in the acceptance of the principle of parliamentary responsibility [86] on at least the supra-national level of integration.

Unless otherwise stipulated, voting in the Assembly is based on the rule of an absolute majority of the votes cast.

(d) *Judicial Review.* In accordance with the ECSC Treaty, the function of the Court of Justice is to ensure the rule of law in the application and interpretation of the Treaty and its implementing regulations. Similarly, under the other two Treaties, the Court's task is to ensure the observance of law and justice.[87] In a number of instances, the Court is even expressly enjoined to take into account economically relevant aspects of a case before it.

The personal and functional scope of the Court's jurisdiction, which is automatic or " compulsory," [88] covers disputes of the Communities with their member States as well as with individuals or business enterprises. The judgments of the Court are executory to the same extent, and in the same form, as the decisions of the executive organs of the Communities.[89]

(e) *External Relations.* The Parties to the ECSC Treaty envisaged distinct " international relationships " of the Coal and

---

[86] See above, p. 348.
[88] See above, p. 238.
[87] See below, p. 660.
[89] See above, p. 346.

Steel Community with non-member States and other international institutions. They, therefore, did all they could to provide the Community with the requisite legal capacity to treat on this level.[90]

In negotiations with third parties on matters concerning coal and steel, the High Authority acts for the member States of ECSC " as a group." ECSC has, however, no monopoly regarding matters in this category. Thus, relations between the Community and the United Kingdom are based on a treaty concluded in 1954 between, on the one hand, the United Kingdom, and, on the other, the High Authority of ECSC, as well as the member States. The Community and the United Kingdom are linked by a Standing Council of Association and mutual representation by ambassadorial missions in London and Luxembourg. The treaty-making power of EEC and EURATOM is more explicitly defined.

As the three Communities have distinct international personalities of their own,[91] they can, in case of doubt, enter into treaty obligations only on their own behalf.[92] However, in the EEC Treaty it is expressly provided that agreements concluded by this Community are binding not only on its own organs, but also on the member States.

7. *Evaluation*

If it is realised that political and functional, or vertical and horizontal, federation are but variants of a common pattern, supra-national institutions fall into their place. While the movement towards the unification of " Little Europe " has fallen short of political federation, the organs of these Communities comply with the tests laid down for functional federation.[93]

It is, however, essential to recall the still rather narrow scope of such functional federation and the necessary implications of this situation. It would, for instance, have been an incongruous and, therefore, unacceptable proposition to satisfy federal purism by establishing a separate federal apparatus for the execution of the decisions of the Communities. Similarly, save for some exceptional competences of EURATOM, it would probably have proved

[90] See above, p. 72.
[92] See above, p. 138 *et seq.*

[91] See above, p. 47 *et seq.*
[93] See above p. 344.

highly inconvenient to give to the Communities, even in their own spheres of operation, exclusive control over relations between member States and third powers. Yet, to be considered as federal, institutions need not necessarily comply with all the' traditional hallmarks of *political* federations.

A view of these regional experiments from the federal angle assists in a clearer perception of the law applicable inside these institutions. We enter here a border land between international and municipal law.[94] In this nexus, legal relations are no longer limited to those between subjects of international law.[95] In each Community, the organs, member States, public and private enterprises as well as individuals, are all subject to the common law of the Organisation. Similarly, as might be expected in relations of such closeness, characteristic features of *jus aequum*, for instance, prohibition of the abuse of rights and powers,[96] become more prominent than on lower levels of international law and organisation.

III—SECTIONAL INSTITUTIONS

The North Atlantic Treaty Organisation (1949), the Brussels Treaty Organisation (1948), subsequently expanded into a Western European Union (1954), the Balkan Union (1954), the Baghdad Pact Organisation (1955—now the Central Treaty Organisation), the League of Arab States (1945), the South-East Asia Treaty Organisation (1954), the ANZUS (Australia, New Zealand and United States) Treaty Council (1951) and the Warsaw Pact Organisation (1955) make up the last group of international institutions which call for consideration.

A. Objectives

On the surface, these organisations invite classification as regional institutions. Besides their military objectives, the more elaborate of these structures serve economic, social and cultural purposes. On closer examination, however, some peculiarities emerge.

In the context of collective security, a region is a functional area in which all States inside it co-operate towards the achievement of common goals. In essence, it is a community concept.[97]

---

[94] See above, p. 45.
[96] See above, pp. 99 and 137.

[95] See above, p. 48 *et seq.*
[97] See above, p. 9.

Yet, in fact, if not according to the tenor of their constituent instruments, these organisations are not open to all States within their radius of operation.[98] Their "collective" defence is not directed against an unknown aggressor in their midst, but against specific, if not necessarily specified, powers.

In some cases, this is more apparent than in others. The League of Arab States, first directed against Zionism at large and, subsequently, against Israel, has made little attempt to hide this objective. In the case of Western European Union this is less obvious, since its object-in-chief is no longer the prevention of a "renewal by Germany of a policy of aggression." Now that Western European Union includes all the States of Western Europe, recognition of its main function as a subsidiary of NATO requires further exploration of its constitution.

B. Functions

The treaties establishing these organisations are political treaties. Thus, they belong to a species of treaty in which words, even more frequently than elsewhere, hide, rather than express, thought. It is well to remember this point, especially in exploring their functions. This assists in perceiving the needs which have given rise to these treaties and conditioned their terminology.

In the first place, with the possible exception of the Organisation of American States,[99] the dovetailed systems of universal and regional collective security envisaged in the Charter of the United Nations have failed to materialise.[1] Moreover, the post-1945 world has become increasingly split into antagonistic world camps directed by hegemonial powers.[2]

Finally, those responsible for the drafting of these treaties on both sides of the world frontier have shown a marked preference for not expressing themselves in the straightforward language of the classical type of defensive alliance.[3] They have found it more congenial to employ the more sophisticated language characteristic of sectional and antagonistic alignments in systems of power politics in disguise.[4]

---

[98] See above, p. 316.
[1] See above, p. 176 *et seq.*
[3] See above, p. 102.

[99] See above, p. 330 *et seq.*
[2] See above, pp. 176 and 352.
[4] See above, p. 179.

The typical function of these treaties and of the institutions which serve to realise their objectives is twofold. It is in the first place to express in legal and institutional forms the political alignments of the parties. Moreover, it is the object of the terminology chosen to assist in approximating these sectional and antagonistic groupings to what they are not: systems of collective security.

C. Significance

The basic structure of sectional organisations is fairly simple and uniform. On the political side, the central organ is a Council on the confederate pattern, with a cluster of committees and a secretariat. On the military side, unified commands—which, in fact, tend to be less unified than it appears from always impressive diagrams—anticipate in time of peace the essential features of the combined commands of wartime coalitions. NATO, with its Council of Ministers, its permanent Council of Deputies, its standing groups, its secretariat headed by a Secretary-General and its Allied Commands Europe and Atlantic, illustrates this pattern to perfection.

The real significance of this type of institution is that it constitutes a perfect catalyst for fashionable day-dreams in the fields of international law and organisation. The study of sectional institutions greatly assists in destroying at least three major illusions.

First, these organisations are concerned with State activities which, to judge by their prominence in national budgets, still appear to enjoy a high priority over more exalted public pursuits. Thus, it is perhaps not entirely coincidental that, in the governing organs of these institutions, the unanimity rule still reigns supreme. While the unified commands of the post-1945 era both east and west of the world frontier may well be functionally integrated to a degree never attained since the days of Genghis Khan, in law each member State still remains free to decide for itself on the *casus foederis*.[5]

Secondly, the problems arising from the need to co-ordinate within each of the various camps giant, medium and small powers are formally resolved on a basis of consent.[6] On this footing,

---

[5] See above, p. 176. [6] See above, p. 138.

it becomes possible to arrange for some powers only to be represented in the most important committees and standing groups, to ensure that forces of the leading powers are stationed in the territories of the other member States, but not *vice versa*, and to retain exclusive or preponderant control of the super-weapons by the super-powers of our age. While a purist self-isolation of the legal element would condemn the student of the law of international institutions to remain blissfully unaware of these realities, an inter-disciplinary study of this subject will enable him to grasp these essentials.[7] In this particular case, it is the phenomenon of hegemony which is his Open Sesame.[8]

Thirdly, the existence of these organisations is a measure of the weakness of the existing world quasi-order.[9] Until this has been appreciably strengthened, it would be sheer escapism to dwell, without the most emphatic qualifications, on the apparent expansion in scope of international law and organisation, the growing concern of functional international institutions with the citizen's every-day life and the inter-penetration of international law and municipal law in supra-national institutions.

The decisive question is hardly the degree of international integration attained inside any of the world camps, but in the relations *between* the antagonistic blocs. A chain is but as strong as its weakest link, and those forged as yet on a world scale appear little more solid than those found wanting in the past.

---

[7] See above, p. 21.
[8] See above, p. 58.
[9] See above, pp. 147 and 172.

CHAPTER 12

PATTERNS OF INTERNATIONAL LAW AND ORGANISATION IN THE NUCLEAR AGE

" The atomic bomb made it clear that the plans which had been laid at San Francisco for the United Nations Organisation would have to be supplemented by a specific control of an instrument of war so terrible that its uncontrolled development would not only intensify the ferocity of warfare, but might directly contribute to the outbreak of war " (*Report of the Lilienthal Committee on the International Control of Atomic Energy*—1946).

PROBLEMS of legal planning—or what Bentham would have called questions of censorial jurisprudence—are as much within the lawyer's province as issues which are examined by the customary methods of analytical jurisprudence or the more novel techniques used in order to reveal the social functions fulfilled by law.[1] It is, however, essential to keep in mind two guiding principles.

There is little sense in planning in the abstract. Every scheme must be related to the specific historical situation in which it is intended to be realised. This test will eliminate a good many blueprints which are theoretically possible, but beyond reach at any particular time.

Furthermore, there is always more than *one* remedy for any social evil. It would, therefore, be incompatible with a detached approach to problems of legal planning to exclude *a priori* from discussion any scheme which, by common-sense standards, is not entirely impracticable. The politician may legitimately argue a case in favour of his own pet scheme or against the desirability of any change in the existing *status quo*. The student, however, must regard it as a matter of honour to put forward impartially all the available patterns. He is fully entitled to make articulate the assumptions and principles of any particular plan and to subject it to criticism from the point of view of practicability and desirability. Yet he must be conscious of the fact that such transcendental criticism is ultimately based on values and

---

[1] See above, p. 9.

convictions which can be honestly stated, but can neither be rationally proved nor disproved in their absolute validity.

From this form of criticism which affects the fundamental aspects of a pattern should be distinguished immanent criticism. Here, the pattern as such is taken for granted. The particular scheme in question is analysed, for instance, from the point of view of whether any of its features are in contradiction to its own basic assumptions, or whether the details of the plan suffer from shortcomings due to deficient legislative techniques. These considerations apply to legal planning in the international, as much as in the municipal, field.

I—The Peculiarities of Classical International Law

A useful starting point may be provided by a short recapitulation of the differences between classical international law and municipal law.

While international law of the pre-1914 variety is ultimately limited by power politics and the rule of force,[2] in the more advanced national and multi-national communities the supremacy of the law is assured. There are very few international persons compared with the number of citizens of a State. Thus, less need exists for abstract rules than in the case of municipal law. Sovereign States, the predominant type of international person, are much more powerful units than any number of individuals within a State. They are closely knit communities, held together by strong emotional loyalties, and they possess formidable means of destruction. For these reasons alone, there is considerably less scope for international law than for municipal law.

While, in international relations, the jurisdiction of courts depends entirely on the willingness of parties to submit disputes to third-party judgment,[3] in any developed system of municipal law it can be taken for granted that judgments can, if necessary, be enforced. Superficially, in inter-State relations the position appears not so different. Yet, such similarity is deceptive; for States consider carefully the effects of an adverse judgment before they agree to submit a case to international adjudication.[4] Unless

---

[2] See above, p. 10.
[3] See above, p. 230.
[4] See above, p. 234.

they are prepared to abide by such a decision, whatever it may be, it lies with them, from the outset, to refuse arbitral or judicial settlement of the issue.

II—The Ideology of the United Nations and the Reality of World Power Politics

On the face of it, international law under the Charter of the United Nations presents a very different picture from classical international law. Yet, in fact, world order under law exists without major reservations only for the bulk of the members of the United Nations.[5] In relation to the world powers, international law is still very much where it stood in 1914.

The anomaly of the position of the world powers is emphasised by their monopoly of thermo-nuclear weapons. The possession of the hydrogen bomb enables three of these powers, for the time being, to indulge in megaton diplomacy, and two of them to claim pre-eminence on the ground of their ability to annihilate each other with medium- and long-range missles adorned with nuclear warheads.

The implications of the monopoly in the super-weapons of our age for international law and organisation are far-reaching. There is no need to think merely in terms of thermo-nuclear weapons and to ignore other methods of warfare which " may constitute as great a threat to civilisation as the military use of atomic energy " (The Atomic Charter, November 15, 1945), that is to say, the more " advanced " forms of chemical and biological warfare.[6]

As distinct from formal equality between sovereign States, nations which are able to manufacture such super-weapons or are relatively immune against their application are alone sovereign in the political sense.[7] They alone have freedom of political decision on any matter in which, owing to the lack of such weapons or of means of effective counter-measures, another State might be forced to act differently from the way it would have desired.

[5] See above, pp. 175 and 276.
[6] See above, p. 189.
[7] See above, p. 275.

At present, the number of States sovereign in the political sense has shrunk below that of the permanent members of the Security Council. Each of these States is a law unto itself—a situation which finds its symbolic expression both in the veto power and in the belief in the majority principle on the part of those permanent members of the Security Council who feel confident of a sufficient following on issues of major importance.

The fear and distrust which result from such a hierarchy of power make it imperative for any world power not to be left behind in the cosmic rearmament race, to secure the maximum quantity of raw materials required for the production of the super-weapons, to prevent potential enemies from acquiring them, and to build up extensive security zones for the protection of its metropolitan territories.

In these circumstances, too much meaning must not be read into the " sovereign equality " of members of the United Nations.[8] The politically sovereign States are attracting to themselves groups of " junior partners," if in one's own camp, or " satellites," if in the opposite camp. Lesser powers are reduced to this position if they are too near to one of the centres of power to be anything but planets of their particular solar system.

In a world rent asunder, trust territories, which have not even reached the status of small independent States, cannot expect to be treated on a privileged footing as compared with lesser powers. Often their importance does not consist in their assets, which may be negligible, but in the value, strategic or otherwise, which their control would give to a potential enemy. Annexation, together with other straightforward terms of classical power politics, has been banned from a vocabulary more hypocritical than that of the empire builders of old. A spurious conception of trusteeship must, therefore, disguise the mixed reasons why States desire to become " trustees " in the mid-twentieth century.

Apart from the quest for raw materials and the desire to deny such territories to potential opponents, the urge for enlargement of security zones and considerations of prestige in general appear to be the decisive motive which inspires the surreptitious

---

[8] See above, pp. 58 and 270.

imperialism of this post-war era. Another novelty of this concept of trusteeship is the privilege bestowed on some of these islands to be singled out as testing grounds for thermo-nuclear weapons.

In the present hierarchy of powers, wars between smaller States endanger world security as little as brawls in a public-house threaten public peace. In any case, the United Nations is amply provided with means of quelling disorders of this calibre. It is, however, constitutionally incapable of preventing a war between world powers, and, in the condition of present-day world society, any all-out war between the world powers is necessarily a world war. Under the Charter of the United Nations it is technically impossible to apply enforcement measures against a permanent member of the Security Council.[9] Furthermore, who would wish to apply sanctions against powers which hold the monopoly in nuclear power or other weapons of comparable destructive force?

Moreover, in an age of cosmic warfare it becomes increasingly difficult to identify the aggressor. Who can say whose agents have planted nuclear bombs in the cloakrooms of the principal towns of a State, from where missiles with nuclear warheads have been discharged, or whose stratospheric aircraft have sprayed the fields of a country with sterilising substances? Any State may fear that, without sufficient evidence, it may be stigmatised as an aggressor. For this reason alone, none of the world powers can afford to consent easily to give up its veto on enforcement measures, unless it feels sure of a ready and comfortable majority in the Security Council.

In the past, aggressors have shown some proneness to expect exaggerated results from surprise attack. In future, the penalty of failure to secure total victory will be still heavier than it has been in wars of the past. Thus, more than ever before, a premium will be put on the most ruthless form of undeclared and pre-ventive war. In an age in which continents have become the battlefields, the future holds but dim prospects for neutrals in any major war. At a time when the powers of the world are engaged in a race for outer space, it is a matter for speculation

[9] See above, p. 285.

where a country ought to be situated in order to enjoy the benefits of a status of neutrality in an all-out war.[10]

It appears still more remote to search for rules of warfare which are to apply in a third world war. The tactics of saturation bombing, as applied in the final stages of the Second World War, and the atomic bombs dropped on Hiroshima and Nagasaki, show that the necessities of war tend to engulf any remaining restraints that, at one time, were imposed by regard for the requirements of the standard of civilisation.[11] If ever there should be a third world war, what is likely to happen is that, in a Judgment of Washington or Moscow, the victorious side will determine retrospectively in which way the defeated enemy has violated the laws and customs of " civilised " warfare.

It may be argued—and it is sincerely hoped that such optimism will be as much justified in future as it has proved to be mistaken in the past—that to draw such a picture is to overemphasise the weakest points in a gallant effort for a brave new world. The answer to this objection is simple. If an existing situation is analysed *de lege ferenda*, it is necessary to stress the darkest side of a landscape which, admittedly, has its proverbial silver linings on the horizon. In any case, the attitudes of *laissez-faire*, " sympathetic " day-dreaming or sheer self-hypnosis are most distinguished by having been disproved by two world wars.

III—A NECESSARY DISTINCTION

The criticism implied in the foregoing analysis of international society both before 1914 and after 1945 is not primarily concerned with technical shortcomings of particular rules of international law. It questions the quasi-order on which, so far, international law has rested.

Within the State, we have become accustomed—as Brierly so rightly reminded us—to take the existence of an effective system of peace and order for granted, and to concentrate on the greater or lesser degree of justice within such a framework. Yet it is not so very long since the modern State has emerged from the jungle condition in which international society is still engulfed.

---

[10] See above, p. 206 *et seq.*
[11] See above, p. 12 *et seq.*

The aftermath of the Second World War in Continental and other countries has shown how easy it is even for a nation to slide back into the primordial state of war of all against all in its most cruel form: civil war.

This reflection suggests that, in dealing with the further development of international law, a clear distinction is required between a narrower and a wider problem. The one is the technical improvement of international law as a legal system to make it commensurate with the needs of contemporary world society. The other is the problem of the international order on which international law may safely rest.

IV—PATTERNS FOR THE DEVELOPMENT OF INTERNATIONAL LAW

Four pairs of possible approaches to the improvement of international law call for discussion. They are related to the objects, techniques, scope and agencies of international planning.

A. Restatement or Reform ?

As in the case of the restatement of American law, much valuable work can be done in the field of international law by a more adequate statement of the existing law. The Harvard Research Drafts on selected aspects of international law show how much still remains to be done in fields not covered by this fruitful enterprise.

In this respect, the most important task which still awaits international lawyers is the systematic presentation of international law as applied by individual States.[12] Yet, even when this stupendous work is completed, it is but a preliminary to the real task ahead.

Only by comparing the State practice of all, or at least most, States will it become possible to find out scientifically, rather than speculatively, what is " international custom as evidence of a general practice accepted as law." [13] Similarly, only by a truly comparative study of the principles on which the world's systems of municipal law are based, will the charlatan's treatment of the third of the law-creating processes of international law, *i.e.*, " the

---

12 See above, p. 34.
13 See above, p. 27, and below, p. 733.

general principles of law recognised by civilised nations," be effectively barred.[14]

The value of a mere restatement of international law may be questioned. It certainly is of a limited character and not as sensational as any proposals for sweeping reforms. It may, however, be open to doubt whether radical plans for changes in the substance of the law, without corresponding changes in the basic international order, are more than innocuous forms of escapism.

A typical illustration is provided by the proposals for Universal Bills or Covenants of Human Rights. Particularly since the incorporation of clauses regarding respect for human rights and fundamental freedoms into the Charter of the United Nations, the drafting of such conventions has become a fashionable hobby. Yet, in a world which is as much split on basic values as is ours, it is more than unlikely that the members of the United Nations will be able to agree on a convention to this effect. Let it, however, be assumed that they did pledge themselves to respect the freedom and dignity of the individual, equality before the law, fair treatment of minorities and so forth. Will the member States of the United Nations submit to examination by the International Court of Justice or any other international body the question whether an alleged infraction of the Convention has taken place? Will it be safe for individuals in the more authoritarian, if not totalitarian, member States of the United Nations to make any complaints or even to give evidence before any international forum?

If it were so provided in the Bill, the Security Council could enforce compliance with the standards laid down in such a convention. Yet this only applies as long as none of the permanent members of the Council is charged with a breach of the Bill. If any of them happens to be the transgressor, the United Nations can enforce its will in this field as little as in any other. Again, the truth must be faced that the modern Leviathans are not yet subject to the rule of law.

It may well be argued that the realisation of such a scheme presupposes some kind of world State. Why then do the advocates of such covenants ask at this stage for a Universal Covenant

[14] See above, p. 29, and below, p. 733.

of Human Rights and not for a world State which is its prerequisite? To proceed in this manner is to put the cart before the horse.

In any case, this illustration shows how closely proposals for improvements of the substance of international law are related to particular patterns of international order. It should, therefore, be the duty of any would-be reformer to relate his particular brand of law reform to the type of international order without which it is likely to remain utopian. Such correlation would contribute to a franker and more realistic discussion of projects for the development of international law.

B. Codification or Common Law Pattern?

It is one of the functions of the General Assembly of the United Nations to initiate studies and make recommendations for the progressive development of international law and its codification. This task is entrusted to the International Law Commission, a subsidiary body of the General Assembly. It consists of twenty-one members, elected by the General Assembly for five-year terms from a list of candidates nominated by the member States. The minimum qualifications of members and the degree of legitimate control exercised by governments over nationals who are members of the Commission are left unsettled in the Statute of the Commission.

In this Statute, adopted by the General Assembly, the language of Article 13 of the Charter [15] has been used to approximate " codification " to restatement, and " progressive development " to reform of international law. In the terminology employed in this Chapter, which is more usual both in international and municipal law, codification means the restatement or reform of legal rules in written form and with binding force. The binding character distinguishes a codification of international law from a restatement by individual scientists or groups of international lawyers. In the absence of international legislative organs in the strict sense,[16] such codification must needs be in the form of multilateral international conventions. In substance, such a condition may either be limited to a restatement of

---

[15] See above, p. 282, and below, p. 703.
[16] See above, p. 141.

the existing law or aim at the improvement of the law as it stands.

Just as the term " codification " may be used in the international sphere only by analogy, so the term " Common Law pattern " has to be applied with reservations. It is not meant to convey that the decisions of international courts or tribunals are precedents in the strictly technical sense of English law.[17] If, however, the Common Law pattern were understood to mean —and the term is used here in this sense—that the statement of international law should primarily be left to international courts and tribunals, this would again leave open the alternatives of restatement and reform. Admittedly, judicial legislation is measured in inches rather than feet. Nevertheless, the development of international law by the World Court is far from negligible.[18]

In order to assess the relative merits and deficiencies of these patterns it is necessary to free oneself from an illusion which, to a great extent, accounted for the popularity of proposals for the codification of international law. In the pre-1914 period it was widely held that most wars could have been averted if only the governments concerned had been aware of their legal rights and duties in the issue involved and been able to refer the dispute to an international court or tribunal.

A minimum of historical sense and reflection on wars such as the Napoleonic Wars, the Crimean War or the Franco-Prussian War of 1870–1871, might have disabused the minds of those who believed that wars were, and are, ordeals by battle and fought in order to prove which party is in the right. Nothing so spectacular as the prevention of war must be expected even from a comprehensive restatement of existing international law by way of codification. If, however, it was implied that it would be possible to smuggle into such a codification a few innocent looking articles by which the basis of the existing international society would be vitally modified, such a flank attack on world power politics is too clever by half, and has never yet led to more than the establishment of systems of power politics in disguise.

The attempts made under the auspices of the League of Nations to codify select branches of international law did not

---

[17] See above, pp. 32 and 244.   [18] See above, pp. 32 and 248.

produce any appreciable results. It is even arguable that they did positive harm in revealing uncertainties in the law in fields where, before, generally accepted rules of international customary law seemingly existed, and the actual disagreement in State practice had not come into the open.

Some of these experiences repeated themselves in post-1945 efforts at the codification and development of international law. It is too much to expect any Foreign Office to commit itself unequivocally in a reply to abstractly formulated questions or with regard to hypothetical cases. Moreover, even if the scope of a codification is as limited as the work of the Hague Peace Conferences of 1899 and 1907, agreement is frequently bought at the price of rules which give merely the appearance of certainty [19] or are purely admonitory but which, in fact, leave everything to the discretion of the parties.[20]

The most significant and comprehensive contribution made as yet by the International Law Commission to the codification of international law is its preparatory work on the legal régime of the high seas. Yet, irrespective of whether the Conventions which were adopted by the Geneva Conference of 1958 [21] will come into force, one thing is clear. The painstaking work of the Commission has greatly contributed to the clarification of the issues before the Conference and assisted it in reaching agreement fairly quickly on a great many uncontroversial items. Moreover, in so far as these are concerned, the law is now codified and, irrespective of ratification, these Conventions will come to be relied on increasingly as *sedes materiae*.

Limited successes of the pattern of codification on a world scale must not be allowed to obscure features of the Common Law pattern which probably still compare favourably with the alternative technique of codification. There are few branches of international law which have not been touched upon by the World Court and the host of international tribunals established under bilateral treaties, and there are many fields of international law which look very different today from the time when international law was the exclusive preserve of chancelleries and writers.

---

[19] See above, pp. 198 and 257.
[21] See above, p. 258.

[20] See above, p. 198.

As distinct from international codification, a decision of an international court or tribunal does not bind anybody but the parties to a particular dispute and only with regard to that particular dispute.[22] It thus presents an experiment which, like the edict of the Roman praetor, is capable of continuous adjustment and adaptation.

Yet the persuasive authority of an international judgment is very much greater than that of any writer or even of judges writing in their capacity as private individuals. This applies especially to the judgments of the World Court. To recapitulate shortly,[23] collective wisdom which, in this case, represents the main legal systems of the world, is superior to individual wisdom. Common deliberation by the members of a world bench is a unique check on subconscious national prejudices and limitations in outlook.

Finally, confrontation with, and final decision on, live issues in a judicial capacity helps to create an atmosphere which is more congenial to the exercise of responsible and balanced judgment than the average conditions under which writers face their problems. Especially if universal judicial institutions, such as the World Court, are available, the cumulative effect of these advantageous conditions appears to weigh the balance in favour of the Common Law pattern as compared with that of codification.

C. Universal or Non-Universal Patterns ?

Restatement and reform of international law, codification and declaration or development of international law by judicial bodies may be attempted on a universal scale. It may also be limited to a particular area. Any geographical region may form such a unit, though it may be a matter of controversy what kind of area constitutes a region. For our purposes, any geographical unit, such as a continent, offers a suitable illustration. There are, however, criteria of close affinity between States other than geographical tests. The ties which bind together the members

---

[22] See above, p. 32.
[23] See above, p. 235 *et seq.*

of the British Commonwealth, or ideological affinities of a religious, political or economic character are instances in point.

A comparison of the work in the field of codification of the Hague Peace Conferences, the League of Nations and the United Nations on the one hand, with that of the Organisation of American States or the Council of Europe on the other, will show that, comparatively at least, the latter have achieved more tangible results.[24]

The position is, however, very different if we look at the development of international law by international courts and tribunals. Here, comparable obstacles to a universal approach do not appear to exist. On the contrary, a judicial pronouncement only gains in weight and significance by its non-segmental character.

In the case of the World Court this is partly due to its permanent character as compared with the *ad hoc* tribunals within the framework of the Permanent Court of Arbitration and bilateral tribunals and claims commissions. Yet, even more important is the additional prestige which accrues to the Court from its universal character. It has enabled the Court to be recruited from among the most distinguished international lawyers in the world. Thus, there can be little doubt that the standing of international judicial institutions appears to be directly related to their universal character.

D. Official or Unofficial Agencies ?

The question whether the restatement or development of international law should be entrusted to official or unofficial agencies presents itself in its most extreme form in the case of codification in the wider sense of the term. It is arguable that a private conference for this purpose is merely so much wasted time; for who, but the governments concerned, can determine the desirable scope and nature of changes in existing international law? It is, however, equally possible to take the opposite stand and hold that, to judge by past experiences, governments are not likely to march further than the pressure of public opinion forces them to march—or crawl.

[24] See above, pp. 330 and 334.

It may be doubtful whether public opinion is as independent and potent a factor as was assumed by nineteenth century liberalism, yet, the Kellogg Pact and other multilateral treaties since the days of Dunant's and Moynier's remarkable campaign for the protection of wounded soldiers prove that there is some substance in this argument.

In the case of a mere restatement of international law, unofficial agencies appear to present obvious advantages. To state the law is predominantly a scientific function. It might, therefore, be thought that it would be best to leave this task to those whose professional function it is to expound international law. To judge by the relative merits of the Harvard Research Drafts as compared with the answers given by governments to League of Nations questionnaires in related fields, it appears fairly certain that unofficial agencies of sufficient standing, and sufficiently well financed to be able to afford at least qualified research assistants, are likely to produce better results than teams of government officials.

The explanation is not to be found in any difference in intellectual calibre between academic and civil service lawyers, but in the former's detachment from practical issues. Nevertheless, the academic lawyer who refuses to be enrolled as a supernumerary civil servant is sometimes slightly handicapped, as compared with others, by the reluctance shown by most governments to publish recent official documents on international affairs.

Actually, any rigid distinction between scholars and government officials has become a myth. Increasingly, the difference between scholars and government lawyers is being reduced to one of degree. This is partly due to personal factors, which tempt scholars to choose what Oppenheim once aptly termed a " diplomatic " treatment of their subject. It is also partly the inescapable consequence of the encroachment of the modern State, and even the democratic State, upon academic freedom. In authoritarian and totalitarian States the problem has ceased to exist, and it makes little difference whether such a country is represented by a government official or scholar at an official or unofficial conference for the restatement of international law.

In these circumstances, the development of international law by international judicial institutions offers unique advantages. Members of international courts combine the authority which is associated with officially appointed or elected individuals, with an, at least subjective, independence which is still associated with the judicial character of their office. Their specific function —and the institutional guarantees by which their independence is protected—make them more immune to temptations of " diplomatic " provenance than the average scholar in a non-judicial position. Although judgments by international courts are binding on States only within the very narrow limits of Article 59 of the Statute of the International Court of Justice, they are of a highly persuasive authority.[25]

No revolutionary changes must, however, be expected from the snail's pace of judge-made law. To do so would be to expect more from judicial institutions than it is fair to ask of them. In a mature international order there would be legislative agencies which would come into operation if there should be a need for a drastic change. In the absence of such organs and in the conditions of a highly dynamic world, the existence of the international order itself remains perforce continuously in jeopardy.

V—CONDITIONS OF INTERNATIONAL ORDER

The problem of international order has been stated throughout the centuries in terms of the elimination of war as a social institution and of attaining a stable peace.

Some of the earlier schemes like Dubois' *De recuperatione terrae sanctae* (1305) or St. Pierre's *Projet de Traité pour rendre la Paix universelle* (1713) were obviously directed against some powers and drafted in the interest of others. Thus, they were never considered as more than rather obvious ideological covers for the foreign policies of the countries championed by their authors.

Others, like de Lacroix's *Nouveau Cynée* (1623), aimed at getting the best of both worlds. They were content to maintain in substance the reality of the sovereign State. At the same time, they wished to see an effective international order established.

[25] See above, p. 32, and below, p. 736.

The experiment of the League of Nations—as other previous failures of the confederate pattern—has proved in our time that it is as hard on an inter-State level as elsewhere to have one's cake and eat it.

What, then, are the minimum conditions to be fulfilled by a blue-print of international order?

First, the cure must be commensurate with the evil that has been diagnosed. If war is merely the last resort of power politics,[26] then the framework of international order must be strong enough to prevent any State, or any likely combination of States, from resorting to war. At least, it must be able to reassert the international order against any actual transgressor.

Secondly, in a world society—at least in the objective and material sense of a single activity area—nothing short of an order of universal scope is likely to offer a reasonable guarantee against a third world war.

Thirdly, the strain on any world order which is merely conceived in negative terms is stronger than it can be expected to bear.[27] The draftsmen of confederate constitutions such as those of the League of Nations and United Nations have rightly emphasised the positive and constructive aspects of peace and shown an imaginative awareness of the inter-nexus between the pacific settlement of international disputes, including peaceful change, collective security and disarmament. Yet confederations of this type are constitutionally incapable of subjecting a world power to the rule of law without that power's consent. It, therefore, appears that it is impossible to speak of a world order proper unless a pattern fulfils seven requirements:

(1) The members of the community must be safeguarded against violation, from within and without, of all rights granted to them by the community.

(2) The community requires for its own purposes adequate governmental and executive powers.

(3) The provision for judicial settlement of international disputes between members of the community is not sufficient. In order to adapt international relations to the requirements of a

---

[26] See above, p. 179.
[27] See above, p. 308 *et seq.*

changing world, international legislative or quasi-legislative organs with discretionary powers are indispensable.

(4) The members of the community must hand over, and refrain from producing, any armaments the retention of which might seriously hamper the community in prevailing over any individual member or any likely combination among them.

(5) The degree of control of the community over its members and the competence of the community must depend on *one* test alone: the minimum of functions and interference which is compatible with the proper working of the community system.

(6) The community needs some measure of direct control over the citizens of the member States in order to create loyalties strong enough to counterbalance existing loyalties of a sectional character.

(7) A community can be based only on the principle of consent. While the unanimity rule would reduce it to impotence, the majority rule is compatible with a far-reaching protection of minorities and of individual member States in spheres which are not essential from the point of view of the community.

To picture world order in such terms may savour of perfectionism. Yet it appears futile to set out an objective and, at the same time, refuse to contemplate the means by which it can best be attained. It is arguable that it is impossible to reach so ambitious a goal, for instance, because the necessary spiritual and emotional motive powers for a drive towards a world State by consent are lacking. Yet this would be merely another way of saying that power politics is the lot of mankind.

VI—Patterns of World Order

A variety of patterns has been suggested from time to time in order to transform the quasi-world order of the League of Nations or United Nations into a world order proper. These schemes, which come into, and go out of, fashion in quick rotation, may be grouped under seven headings.

A. The " One Way " Pattern

It has been suggested that if States solemnly pledged themselves to renounce aggression or resort to war, aggression and war would cease. This pattern is based on the somewhat sanguine assumption of the impossibility or unlikeliness of a breach of international treaties. In addition, such outlawry of war on paper sadly ignores the social, or anti-social, functions fulfilled by war. The frequent breaches of the Kellogg Pact and of bilateral non-aggression pacts in the inter-war period confirm this rather obvious truth.

Even if the formal loopholes of the League Covenant and Kellogg Pact are closed—as has been done in the Charter of the United Nations—and States pledge themselves to renounce the threat or use of force as distinct from resort to war as a means of national policy, not much is gained. Either reliance must be placed on the good faith of all nations at all times or a system of sanctions must be devised which transforms blueprints of this type into those of a different pattern.[28]

Others have considered that comprehensive arbitration treaties for the settlement of all possible disputes provide the solution. If by this proposition is meant the arbitral or judicial settlement of all disputes on the basis of international law, no account is taken of the fact that, as a rule, major wars are not due to the lack of international courts or tribunals. The real problem is not presented by cases of accidental war or emotional resort to war, but by aggression planned for the purpose of overthrowing an existing *status quo* or by the bloodless conquest of a country from within.

Such issues are normally not even within the competence of an international court; for they relate to matters which, by international law, are exclusively or essentially within the domestic jurisdiction of States.[29] This particular difficulty could be overcome by the establishment of quasi-judicial institutions with equitable jurisdiction between States. Yet, to aim at the establishment of an international equity tribunal in isolation would merely amount to tackling one aspect of a more comprehensive problem. It would constitute an attempt to fulfil one, but only one, of the seven conditions of world order.[30]

Similar considerations apply to a direct and isolated attack on the problem of disarmament. Armaments are a symptom of the

[28] See below, pp. 377–378.   [29] See above, pp. 58 and 271.
[30] See above, p. 374.

state of insecurity which is inherent in a system of power politics. Limitation of armaments is something very different from disarmament. This has been temporarily achieved—as, for instance, in the Washington Treaties of 1921-22 regarding naval armaments in the Pacific—and is the expression of a relatively stable balance of power. As soon as there are serious changes in the underlying power equilibrium, such a system tends to become inoperative.

Disarmament in any true sense is not a means of achieving world order, but is its fruit and culmination. *Status quo* powers are well advised to postpone disarmament until an equivalent to national armaments is offered in the form of an effective international order. Revisionist States will prove equally hesitant to renounce war as a means of fulfilling their ambitions, unless more rational and civilised machinery for peaceful change exists than is available in any system of power politics or power politics in disguise.

Thus, the " one-way " pattern is either meaningless or implies a more far-reaching transformation of international society than is apparent. The discussions on the control of nuclear and other super-weapons present a constant object lesson of the futility of the " one-way " pattern.

B. The " Bad Faith " Pattern

The " one-way " blue-prints which have been discussed so far, might also have been described as " good faith " schemes. Each of them must rely on all participant States honouring their pledged word at all times. If, however, they are supplemented by machinery for supervision and the application of sanctions in the case of any breach of engagement, a new pattern emerges.

For the sake of discussion, let us assume that the powers of the world have agreed to create an international agency with exclusive mining rights regarding all minerals required for the production of nuclear energy, and all States have undertaken not to mine such minerals themselves nor to allow anyone within their territories to do so. Then it can hardly be expected that any State will loyally abide by such a convention and risk another State breaking its word, unless there exist both efficient international machinery for ensuring the observance of these obligations by all participant States and overwhelming sanctions in the background against any potential transgressor.

If the production of nuclear energy for destructive purposes alone were prohibited, similar considerations would apply. The amount of supervision required and the constantly expanding means of producing nuclear energy from other substances, and by simplified and cheaper devices, make it obvious that there is only one alternative. This pattern either requires an amount of interference with the economic and industrial life of nations which amounts to the establishment of a world State for the limited purpose of controlling nuclear energy, or it does not provide the amount of security without which a cosmic rearmament race is unavoidable.

C. The Functional Pattern

The progress made since the Napoleonic Wars with international institutions [31] has led some writers to believe that international institutions offer a suitable means for a flank attack on power politics. If the world were gradually covered with a network of international agencies in the most important fields of inter-State life, from communications, international trade and finance to education and science, then one day Foreign Offices would wake up and find that hardly any scope was left to them for playing politics in their traditional manner.

The defect in this comforting picture is that Foreign Offices are not inhabited by vicious dragons who can be cleverly out-witted by gallant reforming knights. They are merely the jealous guardians of vested national interests and, so far, have refused to be tricked into an international community. While, in response to the pressure of public opinion, they have grudgingly agreed to the establishment of a multitude of international institutions in the more innocuous fields, the power of such institutions to act stands in inverse ratio to their freedom to talk.

D. The Regional Pattern

Advocates of intensive regional co-operation fall into several classes. There are those who seek in regionalism consolation from their disappointments on a world scale. There are others

[31] See above, p. 227.

who have resigned themselves to the fact that the time is not yet ripe for achieving international order on a world scale. They hope for the best and attempt to make their region as safe as possible against encroachment from the outside and as free as circumstances allow from the other fears of life in a mechanised mass society. Finally, there are power politicians for whom regionalism is but a new name to cover whatever system of alliances they happen to favour.

Regionalists usually find it difficult to define their chosen area in any but a somewhat arbitrary manner. The history of schemes for Pan-Europe or a European Union amply confirm this impression. The authors of regional schemes also have a tendency to be " land minded." They usually overrate the connecting links formed by land masses and visualise the sea as a barrier rather than the link it can be, and is, for instance, between the Atlantic communities. The cultural links of the Latin American States with Europe offer a relevant illustration of this proposition.

It is still a matter for speculation to what extent co-operation in the Western Hemisphere under the aegis of the Organisation of American States [32] is due to more than the magnetic power of attraction of the Northern giant. Yet even if such an opinion did not allow sufficiently for the genuine enthusiasm of Central and South American States in this venture and for their common interests in continental security, such cases of clear-cut division between different regions are rare. As a rule, the competing claims of various regions on States in border-zones between two or more regions cause additional complications.

It must also be borne in mind that the organisation of an area as a region tends to aggravate relations with the States near to—but outside—the contemplated region. Such States may easily suspect that the regional group is but an alliance directed against them.

At their best, regional groupings are neutral from the point of view of international order. Relations between various regions either remain unregulated by an overriding universal peace system and are then subject to the rules of power politics, or they are co-ordinated within such a universal framework. In

[32] See above, p. 330.

the latter case, the strength or weakness of the world system of which regions form part is what matters, and regional groupings form at most an auxiliary means of buttressing the main structure.

E. The United Nations Reform Pattern

When the limitations of the League of Nations became apparent, it was suggested that it might be strengthened by grafting on to it branches from one or the other of the patterns already discussed. The League was found to be weak in the sphere of peaceful change—an international equity tribunal might provide a solution for this deficiency. The sanctions system of the Covenant was more imposing than real—let an international police force take charge of the matter.

The chief merit of the more elaborate schemes for the reform of the Covenant advanced in the pre-1939 period probably consisted in forcing the opponents of this pattern into the open. Such antagonists found it more difficult to argue that the pattern suffered from insurmountable technical shortcomings. They were forced to admit that they were opposed to the curtailment of national sovereignty involved.

Even the proponents of these schemes only gradually realised that the real problem was of a different calibre. It was—and is—whether the nations of the world are prepared to establish, at least for some purposes, a world State and world government. Whatever their description, the members of an international equity tribunal would be the persons in whose hands would lie decisions which sovereign States most jealously reserve to themselves. Similarly, if the high command of an international police force were authorised to interpret on its own authority standing instructions of a necessarily vague character and to commence actual operations on its own determination of the aggressor, States would have delegated to such an authority the most fateful political decision that a statesman may be called upon to make.

If States insist on reserving to an organ such as the Security Council the question whether enforcement action is to take place, even the existence of a United Nations police force would not essentially alter the picture. In face of the veto, even the most powerfully armed international force might be condemned to inaction. Yet would it not be possible to abolish the veto on enforcement action ?

To put the issue in this way is but another of the many flank attacks on national sovereignty and a statement of the problem of the world State without the necessary frankness. This is the real snag about 'ne welter of post-1945 schemes for peace through Charter reform and disarmament or world peace through world law under a revised United Nations Charter. To change the law of the Charter to the extent postulated in these high-powered blueprints would mean to change a confederation into a federation. At this point, the discussion moves from the reform of the United Nations to a completely different pattern.

F. The " World State by Consent " Pattern

It is possible to emphasise the gradualness of the transition from a strong confederation to a weak federation and then to argue that the difference between both forms of international government is rather one of degree than of kind. Yet, a situation in which enforcement action under the Charter of the United Nations were possible by majority decision, would differ so radically from the present position that such proposals deserve to be granted the distinction of a separate pattern. Such amendments to the Charter would transform the United Nations into an institution with governmental and executive functions. As has been shown,[33] similar considerations apply to schemes for the effective control of nuclear energy.

The difficulties which stand in the way of progress in the direction of territorial or functional world federation are not primarily of a technical character. Co-operation between the Allies during the First and Second World Wars has shown that difficulties of organisation and co-ordination can be overcome when there is the will to do so, and governments are spurred on by a sufficiently urgent common purpose. The obstacles are of a more fundamental, and less rational, character. Prejudices of a national and racial character, differences in economic and social structure or in political ideologies and religious beliefs are elevated into barriers which prevent any further integration of

[33] See above, p. 377.

existing international society. It may be true that to refuse to pay the price of a world federation may mean another inter-war period of uneasy and armed peace. Yet the validity of this argument in the pre-1914 and pre-1939 periods did not prevent the First and Second World Wars, nor has our genera-tion as yet succeeded in terminating even the " Cold War " between the world camps.

G. The " Natural " Selection Pattern

Bearing in mind the limited effect of international law and organisation on world power politics in the past, it may be permissible to reflect on another pattern. Although unpleasant to contemplate, it appears to be more in line with the develop-ment which international society has taken so far. If we look at the political maps of Europe, it appears to have been the function of the successive wars which have taken place in the course of the last five hundred years to reduce drastically the number of legally sovereign States. If by sovereign States are meant States which are sovereign in the political sense,[34] the trend towards the concentration of power is even more potent on a global scale.

In our time there are only two power agglomerations left between which a major war in the nuclear age is possible. If they should not be able or willing to establish world government by consent, they may live side by side for a prolonged period in a state of watchful distrust and fear of mutual co-extermination, with successive periods of strain and relaxation. Yet, until now, such an armed peace has always ended ultimately in an inter-national conflagration.

The victor in such a third world war may find that what has proved impossible to achieve by consent in the inter-war period between the Second and Third World Wars will fall into his lap in a world that may be too exhausted to want anything but peace and order, irrespective of whether it comes from the Kremlin, the Capitol—or the once Forbidden City.

---

[34] See above, p. 58.